THE HIDDEN CASE

OF

EWAN FORBES

*And the Unwritten History
of the Trans Experience*

ZOË PLAYDON

SCRIBNER

New York   London   Toronto   Sydney   New Delhi

Scribner
An Imprint of Simon & Schuster, Inc.
1230 Avenue of the Americas
New York, NY 10020

First Scribner hardcover edition November 2021

SCRIBNER and design are registered trademarks of The Gale Group, Inc.,
used under license by Simon & Schuster, Inc., the publisher of this work.

For information about special discounts for bulk purchases,
please contact Simon & Schuster Special Sales at 1-866-506-1949
or business@simonandschuster.com.

The Simon & Schuster Speakers Bureau can bring authors to your live event.
For more information or to book an event, contact the Simon & Schuster Speakers Bureau
at 1-866-248-3049 or visit our website at www.simonspeakers.com.

Manufactured in the United States of America

1   3   5   7   9   10   8   6   4   2

Library of Congress Cataloging-in-Publication Data has been applied for.

ISBN 978-1-9821-3946-9
ISBN 978-1-9821-3948-3 (ebook)

To defy Power, which seems omnipotent;
To love, and bear; to hope till Hope creates
From its own wreck the thing it contemplates;

Percy Bysshe Shelley, *Prometheus Unbound*

CONTENTS

FINDING EWAN

I first heard about the hidden case of Ewan Forbes on February 16, 1996. I'd been with a group of lawyers working for trans equality, picking over a crushing defeat by the government in the High Court of Justice. We couldn't understand why we had lost. We'd found evidence that trans people had had the sex on their birth certificates corrected in the past without any problems, and we argued that they should be able to correct them now, as a matter of common sense and natural justice. Because the UK has no national identity card, the birth certificate is used as a proof of identity by employers, solicitors and administrators, and it is humiliating for trans people to have their private medical history paraded in front of strangers when their birth certificates are required for such purposes. There are also devastating legal consequences. When the right to have their birth certificates corrected evaporated in the late 1960s, trans people found that their basic civil liberties disappeared along with it. No one seemed to know exactly how that had happened: there had been no debate in Parliament and no new statutes or regulations. But suddenly, although trans people might live their lives like everyone else, they had no employment rights, could not marry or adopt, and if they couldn't pay their car-parking fines, they would be sent to the wrong sex prison, where trans women's rape was routine and yet not classed as rape.[1]

It seemed impossible that an impartial judge could countenance the continuation of this injustice. Yet the High Court had found against us. I was a former chair of the Gay and Lesbian Association of Doctors and Dentists (GLADD), and I'd been working alongside this team of lawyers as an expert in LGBTI human rights, drawing on my years of frontline experience, but neither my colleagues nor I had been able to make sense of our defeat. Then, as I got through the door at my home in Russell Square, London, the phone started ringing. It was one of the lawyers, the solicitor Madeleine Rees, and her news was electrifying.

Maddie had just had a call from Terrence Walton, solicitor in the famous April Ashley trans legal case from a quarter of a century earlier. Terrence, raw about our defeat, had complained to Madeleine that everyone blamed him and April for creating the legal precedent that meant trans people could not correct their birth certificates. But, he said, there had been another, earlier case. In 1969, before he and April went into court, they had been called into the judge's chambers and shown this earlier case, and then informed that they could not refer to it. All traces of it had been removed from the public eye, they were told, and everyone who knew about it was sworn to secrecy—a pact that now included them. Terrence said this secret earlier case ended birth-certificate correction for UK trans people. After that, there was a blanket ban, because, as Terrence put it, "There are some interests that it is more important to protect than the rights of individuals."[2] From then on, trans people would have to live their lives as if they were the sex incorrectly assigned at their birth and suffer the devastating legal, social and psychological consequences.

The existence of this hidden case was astonishing news. The UK's system of common law works by what is known as the doctrine of precedent. This means that the judgment of a key legal case binds all subsequent similar cases, unless that judgment is changed by a more senior court.[3] This system of case law creates the law of the land, so that publicly available law reports of important cases are fundamental to British democracy. Without them, British citizens have no way of knowing what laws they must follow. Terrence's suggestion that an important case had been deliberately concealed was therefore deeply troubling.

I asked Madeleine to ring Terrence back and try to find out more information. Was there really some kind of a conspiracy, and not just a dreadful government error that had turned trans people into outcasts in their own country? But Terrence felt he had already said more than he should have and would give no more information.

I rang two colleagues: the trans campaigner Mark Rees and the academic lawyer Stephen Whittle, a leader of the trans lobbying group Press for Change. We mulled over Terrence's news and decided that we had to confirm or refute it with proper academic rigor. For the majority of proceedings in UK law, the sex of plaintiffs and defendants is irrelevant. But it is crucially important where succession to a title is concerned. Given Terrence's reference to important interests that overrode the rights of ordinary people, our best guess was that if such a case really did exist, it would have been about male-line primogeniture, the law that says certain aristocratic titles and lands can be inherited only by a man, never by a woman.[4] The popular press calls it the "*Downton Abbey* law," after the historical drama television series, which ran a storyline dealing with the primogeniture disinheritance of an elder daughter. In 2016, male-line primogeniture gave Hugh Grosvenor, the young Duke of Westminster, his title and £9 billion estate over his older sisters. It also decided the British monarchy, until the Succession to the Crown Act 2013 gave princesses equal inheritance rights with princes. Male-line primogeniture has been strongly criticized as institutionalized sex discrimination by the Daughters' Rights group, which campaigns against it,[5] and a 2020 United Nations report described son preference as "a symptom of entrenched gender inequality, which harms whole societies."[6]

As a University of London professor, I had the best access to research libraries, and so we decided that I would lead the inquiry. The first step was to eliminate cases we knew about. On February 29, 1996, Stephen faxed me the *Daily Telegraph* obituary of a Scotsman, Sir Ewan Forbes of Craigievar. It described the "ghastly mistake" that meant that Ewan had been "carelessly registered as a girl" at birth in 1912; the correction of his birth certificate in 1952; his subsequent marriage; and a legal wrangle about him inheriting his primogeniture baronetcy, heard in the Scots Court of Session but ultimately decided by the Home Secretary James Callaghan.[7] On the face of it, Ewan was "intersex," born with a variation of external or internal genitalia, and not what was then called "transsexual." It should have been easy to check and dismiss his case quickly.

And so began the mystery of the hidden case of Ewan Forbes, for wherever I looked, Ewan couldn't be found. I enlisted the help of both the Signet Library in Edinburgh and the Scottish Records Office, and they could find no trace in their indexes, files or catalogs.[8] I received no reply to the letters of inquiry I wrote to the Home Office and to the Lord Advocate, the senior Scottish legal authority. This was inexplicable. However, I did obtain a copy of Ewan's birth certificate from the General Register Office, showing his sex as male, and with small print that read, "The above particulars incorporate any subsequent corrections or amendments to the original entry made with the authority of the Registrar General." It was very obviously a corrected birth certificate. The case was definitely worth pursuing.

Fortunately I was still in touch with my history teacher from school, who was then teaching at the University of Glasgow, and he turned up a short newspaper report on the case. With a date for Ewan's case now in hand, I enlisted the help of Dr. Lynne Jones, MP, with whom I co-founded the Parliamentary Forum on Gender Identity in 1994. Lynne wrote formally to the Lord Advocate for information about Ewan's case. The first reply was a simple denial: "no decision of judgment was ever issued in those proceedings."[9] But a second reply suggested otherwise: the Lord Advocate said he had "uncovered some relevant documents, including the determination itself." However, he and the Lord President of the Court of Session felt "it would not be appropriate for me to let you see copy papers or indeed disclose the details which they contain."[10] Lynne wrote back, asking him to confirm that Ewan had the common male XY chromosome pattern. It took a year for a response to arrive.

In that time, I had been in communication with another trans activist, Kristina Sheffield, who had been made unemployable several years earlier by her inability to correct her birth certificate.[11] Since UK trans people had no employment rights at that period, HR managers had been advised that dismissing them would remove any risk of future customers or staff being offended by their presence.[12] Having fallen foul of this practice, and intent on seeking legal redress, Kristina was deeply interested when I told her about the disappearance of Ewan's court records. In March 1996, she told me that she had confirmed with April Ashley and Terrence Walton that they had been shown Ewan's case and had agreed that they would not use it in court or refer to it ever again. This was disturbingly unorthodox. Legal precedents must be available for use in court, and even though a Scots precedent was not binding on an English jurisdiction, it could be pointed to as a persuasive example and certainly could be cited in European litigation. Denying April access to it and making her solicitor, Terrence, complicit in that removed a fundamental civil liberty. And now the disappearance of Ewan's case was affecting Kristina, preventing her from using it in her own legal action. She began to make her own inquiries.

When the Lord Advocate finally replied to Lynne, it was underwhelming. He repeated, "I do not consider it would be right for me to release any of the documents or to disclose the details they contain."[13] Ewan was not just hidden: he was shrouded in secrecy so deep that a member of Parliament, the people's elected representative, was denied access to documents that should have been publicly available.

Meanwhile, frustrated by our failed attempts to see copies of the court papers or find out anything about their contents, Kristina had written to the Home Secretary, Michael Howard, complaining that the UK system of justice was being undermined by this nondisclosure of a case that should be in the public domain. The Home Secretary had raised the issue internally and formally, and a fortnight after the Lord Advocate refused to give any information, Kristina received a letter from the Scottish Records Office.

Apologetic, they explained that the court papers were "spotted by chance" after having been accidentally misfiled for thirty years.[14] No adequate explanation was offered for why they did not appear in any of the indexes, minutes, records or other locations where they should have been listed. But at last Ewan had been found, and in January 1998, nearly two years after I had first heard of the case, a five-hundred-page court transcript was duly forwarded to me.

But by then, as well as my full-time job, I was busy working with a range of stakeholders to improve equality law, National Health Service (NHS) care, the prison service, educational provision and media representation for trans people, as well as collaborating to remove the ban on lesbians and gay men in the military. Consequently, it was only on retirement in 2014 that I had the opportunity to sit back and think about Ewan again and to wonder just what had happened, why his case had been hidden so deeply and how that really had affected trans experience. I dug out the five hundred pages of court transcript, subjected them to a forensic analysis, and then began a five-year research project to reconstruct the narrative that has disenfranchised trans people worldwide.

Ewan left behind no diaries, letters or other personal papers, not even a tombstone with his name on it, for at his wish he was cremated. All that remain are a few newspaper reports, the transcript of the court case and some memoirs that he published, in which he made no mention of the court case or the personal circumstances that gave rise to it. To find Ewan's historical significance, it was necessary to work from archival material surrounding his life and experience: legal decisions, government reports, minority-community ephemera, personal interviews, medical literature, trans confessionals and media coverage. Combined with recollections of him that his family, his friends and the people in his community generously shared with me, the case of Ewan Forbes took form, and its seismic consequences for trans people everywhere became evident.

Most people are unaware that until the late 1960s, trans people lived in complete legal equality with everyone else. Ewan was the reason that changed, and since his life spanned nearly the entirety of the twentieth century, it gives us a glimpse into almost a hundred years of trans history. His story begins in the Victorian period, when the Viennese professor of sexology Richard von Krafft-Ebing published the first medical description of being trans, and it ends in the present day, with increasing attacks on trans people's human rights in the US and UK. On the way, it takes in the experience of well-known trans people such as Lili Elbe, Michael Dillon and April Ashley, and successive waves of trans activism in the 1970s, the 1990s and beyond. It draws on five years of research, thirty years of frontline LGBTI activism and a lifetime in academia. Ewan's hidden court case, finally decided in 1968, marks the tipping point between the trans equality that existed in the past and today's trans discrimination. More broadly, it is also a story of how freedoms we all take for granted can be instantly lost.

PART ONE

1

CHILDHOOD

Craigievar is one of the loveliest castles in Scotland, its faded pink roughcast walls and high, circular turrets giving it an appearance more of a fairy tale than the Highlands. Its ancestral lands march between the river Don and the river Dee, and close by is Balmoral, the Queen's home. At the start of the last century, the Forbes-Sempill family estate included a mansion twenty miles east at Fintray. The family owned the village of Fintray, which for generations had provided the army of servants it required: cooks and gardeners, butlers and kitchen maids, nannies and footmen, grooms and porters and pageboys. Inside the mansion a vast hall opened onto a wide staircase filled with ancestral portraits. At Christmas, the hall became the stage for a glorious pantomime of their own making, in which everyone took part—family, staff and guests—dressing up in whatever came to hand. It is here that we first meet Ewan.

In a photograph of everyone in their costumes, little Ewan has his back to the stairs, standing between two young girls, one with a crown and one with a hat. Ewan is bareheaded, his hair brushed back from his high forehead, his gaze direct and quizzical. His face is thinner than the other children's, making him seem frailer, but his chin is tilted defiantly upward. Dressed in some kind of ornate tunic, his is an androgynous figure when compared with the girls in their frocks framing him. At the rear center of the photograph stands his sister, Margaret, dressed as Britannia, with trident, helmet and Union flag shield, suggesting that the photo was taken at

3

The Christmas costume party at Fintray Manor

the Christmas of 1918, and Margaret is epitomizing Britain's victory at the end of World War I. She was seven years older than Ewan, and since she looks about twelve or thirteen here, Ewan, born on September 6, 1912, would just have been six. Margaret and Ewan's older brother, William, is not there: he was nineteen years older than Ewan, and by the end of the war he had become a colonel in the new Royal Air Force. Ewan will have missed him, for one of his earliest memories was of William arriving in uniform on a motorbike to visit the family, and he grew up hero-worshiping him. But their father, the Lord Sempill, is close at hand, sitting on the floor at the front right in an elaborate robe, a long false ponytail trailing over his shoulder and his face painted like a pantomime Aladdin, while their mother, Gwendolen, the Lady Sempill, sits just in front of Margaret. She looks tired of being in her showy wig of heaped-up ringlets, and her corseted, tight-fitting gown, with its plunging ruffled neckline showing her three strings of pearls. Doubtless she will have been energetically organizing everything and everyone all day.

Fintray House was built in the grand style, imposing, distinguished, fit for its royal and noble guests. Its airy drawing room dwarfed the grand piano; in the dining room, a life-size full-length portrait of Ewan's grandfather, "Auld Sir Wullie," an intimate friend of Queen Victoria, gazed benignly down; the library was filled with vellum quartos and folios, literary treasures older than Shakespeare. The mansion's diamond-shaped windows looked onto elegant lawns and terraces falling away to the broad, mellow, silver Don. But the real, beating heart of the family, the place young Ewan loved to go, was the wild Highlands: Craigievar.

A regular move each summer from the mansion to the castle—"the flitting"—was one of Ewan's earliest and happiest memories. It was heralded by the departure of the head housemaid, two days before everyone else, to alert the Craigievar caretaker and begin making up beds for the family and the rest of their servants. Cook was the next to leave, complete with a milking cow, so that food could be ready for everyone on arrival, and while the chauffeur ferried the rest of the domestic staff in the family's big Siddeley-Deasy limousine, Ewan, his sister and his mother set off on a more leisurely journey.

As soon as he was old enough, Ewan rode his pony for the expedition, while his sister, Margaret, and their mother each drove Shetlands in pony carts. A photograph taken in 1919, when Ewan was almost seven, shows them ready to depart. Ewan, in "ratcatchers" and riding hat, is astride his beloved pony Tommy, impatient to be off. Thirteen-year-old Margaret's legs dangle from the back of her custom-built cart, where she is organizing her Pekingese dog. Their mother, Gwendolen, is between them, with impeccably upright posture, driving that trickiest of all small carriages: a governess cart, where the driver has to sit sideways and steer a true line from a difficult angle—the life skill she would need for raising Ewan.

The flitting

Ewan's brother, William, who as firstborn son was known as the Master of Sempill, had married Eileen, the daughter of the distinguished painter Sir John Lavery, a few months before, and they were pursuing their own adventurous lives in the new aviation industry. The Lord Sempill drove down separately with his butler in a little American car, an Essex, in what sounds like a hair-raising journey since, Ewan said, the butler "risked his life." In a gentler progress, the equestrian group broke their twenty-two-mile journey at Monymusk, a village Ewan's forebears had bought in the 1560s. It belonged by that point to the Grant family, and Ewan's godmother lived at the House of Monymusk, built centuries earlier from the stones of the old Norman priory. Everywhere was steeped in ancestral associations. A couple of miles farther up the Don, nestled in a bend of the river, lay Paradise Wood, which Queen Victoria visited in 1866 to see its spectacular mature larches: perhaps she, too, had been on the way to Craigievar Castle. Beech trees lined the castle's main drive, the falling sun making their shadows a ladder of light, which Ewan rode up to the castle door. Here he lived between the castle, warm welcomes in local farm kitchens, and the country separating them. Craigievar was wild to Fintray House's domesticated, a tall tower to its spreading rooms,

Early nineteenth century lithograph of Craigievar Castle

heath, hill, moor and forest, not gardens and greenhouses. Craigievar was adventure.[1]

The Forbes-Sempill family was discreetly distinguished. Ewan's father held two titles, a baronetcy ("Sir") and a barony ("Lord").[2] Both titles were among the oldest in Scotland. The family had long-standing royal associations: not only had their ancestors been friends of Scots national hero Robert the Bruce, but they had played a part in the release from English captivity of King James I, who conferred their knighthood in 1430.[3] Friendship with and service to the monarch became an enduring theme for the family, and in 1488, King James IV upgraded the knighthood conferred by James I to the Barony of Sempill. The Forbes lineage was similarly honored, so that in 1630, Sir William Forbes was created a baronet of Nova Scotia. Both the Sempill and Forbes dynasties converged in Auld Sir Wullie, who was the 8th Baronet Forbes of Craigievar and the 17th Lord Sempill. As well, in the Scottish way, the Forbes-Sempills were also lairds, the ancient Scots clan title held by estate owners who place the welfare of the land and its people at the heart of their work and lives.

Ewan's father, John, whom he referred to as "the Auld Laird," inherited both the titles and the close royal connection, becoming an aide-de-camp to King George V. But he was also a dark, unpredictable, somewhat obsessive character. In World War I, General Kitchener had tasked him with raising a new battalion of the Black Watch, the Scottish infantry regiment traditionally associated with the Forbes-Sempill family. After leading his men "over the top" in trench warfare at the Battle of Loos, the Auld Laird was struck in the spine by shrapnel and lay paralyzed all night in no-man's-land, his life saved only by his orderly, Corporal Smith, who found him the next morning and got him to safety, to be invalided home. Two of his brothers were killed at war: only the youngest one, Lionel, survived unscathed, as a rear admiral in the Royal Navy.

Those terrible experiences perhaps had something to do with the Auld Laird's difficult relationship with William and Ewan, who were very attached to each other despite their age difference. Ewan observed that "his father's tantrums and tempers were constant, and the unfairness of things that were perpetrated on us had to be experienced to be believed."[4] When Ewan was grown-up, his mother told him that when William was born, and she proudly showed him to their father, the response she got was, "You go to hell, I don't want a son, I wanted my brother Douglas to succeed." Douglas would have been next in line, and it was not uncommon for eldest sons to feel that a sibling was "the better man" or that they would cope better with the duties of rank, which included sitting in Parliament in the House of Lords.[5] Simply by being born, William had seemingly thwarted his father's wishes: he attributed the Auld Laird's black moods to that and told Ewan to ignore them. But there was also a certain stubborn dogmatism in the family. Ewan's great-grandfather had preserved Craigievar Castle in the baronial style of its original, seventeenth-century building, and

Left to Right, the 18th, 19th and 17th Lords Sempill:
the Auld Laird, William, and Auld Sir Wullie

his father was determined to do the same. Hence the annual "flit-ting"—Craigievar's paucity of modern plumbing, heating or light-ing meant that even by early twentieth-century standards it was uncomfortable to live in during the winter.

But Ewan was happy, in spite of these restrictions and his father's moods. He was a patient and biddable child who did his best to comply with whatever was required from him. His father insisted that everyone learn to speak, read and write in Doric, the Scots vernacular, which Robbie Burns used in his verse, and so Ewan did. His father's family were Old Covenanters, rigorous Presbyterians, and Ewan not only attended worship faithfully but later in life became an elder at his local kirk, as Presbyterians call their church. Engagement with Scots folk culture was another family imperative, and like his grandfather, father and mother, Ewan became an accomplished Scots country dancer, eventually founding his own troupe, the Dancers of Don. At the same time, mindful of Scots historical friendships and trade with continental Europe, Ewan's father expected everyone to be able to speak two or three European languages, and Ewan dutifully complied. It was as if he had the resilience, intellect and imagination not only to take in his stride every austerity and duty his father demanded, but to enjoy and thrive on them. At least, every demand but one, and it was in that matter that Ewan's mother, Gwendolen, came to the fore.

A photograph of Ewan's parents outside Craigievar Castle shows Gwendolen's strong, good-humored face, erect carriage and firm jawline, and where the Lord Sempill could be flinty, dour and grim, the Lady Sempill was gentle, caring, and fun. Her family was of Welsh and Cornish descent, from the distinguished Ap Roger line, which came over with William the Conqueror, and she was a close friend of Queen Mary, who admired her gardens at Fintray. While her husband was away at war, Gwendolen ran the estates of Fintray and Craigievar, and on rainy days she sat toddler Ewan on a cushion inside a large, upside-down turtle shell and told him to "go on a voyage" while she wrote business letters. Using his hands as paddles, he sailed round the vast room, "negotiating chairs, tables and all sorts of cabinets and ornaments as rocks," guarding the trust his mother placed in him—not to hit the Bühl table or Louis XVI cabinet—with fierce, childish honor.[6] An accomplished musician—she played five instruments, but the harp was her favorite—Gwendolen took her aristocratic responsibilities seriously. During World War I, she established a hospital for wounded Belgian soldiers at Fintray House, donated four ambulances to the Red Cross, and entertained British walking wounded at tea every Sunday. She paid at least one visit a year to each of the estate's 120 tenant farmers and employees, more if there was illness in their family, and she paid

Ewan's parents outside Craigievar Castle

for a doctor for those who could not afford to do so themselves. And she focused all of that willingness to empathize, nurture and care on Ewan.

He had been assigned as female at birth, christened Elisabeth, and raised as a girl. Because his external anatomy was visually consistent with that of a baby girl, there was no reason for his parents to imagine he was anything other than female until he got older. But as far as Ewan was concerned, he was a boy, and his certainty about this was so firm that his tranquil memoir, *The Aul' Days*, published when he was seventy-two, mentions no other possibility. Ewan was in every other way an obedient child: he loved learning to play the harp like his mother, becoming an accomplished traditional dancer like his father and grandfather, and doing his lessons in the airy schoolroom at the top of the castle. But Gwendolen could see that there was something quite different about him from his older brother and sister. Although they had been sent to boarding school from the age of six or seven, William eventually going to Eton, and Margaret to Queen Margaret's School in York, Gwendolen understood immediately that Ewan needed a quite different learning environment, and she employed governesses and tutors to teach him at home. School would be disastrous for Ewan, for it would treat him as if he was a girl, causing immediate distress and enduring psychological damage. But in the protected environment of homeschooling, Ewan could thrive. Strongly receptive to Ewan's needs, Gwendolen called him "Benjie" at home, not "Elisabeth" or "Betty," encouraging family friends to do the same, and saying it was because, like Benjamin in the Bible, he was so much younger than her other children. It worked: thirty years later, the Marquess of Aberdeen still opened her letters to Ewan with "My Dear Benjie."

When Ewan was six, Gwendolen decided that she had to do something because, as we now know, it is between the ages of six and seven that children develop the understanding of gender consistency and stability, which Ewan had clearly developed.[7] His former experience of healthcare had been literally limited to horse medicine: for coughs and colds Gwendolen dosed him with a fluid called Globena—declaring, "Of course it will cure you, it saved the life of your father's horse in the South African war"—and for sprains and other injuries with "Elliman's Embrocation as prepared for horses."[8] But when he was six, Gwendolen took Ewan to a pediatrician, in what was to become the first of a long series of medical interventions. The pediatrician referred them to Professor McKeren, a urologist at Aberdeen. In later life, in spite of his medical qualifications, Ewan would say little about his childhood treatments, politely claiming that he never knew quite what was going on: his body, and especially his genitalia, were his business, and not for public inquiry. But it is clear that Gwendolen now brought into play all of the family's powerful connections to do everything she could to solve Ewan's dilemma.

Time was not on their side. As the caring parents of all trans children know, Gwendolen and Ewan needed to find a solution before he went through the wrong puberty. In the early 1920s, this was a difficult task, with only a limited chance of success. They hoped for the best and prepared for the worst.

The power of the Forbes-Sempill family gave her hope. The family connections were wide and various. As well as the family's links with the aristocratic and crowned European elite (the Queen of Spain was a houseguest), Gwendolen's family had money. A cousin, Ernan Forbes, was the head of MI6 for Austria, Hungary and Yugoslavia, and his wife, the American writer Phyllis Bottome, was part of the international avant-garde, friendly with Ivor Novello, Ezra Pound, the poet Edna St. Vincent Millay and the American journalist Dorothy Thompson and her husband, the novelist Sinclair Lewis, the first American writer to receive the Nobel Prize for Literature. Gwendolen's energy was a family legend: when someone complained there were not enough chairs at Craigievar, Gwendolen responded, "Chairs? What for?" since, as everyone knew, she was too busy to sit down. She swung into action. Whatever could be done for Ewan would be done.

A massively influential medical text, Richard von Krafft-Ebing's *Psychopathia Sexualis*, was current among the intellectual set. First published in 1886, it was still sold in an English edition in 1947, and it shaped medicine's thinking about trans people until the 1960s. In Radclyffe Hall's famous 1928 novel *The Well of Loneliness*, her trans man hero, Stephen, finds the book in his father's study. It is a landmark medical book for trans healthcare, since it provided the first set of diagnostic criteria for what Krafft-Ebing called "metamorphosis sexualis without paranoia." These diagnostic criteria operated by setting out the patient history of several trans men and women and deducing from this what is known as a "typical patient narrative." If a patient presented with a history that corresponded to Krafft-Ebing's typical patient narrative, then they would be diagnosed as experiencing "metamorphosis sexualis without paranoia," or, as we would say today, being trans.

But there was a vicious sting in the tail of Krafft-Ebing's diagnosis. What he meant by "without paranoia" was "not being gay." Male homosexuality was illegal, and *Psychopathia Sexualis* was written primarily for the criminal courts, to enable juries to distinguish between gay men (go directly to jail) and people with apparently similar but actually different "diseases." For at that time, to be gay was to be diseased or degenerate. Either you had been born with your biology broken in some way or you had been corrupted by society. To support this idea, Krafft-Ebing described what he called the "law of the sexual homologous development."[9] It was claimed as a matter of scientific "fact" that "cerebral development" must match genital development: right-minded people were right-bodied people, and right-bodied people were heterosexual. Gay and bisexual people were unnatural and possibly criminal. But where gay men and lesbians were mentally ill, "diseased and degenerate," being trans was simply a form of physical intersex, people who were biologically different, and natural justice demanded that they be supported and accepted, not persecuted.

Krafft-Ebing's work impacted several generations of psychiatrists. *Psychopathia Sexualis* went to twelve editions, was widely translated and was cited by other sexologists, including Sigmund Freud. And it carried its homophobia with it. Decriminalization of male homosexuality did not begin until 1961 in the US and 1967 in the UK.[10] This meant that trans people were conscripted into institutionalized homophobia: unless they presented with a history that explicitly rejected same-sex intimate relationships, they would not get medical care. That medical imposition created tensions that still endure today for some members of LGBTI communities.

But to be fair to Victorian medicine, we should recognize that belief in the law of the sexual homologous development was general. Nowadays we take sex to mean biology (intersex, female, male), sexuality to refer to love (bisexual, gay, straight), and gender to denote cultural conventions for dress and behavior (androgynous, masculine, feminine). But the Victorian error, which in philosophy is known as a "category error," made no distinction between sex, sexuality and gender. The false but enduring idea they gave us was that to be female was to be feminine and heterosexual, and to be male was to be masculine and heterosexual. Anything else was "abnormal."

The politics of the day turned this category error into a persistent pseudo-medicine, separated from real, empirical, scientific medicine by a "stubborn will to nonknowledge."[11] Pseudo-medicine refused to recognize the obvious biological evidence that humanity's variety incorporates variations in sex development, differences in sexual preference and diverse personal expressions of social identity. Since homosexuality was illegal or illicit during the nineteenth and twentieth centuries in most of the developed world, including Europe, North America and Australia, this new pseudo-medicine supported both the imprisonment of gay and lesbian people as criminal and their abuse by medical "cures."[12] Similarly, the category error determined the shape of Krafft-Ebing's "typical patient narrative," supplying its notion of trans people moving from one binary pole of sex, gender and sexuality to another, ultimately engendering the concept of "transition," which is still used to disauthenticate and diminish trans people today.

Even so, Krafft-Ebing's description of "metamorphosis sexualis without paranoia" had left a medicolegal loophole for trans people, and it was this affordance that Ewan and Gwendolen used. Medical research was challenging established views, and by 1910, Dr. Magnus Hirschfeld had published his landmark work *Die Transvestiten* (*The Transvestites*). Without using those terms, he began to distinguish recreational cross-dressing from homosexuality and both from being trans, while mounting a powerful defense of all three. In July 1919, when Ewan was six, Hirschfeld opened his renowned Institute for Sexual Science in central Berlin, to the great interest of the European gay avant-garde: the playwright and diarist Christopher Isherwood lived next door, and his friend and some-time lover, the famous modernist English poet W. H. Auden, vis-ited the clinic. Hirschfeld's institute worked closely with Vienna's Institute for Experimental Biology, where pioneering endocrinolo-gist Eugen Steinach had been using transplants of animal tissue to rejuvenate and improve the sexual performance of elderly men.[13] Sigmund Freud and W. B. Yeats both attested to the effectiveness of the Steinach procedure, although, like Serge Voronoff's contempo-raneous process of implanting monkey glands, it in fact operated only by a placebo effect.[14] But work of this kind introduced the idea that endocrinology could affect the boundaries usually drawn in human experience and meant that research was carried out to syn-thesize hormones such as estrogen, testosterone and progesterone. In 1923, a film made by Steinach that explained basic endocrinol-ogy and the effects of "glandular juices" on shaping human bodies and minds as female, male or intersex had been screened across Germany and Austria.[15] Hirschfeld's institute had "developed 'ovarian' and 'testicular preparations' to be injected as a primitive form of hormone therapy,"[16] and in the 1920s and 1930s, Nobel Prize–winning American and German biochemists had increas-ing success in producing the preparations that form the basis of modern hormone replacement therapy (HRT).[17] This meant that there was information and at least experimental solutions available to those trans people and their families who had the wherewithal to access them.

During his preteen years, Ewan was allowed to run wild with his male cousins and the other boys on the estates, riding, skat-ing, organizing races and wrestling competitions, hunting for rats in the estates' granaries, lassoing the farm cattle, and every other boisterous boyhood activity. Whenever he could, he wore either riding breeches or a kilt, and a childhood picture shows him short-haired, in a jumper and breeches, trick-riding his pony Tommy by standing on his back. Visitors being shown round Craigievar—the great American novelist Henry James was one such—discovered that an air rifle and a bowie knife were given pride of place in Ewan's room.[18] His mother would explain, "Oh, these belong to my youngest child, such a queer child, you know, sort of tomboy and very masculine." But such visitors and other formal social events were a torment to young Ewan, who was expected to behave "properly" and to wear what he called "frilly things or dresses and things of that kind." His life was shaped and often constricted by such implacable family duty, so that when he was eight years old and running wild with other boys at Craigievar, Ewan had to put on a dress to join his older sister, Margaret, in a ceremony to commemorate the people of Fintray who had died in the war. They listened quietly to lengthy prayers and speeches from their father and other dignitaries, before stepping forward to unveil the new war memorial. Occasions like these must have been deeply distressing even to an obedient child. To make matters worse, the public press always referred to Ewan as "the Hon. Elisabeth Forbes-Sempill" even though no one called him that at home.

Of course, Ewan had no choice but to comply, and speaking forty-five years later, he said somberly that it made him feel "like a bird that had had its wings clipped." He did his intrepid best to avoid such occasions. At Craigievar, where there was only one door in or out, he was thin enough to squeeze through the kitchen window on the castle's ground floor, while if unexpected visitors turned up at Fintray, Ewan jumped the twelve feet out of the schoolroom window and ran away as fast as he could, so that he could honestly say that he had never heard his name being called. Perhaps the occasional mischief he got up to was him compensating for those restrictions: dropping a huge stone down the kitchen chimney to put the fire out, or catching bees and putting them in the kitchen cupboard as a surprise for the cook—there was no oatcake treat for him that day! Gwendolen did her best to occupy him. One of Ewan's jobs was cutting up the family's annual supply of laundry soap, bought in a two-hundredweight (one-hundred-kilogram) lump from Glasgow Drysalteries. He had to turn it into small squares and stack them up in neat arches to dry out. He had been sensible and responsible enough to be trusted to take messages on his pony when he was just five years old, so that by the time he was nine, he was delivering buckets of soup, balanced on his saddle, to local families stricken with the flu.

Ewan's brother, William, had given Gwendolen a firm grounding in dealing with children who knew themselves to be different. William and school didn't mix, and in 1907, the newspapers were full of the schoolboy who had run away from Eton, seen the sights of London and then taken himself home to face his parents. Gwendolen's solution was to allow William to leave school when he was fifteen and take up an engineering apprenticeship at Rolls-Royce, where he started work at six in the morning with all the other apprentice mechanics. She operated to the principle that people knew their own hearts, and she would do her best to make sure her children got what they needed from the world. What's more, his older brother provided Ewan with an inspirational model of independence. As Ewan was becoming a teenager and starting to meet his own personal challenges, William was becoming known worldwide as an aeronautical expert, leading advisory missions to Japan, America and Greece, flying everywhere in his de Havilland Moth, breaking international records and supporting the new British aerospace industry. William's title, Colonel the Master of Sempill, and his intrepid life made him a real-life version of a cinema hero. Ewan worshipped him.

When he was six, Gwendolen had established that Ewan had a normal female anatomy, and later, she warned him that he might menstruate, saying, "You know what may occur," and questioning him frequently about it. At least menstruation was likely to occur later in those days, perhaps not until sixteen.[19] By the age of thirteen, Ewan was holidaying in St. Moritz with his uncle, the Reverend Charles Prodgers, making friends with the Cartier children, winning a bobsleigh race with them, and falling desperately in love with his eighteen-year-old female cousin. St. Moritz was famous as a health spa before it became a leisure resort, and perhaps his visit was also a part of his healthcare. Certainly, it gave

Ewan much-needed companionship, since at home his society was mostly adults who worked on the estates: Annie, who gave him glasses of milk that were half cream; Jimmie, who told stories about smugglers on the Don; and Postie Lawson, who showed him endless ingenious inventions.

Ewan's sister, Margaret, was at boarding school for most of the year, often staying with friends during holidays, and their almost seven-year age difference meant that they had little in common when she was at home. She returned from finishing school to be presented at Court as a debutante, and ten-year-old Ewan was "dragged over the border" into the London Season's fashionable parties and dinners, which he found "a very wild and hectic time of society nonsense." They were never very close. Every now and then Margaret would deign to play with Ewan: once they rooted through the outbuildings and "collected together all the strange commodes and conveniences of a bygone age, including some with cute little steps to climb up to some of the four-posters about five feet off the ground." Titling their assemblage "Baronial Sanitation throughout the Ages," they presented it as an entertainment to dinner guests. But for the most part, Margaret simply wanted to spend her time with her Shetland ponies and her friends, grooming, cleaning tack and preparing for shows, and while Ewan was allowed to watch, he was not trusted to touch. Yes, he rejoiced when his cousins David and Patrick came to visit, and they could organize rodeos or ice hockey or a carnival, and reassemble their impromptu musical trio of melodeon, mouth organ, and paper and comb. But those were the high days. For most of the time at Craigievar, his only constant companion was "the mannie," a red-haired mummified head, "which my father had picked up in the desert beside Wadi Halfa" and who, Ewan said, "was really a very sincere friend." Similarly, at Fintray he was "often lonely," finding solace by lying down among the ponies and horses and putting "my head on their warm comforting rumps."

This sense of personal isolation, so familiar to many trans children, was accompanied by an equally familiar increase in risky behavior. Back home, Ewan began to imitate the skijoring he had seen in Switzerland, an extreme sport in which a skier is towed by a galloping horse. Even in today's controlled conditions, on flat, groomed racetracks, wearing modern full-body protective clothing and helmets, with emergency ambulance services on standby, it reportedly gives an adrenaline rush like no other. Fourteen-year-old Ewan, though, "tore along the roads at home which were usually very ice-bound, even with the modest amount of traffic in 1926," with the added danger of being trampled if he overtook "the horse going down steep braes," and only able to stop with "vigorous stemming." It was a radical level of risk-taking.

But everything was about to change. In spite of his social isolation, Ewan was a gifted student. The most complicated steps in traditional Scots dance were always the ones he most enjoyed learning, while his horsemanship was as skilled as it was extreme. And his homeschooling had given him excellent support. By the time he was fifteen, fluent in French and German, he was allowed to attend a coeducational college in Dresden, where he relished the days filled with lectures, visits to operas, weekends skiing, skating and wandering in the forests, and still more advanced lessons in music and the harp. It seems to have been one of Ewan's happiest times. His remarkable outdoors experience, gained running wild in Scotland, stood him in good stead. Although he was the youngest in his group, he led the cross-country skiing in Bavaria's deep forests: the others called him the "Wichtel Männchen," or "good elf," because of his ability to guide them safely and securely. He relished the new companionship.

Against this background of Ewan's life as a student and woodlander, Gwendolen arrived in Dresden. She had done a good job. Letting Ewan live, dress, play and be named as he wished at home allowed him to develop a sense of himself as an individual, and it meant Gwendolen could be certain that he was trans, rather than just "going through a phase."[20] In spite of the loneliness and risk-taking of his term-time life, Ewan had been able to form a positive sense of himself and his abilities and to relish learning and life.

This was vital to surviving the social traumas that he endured as his part of the bargain, for the wonderful support Gwendolen gave him came at a price.

Intelligent, liberal and caring though she was, Gwendolen had still been brought up with Victorian values of propriety, and the Forbes-Sempill family was a focus of attention locally and distinguished nationally. Ewan's father had a strict code of personal honor, and a sense of duty that demanded that family members fulfill their social obligations. What's more, Gwendolen cared a great deal about her husband's profile and presentation. Trying her best to manage the tension between the demands of social position and the needs of her children, the trade-off she made with Ewan for all the help and support he received was that he played his part and didn't rock the public boat. Put simply, on some formal social occasions his parents gave Ewan no choice but to dress as a girl. The Victorian values that overshadowed the early twentieth century made it a brutal period for any child who was different. Before William was allowed to become an apprentice at Rolls-Royce, he was sent back to Eton, where he was birched—held down by two other boys and ritually beaten, mercilessly, on his bare buttocks with a bunch of thin, whip-like twigs, designed to cut and mangle—in front of the other pupils as a lesson to him and them. Ewan paid his price in mental rather than physical anguish, but it was no less humiliating or painful.

It would be decades before Ewan finally rebelled against family duty and publicly changed his name and corrected his birth certificate. At fifteen, he was just beginning his journey into autonomy, springing from his positive experiences of life in a different country, ready to find out how the world might help him. And putting aside her problems in managing her husband's iron inflexibility in matters of protocol, Gwendolen's wartime experience had made her into an excellent guide. By managing the hospital that Fintray House had become and organizing the Aberdeen branch of the Red Cross, she had gained a practical knowledge of medical circles and a healthy respect for the mysteries of medicine. Sphagnum moss was just one of these. Writing to the *Aberdeen Press and Journal* in 1917, Gwendolen encouraged others to follow her example, saying, "I started a two-hour Saturday afternoon meeting (of course attending regularly personally) last September, gathering moss whenever weather permits and drying it in a laundry loft in cricket bags."[21] Sphagnum moss was in great demand for the treatment of war wounds at the front, for it was a far superior dressing to cotton wool, which was being commandeered for explosives manufacture anyway. It was much more absorbent and had antiseptic qualities that science recognized but couldn't explain. The filthy conditions of the trenches meant that bullets and shrapnel carried sewage bacteria from contaminated clothing deep into wounds, frequently resulting in amputations to avoid septicemia. Sphagnum moss absorbed the blood and pus and mysteriously healed the infection where chemical antiseptics failed. Gwendolen encouraged local people to collect the moss, prevalent on bogs and moors, with the aim of Aberdeenshire supplying 150 bags of it a week. She might not have known the science, but she knew what worked.

When he was fifteen, then, Ewan and his mother began a series of visits to European specialist doctors, beginning in Dresden, moving on to Prague, Vienna and then Budapest. Their remarkable expedition into trans healthcare was neatly disguised as a cultural tour, and en route they saw the sights together: the castle in Prague; the Schönbrunn Palace in Vienna, where Ewan made friends with the grooms of the famous Lipizzaner horses; museums and galleries in Hungary; and a period in Paris when, Ewan said, he attended classes at the Sorbonne. But much as he liked to talk about his travels, Ewan was reticent about the medical treatment he received. In Dresden, the doctor arrived "on the instructions of my mother" and he "got something to take," while in Paris, his first consultation was attended by "a terrible plague of boils and pimples" and his second was with a Dr. Block, who sent him to the Laboratory de Tuille for investigation. Ewan says that there was a vaccine, "a particularly vile one," and "various other forms of treatment," with the consequence that the "boils still went on" and that at age sixteen, he "began to have erections and emissions." When they returned to Aberdeen, Ewan's mother took him to "Dr. Tom Fraser and he produced some more vaccine, and I had a further course of injections," after which the boils stopped temporarily.

Even today, when preparations are far more refined and prescribing far more accurate than in the experimental days of the 1920s, trans boys and men are warned that some acne can appear as a result of taking testosterone, and it is clear that, almost a hundred years ago, Ewan was a guinea pig for early endocrinology. If cross-sex hormones are continued, then they stimulate a male puberty, just as Ewan experienced, thanks to the careful arrangements made for him with Dr. Fraser when they returned home.

Their journeys were a travelogue of famous names and connections. In the spring of 1931, Ewan visited his mother at Baden-Baden, where she was taking the waters, for a series of consultations with Phyllis Bottome's physician, Dr. Eddy Schacht, whose brother was then president of the Reichsbank and later became Hitler's minister for economics.[22] That year is another landmark in trans history as the date of the first documented gender-confirmation surgery, provided for a trans woman named Dorchen Richter. Her vaginoplasty, carried out at Hirschfeld's institute, was a milestone in surgical reconstruction and heralded a new era in trans healthcare. The same year was also a turning point for Ewan. Medical understandings of being trans were changing radically, and although Dr. Schacht said only a little to Ewan—at eighteen, he was still regarded as a minor—he spoke at length to Gwendolen. Ewan reported that:

> he must have said something to my mother which gave her a far better understanding of the situation, because after the visit to Dr. Schacht, that was the first visit, there was far less restriction put upon me, and I was allowed more to dress as I liked, and I could smoke my pipe in the house, and that kind of thing, otherwise I always had to go outside and smoke it.

Eighteen months after first consulting Dr. Schacht, in the winter of 1932, Ewan moved to Munich, to stay with his cousins Ernan and Phyllis for nine months. It was essentially an elective period of counseling and psychotherapy. Ernan and Phyllis had both gone into analysis with Dr. Leonard Seif, whose approach followed that of the famous Alfred Adler's individual psychology, and Ernan had trained as an Adlerian psychotherapist. Together, he and Phyllis opened a residential school at the Villa Tennerhof, in the Tyrolean ski resort of Kitzbühel. They specialized in treating and teaching wealthy troubled youth, but it seems as though Ernan also scouted for talent for the British secret service. One of his pupils was the creator of James Bond, the writer Ian Fleming, who had been troublesome at both Eton and Sandhurst and who left Ernan's school first to work as a journalist for Reuters, and then to join military intelligence. Fleming's devotion to Phyllis is described in detail by her biographer, and Ewan gets a brief mention, as "a strictly-brought-up young Scottish cousin of Ernan's."[23] Ewan said simply that he had "a wonderful chance to study at the University of Munich under Dr. Seif, who was professor of Adlerian Psychology."[24] However, since the Adlerian approach was to reeducate, clients were often referred to as "pupils," and in this sense, for example, the sculptor Barbara Hepworth was another of Ernan's "pupils" in his profession as a therapist.[25] As a "pupil" of Dr. Seif, Ewan was in therapy with him while at the same time continuing his endocrinology appointments with Dr. Schacht. Schacht's HRT was effective, since at this time, Ewan said, "I found it necessary to shave, because I had quite a lusty growth of hair on my chin and cheeks, and there also, of course, was hair growth on my body, on my chest in particular." His elective counseling support from Dr. Seif also seems to have been effective. Adler's approach had three key tenets as a framework for life: work, love and social engagement. Ewan's future life—his medical practice; his devoted relationship with his wife, Patty; and his deep engagement with his local community—was to reflect those principles in full.

The Auld Laird had played no part in the arrangements Gwendolen made for Ewan. His own father, Ewan's grandfather, had been a larger-than-life figure, fighting in the Crimea, marrying three times and spending recklessly: he brought back the billiard table at Fintray House from the officers' mess in the Crimea at huge expense, and a romantic, full-length portrait of Auld Sir Wullie in full Highland dress still loomed over Fintray's dining room. It can be hard growing up in such an irresponsibly glamorous shadow, and Ewan's father had struggled at Eton, his master reporting in 1877 that "now and then he takes a naughty fit" and was "kept clean of scrapes" only "by dint of curtailing his liberty and requiring him to do all his work under my eye."[26] After Eton, in 1883, Ewan's father joined the army, but Sir Wullie's fecklessness dogged him. As the eldest of a large family of children, it was the Auld Laird's unenviable duty to write to his father in 1890, just as Sir Wullie was about to marry his third wife, pointing out that it was "entirely through you that the family have been brought into their present poverty-stricken condition" and asking him why he was marrying again when he was "unable to support in a manner suitable to their station in life" the family he already had.[27] Apparently unable to pay even the household bills, Sir Wullie had casually borrowed £1,000 (present-day value £130,000, or $177,000) at an exorbitant rate of interest from moneylenders.

Perhaps the Auld Laird became such a stickler for the rules because his own father had paid so little heed to them. He is first recorded in the company of Ewan's mother, Gwendolen, at the Wiltshire Society Annual Ball, held in London in 1888, and at that period, such a coupling in the public eye was tantamount to engagement. A family story says that the Auld Laird had made one too many social calls on Gwendolen, obliging him to marry her to save her reputation, and, certainly, the motive fits well with his character: duty was everything. Four years later, in 1892, the Auld Laird left the army and married Gwendolen at St. Paul's Church in Knightsbridge. Nine months later, William, the son he didn't want, was born.

The Auld Laird didn't have any better of a relationship with his children than his own neglectful father had, and part of his motive in joining the Lovat Scouts to fight in the Boer War in 1901 may have been to get away from his family. The Scouts were a precursor of today's special forces, recruited from lairds, ghillies and game-keepers for their fieldcraft and shooting skills, and in his slouch hat, khaki tunic and riding boots, Ewan's father cut as romantic a figure as Auld Sir Wullie.[28] He commanded the 100th Company, and even when he was wounded in a Boer nighttime attack, he mustered thirty-five men and continued fighting. Less glamor-ously, he rode for a day to take terms for surrender from the British chief of staff, Lord Kitchener, to a Boer commando unit. The Boers refused the terms and took the Auld Laird's horse and boots, oblig-ing him to walk back barefoot in humiliation.[29] Twelve years later, in 1914, two years after Ewan's birth, having "received a telegram from Kitchener asking him to command the 8th Battalion Black Watch,"[30] the Auld Laird fought in World War I. But by then he was fifty-one, too old to do well in the harsh conditions of trench warfare, and it is unsurprising that he fell to enemy fire, though perhaps it was his inflexible sense of duty and propriety that was his real enemy.

Gwendolen was aware that her husband was a difficult man, for whatever reason, and like other women of the period, she accepted that it was her job to "manage" him. He was not sociable, and when they had titled visitors to Fintray House, he would go and clear the field drains and leave Gwendolen to make his excuses and do all the entertaining. He preferred the company of ordinary people, where he could show his puckish sense of humor. One of Ewan's favorite stories was about his father being mistaken for a game-keeper by a workman. The workman asked him how long he had been a keeper, and using Doric rather than his usual upper-class English accent, Ewan's father told him, "O a gey lang file, but I'm nae gaun tae bide" ("Oh, a right long time but I'm not going to stay"). The workman asked him why he was leaving, and "I canna thole the laird" ("I can't stand the laird") was the prompt reply. Of course, Ewan's father *was* the laird, though he didn't look like it in the old clothes he was wearing. But he was more often dour than jolly, as far as Ewan was concerned. After the angry reception he had given to William's birth, it can have been no surprise to Gwendolen that the Auld Laird went out fishing when Ewan was being born, and if he was out of temper at having a new child, she could tell everyone it was because he had failed to catch anything. Gwendolen put herself between her husband and her children as best she could, and she occupied herself with her garden, took an annual sketching holiday abroad and clearly delighted in the many and varied friendships that enabled her to find help for Ewan. But she couldn't always intervene. It was doubtless the Auld Laird's obsession with duty and family honor that sent William back to Eton to be flogged, and he treated Ewan with the same inflexibility.

He didn't oppose the treatment Gwendolen found for Ewan— major difficulties are caused when one parent is unable to come to terms with having a trans child—but Ewan could never do anything right for him. Trying to emulate his father's sharpshooting, Ewan practiced target shooting with his air rifle, and when he was seventeen, his father let him go out with the keeper with a cheap second-hand shotgun to shoot the rabbits that were destroying the farm's crops. Ewan killed twenty-three with twenty-six shots, a remarkable performance, which meant that "no adverse comment was made and shortly permission was given to shoot game." But the Auld Laird seemed incapable of praise, even about an area in which they had common ground, so that "if other guns praised my shooting, he could be very annoyed," but if Ewan did not shoot well, "scolding inevitably followed, so whichever way things went, I was in the dog house." Gwendolen had to sort out and try to put to rights these constant injustices and jealousies on her husband's part, and a major part of her effort was spent mitigating his deficiencies as far as she could. However, as every parent who deals with such a difficult partner knows, protection can never be complete.

Gwendolen was powerless to prevent the Auld Laird from forcing Ewan to comply with the social observances he believed fitting to the family name. So, in 1930, even though the HRT he had received on his European tour had begun to produce hair on his chin, cheeks and chest, Ewan was given no choice but to be presented to the Queen as a debutante.

This process of "coming out," which Margaret had already followed seven years earlier, was an elaborate ritual. Only the daughters of selected upper-class families could take part in this ornate court ceremonial, and its rules were very strict. Ewan had to wear the required long white dress, with a train no more than two yards (1.8 meters) long and no less than fifty-four inches (1.3 meters) wide at the end, a headdress of three white ostrich feathers worn slightly to the left, and long white gloves. After making his curtsies to King George and Queen Mary, Ewan left their presence by walking backward—not easy in the long dress and train—for even though they were family acquaintants, proper etiquette would be maintained at all times. Presentations began after Easter and were followed by a summer of the London Season's round of garden parties and events, which Ewan liked even less. He attended one dance and a couple of London parties "under protest and duress," as he put it, "and after that I made my escape and I never went back." At home, Ewan was allowed to dress as he pleased and smoke his pipe. But until he was twenty-one, whenever the Auld Laird required it, he was forced to appear in public as "the Hon. Elisabeth," looking precisely like what he was: a young man forced to wear a dress.

In late summer 1933, Ewan left Munich and returned home to celebrate his twenty-first birthday and to attend the Lonach Highland Games, instituted by Clan Forbes a century earlier. A photograph, taken at the Lonach ten days before his birthday, shows Ewan in traditional male Scots attire, bonnet decorated with the usual Forbes badge of a sprig of broom, cromach in hand, chatting cheerfully to guests in the Craigievar party. He marked his adulthood on September 6, 1933, by choosing three guns to accompany him on a shoot, taking the sixteen-bore gun he always preferred to the usual twelve-bore, and bagging a record "seventy-five brace of partridges."

But in 1933, things were changing in Germany. Hitler had

Left to Right, Miss Deal, Miss Reynolds
and Ewan at the Lonach, 1933

become chancellor, the Reichstag had been burned down, and while Ewan and his friends were shooting game birds in the Highlands, a horrific "cleansing" had begun in Berlin. On May 6, 1933, Magnus Hirschfeld's Institute for Sexual Science and his private home were ransacked and demolished by Nazi storm troopers. Four days later, over twelve thousand books from the institute's library, along with its collection of thirty-five thousand pictures, were destroyed in the public *Säuberung*, or book burning, together with thousands of volumes of Jewish, communist and other supposedly "degenerate" literature. A bust of Hirschfeld, who was at once gay, socialist and Jewish, was carried in torchlight procession and thrown on the bonfire: Hirschfeld himself was on a lecture tour in Paris and never returned to Berlin, dying two years later in exile in France.[31]

The Nazis made no distinction between trans women, gay men and cross-dressers: all were made to wear the pink triangle and sent to camps like Dachau, Auschwitz and Sachsenhausen, while trans men, classed as lesbians, were marked by the same black "antisocial" triangle as communists and intellectuals. People with pink triangles were singled out for extreme brutality by both the Nazis and other inmates. They were segregated into "queer blocks" and given the deadliest work assignments. For those with pink or black triangles, death arrived not by extermination in gas chambers but by so-called indirect mass annihilation, a combination of "terror work," induced starvation and pitiless punishment. Their lives were ended by a few weeks of deliberately prolonged torture, justified by the Nazis' decision that they were not "real women" or "real men."[32] This was the regime Ewan had narrowly avoided.

The Third Reich's horrific attitudes reflected a colonial mindset that was centuries old. From Columbus's voyages to the Americas onward, Europeans had defined countries they colonized as terra nullius, empty lands, and the people who lived in them as Homo nullius, savages, non-people. And they had ranked them: Carl Linnaeus's Systema Naturae, an international classification system for plants, animals and minerals, provided six categories for Homo sapiens, with the sixth being "monster."[33] Similar taxonomies included in the "monster" category "persons who have changed their sex."[34] People are subordinated and dehumanized by this kind of rationalizing, dissociative classification, and Darwin's cousin, Francis Galton, was a leading expert in it. He gave us the idea of "nature or nurture," that people might be formed by biologically inherited traits or by education, and he was clear that nature always predominated: that was why the aristocracy was always fittest to rule and why colonial subjects could never be equal to their

British masters. Or women to men, for that matter. The best that could be hoped for was turning them into fit servants of empire by eugenics, the process of weeding out the weakest, as one would breed plants and animals. It was an idea popular not only with the Third Reich but with people as varied as H. G. Wells, Winston Churchill and John Harvey Kellogg of cornflakes fame.

Eugenics ranked other people's appearance and physiology against that of white, European, elite, heterosexual men, creating a violent binary between "civilized" and "degenerate" humans.[35] Part of colonialism's sinister eugenic ranking was "orientalism," the process of objectifying other people into items for study and display.[36] Sometimes this was done literally in human zoos, like the Filipino people displayed at America's 1904 World Fair, or the African family that Ewan could have seen exhibited at the Berlin Zoo in the 1930s, as if they were animals. Orientalized people, including trans people, were at once thrilling and repellent, fascinating and reprehensible, remarkable and pathetic, imbued with dangerous secrets and knowledge, necessitating control by "superior" Europeans. More subtly, orientalism operated by pseudo-medicine and the law defining specific groups of people as physically, mentally and morally inferior and exhibiting them in the "virtual zoos" of medical textbooks and illicit erotica.

LGBTI people were subjected to this toxic bigotry, formed by "nature" as naturally diseased, or turned by "nurture" into something depraved. They were viewed as tainted and in need of control, cure or eradication. It was as though the colonial eye had turned inward, to gaze on European citizens, and found them as wanting as the "savages" and "natives" of other countries.

Intellectually degraded as it was, pseudo-medicine was closely intertwined with pornography. While Krafft-Ebing was publishing his catalog of sexual practices, an English textile merchant, Henry Spencer Ashbee, was producing a three-volume catalog of erotica. Both works map and classify minority sexes, sexualities and genders as freaks, both use Latin for things they think too indecent to say in English, and both write with a tone of authoritative finality.

The only real difference between them is that Krafft-Ebing's tone is judgmental and reproving while Ashbee's is an arch, shocked, titillating enjoyment. At least Krafft-Ebing gave a measure of protection to trans people while Ashbee just mocked them, but both of them appropriated LGBTI experience for their own ends.

These were some of the ideas lying behind the Holocaust and Hitler's demand for *Lebensraum*, or "living space," for his master race. Inferior creatures were intruding onto space that should rightly be reserved only for superior, "real" people. Consequently, Nazis were ruthlessly closing down the city's trans-friendly cafés, clubs and bars, so that in 1933, being associated with Hirschfeld's institute or Berlin's gay scene was a death sentence for trans people. It is a stark reminder of what happens when a society defines some of its citizens as not "real" people.

Ewan was still in Munich with Ernan and Phyllis for the first part of 1933, and he would have seen the Nazi banner unfurled on its city hall in March of that year. Phyllis was a close friend of the American journalist Dorothy Thompson, who had interviewed Hitler in 1931 and dismissed him as a mere "drummer boy" who "will be extinguished" and whose "startling insignificance" made it inconceivable that he could persuade a sovereign people to vote away their rights and make him dictator.[37] She realized her mistake too late and went on to write endless articles exposing his brutality. But as Ewan said, in the first part of 1933, "we still thought it was all a joke." When he visited the Countess von Soden in Munich, she ordered the curtains to be drawn to block the view of a Brownshirt torchlight procession, seeing them as simply a temporary social inconvenience and telling her guests that watching Ewan dancing was far more important. Ewan went with a group of fellow students to hear Hitler speak at Munich's Exhibition Park, and he noted how orchestrated the events were: "a brown-shirt would rush across an open space shouting, 'Der Hitler kommt,' then several others were organized to shout, 'Where? where? where?,' followed by more martial music, and further shouting that Hitler was about to appear." When he did arrive, Ewan said, he screamed into the microphone to crowds that filled the building and spilled over into the snow outside, to orchestrated shouts of *Sieg Heil!* and martial music. It all seemed contrived and contemptible. But just weeks later, Hirschfeld's institute was looted and the persecution began.

While we do not know how Ewan reacted to these specific events, both the destruction of the Institute for Sexual Science and the bonfire of the books were reported in *The Times*, and since the world of trans medicine was so small, Ewan and Gwendolen must have understood their significance. Most of the rest of his life was to be lived within a fifteen-mile radius, between Craigievar Castle and Aberdeen Medical School, in the village of Alford, where he practiced as a family doctor, and at Brux, where he bought an estate. His brother, William, would fly quite literally all over the world, including a solo flight to Australia and back, but Ewan was a homebody, wanting the quiet life, his deeply personal battle fought, won and ended. Or so he thought.

2

THE MEDICAL STUDENT

Ewan was twenty-one and desperate to find an independent place in the world. He had tested out a career in the media, making recordings of harp solos and the verse of the Scots poet Charles Murray for Beltona Records in London when he was eighteen, and two years later he had made four broadcasts for BBC Scots Regional Radio, reading verse and appearing in a radio play. But there was not enough interest in Doric literature to make that a career, and so Ewan asked his father for funding to study medicine at the University of Aberdeen. An academic life was surely something to which his father could not possibly take exception, since in the 1600s, their ancestor Dr. John Forbes of Corse had been Professor of Divinity at the University of Aberdeen.

The Auld Laird's response to Ewan's request was a "frank refusal to be bothered paying out anything more on me."[1] It was a crushing disappointment to a mind hungry for higher education. Ewan said he was "wounded to the core" by this brusque dismissal of him as a worthless investment and "had no hope of achieving a life of my own."

Temporarily defeated, Ewan threw himself into learning about farm management and worked for his keep alongside the other staff on the Craigievar and Fintray estates, planting trees, fencing and doing all the driving jobs needed. It would turn out to be invaluable experience for the future.

His father, meanwhile, was preoccupied with William, who would inherit the Forbes-Sempill titles and estates. But William was not interested in farming or forestry or estate management. His head was in the clouds with his aircraft. He couldn't tell one crop from another, and he was not a good businessman, his household and personal accounts a confused mess, and documents and letters forgotten or ignored. Further, William's children were female, and although the barony of Sempill could pass down the female line, the baronetcy of Forbes was limited by primogeniture, so that only male children could inherit it. What would become of the estates when William died?

William had his own worries. After being awarded the Air Force Cross at the end of the war, he had led a mission on behalf of the British government to help its ally, Japan, create an air force. One of William's daughters was born in Japan, and he fell in love with its traditional culture. The emperor rewarded him for his service with the Order of the Rising Sun, together with a traditional Japanese house, which was transported to Craigievar for him, a regular Christmas gift of £100, and a Japanese naval rating as his orderly. But unknown to William, MI5 was on a "fishing trip" and angling for him. With its peacetime budget reduced by two-thirds, its staff decimated, and under siege from MI6 and Special Branch, who wanted to divide its role between them, MI5 was desperately looking for suspects to justify its existence.[2] William became a target largely, it seems, because he had been in Japan and had a Japanese orderly: orientalism and racism were rife in UK society, epitomized by the popular novels and films about the diabolically evil Dr. Fu Manchu. But in spite of all they did, MI5 could find no material evidence against him.[3] William went on to become something of a household name for aviation, an advisor to Sweden, Norway, Chile, Brazil and Argentina, continuing to break records, and famously landing a small seaplane on the Thames to lunch at the Savoy to show the flexibility of light aircraft. But MI5 were smarting from their failure, and they were to go fishing for William again.

The tie between Ewan and William was so great that after escaping the emergent Third Reich in 1931, Ewan had agreed to travel back with William to Eichstätt, in Bavaria. William's wife, Eileen, was Catholic, and William had decided to be received formally into the Catholic Church. Unlike the rest of the family, who were rigorous Presbyterians, Ewan had no objection to his beloved brother's association with the Catholic faith and was pleased to accompany him to St. Walpurga's Monastery, a venerable site of Catholic worship and tradition. They were invited to meet the nuns, and at the request of the Lady Abbess and the Bishop of Eichstätt, Ewan gave an impromptu performance of a favorite Highland dance, the *Seann Triubhas*, to an accompaniment whistled by William, and the next day William was received into the Catholic Church. The decision came at a cost. The dark family tradition was that if an heir to Craigievar forsook the Presbyterian faith, then "the Lands of Craigievar would surely be taken from them," and Ewan surmised that William's conversion had broken the ancient Covenanters' Oath.[4] The Auld Laird was so generally angry and disappointed with William that in his will he left William only a life interest in the estate. William could receive the benefits of the property during his lifetime, but he had no say in its future disposal. However, given the Auld Laird's fixed notions of propriety and his experiences of Auld Sir Wullie's financial recklessness, it seems as likely that the motivations were anger at William for ditching Eton for engineering and a desire to protect the estate from William's careless business management and ignorance of agriculture, rather than the curse of the Covenanters' Oath come to rest.

Experiences like these can only have cemented Ewan and William's friendship more closely. They trusted each other, they respected each other's individuality and they supported each other unconditionally. It must have been a relief to them when their difficult relationship with the Auld Laird was ended by his death in February 1934, a few months after Ewan's twenty-first birthday. William became the 19th Baron Sempill and the 10th Baronet Forbes of Craigievar, and he made sure that the new order worked to Ewan's benefit by paying Ewan a salary to manage the Craigievar and Fintray estates. William's interests lay in flying, in Gaelic culture (he was both a Cornish bard and a Druid) and in his new religion—not in agriculture. Accustomed to working just for his keep, this salary must have been a handsome reward to Ewan. In return, in his enterprising way, Ewan introduced direct marketing of produce from the farms and game from the moors, selling them to the public from a small beige van, which he drove on a regular circuit round the local villages. This became his new life, although his intention of becoming a doctor had not wavered. He had decided to self-fund his medical education, at a cost of £1,000 (about £65,000 or $88,000 at today's spending value). Now, with the role William had given him, he had a real possibility of saving money to pay for the future he wanted. Meanwhile, as well as work he was good at, Ewan had his friendships with local people to sustain him, invited by all the farmers to take his accordion to harvest suppers for what he called "an enthusiastic evening of richt Scots tunes." His aristocratic circles were used to a wider range of individual expressions and personal relationships than the rest of society. Perhaps it was because their marriages were expected to be with "appropriate" partners, not quite arranged but certainly engineered. Like Ewan, they maintained a public profile of cisgendered, heterosexual respectability, while living their private lives as they wished. Prince George, the Duke of Kent, for example, gave a perfect public performance of social "respectability" while in private carrying on a passionate affair with the playwright Noël Coward. They both attracted the attentions of the security services by cross-dressing and walking through London together (where the police once attempted to arrest them for "soliciting," the usual false accusation against male cross-dressers), but in their social circles that was regarded as absolutely their own business.

Ewan's solution to the friction between his private and public lives was typically imaginative. In 1933, when he was twenty-one, he formed a dance team, the Dancers of Don, which had a very successful round of public performances. Since the team was largely women, many of them danced the men's part, like their leader, Ewan. It was a way of doing what he loved while being male in public, in full dress kilt, jacket, waistcoat, shirt, jabot, *sgian-dubh* and sporran.[5] Newspaper reports would still use his birth name, for, accustomed to appeasing family proprieties, Ewan had not yet legally changed his name, but no one who saw him perform could doubt his sex was anything other than male. The Dancers of Don took part in music festivals and competitions, and when he was twenty-five, in 1937, the troupe appeared on BBC television demonstrating Scottish country dances. People who recall Ewan say he could dance on a sixpence, and he himself was very particular about accuracy and precision, insisting that the arms in the *Seann Triubhas*, which imitate a stag's horns as it outwits a hunter, should be curved evenly, not bent at the elbow, that turning should be swift, and each step have precisely the right amount of bounce and spring.[6]

On other local public occasions, Ewan now habitually wore a men's suit. He did his best to avoid high society "because the sex assigned to me was not what I felt it was, and I felt if I had to dress up and conform as they thought I should, dress in female clothing, I felt as if I was acting a false part, and I could not be happy in it."[7] And yet, his compliant, generous nature meant that while his mother was alive, if she absolutely insisted, he gritted his teeth. The last time he wore women's clothes was to escort Gwendolen to the Duke of Kent's garden party at the Palace of Holyroodhouse in Edinburgh in 1935. Royal protocol demanded he wear a dress or not attend at all. He and Gwendolen had once "dressed up like tinkies" to play a prank on a French baron staying in a neighboring house, and perhaps he put the garden party into the same category; or perhaps he knew that Prince George cross-dressed and thought he'd do the same; or perhaps he was bowing to family duty once again to support his recently widowed mother in the social role she valued.

Trans people in the public eye had a very fine line to tread, even in Ewan's relaxed circles, and he will have been reminded of this by the publicity in 1933 that surrounded the English translation of Lili Elbe's *Man into Woman: An Authentic Record of a Change of Sex*.[8] Newspaper stories about so-called sex changes were popular, with twenty different cases being reported in the 1930s, but they were predominantly about trans men and gave little insight into the trans experience. Being trans was a mystery, and trans women, who were considered far rarer than trans men, were especially mysterious. Now, though, there was a full-length book about a trans woman, and according to the Harley Street sexologist Norman Haire, who wrote the introduction, it was all true.

Except that it wasn't, quite. The idea that *Man into Woman* is a faithful biography, recording only actual events as they unfolded, has been an enduring one. It is repeated on internet sites and has found its way into the blurb of a novel based on Lili's life, *The Danish Girl*, "loosely inspired by a true story."[9] It *is* true that the woman we know as Lili Elbe was a trans pioneer, a painter who was married to another artist, and who lived contentedly, until she was killed by an overambitious medical procedure in 1931. Like Ewan, Lili's focus was on presenting a public image that allowed her to gain acceptance and negotiate a successful life.

Crucially, though, *Man into Woman* is a far more radical and subversive piece of work than a mere biography. As well as its surface story, it contains a hidden narrative, a kind of underground railroad or secret route for trans women eager to access medical support. It is, in fact, the first extended piece of trans activist writing, and trans people like Ewan, to whom it would have been irresistible, would have been able to read between the lines to the message that followed.

Lili's hidden story was a retelling of medicine's typical patient narrative for trans women, which in turn was based on Krafft-Ebing's famous Case 129.[10] Case 129 comprises a long and detailed letter to Krafft-Ebing from an anonymous trans woman, a physician herself, in which she describes her experience of "metamorphosis sexualis without paranoia." She became Krafft-Ebing's type specimen for trans women, and the typical patient narrative that her story formed protected them from prosecution as gay men. It is such an extraordinary loophole, and we know so little about

Krafft-Ebing's life, that sometimes there is speculation that Case 129 was actually Krafft-Ebing's own, personal narrative. Either way, by faithfully following Case 129's typical patient narrative, trans women could escape criminalization and access the newly available medical support from endocrinology and surgery. The key to success was to stick to the story as closely as possible, while personalizing it with enough minor variations so that it wasn't an obvious copy. Lili was telling other trans people what to say to get medical care without ending up in prison or confined in a mental hospital.

As well as telling other trans people *what* to say, Lili signposted the way to say it, by playing into a newly popular "real-life" format. By the 1930s, an American magazine called *True Story* had become a bestseller in the UK and the US. It was aimed at working-class women who fondly imagined that its lurid tales were "stories that actually happened to people. They are true life experiences."[11] Its anecdotes operated within the literary genre known as "conversion confessional," a "sin-suffer-repent" formula in which heroines atone for their errors by marriage, childbirth or death. *True Story* popularized a formula that became an enduring commercial success, in soap operas, blockbuster serials and, of course, the many magazines that still follow its tradition. Lili was playing into this market, calling her account "my Confessions," borrowing from popular erotica to keep the reader engaged and saying she was writing a commercial book "to be able to provide for my material existence."[12] It was not so much a "true story" as the kind of story that people were willing to believe was true.

Finally, the introduction to *Man into Woman* has a veiled warning to trans people. It was commissioned from Norman Haire, a somewhat flaky Harley Street character, who wrote medical advice for the popular Australian magazine *Woman* under the pseudonym "Dr. Wykeham Terris." He was a pompous, self-opinionated bigot: "The black races produce fewer males than the white,"[13] he wrote in one column. This addition of an introduction by a "medical doctor" was meant to give Lili's story legitimacy and to strike a cautionary note to anyone who might wish to follow in what he called Lili's "unwise" footsteps. But although Lili had used his transphobic views to make her narrative credible, she was also very clearly warning her trans readers that not all doctors were helpful and that they must be careful to avoid Norman Haire's type if they were to access proper healthcare.

Lili's book used Case 129's typical patient narrative and the *True Story* format to negotiate her public identity, while also writing a bestseller and guiding other trans women in how to present to a doctor in order to get medical help. Accordingly, her confession began with a description of her childhood: "Mother loved to dress me up. I was never clad finely enough for her," and, "I had long, fair locks, snow-white skin, and dark eyes, so that strangers often took me for a girl."[14] At kindergarten when she was five, Lili "played with eleven girls, I was the cleverest of all the children in knitting and embroidery." When she was eight, she said, "my two brothers often bantered me on account of my 'girl's voice.' "[15] At school, a girl put her hat on Lili's head, saying, "Doesn't he look like a proper girl?" and everyone laughed in agreement. She reproduced precisely Krafft-Ebing's typical patient narrative for childhood: looked girlish, dressed girlishly, preferred playing with girls, taken for a girl by strangers and teased for being girlish by her brothers and schoolmates. Ewan's narrative about his childhood was a mirror image of Lili's narrative.

In adolescence, Case 129 told a friend of her "wish to be a girl," and for Lili, her desire to be an artist—an acceptably "feminine" pursuit—was proxy for that. At twenty, Lili met and married Grete, some two or three years younger than her. They were both artists, living in a studio in Copenhagen, part of the demimonde, and this unconventionality sets the stage for a stock piece of light erotica: enforced cross-dressing. Case 129 cross-dressed at the insistent invitation of women friends, while Grete persuaded "Andreas" (Lili's birth name) to cross-dress to help her out in an emergency:

About this time Grete painted the portrait of the then popular actress in Copenhagen, Anna Larsen. One day Anna was unable to attend the appointed sitting. On the telephone she asked Grete, who was somewhat vexed: "Cannot Andreas pose as a model for the lower part of the picture? His legs and feet are as pretty as mine."

While Grete was talking to Anna Larsen on the telephone, I had been busy cleaning my palette. I was smoking a cigarette and scarcely listened when Grete informed me of Anna Larsen's proposal. At first I declined rather shortly. Grete chaffed me, abused me, implored me, petted me, and a few minutes later I was standing in the studio in costume and high-heeled shoes. We both laughed as though at a great joke. And to make the disguise complete, Grete fetched out a carnival wig from the depths of a trunk, a fair, very curly wig, and drew it over my head. Then she attacked me with rouge and powder, while I submitted patiently to everything.

When all was ready we could scarce believe our eyes. I turned round and stared at myself in a mirror again and again, trying to recognize myself. Was it really possible, I asked myself, that I could be so good-looking? Grete clapped her hands delightedly. "The most perfect ladies' model," she cried again and again. "You look just as if you had never worn anything but women's clothes in your life."

And I cannot deny, strange though it may sound, that I enjoyed myself in this disguise. I liked the feel of soft women's clothing; indeed I seemed to take them as a matter of course. I felt at home in them from the first moment.[16]

Enforced cross-dressing had been popular mass entertainment from Charlie Chaplin's *A Woman* (1915) onward, while the crossover between erotic confessional and sexological case history was well-known enough to be mockingly pastiched by James Joyce in *Ulysses*, in 1922.[17] Renaming the individual was a significant feature of such narratives, and this happened immediately in Lili's case, as Anna unexpectedly turned up for the sitting after all. At first she did not recognize Lili, but as soon as she did, "she asserted that I was very much prettier as a girl than as a man," and said, "Nature has made a mistake with you this time." Accordingly, "I will christen you, my girlie. You shall receive a particularly lovely, musical name. For example, *Lili*. What do you say to *Lili*? Henceforth I will call you Lili. And we must celebrate this!"[18]

Following Case 129's lead, Lili went into the larger world and was comfortable there, just as Ewan negotiated his own entry to society with the Dancers of Don. Thereafter, Lili began to live with Grete as two separate people, so that "if Lili was not there, we spoke of her as of a third person." Grete became increasingly attached to Lili and was distraught at any thought of losing her, but fortunately, just like Case 129, a culminating illness ended that possibility. What was horrific for Case 129 was liberating for Lili:

> I was then attacked for the first time by strange haemorrhages. I bled mostly at the nose, but in so unusual a way that Grete became anxious. . . . When the attack was over, however, I felt as if liberated, just as if something torpid in me had been dissolved; as if something new, something never before felt, was stirring. My whole being seemed as if transformed, as if a dam had suddenly burst.[19]

Lili noticed a "strange alteration in the contours of my body," just like Case 129, and after consulting medical textbooks, explained her physical and psychic transformation in the sexological framework then current, that, "I was both man and woman in *one* body, and that the woman in this body was in the process of gaining the upper hand." The press consistently used the term "man-woman" in the 1930s, so this concept of an internal biological struggle was familiar to the book's intended readership. But there was a danger Lili had to avoid. Pseudo-medicine's category error, of collapsing together sex, gender and sexuality into one, required trans women to be explicitly homophobic in order to escape criminalization as gay men. So when Lili wore her male clothes and a gay man propositioned her, she violently repudiated him, saying, "A very little more and I should have been obliged to challenge this poor creature to a duel with pistols."[20]

Then, with Grete's support and assistance, Lili sought reconstructive surgery. In clinical terms, four surgical procedures were performed, including vaginoplasty and an attempt to implant ovaries. A final procedure, to implant a womb, led to her death in 1931: doctors had still not become aware of the problems surrounding tissue rejection, believing with Voronoff and his "rejuvenating" monkey-gland implants that organs from one body would automatically be assimilated by another. But Lili's narrative provided tropes that would be repeated in future trans confessionals: waking up with "violent pain"; a vocal change to "a splendid soprano voice"; and different handwriting—pseudo-medicine believed that it could distinguish between a man's and a woman's handwriting, so Lili prudently altered her script. Lili's marriage to Grete was dissolved by the Danish government in 1930, and Grete remarried, leaving Lili free to do the same. But post-surgery, she presented herself as hyperfeminine, too modest to ask the doctor about its results, accepting a marriage proposal with an emotion of "something blissful, something frightening," and needing permission to do so from her fatherly surgeon. Finally, she opted for her last, fatal operation because "I want so much to become a mother"[21]—that is, to fulfill the heteronormative role ascribed to all women.

Man into Woman established trans confessional writing as a new, niche genre in literature. It was to prove an enduring means for trans people to articulate a public identity. Even more importantly, Lili had provided a road map for all of her readers, written in a popular form that ensured it would be widely read. This was hugely significant. *Psychopathia Sexualis* was on restricted sale and not easily available to members of the general public in case it damaged their morals, although the upper classes, like those in Gwendolen's milieu, were deemed to be above such dangers. At the same time, press coverage of trans people in 1930s UK often cited the surgeon Mr. Lennox Broster at Charing Cross Hospital, and contemporary trans people thus knew the name of someone who could, potentially, offer them medical help. Lili's narrative showed them the script they would have to follow to access endocrinology and reconstructive surgery.

It cannot be emphasized too much that at this point in history, being trans was an intersex condition, a variation in sex characteristics, part of biopsychosocial diversity, as we would say today.[22] Lili's narrative claimed that she may have had vestigial ovaries, and although this was never confirmed, it was a claim that helped to validate her surgical procedures, and it, too, became a staple of later trans confessionals. Turn up at Broster's clinic with the wrong narrative, and you would be dismissed, or worse: he had a ferociously homophobic guard dog, psychiatrist Clifford Allen, who claimed to be able to determine someone's sex and sexuality by analyzing their mental outlook and behavior. Get your story wrong and you were sunk by the same violent prejudice that destroyed the lives of gay men and lesbians. Lili was telling a story—she used invented names for the real people in her book—that was explicitly emancipatory, as a deliberate piece of trans activism.

We can expect that Ewan read *Man into Woman* while he was preparing to go to medical school, since the book was widely publicized and sexology was part of his university curriculum, but we do not know his response to it. Ewan's early access to endocrinology meant that he did not go through the wrong puberty, and so he did not need Lili's "before and after" narrative, with its culminating "change," which was to give rise to the ideas of "sex change" and "transition," to form part of his story. In the same way, he didn't need to lay claim to any of the other "changes" Lili listed: as far as Ewan was concerned, he had always been a boy and a man. But he will certainly have understood the notoriety that gathered round Lili's book and the dangers that other trans people faced, and he must have felt glad that his early medical care had saved him from that.

By 1939, when he was twenty-seven, Ewan had gathered together enough money to pay for university fees and lodgings in Aberdeen, and with William's enthusiastic support, he went to start life as a medical student. The University of Aberdeen was already familiar to him, since he had attended Alfred Adler's public lecture series there in 1937. Choosing Ewan's cousin Phyllis to be his official biographer, Adler had become a family friend, and Ewan drove him round the countryside between talks. Adler died from a heart attack before completing his lecture tour, his funeral taking place in King's College Chapel with the full university court in attendance: inevitably, the Forbes-Sempill family will have been present, so even before his admission, undergraduate Ewan would have been on social terms with the university's vice-chancellor, rector, senate and other academic dignitaries. Then, too, there were family associations, since the Royal Aberdeen Hospital for Sick Children, which was intimately connected with the medical school, held the Gwendolen Janet Forbes-Sempill Cot, endowed in memory of a sister of Ewan's who had died of peritonitis when she was twelve, two years before he was born: the Auld Laird was not completely unfeeling for his children.

Ewan loved medical school and his studies in medicine, anatomy and surgery. He had always wanted to be a doctor, and his class of 1939–44 gave him an enduring sense of community and companionship with both his fellow students and their lecturers. Ewan's yellow Labrador, Bran, the first gun dog his father let him own, accompanied him to his lodgings in Aberdeen, where he lay at the garden gate waiting for Ewan or sometimes went for "ploys" on his own, being petted and fed at various houses on the way. When Ewan moved from his digs to live at 27 Lewis Hill Avenue, "with a friend," Bran went with him. Tram fares were only a penny, and Ewan took them everywhere, exploring Old Aberdeen, set on the banks of the river Don, and "New" Aberdeen, the commercial center, which lay along the river Dee. Ewan lived in Old Aberdeen, close to his studies at King's College, the first medical school in the UK, established by papal edict in the fifteenth century, part of "the effort to realise the unity of Europe through the unity of learning,"[23] which resonated with his family's Eurocentric tradition. The original chapel and Crown Tower still remain, built in a warm golden sandstone that contrasts with the austerely lovely silver granite of its nearby contemporary, St. Machar's Cathedral. Together, the university and cathedral formed the academic and spiritual home of Aberdeen, half an hour's easy walk from Castlegate, the city's old marketplace, huddled by the clamorous, lively docks. When Ewan stood at the Mercat, as the decorative seventeenth-century market cross is known, and looked along Union Street, he saw both medieval streets like Correction Wynd and the turreted Victorian neo-Gothic Town House, the center of the city's municipal offices. Like Ewan himself, the city was a mixture of old and new, tradition and individuality, building on the past to secure a new future. He must have felt sure that, despite the challenges of his early life, he could look forward to a happy time ahead.

Part of Ewan's medical studies took place in the university and part of them in the hospitals associated with it. Aberdeen was as proud of its innovation as it was of its ancestry, billing itself as "the first Scottish university to have a swimming pool of its own" and having just built a new medical school two miles west of King's College, at Foresterhill, where all the Aberdeen hospitals were concentrated. But it was a demanding time for Ewan. The outbreak of World War II meant that medical students were expected to support the war effort with fire watching and auxiliary ambulance and mortuary services. What's more, Ewan was a mature student, ten years older than the rest of the group, and he felt shy. Happily, his new family welcomed him in. The other forty-seven men and nineteen women nicknamed Ewan "Wink," because of his habit of winking, and helped him with his chemistry and math, and Ewan became part of a jolly group of high-spirited medical students. They needed their high spirits to cope with the grueling combination of study and war work. Although London was the most heavily bombed UK city during World War II, Aberdeen was the most frequently bombed. Both the university and the hospitals were bombed, with twelve bombs being dropped on the psychiatric hospital during the April 1942 blitz, so that Ewan's studies were constantly interrupted by warning sirens, while being on the wards in the hospitals was as dangerous as being in Aberdeen's streets during air raids.

Ewan's picture in his
medical student yearbook

His brother William's war was quite different. Part of the Naval Air Branch in the Admiralty, William was president of the Royal Aeronautical Society and a Conservative peer. But he was still on MI5's watch list, and once again, they tried to prove that he was spying for the Japanese, who were now potential enemies. They presented his annual £100 gift as payment by the Japanese for espionage, though MI5 obviously knew that they themselves paid twenty times that to quite ordinary agents, let alone someone as highly placed as William. And they tried to use William's stubborn, injudicious loyalty to old colleagues against him. He had been writing to Japanese friends before Japan entered the war, sending his letters through the ordinary post, doubtless aware that they were being opened: he felt he had nothing to hide. But after the attack on Pearl Harbor, he was intercepted phoning the Japanese embassy, presumably from concern about his Japanese friends. Of course, he should have known better than to place more importance on personal relationships than on national politics. But William was a curiously unworldly character as well as a dogmatic one, hopeless with money and paperwork, his strongly romantic temperament obsessed with Celticism and Catholicism as well as flying and airplanes.

Although no smoking gun was found, an irritated Winston Churchill suggested William should be posted out of harm's way.[24] Refused an inquiry into why MI5 was accusing him, and what of, William resigned his commission and left for Canada. A rare combination of mechanic and pilot, with unrivaled experience of the aerospace industry, he must have been a loss to the war effort. A newsreel clip of the day shows him in 1939, just before the outbreak of war, marching in procession at the eisteddfod, one of the leading Druids, wearing the blue robes and distinctive headdress of a Cornish bard.[25] Perhaps that profiled him as eccentric and therefore unreliable in MI5's mind or perhaps his love of Japanese culture, liking his children to call him "Papasan" and being photographed in Japanese traditional costume, meant he was regarded as having "gone native," as the racist term of the day put it.

Meanwhile, back at Aberdeen Medical School, in between Nazi bombing raids, Ewan was working through his medical curriculum. At that time, medical education used "the medical model," in which doctors detect disease in patients by taking a patient history, then examining and testing them against a set of symptom descriptors and typical presentations of illnesses. Its focus was on measurable evidence, so that patients were positioned as "diseased bodies," objects for medical inspection and repair, in a broadly mechanistic way. Ewan's first year focused on the sciences: chemistry, physics, zoology and botany, which prepared him for his second-year study of anatomy, physiology, embryology and biochemistry. Year three moved into bacteriology, pathology, and then into forensic medicine, public health and infectious diseases, tropical medicine (for many doctors served the empire and many servants of empire returned home with conditions contracted abroad), and psychopathology, the study of mental disorders.

It is the last subject that must have fascinated, alarmed and reassured Ewan. Learning the history of medicine is a fundamental part of a medical degree, and Ewan will have known that a considerable body of work had developed since Krafft-Ebing's landmark *Psychopathia Sexualis*. Much of it had been linked to Magnus Hirschfeld's institute, which had initiated a series of International Congresses on Sexual Science in 1921.[26] A striking case study about a "sexual intermediary" had appeared as early as 1907, Karl Baer's *Memoirs of a Man's Maiden Years*,[27] and by 1926, Hirschfeld had renamed Krafft-Ebing's "metamorphosis sexualis" as "total transvestitism."[28] But from the 1930s onward, Nazism had viewed being trans as a form of degeneration, and during World War II, "psychiatrists within the US army were promoting the concept that homosexuality was a pathology and making a concerted effort to eradicate homosexuals from their ranks."[29] Psychiatry of the day, as taught in medical schools, was strongly Freudian, conflating sex, gender and sexuality and promoting attitudes to them that were ambiguous at best and deeply punitive at worst. Faradisation, as electric-shock treatment was known, was being used on so-called shell-shocked patients, while the range of conditions labeled as "schizophrenia" was treated with insulin-based comas, and the US was enthusiastically spearheading the use of frontal lobotomies, performed with a carpenter's hammer and an ice pick inserted through the eye socket.[30] Ewan must have felt deeply relieved that the work of Hirschfeld and other sexologists classified him as intersex rather than mentally ill and that his medical care had been affirmative, not punitive.

In his fourth and fifth years, Ewan followed a range of special subjects for in-depth study, doubtless spending time observing in the hospitals that shared the medical school's campus and becoming particularly adept in surgery. But as well as this formal curriculum, the "hidden curriculum" was an equally enduring influence. Medical students are strongly bonded groups, partly through the initiation ritual of dissection that distinguishes them from other university students, partly from the contemporary "medical firm" structure, which creates tight-knit teams in clinical settings, and partly from the need to support one another through long hours.[31]

In the 1930s, many students practically lived in the hospitals where they worked, often being allowed just a two-hour visit once a week from a family member. It was an intense experience, added to by the harshness of working in wartime conditions, risking their lives to save those of others. Combined with the medical model of treatment, which effectively reduced patients to objects for treatment, this could give rise to a defensive insidership, in which doctors felt they were fighting the ignorance of laypeople as well as their diseases, in a battle that only other doctors truly understood. It was a powerful camaraderie, creating deeply enduring relationships that were to stand Ewan in good stead thirty years later.

Ewan's study necessarily included the contemporary preoccupation with the "science" of eugenics. Medicine was deeply involved in colonialism, and his anatomy lectures automatically included interpreting non-European human skeletons as deformed or ape-like when compared with the European ideal, and measuring skulls to show that male European brains were bigger and better than anyone else's. The lectures in psychopathology doubtless included the "scientific evidence" for the degeneracy of gay and lesbian people and the brutal remedies for their "cure." Perhaps in surgery or in gynecology, he discovered the widespread policy of sterilizing people with congenital intellectual impairment, prevalent in the US, Canada, Japan, Germany, Denmark, Sweden, Norway and Finland.[32] And embryology taught the latest research into variations of sex characteristics, which became a hot topic during the 1936 Berlin Summer Olympics.[33]

The popular British press supported the idea that people assigned as female at birth might reasonably develop as male at a later stage of their lives. In contemporary medical literature, this was believed to be through a process that leading authority Mr. Lennox Broster called "virilism," "the appearance in the female of male secondary sex characteristics."[34] The UK field athlete Mark Weston was regarded as one such "man-woman." He had been one of Broster's patients, receiving the standard letter reading, "This is to certify that Mr. Mark Weston, who has always been brought up as a female, is a male, and should continue life as such," and marrying ten weeks later.[35] Mark became well-known because his championships in women's sports were challenged when he was known to be male. The view was that if he was a man now, he had always been a man, and accepting this, Mark offered to relinquish those awards. But these newspaper reports about Mark coincided with the 1936 Berlin Olympics to create a new preoccupation with "sex testing" in athletics generally and women's sports in particular. In fact, "sex tests" were not introduced to the Olympics until 1968, when the general medical viewpoint about trans people had changed radically, as Ewan was to find out at his cost. But in the 1930s, medicine recognized that sex might be fluid rather than fixed as male or female. One doctor in particular made it his business to explain these complexities: Michael Dillon.

While Ewan was graduating from medical school in Aberdeen, another young trans man was beginning his medical degree in Ireland. Michael Dillon already had a humanities degree from Oxford, and after graduating, he had started to take testosterone. In 1942, he had a bilateral mastectomy, and in 1944, he corrected his birth certificate to male. In England and Wales, it was easy to do this, simply by taking a letter from an appropriate medical authority, such as the one Lennox Broster gave to Mark Weston, to the General Register Office, and while it was a little more complicated in Scots law (which is different from English law), it was still a straightforward thing to do. Then Michael had his Oxford degree migrated to a men's college and secured a place at Trinity medical school in Dublin. When we watch the annual Women's Boat Race between Oxford and Cambridge, it is courtesy of Michael: he instituted the first side-by-side race between the two teams, and was stroke for Oxford, in 1936. The *Daily Mail* tabloid rewarded him with a photo of him in the boat club's uniform of cap, blazer and flannel trousers, captioned "How Unlike a Woman!" and asking readers, "Would you have guessed this is not a man?"[36]

In between Oxford and Trinity, Michael had been writing a short book, *Self: A Study in Ethics and Endocrinology*, published in

1946 in the popular "Medical Books" series, which included Magnus Hirschfeld's lectures. In 1945, he had met the groundbreaking plastic surgeon Sir Harold Gillies, who carried out Michael's long series of operations for phalloplasty. By the time he published *Self*, therefore, Michael had undergone similar medical therapies and surgical procedures to those available to trans men today, and he had been accepted legally as a full, equal, male citizen. He was writing from personal experience, and his message was that "where the mind cannot be made to fit the body, the body should be made to fit, approximately, at any rate to the mind."[37]

Self sets out a biological etiology for being trans, building on Lennox Broster's research into virilism and Alexander Cawadias's work on intersex conditions. In 1943, Cawadias's landmark book, *Hermaphroditos: The Human Intersex*, had described the endocrinological basis for variations of sex characteristics, including being trans. As far as Cawadias was concerned, few people were wholly male or female, and only social convention defined them as such: individuals' hormonal, psychic and other sex characteristics were various. The general use of the term "hermaphrodite" was a misnomer, therefore, since in reality, "the human intersex shows many gradations and shades" while "so-called pseudo-hermaphrodites and hermaphrodites" very rarely occur.[38] He believed that most women had vestiges of testicular tissue in their ovaries and many men might have ovarian tissue as well as testes. For Cawadias, HRT was an obvious remedy to redress imbalances that individuals might experience. Similarly, surgeon Lennox Broster took the view that trans men and women should reasonably be provided with whatever surgery they required to improve their lives and health. Specifically, Michael was deliberately writing against psychiatrists like Clifford Allen, who claimed that "sexual abnormalities" were their province. *Self* asserted that "it is for the individual to judge" what was best for them, and Michael knew from his own life that hormone therapy and elective surgery worked for trans people, whatever claims psychiatrists might make.

Both Cawadias and Michael refused the idea of "trans masquerade." Racism in the US had led to repulsive blackface lampoons, such as "Jim Crow," a vaudeville act that toured America and Britain in the mid-nineteenth century. Then, as now, brutally demeaning caricatures were a way of trying to delineate, enforce and sanitize boundaries between a "natural" elite and an "unnatural" Other. As the political philosopher Frantz Fanon put it, "The white man is sealed in his whiteness. The black man in his blackness."[39] In turn, this had created a fear of people who "passed," light-skinned people of mixed race who lived in "stealth" and were "read" as Europeans. This demeaning language was also applied to gay men and lesbians who were indistinguishable from heterosexuals, and subsequently to trans people who were indistinguishable from cisgendered people. It is a discourse that is intended to humiliate and disauthenticate minority communities by suggesting that their lives are masquerades and they are deceptive playactors.

The argument in *Self* is that trans people are not emulating or parodying, they are not masquerading or passing: they are who they say they are. Trans men are both the same as and different from other men, and trans women are similarly the same as and different from other women. Biology is infinitely variable, and people come in all shapes and kinds. This simple scientific fact needed to be recognized and accommodated if a society was to regard itself as ethically based.

This was precisely Ewan's view of himself, moderated only by a sense of duty that left his public name unchanged. It is tempting to wonder whether Ewan and Michael ever met, and if so, what they said to each other. But we know so little about Ewan's personal life, outside the memoirs he published and the record of his court case, which was itself hidden for so many years. There are no diaries, letters or personal papers remaining. However, the subject of Michael's book and the series it was published in mean that it will have been both irresistible and easily available to Ewan. And both the author and his subject were similar to Ewan's own experience in ways that Lili Elbe's narrative wasn't. When the press pilloried Michael, it was uncomfortably close to home for Ewan.

Like Ewan, Michael was from an aristocratic family, and correcting his birth certificate had put him in line for the baronetcy of Lismullen. This information was ferreted out by the press, and in 1953, while Michael was serving as a ship's doctor, the *Sunday Express* outed him. Such intimidating outing and bullying of trans people were to become enduring media practices. Ewan will have read these reports and understood what they meant for him and how vulnerable he could easily become.

Like the thousands of trans people who were to suffer public humiliation subsequently, Michael found that there was no right of reply:

> I wrote . . . to the editor of the *Sunday Express*, asking him whether he had stopped to think before publishing what might be the effect on a doctor's career of such a denouement. Since I had committed no crime and was undeserving of publicity, what justification had he? And I enclosed a defensive article entitled *A Ship's Surgeon Speaks*, for publication, putting right many of the printed errors and calling for a better sense of values. Needless to say, it was not printed.[40]

Always a private person, Michael found himself in "an impossible situation. Boarding any new ship, I would have been the target for speculation and whispers."[41] He gave all his considerable wealth to charity and pursued his interest in a spiritual life, arriving in India to study Tibetan Buddhism in 1959, the same year the Dalai Lama escaped from Chinese-occupied Tibet. There, he changed his name to Jivaka, devoted himself to an ascetic life of poverty and contemplation, and died on May 15, 1962, at the age of forty-seven. Michael was estranged from his family, and although he had written an autobiography, his brother Robert made it clear he would legally oppose any attempt to publish it: fifty-five years after Michael's death, it was printed for the first time, in 2017.

Michael had been vulnerable to public opinion because he was a doctor and the potential heir to a title. The cultural assumptions and expectations associated with medicine and aristocracy formed a very specific "virtual social identity"—he was expected to meet a standard of perfection that was higher than that for everyone else.[42] But the "masquerade" trope, with its demeaning inferences of freakishness and falsehood, had stigmatized him for being trans, recasting him as blemished and disgraceful. How would Ewan manage his social identity to avoid the stigmatization that had ruined Michael's life?

3

MARRIAGE

On March 2, 1944, while Ewan was still at medical school, Gwendolen died. A soft, grainy photo from the local press shows Margaret and Ewan carrying their mother's ashes for interment in the ancient family burial ground of St. Medden's Kirk, a few hundred yards away from Gwendolen's wartime home at Cothal House, on the banks of the river Don.[1] A piper leads them, playing the traditional lament "Flowers of the Forest," written for the dead at the Battle of Flodden in 1513. He is followed by the minister, who is wearing military dress, while Margaret and Ewan wear the Forbes clan tartan, Margaret's kilted skirt a little below her knee and Ewan's kilt breaking right on the knee and accompanied by a sporran: only men wear the sporran and the kilt on the knee. Behind them walk William's second wife, the noted sculptor Cecilia Dunbar-Kilburn, now the Lady Sempill—the 19th Lord Sempill was "on Government service in America," the paper said—and the Marquess of Aberdeen.

Gwendolen had always put people first. It was not just her family: she would walk miles to visit sick tenants if no transport was available, and when the wife of one of the estate's foresters was dying of cancer, she went and stayed in their cottage, cooking for him and caring for his wife during the end stages of her life. Gwendolen's other passion had been flowers: her gardens were much admired, she had exhibited at the Chelsea Flower Show, and she had bred a dahlia that was a particular favorite of her friend Queen Mary. But spring comes late in the Highlands, and so Gwendolen's

catafalque was heaped with catkins, Scots fir tips and grape hya-
cinths, as well as the Forbes clan badge of broom, taken from her
own garden. They memorialized a life given to service for her community and a steadfast, fierce love for her family.

Six months later, when he was thirty-two, Ewan graduated from
Aberdeen Medical School, becoming first junior casualty officer,
then senior casualty officer, at the Aberdeen Royal Infirmary. He
spoke warmly of his time there, acknowledging the debt he owed to
nursing staff (as all junior doctors should) for helping and guiding
him in this first, crucial year of full-time, real-life medical practice.
Like doctors in emergency medicine today, Ewan saw a wide range
of cases—burns, births, bleeds and broken bones—and many of
them required surgery: the casualty department had a stash of old
car tires to make cast sandals for patients who had their feet and
legs plastered.

His teachers knew Ewan was a talented doctor. The heads of
orthopedic surgery and of ear, nose and throat surgery had both
invited him to become their house surgeon, a prestigious vote of
confidence that was not easily earned. A surgeon requires "good"
hands, resilient nerves and the ability to navigate well—in real life,
the insides of individuals look rather different from the illustra-
tions in anatomy textbooks. Ewan's accomplished harp playing
gave him a strong, sensitive touch, his daring horsemanship spoke
to his nerve and navigation came as naturally to him in the operating theater as it did in the Dresden forests. But debates were rag-
ing in the medical world about the government's proposals for a
national health service, and much of the discussion was about the
employment and payment of doctors in the future. It seemed likely
that hospital-based doctors, such as surgeons, would get a fixed
salary, while community-based doctors would be paid according to how much work they did. Experience in emergency medicine is an excellent grounding for general practice, and always a
good businessman, Ewan decided to leave hospital medicine and
become a family doctor at his local market town of Alford, twenty
miles west of Aberdeen.

The road to Alford follows the river Don, gradually opening out from the city into neat pastures edged by drystone walling. There are glimpses of the river beyond them, and at the roadside bright yellow clumps of broom meet slender birch and spreading beech woods. The wild splendor of the Cairngorm Mountains dominates the horizon, and even in late spring you can start out in bright sunshine and find yourself in a hailstorm, for as the local people say, it is the land of "four seasons in a day." Pine and spruce mix in with the woodlands that run down to the sinuous, silvery Don, while road signs tell you that you are on "the Castle Trail," for the road to Alford is also the road from Fintray to Craigievar. Little lanes lead to villages with tantalizing names—Echt, Lyne of Sken, Tilly-fourie—and then the road drops from the forests and moors into a broad valley, where many small burns flow into the river Don. This is the Vale of Alford. Five miles away, William, the 19th Lord Sempill, was living in Craigievar Castle with his second wife, Cecilia, and celebrating the recent birth of their third and youngest daughter, Brigid, while Ewan's sister, Margaret, lived twenty miles to the east in Little Fintray, in one of the family's cottages.

Fintray House was gone. During World War II, Gwendolen had again offered it for use as a military hospital, moving herself to the smaller family property, Cothal House, a little way downstream but still right next to the river Don. But this time, Fintray House had been left in such a state of disrepair that it was not really habitable. Tragically, it was demolished three years later, in 1947, just a few weeks before a new town and country planning act would have made it a listed building, eligible for restoration. Gwendolen's famous rock gardens, which she had designed to look like a natural mountain torrent and which had attracted horticultural experts from across the world, were gone. The spacious courtyard from which the annual flitting began was obliterated. At least Gwendolen did not live to see those losses.

Ewan's new home of Alford was then a thriving market town, its railway connection to Aberdeen making it the center of the local farming economy. Still today, as you drive into the village, you can see on your right the large, well-proportioned house Rosemount, where Ewan both lived and set up his surgery. Built substantially in stone, the house has two small wings and an ample garden. The main part had four bedrooms and three reception rooms, and the west wing had an additional four rooms, which Ewan used as his surgeries and waiting rooms. It is here that Ewan started out as a general practitioner on November 1, 1945, first single-handed, and a year later, with an assistant, Dr. Laura Thompson, who had been in the class above him at medical school.

Ewan had abandoned his inherited title. Instead of "the Honourable E. Forbes-Sempill." he became "Dr. Forbes-Sempill," often contracted to "Dr. Sempill," or, to most of his patients, simply "Doctor." He was deliberately managing his public image. Of course, all of his patients would know his family background, but Ewan was signaling a new life. He was also solving the problem of "spoiled identity," which was to lead to Michael Dillon's downfall. By continuing to live among the same people who had known him all his life, he was refusing to conceal himself. He was just the local doctor, and the fact that he always wore a gentleman's suit was explained to his young nieces by their nanny as the need "to get in and out of the car a lot on doctor's rounds."

In the next few years, family medicine and hospital medicine were to go in very separate ways in the UK, but in that period before the creation of the NHS, many surgeons practiced part-time as GPs and many GPs did surgery, usually in local cottage hospitals. In rural areas like Alford, GPs did practically everything for their patients, even major operations.[2] Ewan's period as a casualty officer had prepared him admirably for this new role. The geographical area of his practice was massive, covering all the hill farms and villages: two hundred square miles and four thousand people. Just getting to patients could be a challenge, but Ewan vowed that he would always attend any call. In the very severe winter of 1947, he drove through the snowstorms in a Studebaker M29 Weasel, an American Special Forces light transport vehicle with caterpillar tracks instead of wheels, perfect for snow, able to reach the remotest hill crofts. When the Studebaker had gone as far as it could, Ewan took to his skis or snowshoes or rode on a borrowed Clydesdale horse—no mean feat, for they are tall, broad-backed draft horses, not meant for riding, and Ewan would have had no saddle and only improvised reins.

As well as his Scots patients, Ewan also attended thirty German prisoners of war who lived in Alford. World War II had ended only a few weeks before he opened his new practice, and there were around 350,000 prisoners of war in Britain. Conscription to the armed services had caused a severe workforce shortage, especially in agriculture at harvesttime, and prisoners of war supplied that need, working to the same hours and being paid at the same rate as British workers. Like Ewan's thirty new patients, many were "trustees," who lived at their places of work, under the supervision of their employer, and Ewan said that they "were very polite and cooperative and delighted to find a doctor who could speak to them in their own language, so that symptoms could be explained direct from patient to physician."[3] Another eight hundred men, mainly German but with a few Italian and Ukrainian inmates, were housed at Monymusk Prisoner of War Camp, just half a mile away from Monymusk House, where Ewan, Gwendolen and Margaret broke their journey from Fintray to Craigievar during the flitting, and Ewan's fluency meant that he was asked to take on their care as well. The quality of prisoner-of-war camps varied greatly, but Monymusk was one of the good ones. Its huts were strongly built, and thirty-five men slept in each of them on simple wooden bunks, with a pot-bellied stove to provide heating. There were blocks for latrines and wash houses, a cookhouse, boiler house, canteen, stores and medical area, while sporting activities, workshops, concerts and lectures were put on inside the camp. A group of Catholic inmates built a small chapel in one of the huts, making the altar from wood, cardboard and tin, decorated by a Ukrainian artist with paintings of saints, while an elaborate chandelier made from biscuit tins illuminated over the altar his copy of Leonardo da Vinci's *Last Supper*.

Ewan was given four assistants, all prisoners of war, one with a trolley and equipment, one with a mobile washstand, one with towels and one taking down medical notes, and he said, "I was never waited on in such a kindly and efficient manner."[4] Some prisoners of war had serious illnesses such as tuberculosis and pneumonia; stomach complaints were common, as were scabies; and many suffered from malaria contracted while on military service for their countries. When Ewan attended them, malnutrition was a problem, for many of them had arrived from "a camp in Belgium where food supplies had been short." In his memoirs, Ewan wrote:

> One man 6 feet 7 inches tall weighed less than six stones. It so happened that I had been very thin following flu and bronchitis after a hard winter's work and had bought some Keppler's malt and cod liver oil to buck myself up. I felt that this poor man was in far greater need, and took the jar down to Monymusk. It certainly did both of us a lot of good.[5]

The camp usually had two medical officers—one German and one British—and an interpreter so they could co-consult, but Ewan performed all three functions and was duly recompensed. All of Britain's prisoners of war would not be repatriated until the end of 1948, and the pay helped Ewan build his fortune. The rules of primogeniture meant that the Forbes-Sempill property and finances were automatically tied to the next male in line, but Gwendolen had had some money of her own, which her will divided between Margaret and Ewan: £3,700 each (£165,000 or $225,000 in present-day value). This was the money that enabled Ewan to buy his medical practice at Alford. And since he would go far and wide to attend patients as a matter of duty and personal honor, the NHS remuneration system, which at its inception was based on a payment per patient, worked in his financial favor. The picture painted by his former patients was of a caring, much-loved doctor. One patient, whom Ewan attended at home when she was a little girl, said that "the Doctor"—as he was generally known—was "very nice, very kind." He was especially good with children: to lance a boil on the arm of a nervous little boy, he visited him at home, said, "Oh, just look out of the window, Johnnie," and by the time the little boy turned back round, the boil was gone.[6] Ewan said that he felt that he was "amang my ain fowk," living in the community as someone "who knew their ways and could speak their language." To ordinary working-class people in the 1950s, doctors were like gods, and to have one who would greet you with a warm Doric "Fit are ye the day?" rather than the chilly English "How are you today?" must have created an instant rapport. Ewan and Dr. Thompson, a tall, commanding woman who rapidly took charge of the local Girl Guides, were made very welcome.

As World War II ended, the old traditions were being revived. The 1946 Braemar Games were the first since the start of the war, part of a nine-hundred-year-old tradition in which clan chiefs acclaim the monarch as Chieftain. The practice of raising clan banners was restored, and the first to be raised was that of Clan Forbes, by Ewan, because William was in France "by reason of divers weighty affairs," it said in the antique language of the "commission and warrant" traditionally required to delegate this responsibility.[7] As expected, the King and Queen were present, together with Princess Elizabeth and Princess Margaret, and Ewan's sister, Margaret, was one of the dignitaries presented to them. Three weeks later another important tradition resumed: the Scottish Gaelic arts festival known as the Mòd. This was a Victory Mòd, replacing the usual Royal National Mòd and reinstituting the tradition. It took place at Aberdeen's premier concert venue, the Music Hall, and was attended by the Queen and princesses, who were received by Margaret and her fellow organizers. The country was coming back to cultural life after its wartime deprivations. Ewan was called on to judge dancing competitions everywhere—at one fête in aid of Boys' Clubs, at another in aid of Scottish Youth Hostels, and at numerous Aberdeenshire sports festivals. In 1947, he and the Dancers of Don were commissioned by the Caledonian Society in Mexico to make a short, Technicolor instructional film on traditional Scottish dance. They shot it with Craigievar Castle as the backdrop, first demonstrating the dances step by step, and then dancing in full fling, in a riot of color, movement and open-air joy.

Every year Ewan was out shooting, opening the Glorious Twelfth (the start of the grouse shooting season on August 12 each year) on Corse moor, apart from once when he had to attend a home birth: he laughingly called the baby "my little grouse." His love of the countryside was enduring, and by 1947, he had saved up enough money to buy an estate at Brux, a few miles upriver from Alford, from his relative, the 21st Lord Forbes of Castle Forbes. Now, as well as his general practice, he owned a farm and three thousand acres of exquisite countryside, farmland, moors and fells, almost encircled by a loop of the river Don, entitling him to be known as Laird of Brux. What is more, it had associations that Ewan valued: traditionally, Brux was occupied by "the second son of the family" at Castle Forbes, and close to it, on the other side of the river, was the Nine Maidens' Well, where the legendary family founder, Ochonocar, slew the mighty bear that gobbled up young women and gave the family the bear on their coat of arms. In Gaelic, Ewan said, "Brux" means "sheltered bank," and he must have felt that he had found a physical haven to match the sanctuary he had made in his work. As he said later, "I felt the right to have my own wife and my own house and take my place as other ordinary individuals." In 1950, Ewan decided to ask Isabella Mitchell to marry him.

Traveling west from Craigievar, the road rises sharply up to the Cairngorm Mountains, weaving through a network of narrow glens, guarded by heather-covered heights. Even on a hot, blue-skied August day, snatches of mist roll over the stretches of boggy moorland that separate the mountains' purple-gray summits: this is the land of whisky and hard hill farming, where pure spring waters tumble from steep, rocky mountainsides into famous distilleries, and sheep pebble the neat pastures that form the bottom of the glens. Isabella Mitchell's family came from the farming community in one such glen, Glen Rinnes, running parallel to Glen Fiddich, ten miles of winding road between Dufftown and Glenlivet, its edging of purple fireweed and gray thistles occasionally broken by the riotous reds and yellows of an outlying cottage garden. Even tinier roads fall away into the valley bottom, where the Dullan Water runs, and it was down one of those that Alexander Mitchell had his house, on the estate known formally as Mether Cluny but referred to by everyone as Glenrinnes, and owned since 1897 by James Eadie, the successful brewer and distiller who was deputy lieutenant of Banffshire.

In the census returns, Alexander Mitchell is described as a "forester," an ambiguous term that can mean anything from an estate owner to a farmer to a huntsman to someone who lives in a forest. In Alexander's case, though, his handsome, stone-built, double-fronted farmhouse with its winged outbuildings almost enclosing a square courtyard indicates that he was a tenant hill farmer, one of the more well-to-do members of the community, as he needed to be to support his extensive family. Alexander's first wife, Jessie, gave birth to five children in eight years before dying of rheumatic fever and heart failure in 1909. He married Jane Anderson two years later—they already had a one-year-old child, named Alexander after his father—and on March 7, 1912, Isabella, or "Patty" as she was always known, was born.

She was just six months older than Ewan, and while he was running wild on Craigievar's estate, she was growing up in a farmhouse on the Glenrinnes estate similar to the ones where young Ewan had his grown-up friends. Instead of the towers of Craigievar Castle, Patty had the soaring slopes of Ben Rinnes sheltering her, its almost three-thousand-foot outline as beautiful and distinctive in its own way as Craigievar's fairy-tale appearance. There were eight children in the family—Patty was the seventh—and as is the way in such households, all of them will have had their own jobs to do, from small children's tasks such as collecting eggs to the adult work of sheep husbandry, lambing, shearing, winter feeding and all the tough hill work of shepherding. Perhaps little Patty had a "wee lammie" to feed by bottle in the farmhouse kitchen, one that had been deserted by its mother and needed special care, or her own chickens to feed, as well as learning all the housekeeping tasks from an early age. While Ewan was being homeschooled by governesses, Patty would have been attending the local school and the kirk's Sunday school, with all the other children of the estate. In addition, one of her older sisters was named Jane Eadie, after the estate's owner, and the Mitchells had the reputation of being a more than usually educated family. It is likely that there were the same cordial relationships between the Eadies and the Mitchells as there was between the Forbes-Sempill family and their favorite Craigievar tenants, so that the families were friends, and Patty had access to more refined society and sensibilities than her schoolfellows. But her education didn't stop at book learning. Five of the eight children were boys, and in the old-fashioned way of the day, it will have been the three girls, Patty, Ella and Jane, who were expected to help their mother with the cooking and cleaning, as well as the dairy, poultry and kitchen garden, making butter and cheeses, preserving fruits and berries in season, and marketing any excess produce. Had they been twenty miles to the southeast, on the Craigievar estate, the Mitchells' farmhouse would certainly have been one of those welcoming adolescent Ewan with his melodeon for an evening of "richt Scots tunes" to celebrate harvest home.

During World War II, when Ewan was entering medical school, Patty will have been one of the many women who took a greater lead in local agriculture, either on the Mitchells' own farm or on that of a neighbor whose men had all gone to war. She will have been joined by some of the army of land girls who moved from town to country to provide wartime farm labor and escape the Blitz, and this will have given her early experience of management responsibilities. By the end of the war, therefore, Patty had greater ambitions than staying in Glenrinnes. She had had a broad and thorough education in everything that was needed to produce and prepare food and to run a household; she was comfortable with a wide range of society; and she had the kind of grounded view that Scots poet Nan Shepherd attributed to life in the Cairngorms, a calmly holistic acceptance of life's variety, a sense that "the disintegrating rock, the nurturing rain, the quickening sun, the seed, the root, the bird—all are one."[8] From this rich background, Patty left the austere life of hill farming and moved to Tomintoul, the highest village in the Highlands and the largest community on the Glenlivet estate, to become head waitress at the Richmond Arms Hotel. Built originally as a fishing lodge in 1858, to cater for the upper-class London visitors who followed Queen Victoria to the Highlands, the Richmond Arms is still an imposing twenty-five-bedroom hotel, and Patty's post was a significant front-of-house position: essentially, she was the "lady of the house," ensuring her guests received a warm welcome and were escorted to the lounge bar for preprandial drinks, and overseeing an impeccably run silver service, which as a matter of course will have operated to the same conventions as formal dining at Fintray and the other mansions and castles in Aberdeenshire.

Had chance fallen out that way, Patty might well have met Ewan at the hotel, for it was a popular destination for dining. But in fact, Ewan first met Patty as a patient. In spring 1946, Patty fell ill while visiting her favorite sister, Ella Thomson, in Aberlour, which was part of Ewan's large practice. When Ella called the doctor, Ewan arrived. Ewan had been strongly attracted to Patty from that first meeting, and Patty was sufficiently impressed by Ewan to take on the role of housekeeper and medical receptionist for him and his assistant, Dr. Laura Thompson, nine months later. Running the house and running the surgery will have been easy for her, and perhaps she was glad to move to the gentler country of the Vale of Alford after bleak winters in Tomintoul. Certainly, when Patty moved into Ewan's home and surgery at Rosemount House, Alford, on January 3, 1947, they were in daily contact, and it was there that she and Brux, as his family and friends now called Ewan, fell in love. It did not happen overnight. Ewan was involved with another woman for some time, and in any event, he was professionally very proper, so much so that, for example, he always dressed in a suit to attend patients, since within medical society it would not be regarded as entirely appropriate to wear the kilt for such occasions. Consequently, it took a while for him and Patty to get on familiar terms. But their daily contact meant that they got to know each other well, and in June 1950, Ewan proposed marriage.

Patty turned him down. She said that she felt that his life had been "so battened down" that he needed to be free, rather than tied into a permanent relationship. That, at least, was their official story. But since the records show that Dr. Laura Thompson left Ewan's practice a year later, it is also possible that Ewan's relationship with his medical partner had been more than just professional and that Patty made her departure a condition of marrying Ewan. Either way, during the next year, Ewan's and Patty's feelings for each other endured, and so Ewan set about preparing the ground for their marriage.

It was a momentous decision. Ewan could not legally marry Patty without a male birth certificate, and on his, the sex was shown as female. It is true that the UK does not require people going through a marriage ceremony to show their birth certificates, and some LGBTI people took advantage of that to marry without the celebrant realizing that theirs was a forbidden relationship. But going through a marriage ceremony in that way meant that the relationship had no legitimacy: it was void ab initio, invalid from the start, and neither "husband" nor "wife" had any legal standing or legal obligations to each other. What's more, it was a highly illegal act, since in going through the ceremony the couple both committed perjury: they had made a false oath and faced a penalty of two years in prison and a heavy fine if they were discovered and prosecuted. Witnesses to the ceremony who were aware that the couple were acting illegally could also face the same penalty.

Perhaps if Ewan and Patty had moved from Alford to London, changed their names and slipped into the obscurity of new identities, they might have gotten away with such an illegal wedding ceremony. But leaving aside human dignity and personal pride, that was not practical for Ewan, for he was registered with the General Medical Council, and that record, naming him as Elisabeth, would

Ewan with Bran at Brux, September 1952

follow him everywhere he went to work as a doctor. Anyone could go into their local library and find his entry in the General Medical Register, just as today, anyone can go online and check a UK doctor's qualifications on the General Medical Council website. Ewan knew that to marry Patty, he would have to get his birth certificate corrected to male.

He was facing the first crucial turning point of his life: refusing the bonds of family duty that he had followed all his life. In a fascinating glimpse into the informal trans community network that existed at the time, he was aided by a family friend, Miss Aline Scott Elliot, who introduced him to a man who had seen and been helped by Professor Cawadias, the expert on intersex who had influenced Michael Dillon's *Self*. We know little of Miss Elliot beyond her name and the fact that her father was a military friend of the Auld Laird, and we have no clues to the identity of the trans man whom Ewan met.[9] But in 1951, Ewan traveled to London to consult Professor Cawadias, whose book, *Hermaphroditos*, set out the generally accepted medical viewpoint that being trans was a biological, intersex condition. All of Ewan's records of his visits to early endocrinologists on the Continent had been swept away by the war. Without that medical history, Cawadias probably viewed Ewan's condition as what we now call androgen insensitivity syndrome (AIS), in which an otherwise conventional male fetus fails to respond to testosterone and so develops a partially female external anatomy. He recommended testosterone (which Ewan had been taking for many years) and, Ewan said, speculated that there could be testes present. However, the purpose of the visit was not so much diagnosis and treatment as credentialing. On Cawadias's advice, Ewan wrote to Professor Sir Sydney Smith, Regius Chair of Forensic Medicine and Dean of the Faculty of Medicine at Edinburgh University, to seek support for his reregistration as male under Scots law.

The idea of "virilism," which Lennox Broster had so enthusiastically propounded, must have been helpful to Ewan. Ironically, too, the eugenic mindset, which was still current in medicine, also came to his aid. One of the reasons that "virilism" and trans men were so culturally acceptable to medicine was the notion that the apogee of human development was men, like God's original creation, Adam, and heteronormative European men in particular. Combined with the notion of natural selection, which was deemed to have made "white" races superior to all others, it gave rise to the idea that humanity's natural development was toward being male. Trans men, therefore, represented a natural biological impulse toward this perfection, one that nature hadn't been able to manage on its own, but one that should nevertheless be rewarded with help—especially when the man concerned was from a distinguished family like Ewan's and a fellow clinician to boot.

In England and Wales, correcting birth certificates was a relatively easy process. Doctors provided an official letter, which their trans patients took or sent to Department D6 at the General Register Office at Somerset House in London, together with a nominal sum for administrative costs. Scotland has a separate system of law to England and Wales, though, and Ewan needed the signatures of three doctors to get his new birth certificate. But this was not a problem. His new assistant, Dr. William "Wullie" Manson, who had just replaced Dr. Thompson, was one signatory, and the others were Mr. James Phillip, who had been one of Ewan's lecturers at medical school, and Dr. John Reid, a former fellow student from the year below Ewan. Ewan sent this evidence to Professor Sir Sydney Smith, whom he already knew socially through family connections, and Smith spoke personally to the registrar general. The registrar general then wrote to Ewan and the sheriff clerk of Aberdeen, Kincardine and Banff to make the necessary correction to the record. Ewan had lined up all the big guns neatly, and shortly after he received his new birth certificate, showing his name as "Ewan" and his sex as "M." Small print below the entry reads, "The above particulars incorporate any subsequent corrections or amendments to the original entry made with the authority of the Registrar General." The contemporary legal convention required a change of name to be announced publicly, and on September 12, 1952, four lines appeared discreetly in the public notices section at the back of Aberdeen's *Press and Journal*: "Dr E. Forbes-Sempill, Brux Lodge, Alford, wishes to intimate that in future he will be known as Dr EWAN FORBES-SEMPILL. All legal formalities have been completed."[10]

Both the national and international press leaped on this announcement, noticing that Ewan was now next in succession to the Forbes baronetcy and speculating that Ewan's reregistration was to enable him to marry.[11] There was little Ewan could do about the unwanted publicity. He issued a statement to "clear away untruths and misunderstandings" and asked to "be left to live my life in my own way and in peace." But reporters harried him, preventing him from doing his medical rounds by blocking the road from Brux. Ewan had bought a Land Rover after learning from Princess Margaret that the King had acquired one, and he simply drove it over the hills and moors to his surgery in Alford.

The news had not gone down well with his family. When Ewan telephoned Craigievar, William was already in bed, and his wife, Cecilia, answered the phone. In an attempt at lightheartedness, Ewan told her, "I've transmogrified," but while Cecilia was always a strong support for him, William was upset at having had no advance warning and being unable to help as he might have wished. "He should have *told* me," he said, striking his hand against the steering wheel as he was driving his family, to the alarm of his young daughters. Perhaps the cooling in their relationship dated from that time. Margaret, too, was offended at being told the news by Cecilia, not Ewan, and they grew increasingly distant from each other.

A month later, on October 12, 1952, Ewan and Patty married at Brux Lodge. It was a love match, not a society wedding. Sweet-faced and slender, with thick, wavy, shoulder-length hair, Patty was a quiet, unassuming, caring person. She was half a head taller than Ewan, defying the convention that dictated that the bride should be shorter than the bridegroom, carrying herself with a quiet dignity, never seeking the limelight. The *Evening Express* reported that "the ceremony took place in the greatest secrecy," at night. The first Ewan's neighbors knew about it was when, returning from a dance in the neighboring village of Kildrummy, they heard the music and saw the lights at Brux. Only twenty guests attended, including William, with Ewan's favorite cousin, David Forbes, as his best man, and Patty's sister Ella as matron of honor. When asked about the ceremony, the minister, Peter MacEwen, would say only, "My lips are sealed."[12]

Of course, fear of further press harassment would dictate discretion. But there is an additional tenuous but interesting possibility. The royal family had always been frequent visitors to Craigievar Castle and Fintray House, and a tantalizing scrap of a letter from William found abandoned at Brux Lodge many years later refers to "the wonderful afternoon you all had with the Queen Mother and the great time she and Jaimie had with you both at Brux."[13] It is one of the very few shreds of Ewan's unpublished papers that have survived, and it indicates that Ewan, too, received royalty.

Ewan and Patty's wedding

Young Queen Elizabeth and Princess Margaret were at Balmoral—the press reported that they returned to London on October 13, 1952—and in the popular imagination, either they or their mother might have been guests at Ewan and Patty's wedding. It was, after all, before the formal coronation of Queen Elizabeth II, when a certain latitude might still have been taken, especially when on holiday, with a discreet visit to a family whose friendship stretched back to her great-great-grandmother Queen Victoria.

Using almost exactly the same words as Robert Allen in his biography *There but for the Grace*, Ewan had told family friends that he had corrected a "grievous error which had occurred at my birth and had led to my being registered as a girl instead of a boy."[14] Fortunately for him, natural good manners, Scottish reticence and his own popularity ensured no further information was needed.

He supported local concerts, and he cared for the ill and infirm with unflagging, good-humored solicitude: everyone knew that in the great gale of January 1953 he traveled by Land Rover and skis to reassure the family of one injured patient—whom he had housed at Brux—that all was well. Ewan's local community appreciated his care for them and organized a presentation for him and Patty in Alford Village Hall. His patients had clubbed together to buy him and Patty handsome wedding gifts of a desk and a dirk for Ewan and a set of luggage for Patty, which were received with all Ewan's usual wit and good humor and Patty's quiet pleasure.[15] And a special dance had been composed in honor of Ewan and Patty, called "The Doctor's Waddin'," to celebrate the occasion in true traditional fashion. Finally, the minister who had married them gave Ewan an encomium: "No matter how deep the snow, no matter how high the river or wind, the doctor is always there when we need him." Ewan's married life continued on an even course. But the world was changing, and in both the UK and the US, trans experience was becoming increasingly sensationalized.

Both Ewan and Michael Dillon might have seen a condemnatory article called "Psychopathia Transexualis" published in 1949 in *Sexology*, a popular American magazine that printed lurid "sex science" stories under the guise of education. One of its regular contributors, Dr. David Cauldwell—he was not a practicing clinician—described a certain Earl, whom he said asked him for help accessing testosterone and surgery, which Cauldwell refused. Earl goes into a decline, is expelled from college and becomes a vagrant, and although Cauldwell takes him in for a little while, he cannot tolerate Earl's insistence on dressing and being treated as a man. Earl's family pay him to move away from them, to another city, and Cauldwell gloomily predicts that soon, Earl will end up in prison, for he is "a psychopathic transexual," with "a pathologic-morbid desire to be a full member of the opposite sex," someone who "is mentally unhealthy and because of this the person desires to live as a member of the opposite sex."[16]

Of course, *Sexology* was just a smuttier version of *True Story*, but this particular article was significant. While scientific medicine continued to treat trans people as biologically intersex, pseudo-medicine, with what French philosopher Michel Foucault called its "stubborn will to non-knowledge," was starting to construct them as mentally ill. Cauldwell's psychopathologization—classifying people as mentally ill—was a landmark in transphobia, its title an obvious pushback against Krafft-Ebing's assertion that the absence of psychopathology was a defining feature of being trans. And the name, "transsexual" (whether with one "s" or two), somehow stuck, as a definitive label, limiting and circumscribing trans people and their experience. The use of "sexual" rather than, say, "transexed" implied eroticism rather than biology, and the meaning attached to "trans" was not of movement across or between, but as "beyond" or "outside," seeking to consign individuals to perpetual exclusion, to a libidinous life beyond the pale.

But in the same year that Cauldwell's mean little story pandered to lowbrow sensationalism and prejudice, France produced a new, remarkable view of sex, sexuality and personal identity. Simone de Beauvoir's *The Second Sex* made a clear distinction between biological sex and the cultural standards that constituted gender: dress, occupation, law, acceptable behavior. As far as sex was concerned, she refused a simple male-female binary, saying:

> there is no rigorous biological distinction between the two sexes; an identical soma is modified by hormonal activity [which] can be diverted in the course of the fetus's development. . . . Some men take on a feminine appearance . . . and sometimes girls as well—athletic ones in particular—change into boys.[17]

But her main focus was on gender, the process in which women were constructed as "feminine" and men as "masculine." De Beauvoir's famous statement "One is not born, but rather becomes, woman" exposed the social constraints that define "the figure that the human female takes on in society."[18] They were deliberately disempowering, she said, since "only the mediation of another can constitute an individual as an *Other*," and like Michael Dillon, de Beauvoir pointed the finger at Freudianism. Freudian psychoanalysts, she said, accepted "masculine-feminine categories as currently defined by society"[19] and these categories legitimized worse treatment—economically worse, socially worse, politically worse—for females. They were responsible for defining homosexuality as "a deliberate perversion" when it was really "an attitude that is *chosen in situation*; it is both motivated and freely adopted." Lesbianism was simply "one way among others for woman to solve the problems posed by her condition in general and her erotic situation in particular."[20] Nothing was deterministic, de Beauvoir said, not "physiological facts, psychological history or social circumstances" and, accordingly, the question for every person was how they live their life, "whether it is lived in bad faith, laziness and inauthenticity or in lucidity, generosity and freedom."[21]

These were stirring, wonderful words for everyone who had what de Beauvoir called the "strange experience" of exclusion, of knowing themselves to be "subject, autonomy and transcendence" but discovering they were regarded as having "inferiority—as a given essence." But they did not represent the general view of the world. Trans people had to find their way as best they could between Cauldwell's lurid journalism and de Beauvoir's philosophical deconstruction of sex, gender and sexuality. That was the lesson learned in the US by Christine Jorgensen and in the UK by her contemporary, Roberta Cowell, at the start of the 1950s. Their publicity coincided with Michael Dillon's outing and bullying by the press. All of this newspaper coverage must have given Ewan, as well as other trans readers, deep cause for concern.

Christine was born in the Bronx, New York, in 1926 and Roberta in Croydon, a southern suburb of London, in 1918. They both came from professional families: Christine's father was a craftsman and contractor, and Roberta's a distinguished doctor, a major general and honorary surgeon to the King. Both Christine and Roberta served in the military, and on their discharge, both of them found ways and means of affirming their sex as female, at almost the same time, Roberta in 1951 and Christine in 1952. But from their different sides of the Atlantic they both faced the same difficult issue: As trans women, who were they allowed to be, and what life story were they allowed to tell?

The stakes for saying the wrong thing had become considerably higher. In 1948, Alfred Kinsey's *Sexual Behavior in the Human Male* report had indicated that 37 percent of American men had had orgasmic homosexual experiences and suggested that everyone was homosexual to some degree. The Kinsey Report was to be a liberalizing influence in the long term, but in the short term, it tended to increase public anxiety about gay men and lesbians. Consequently, because psychotherapy was seen as ineffective in treating gay men, more draconian measures began to be taken.[22] Electric shocks, drugs to induce vomiting or sustained verbal humiliation were used as behavioral conditioning, which operated alongside chemical castration, electro-convulsive therapy, induced comas and frontal lobotomies. There were no general protocols or ethical guidelines: individual clinicians simply did whatever they wished to LGBTI people. Whether they called it aversion therapy, conversion therapy, desistance therapy, reparative therapy or any other term, it amounted to the same thing: a degrading, violent, medically and legally sanctioned attack on individuals who did not conform to heterosexual standards.

The term "therapy" is still misused today for actions that are more accurately termed "abuse" or "assault" or simply "torture." Their practice brings into sharp contrast the deficiencies of pseudo-medicine, starkly illustrating the penalties Christine and Roberta then faced for telling the wrong story. Whichever side of the Atlantic they were on, trans people had to find affordances—available possibilities—for personal action in a potentially dangerous collective culture.[23] Although the postwar period resonated with new ideas about individual liberty, self-determination and equality, trans people still had to be very careful what account they gave of themselves if they were not to be humiliated, bullied and intimidated by the general public, egged on by a deeply transphobic press.

Both Christine and Roberta attempted to influence press coverage and supplement their incomes by serializing their life stories in popular magazines, Christine in five installments of *American Weekly*, commencing February 1953, and Roberta in seven issues of *Picture Post* from March 1954 onward. Christine took the safe route and followed Lili's narrative, just as Lili had followed Case 129's. She said that she was a frail child who preferred "the girlish activities" of jumping rope and hopscotch, and that she prayed to God when she was five for "a pretty doll with long golden hair" for Christmas. At summer camp, she was teased as a "sissy" and asked if she "was really a girl dressed in boy's clothes." At age nineteen, when she was drafted into the US army, comparing herself to other GIs, Christine said:

> My body was not only slight, but it lacked other development usual in a male. I had no hair on my chest, arms, or legs. My walk could scarcely be called a masculine stride, the gestures of my hands were effeminate and my voice also had a feminine quality. The sex organs that determined my classification as "male" were underdeveloped.[24]

After her army service, Christine self-medicated with HRT, enrolling at Manhattan Medical and Dental Assistants' School to get the credentials necessary for purchasing it and to learn more about how medicine viewed her. Then, discovering that US surgeons would not provide the surgery she wanted, Christine drew on her half-Danish ancestry and traveled to Denmark for medical help. What she found was brutal. The idea of masquerade had found its way into Danish medicine, and Christine was categorized as a "transvestite," as a man who wanted to look like a woman, rather than as a person who was a woman. And so her surgeons gave her the choice of surgery that would remove all possibility of intercourse and orgasm, or no surgery at all. It was a cruel choice, but as a generation of trans people was to learn, you took what clinicians were prepared to offer or you got nothing. Christine accepted what was on offer, and when she returned to the US, she had further surgery to create a vagina and labia.

A professional photographer and filmmaker herself, Christine was careful to present a glamorous, feminine image to the newspapers when she flew back to America in December 1952. She dressed within the conventions of middle-class respectability and posed with an indefatigably upbeat starlet's smile that supported the *New York Daily News* headline "Ex-GI Becomes Blonde Beauty." As the US trans historian Joanne Meyerowitz puts it, she had "sailed smoothly into the womanly realm of glamour without going overboard into the camp world of gay male drag."[25] By playing into the category error that collapsed sex, gender and sexuality together, in accordance with Krafft-Ebing's law of the sexual homologous development, Christine was able to earn a living as a stage and television performer, moving on to the lecture circuit after the publication of her autobiography in 1967.

Just as Ewan was male, masculine and heterosexual, so Christine was female, feminine and heterosexual. But Christine's career was in public, and although she was a well-acknowledged, popular performer, she was also often ridiculed, so much so that she recorded that "almost everybody I met had a Christine Jorgensen joke."[26] Officialdom's responses to her were often degrading: for example, the army refused to cover news about her in its service newspaper, on the grounds that she was bad for moral welfare;[27] in Washington, police told her that she would be arrested if she used public toilets;[28] and Boston refused to let her onstage without a formal medical examination.[29] At least the newspapers were simply tomorrow's rubbish: a malicious calypso, "Is She Is or Is She Ain't?," by the then popular singer Gene Walcott, which described Christine as "the amazing freak of the century," is still available to purchase or hear on YouTube.[30] Watching this play out must have made Ewan even gladder that he had corrected his birth certificate and kept as low a profile as possible.

Roberta's approach was bolder. The first half of her autobiography, published in book form in 1954, describes her life as an adventurous schoolboy who became a racing-car driver and then a fighter pilot in World War II, before being shot down and interned in a German prisoner-of-war camp. But then, in peacetime, she saw an intense, dark film, *Mine Own Executioner*, in which the protagonist, who is also a Spitfire pilot like Roberta, was similarly shot down and taken prisoner. As she watched it:

> For a moment I was back again in the cockpit, with the familiar mirror above my head, and that bulbous Perspex cockpit hood with its ball-ended rubber jettison handle.
>
> As the aircraft was hit and crashed in flames I felt all the pent-up emotion I released that I must have experienced when my own plane was shot down but this time I was an observer and not so preoccupied with what I was doing that I could feel no emotion. Now I felt the full impact of stark terror. Fear that I would be burnt alive, fear that I would be lynched by the soldiers, fear that I would be terribly injured by the crash.[31]

The shock of this vicarious reliving of trauma, Roberta said, "upset my glandular system and my feminine characteristics became more marked." Her marriage had failed, and she looked for a sympathetic psychiatrist, finding one on the third attempt and subsequently getting hormone therapy and reconstructive surgery. The experience she had relived had spontaneously released her physical potential to be female, she said, and she believed herself to be unique, quite different from other trans people such as Christine Jorgensen, whom she contemptuously called "transvestites."

Roberta was asserting her right to interpret her life on her own terms, irrespective of factual accuracy. It is a narrative approach termed "herstory," history as affinity, foregrounding the personal and emotional and distancing the significance of recorded "fact." Herstory is concerned more with the imaginative significance of events than with the events themselves, and it supports individuals' autonomy by accepting their understandings and perceptions as valid in themselves, without external material definition. Fifteen years later, herstory was to become a staple of radical feminist writers such as Robin Morgan and Mary Daly, whose free retellings of women's history were a clarion call to a generation's emotional experience.[32] We find elements of it, too, in Ewan's memoir, *The Aul' Days*, written in 1984, which avoids all mention of his being trans. Roberta was an early innovator.

Underlying Roberta's herstory, though, was a sequence of unacknowledged events. Her father was an honorary surgeon to King George VI, and so she was a medical insider, able to pick and choose among the treatments on offer. Then, as now, many trans people took hormones before approaching a doctor, and this would have been easy for Roberta, who already had access to benzedrine and other amphetamines.[33] In an unusual turn of events, she had met Michael Dillon, after reading his short work *Self*, and Michael had fallen in love with her. Michael risked his career by performing Roberta's orchidectomy, a procedure that was illegal for a medical student to perform. After the operation, which would have ended his medical career had it been discovered, Michael introduced Roberta to Sir Harold Gillies, the surgeon who had performed his phalloplasty two years earlier, and who carried out Roberta's vaginoplasty. Roberta's herstory was of a unique, unpremeditated transformation. But her medical history was the same as that of every other trans woman, differing only because, like Ewan, she had privileged access to medical expertise.

Pseudo-medicine's enforced homophobia required both Christine and Roberta to distance themselves from gay men. Christine told a story about a gay man who offered to buy her a drink:

> I knew immediately that I was being confronted by a homosexual and, even more startling, that he considered me one, too. For the first time to my knowledge, I had been classified openly. I stifled an impulse to throw the drink in his face. Instead, I raised my glass and using the Danish salute, I politely said, "Skoal." As soon as I could, I made my excuses and left.[34]

Roberta's reaction is far more violent, saying that if she met a gay man: "It is true that I had become a little more tolerant in this direction, and had I met one I would have refrained from actually kicking his spine up through the top of his head, but only with an effort."[35]

The medical, legal and social narratives required from trans people were still highly restricted and strongly policed. Christine and Roberta were obliged to follow the conventions established by Krafft-Ebing and demonstrated by Lili Elbe, including validation by male sexual approval. Roberta described a whole host of changes that we would think of as being stereotypically sexist today, but pseudo-medicine held these as absolute truths in the 1950s: she had "greatly increased powers of intuition" combined with slower mental processes;[36] her handwriting changed, as did Lili's in the 1920s, so that it was "rounder and neater and had acquired some flourishes";[37] her "nature was becoming milder and less aggressive"; she "found it much more difficult to summon up willpower";[38] and her interests changed, so that "for the first time in my life, I could read stories and novels with sustained interest."[39]

The UK and the US press were equally bad in their treatment of trans people, and on her side of the Atlantic, Roberta also received abusive coverage. On March 14, 1954, a front-page headline in the tabloid *Sunday Pictorial* read, "Cowell Sensation," claiming that "experts think he is not a complete woman." To corroborate this, the newspaper provided as scientific fact criteria by which "real women" might be identified: "Even if uncut, a white man's hair does not grow below the shoulders" and "Woman walks by placing one foot directly in front of the other. Man walks with his legs parallel."[40] *The People* continued the story with a front-page headline a month later, "Roberta—The ghastly truth at last,"[41] asserting in its next edition: "Cowell should face the fact that he is now nothing but an unhappy freak, and so, if he wants to come back to this country, he should go into a home and so avoid contacts that might lead to normal relationships."[42]

As was usual in those days, Roberta's birth certificate had been corrected to show her sex as female after she had produced a letter from Harley Street gynecologist Dr. George Dusseau. This angered

The People still further, and they demanded that the correction be challenged in Parliament.

But in America, there were some positive results from the publicity given to Christine's case. It led to her meeting endocrinologist Harry Benjamin, a former student of pioneering endocrinologist Steinach and an admirer of Magnus Hirschfeld's work at his Berlin Institute for Sexual Science. It was a significant moment for trans activism. Christine set out to provide an acceptable face for trans women—poised, successful, polite, moderate—while in 1953, Benjamin set out an emancipatory medical position in the *International Journal of Sexology*.[43] He was clear that all intersex conditions, including being trans, were a natural biological variation resulting from differences in individuals' endocrinology and genes. Attempting to cure a physiological condition by psychotherapy was wrong and useless. Surgical reconstruction in conjunction with pharmaceutical intervention was the only reasonable and effective clinical route to take. The collaboration between Christine and Harry Benjamin meant that many trans people found their way to Benjamin, who provided endocrinological support and referred them to surgeons such as Dr. Georges Burou in Casablanca for treatments that were unavailable in the US.

In the UK, though, a week after the *Picture Post* published the first installment of Roberta's story, an anonymous article in the *British Medical Journal* took a very different approach.[44] It typified trans people as suffering from "a psychological aberration" and cited a Church of England report on the "Problem of Homosexuality" to advocate for "sublimation" rather than medical care for trans people. In the same issue, another anonymous article titled "Sex and the Law" pointed out that there was no legal definition of sex, and there would be none "until the question arises directly for determination in the courts or is determined by Parliament."[45] The two articles sparked an acrimonious debate in the *BMJ*'s next two issues, with psychiatrist Clifford Allen arguing against endocrinological and surgical support for trans people, on the grounds that "change of sex from adult male to female is not possible."[46] A week later, Professor Cawadias responded that people "who feel they belong to the opposite sex and want to live, dress, and work like members of this opposite sex" were "in fact hermaphrodites" and should be treated as such.[47] Allen responded even more violently in the next issue, describing trans people as "maimed and mutilated into travesties of the opposite sex,"[48] and the editor closed the correspondence. As a member of the British Medical Association, Ewan would automatically have received his weekly copy of the *BMJ* and had an opportunity to read Allen's transphobic views. Who Ewan was or who he was allowed to be were being increasingly debated, both by the media freak shows of Christina and Roberta, and then by transphobic pseudo-medicine. All of this publicity must have caused Ewan considerable anxiety, although at this date, he could not have been aware that these transphobic trends were to have devastating personal consequences for him.

At a deeper level, Christine and Roberta became a new focus for cultural insecurity. Marilyn Monroe in Hollywood and Diana Dors in British film had made popular the "blond bombshell" image of femininity, and adverts reading, "If I have only one life, let me live it as a blonde," resulted in three out of every ten American women dyeing their hair blond to gain self- fulfillment.[49] Christine and Roberta both espoused this idealized image of white womanhood and its norm of respectable domestic heterosexuality. It was their form of self-protection, since as Betty Friedan's foundational feminist text *The Feminine Mystique* pointed out, the blonder you were, the whiter you were, the more unsullied, pure, idealized, and desirable you were. But this obsessive focus on whiteness concealed an anxiety about blackness, epitomized as the racist motif of "passing." Were white women really genealogically white? Were blond women really the passive "dumb blondes" they were supposed to be?

Both Christine and Roberta were strong self-publicists, and there was press coverage and speculation about them everywhere. Much of it was a prurient focus on their sexual potential. The media wanted to know whether it was legal for them to marry? (It was, if they had had their birth certificate corrected—Roberta had, Christine hadn't.) Could they give birth to children? (They couldn't.) Could they have sex? (They said they did.) More crucially than any legal or medical concerns, though—were they found desirable by heterosexual men? (Apparently they were, or there would have been no anxiety.) And an even more anxious question: Could a heterosexual man distinguish them from other women? (No. They couldn't.)

Unlike Marilyn Monroe and Diana Dors, who were sanitized and contained by their film images, Christine and Roberta were real-world "blond bombshells," and trans academic Susan Stryker suggests that uncomfortable cultural anxieties about power, masculinity and whiteness underlay the publicity given to them. As the Cold War developed, both the UK and the US press were filled with postwar anxieties about the actual bombshells of a potential nuclear conflict; consternation at the growth of the American civil rights movement and the first rumblings of second-wave feminism; concern about the growing visibility of gay men; and unease at the first stirrings of post-colonialism. Roberta and Christine destroyed the stable materiality of biological sex: they seemed to demonstrate that American and British manhood, already feeling under siege, "could quite literally be undone and refashioned into its seeming opposite through the power of modern science."[50] At least Christine had had the relatively feminine occupations of photography and filmmaking and had become a stage performer. Roberta's career had been the most masculine of pursuits, racing-car driver and fighter pilot, and what was worse, she showed no sign of giving them up: in 1957, she took the women's hill-climb championship at Shelsley Walsh, while also training for an air record for the non-stop flight from England to Brazil. This was a far cry from demure publicity photographs of her posing in the kitchen.

The media coverage given to them was both patronizing and repressive, appropriating them for sensationalism while repudiating them as masqueraders. Above all, though, it was publicity, and for trans people such as Ewan at Brux, who wanted only a quiet life with Patty and his community, such public notice was a source of concern. They could not have avoided seeing it, since every newspaper stand was filled with Roberta and Christine stories. The attack on Roberta's birth certificate must have made Ewan feel worried for his own. Still worse, Roberta devoted two paragraphs of her 1954 hardback biography to Ewan, referring to him as an "unfortunate intersex." While she didn't name him, as she did other trans people, she gave readers the details they needed to identify him: Ewan's change-of-name announcement in the *Aberdeen Press and Journal* from September 12, 1952.[51] This was unwelcome attention, and happy and loved as he was, his tranquil retreat was soon to be entirely disrupted by a death in the family.

PART TWO

4

A DEATH IN THE FAMILY

Ewan had disbanded the Dancers of Don before he married: their last public performance was in aid of "the war-blinded of St. Dunstan's Hospital, Edinburgh" on April 10, 1952.[1] After that, Ewan said, he was too busy professionally to continue dancing, although he did accept the honor of becoming the first chairman of the Aberdeen branch of the Royal Scottish Country Dance Society. Perhaps this disbanding was another condition laid down by Patty, for there are hints that Ewan's relationship with at least one of the women dancers, Tibby Cramb, was personal as well as professional. But the dancing didn't end, for one of the dancers, Alice MacLennan, re-formed the team as the St. Nicholas Dancers, named after the patron saint of Aberdeen. She and her sister, Margaret A. Catto (always known as Mac), had invented a dance in honor of their leader, Ewan, called "Bonnie Brux," danced as a strathspey that "suddenly changed into a reel called 'The High Road to Alford' ending with the dancers forming a circle and on the last note raising their hands towards the centre with the 'Laird' doing a solo step and the dancers shouting 'Brux!' "[2] Ewan was delighted at his lasting contribution to Scottish dance being memorialized by his community for future generations.

He wanted as little publicity as possible, especially after all the fuss attending his name change and subsequent marriage. Consequently, Ewan hid himself away for the next decade so that we have only occasional glimpses of his and Patty's farm life at Brux. News reports about trans men continued to appear in Britain throughout

89

the 1950s. In 1951, the High Court ruled in favor of Wynsley Swan, confirming that he was the same person as Wynifred Swan, a former lieutenant colonel in the Women's Army Corps who corrected his birth certificate and married in 1927. After his death, Wynsley's wife was able to benefit from bequests made to him in his female name since, the High Court decided, "the change of sex" was irrelevant to inheritance.[3] Making the decision, Mr. Justice Vaisey said, "There is nothing to be ashamed of." In 1956, a primary-school teacher, Oliver Berry, corrected his birth certificate and continued to work at Shaftoe Trust School in Northumberland, with "the same happy and cordial relationships" with pupils and staff.[4]

Media coverage of trans women was more alarming. After the sensationalized coverage given to Christine Jorgensen and Roberta Cowell, negative media reportage about trans women began to increase. In 1954, the Danish Ministry of Justice was quoted as being concerned about a possible "invasion of American transvestites,"[5] although US citizen Tamara Rees had her reconstructive surgery in Holland before marrying in 1955, according to a story mockingly headed "Sex-Changed Father Becomes Bride of Another Father."[6] In the same year, trans woman Elizabeth Wind, who appeared in court to defend her right to publish her autobiography, was described as wearing more makeup than her ex-wife: her story was published subsequently by *The People*, which advertised it as "one of the strangest, most intriguing true-life stories of all time."[7] The same newspaper published a photograph of trans woman Coccinelle, who worked as an entertainer in the Paris nightclub Le Carrousel, and asked six doctors, "Would you be prepared to accept sworn evidence that this is a man?"[8]

The press practice of sensationalizing trans women for entertainment was replicated in the theater, although with less success. A review of Rae Whistler's play *Woman of the Year*, presented at the Embassy Theatre in London in 1954, which caricatured the romantic complications of a trans woman central character, concluded "the production is as crude as the play."[9] William Douglas Home's satire about a trans woman, *Aunt Edwina*, performed at the Fortune Theatre in 1959, tried "to get fun out of these rare surgical phenomena" but "lacks wit," the reviewer said.[10] Both plays used male actors to represent their trans women characters. Meanwhile, the *Sunday Mirror* lampooned Christine Jorgensen's third engagement with the headline " 'It's Love Again,' Coos Sex-Change Chris" and implied that sex with her was sodomy.[11]

In 1957, Perth sheriff's court, in Scotland, refused to correct the birth certificate of a trans woman. We know her only as "X," and we have just a few sentences of court record and newspaper reportage about her. She didn't tell the right story. X followed Roberta Cowell's medical narrative of a laddish boy's sudden transformation, but without Roberta's influential connections, she had no chance of success. Instead of identifying her as intersex, doctors at the infirmary where X was a patient said "he" was "a genuine case of the very rare condition of trans-sexualism." The court reported that "skin and blood tests still showed 'X''s basic sex to be male and that the changes had not yet reached the deepest level of sex determination." It was an obviously unscientific decision, since even in the 1950s geneticists knew that chromosomes were not a reliable indicator of someone's sex. Perhaps the Sunday newspapers' scandalmongering about Roberta influenced the courts, or perhaps X's doctors were less cooperative. Certainly, the court felt it was "not without significance that throughout the medical report X is referred to by the personal pronoun 'he.' " Consequently, "while 'X' could be described as an abnormal male, it would not be possible to describe him as a female," and the sheriff ruled that alterations to birth certificates should only be "directed towards the correction of an entry which was erroneous when the information was given."[12] Exposed to publicity by "a friend of the family," she was sensationalized and misgendered by the press as "once a burly, heavily bearded man, fond of tweeds, he now wears women's clothes and uses lipstick and powder."[13]

It was easier to be an English trans man than it was to be a Scottish trans woman. Six months after the Perth sheriff dismissed X, in England in 1958 former wartime ferry pilot Jonathan Ferguson corrected his birth certificate and continued to work at the Ministry of Supply.[14] Or perhaps it was just easier to be a man: Jonathan's success was in sharp contrast to a divorce court case in the same year, *Dolling v. Dolling*, where both the medical and legal verdicts on the trans woman concerned were that she was "suffering from a mental illness." Ms. Dolling had left the family home and "was employed as a woman in a clerical capacity for British Railways." At least the court decided that Ms. Dolling did not intend cruelty, since she "could not help it any more than any other illness."[15]

This newly emergent transphobia, as well as the unwelcome publicity Roberta Cowell gave him, may have contributed to Ewan's decision, in 1955, to step back from his medical practice to concentrate on running his estate at Brux. He said that his "grieve," or estate manager, had been so incompetent that he had to take over the task himself, leaving his assistant Dr. Wullie Manson in charge of the Alford practice. Ewan was still "the Doctor" to the people of Alford, but he was also "Brux," and his time spent working on Craigievar's estates had paid off. Over half of Brux was farmland, and Ewan raised a herd of Highland cattle, a small flock of Hampshire Downs pedigree sheep, a pedigree herd of Jersey, from which he supplied milk to Aberdeen, and crops of cereals, hay and winter wheat. And as "Brux" he continued to be part of his community's life, winning a prize for the best Jersey cow at Alford Show in 1959: Ewan had named it "Bridie-Genesteae" after his youngest niece and the Forbes clan emblem, telling his niece, "I chose one with a very silky nose for you." Prize-winning cattle have an especial significance in Alford, since it is where the world-famous Aberdeen Angus breed began, and his little niece wanted to take the silky-nosed Jersey to boarding school with her. Uncle Ewan said he'd keep it safe until she got back.

Ewan embedded himself more deeply in his community, becoming an elder at Kildrummy Kirk and being quietly involved with the Aberdeen branch of the Scottish National Party. But although he continued to introduce the performers at concerts of Scottish music and dance, Ewan and Patty's focus was on their happy, shared life at Brux.

However, although Ewan's life and community insulated him from the popular press's increasingly hostile view of trans people, he must have been worried by news in the medical press of a radical shift in trans healthcare. In 1960s UK, there were some endocrinologists and surgeons who viewed being trans as an intersex condition and who wished to help their patients lead a healthy, authentic life. Their patient notes would describe trans people's condition as "sexual intermediacy," "psychic hermaphroditism," "congenital absence of vagina," or (as the pioneering plastic surgeon Harold Gillies did for Michael Dillon) as "acute hypospadic," and they would readily agree that both ovarian and testicular tissue might be present in trans people.[16] If you could find your way to these clinicians and give an appropriate typical patient narrative, you could correct your birth certificate and marry, work and live with full equality in your real sex.

But as the cases of X and Ms. Dolling demonstrated, another group of clinicians was taking a different view. To them, trans people were delusional, seeking to masquerade in the wrong sex, diseased at best and depraved at worst. They required confinement and control, not support and autonomy. A new way of thinking about trans people was emerging in the US, supported by a mass political attack on LGBTI people and stimulated by toxic medical research.

Everyone knows about the "reds under the beds" scare about communism that swept 1950s America, obsessively driven by Senator Joseph McCarthy and the Committee on Un-American Activities. Its moral panic caused widespread censorship, blacklisting, and the dismissal of people suspected of being communists. The usual rules of evidence did not apply: being accused or suspected of having communist sympathies was enough to destroy the livelihoods and careers of hundreds of people, like, for example, top screenwriter Dalton Trumbo or actor and singer Paul Robeson. What is less well known, however, is that at the same time as the FBI was investigating American citizens for communist sympathies, they were also carrying out a parallel persecution of LGBTI people. J. Edgar Hoover, the head of the FBI, believed in the "hom-intern," a homosexual conspiracy supposed to be like Vladimir Lenin's international communist organization, the Comintern. He claimed that LGBTI people had infiltrated positions of power, where they inevitably undermined national security because, auto-matically, they would "form stronger allegiances to others of their own kind, across national boundaries, as well as across other social subdivisions such as classes, than to their fellow nationals."[17] From this bigoted viewpoint, cultural relationships with "others of their own kind" made LGBTI people inherently untrustworthy. Hitler had applied the same conspiracy theory to Jewish people.

The notorious question "Are you now or have you ever been . . . ?" that was used to pillory people suspected of communist sympathies was applied to people suspected of LGBTI "tendencies." In the pub-lic mind, McCarthy's reckless witch hunt intertwined with Hoover's homintern, so that to be LGBTI was to be subversive, an enemy of the political, social and cultural values of the free world. This was the start of what was to become a generally assumed right for any-one to interrogate LGBTI people about their lives and private medi-cal histories. Scores of LGBTI people were accused, intimidated, smeared, dismissed or barred from employment.

This political persecution was bad enough. But Ewan will also have been aware that trans people were being redefined by the medical world. Disaster had struck in the form of a new US medi-cal protocol for symptomatically intersex babies—neonates whose variation in genital conformation was evident at birth. It was, and in some places still is, usual for doctors to treat such babies sur-gically as soon as possible, to make the appearance of their geni-talia stereotypically male or female, not for medical reasons but because of social prejudice. Parents were and are advised that such very early surgery is in the baby's best interests, even though it is extremely rare for such variations to be threats to health. The idea that children might prefer to make their own decisions later in life, with no surgery at all being a valid choice, was unthought at this time. Consequently, doctors had a problem: How to deal with the intersex children who grew up unhappy with the sex that surgeons had chosen for them?

A scientific response would have been to stop intervening, unless there was a threat to health. But instead, pseudo-medicine took over, and a team of three doctors at the Johns Hopkins Hospital in Baltimore, John Money, John Hampson and Joan Hampson, created the so-called optimum gender of rearing model of child development.

We might think that the optimum gender of rearing is surely the one each individual discovers for themselves, but Money and his colleagues had a different idea. In an article in the influential *Bulletin of the Johns Hopkins Hospital* in 1955, they argued that what they called "gender identity" was malleable until the age of two or three, after which a so-called "gender identity gate" closed.[18] Provided parents were committed to what Money and the Hampsons called "gender-appropriate rearing," which included keeping their surgery secret from their children, the child would experience no problems. It did not matter what sex the surgeon made their genitalia, because proper parenting would ensure that the child went through the "gender gate" in the prescribed direction. If they didn't, it was the fault of the parents (especially the mother), not of the surgeons.

What was important to them was that doctors should "settle the sex of an hermaphroditic baby, once and for all, within the first few weeks of life, before the establishment of a gender role gets far advanced."[19] Once "boy" or "girl" was chosen, surgeons could operate according to "the morphology of the external genitals and the ease with which these organs can be surgically reconstructed to be consistent with the assigned sex."[20] As the crude in-joke put it, "It's easier to make a hole than a pole," and the surgeon was free to take the simplest solution available. According to Money and the Hampsons, "gender-appropriate rearing" would not only ensure that people were comfortable in whatever sex the surgeons assigned them to, but it would also create a heterosexual orientation. The idea was that "most people, including intersex people, could be conditioned to be either men or women with suitable, and psychologically healthy, heterosexual desire," as American historian Elizabeth Reis puts it.[21]

How do we make sense today of this heady brew of pernicious nonsense? First of all, we might notice the reemergence of colonialism's Homo nullius, non-people. Money and the Hampsons regarded intersex as no sex at all. However, by imposing a "gender identity" on such people, they could be turned into passable imitations of "normal," heterosexual people, just as "savages" could be "civilized" into useful servants. This positioned intersex people in a permanent masquerade, citizens without a sex pretending to have one: the law insisted on that by refusing them their real, intersex identity and requiring birth certificates to record them as "male" or "female."

Second, we might notice how Simone de Beauvoir's careful distinction between being physically sexed and culturally gendered has been appropriated and distorted. "Gender" has become a biological feature in the form of a "gender identity gate" that swings to and fro somewhere, and which can suddenly close and leave you on the wrong side. De Beauvoir's focus on achieving equality by changing society's cultural values has been twisted into maintaining the status quo by socially conditioning "defective" people. To be effective, such conditioning had to begin early: adolescent and adult trans and intersex people were doomed, since if "a change of sex was imposed later than early infancy, the life adjustment was not significantly improved and was often made worse."[22]

A mass of general social anxieties about difference, authority and hierarchy was displaced onto LGBTI people by Money and the Hampsons, reiterating the Victorian category error that created Krafft-Ebing's law of the sexual homologous development. Pseudo-medicine began to operate at full swing. LGBTI people were redefined as badly nurtured by their parents, who had not carried out "gender-appropriate rearing." Ideology was made flesh. LGBTI people were aberrations in nature's plan on the one hand, while on the other hand they were guilty testaments to poor par-

enting. Like every colonized person, they were degenerate bodies, naturally inferior to the elite, Europeanized ideal, in need of
appropriate nurture to control and limit their depravity. Pseudo-
medicine claimed to cure and care for them, and to convert them
into good citizens.

John Money was a big fish in the small pool of trans healthcare.
Johns Hopkins Hospital is one of the top hospitals in the US, and
in the 1950s, its clinicians were used to wielding absolute power.
In 1951, the eminent cancer specialist at Johns Hopkins, Dr. Richard TeLinde, had produced the world-famous HeLa immortal cell
line by harvesting cells from black patient Henrietta Lacks without
even informing her, still less asking for her consent.[23] Like TeLinde,
Money was a charismatic character, intent on furthering his ideas
and career, and his flawed research made a major contribution to
an emerging "turf war" between endocrinology and psychiatry.

The battle lines had been drawn at a US symposium spon-
sored by the *American Journal of Psychotherapy* in 1954. Dr. Harry
Benjamin, who collaborated with Christine Jorgensen to provide
elective endocrinology and surgery for scores of trans people, presented his experience of successful trans clinical support. He was
attacked by psychoanalysts, psychologists and psychiatrists, who
said that since endocrinology could not prove a biological basis for
being trans, it must be a mental illness. They claimed it as a form
of homosexuality combined with "sadomasochism, narcissism,
scopophilia [voyeurism], exhibitionism, and fetishism" caused by
childhood experience in which "the patient's mother plays a pivotal part."[24] Trans people were floridly psychotic and should not be
indulged in their fantastic claims and masquerades.[25]

By these standards, Gwendolen's remarkable support for Ewan
had been abusive, an extension of the wholly inadequate parenting that had prevented him from ending up on the right side of
the "gender gate." She had willfully caused him extended distress
and damage while pretending to protect and help him. According
to this reiteration of pseudo-medicine, Ewan had a raft of underlying problems from elsewhere, which he was expressing through

being trans. Listening to him and helping him on his own terms only made matters worse. He needed to be cured of being trans, through some kind of extensive therapy, though precisely what therapy, how it was selected and for how long it had to be administered only became clear when the first gender identity clinic was set up in 1962. It must have been terrifying for Ewan, as a medical insider, to see a generation of trans-affirmative work by Hirschfeld, Cawadias and Benjamin vandalized and dismissed in this way. Suddenly his life was no longer as secure as it had been, his medical family no longer so comprehensively welcoming. Perhaps it was this attrition of his intellectual home that pushed him toward the kirk, to seek consolation through a deeper affiliation with his spiritual locus. Certainly, he began to become more uncompromisingly Presbyterian, as if doctrinal precision might provide the protection that pseudo-medicine was stripping from scientific thought.

In the US, it was a stand-up fight between empirical, scientific medicine and pseudo-medicine's bigotry. The leading American endocrinologist, Harry Benjamin, was elderly and in no mood for a fight, and his colleagues were confounded by the demand for a specific biological etiology. In fact, many medical conditions have no clear etiology: a description of how a medical condition presents and proceeds is not at all the same as an explanation of how it arises and develops. As Ben Goldacre points out in *Bad Science*, "We do not know *how* general anesthetics work; but we know that they *do* work and we use them despite our ignorance of the mechanism."[26] Psychiatry was unable to show cause and effect either, but pseudo-medicine rooted itself in prejudice, not knowledge, and could get away with vague references to Freudianism, bad mothers, complex psychodynamics and inherently flawed dispositions without empirical data. And if data were required, they could fall back on all the gay men who had avoided prison or further treatment by claiming that aversion therapy had cured them. Pseudo-medicine had won, and it was a bleak future for trans people.

Meanwhile, Ewan continued to live his quiet life. His former medical practice in Alford was being run ably by Dr. Wullie Manson, who had become popular with local patients. For a while he had moved to another practice but was enticed back when Ewan retired. Salaried GPs were the exception rather than the rule in those days, and so Dr. Manson would have had to buy the practice from Ewan, and we do not know how he managed to raise the money to do that. But since Ewan wanted it to be in good hands, perhaps he took payment in installments or stayed as a sleeping partner to keep the price low until Wullie Manson could afford the whole thing. Either way, they were firm friends, Dr. Manson frequently shooting at Brux and becoming intimate with Ewan's family.

Ewan's youngest niece, the one he had named the Jersey cow for, was back from boarding school, much to her relief. Like Ewan, she loved Craigievar and the wild animals she had befriended there, a tame hare and a blackbird, and he had a particular soft spot for her. Ewan liked to recite Doric poetry, his favorite being Charles Murray's "Ay, fegs, an fat dae ye think o my legs?" with its refrain "Gin't hadna been for my legs / O I would be a cold corp noo" ("Ah, faith, and what do you think of my legs . . . If it hadn't have been for my legs / Oh, I would be a cold corpse now"). His young niece would recite back to him a poem by John Caie, "The Puddock" (Doric for "the frog"), about a boastful frog that was eaten by a heron. Doubtless Ewan was amused at the implication that this self-congratulatory poem made him seem like the frog, and his niece was nicknamed "McPuddock" to honor the connection between them. She liked to help him with the "coos and caafies" (cows and calves) and wrote enthusiastically to her mother that on one visit, "Uncle Ewan gave us some clothes." These were not fashion items from grand shops, but hand-me-downs, and his niece reported happily that "I got a blue shirt, pair of grey shorts and beezer shammy leather waistcoat. It is lined with white and red stuff and it fits me like a glove," although "it is rather dirty and nanny says I must have it dry cleaned." She sent Uncle Ewan a napkin ring with the Craigievar cock on it by way of a thank-you gift.

Ewan adored all his nieces. They stayed at Brux with him and their aunt Patty during their summer holidays, learning to fish and shoot. Patty was a gentle carer and a very good cook, and after breakfast, the visiting niece would climb into the Land Rover with Uncle Ewan and set off for a day's tramping up the steep, hilly moors of Brux. Ewan's practice with his air gun as a child had made him into an excellent shot. He had the capacity to remain calm, take his time and shoot unhurriedly, even in difficult circumstances. Halfway across a fence with his sixteen-bore open and empty, he saw two snipe—small, quick birds—taking off: calmly, Ewan fed in two cartridges and bagged them both. The day's shooting would be broken by Patty joining them for lunch in the Land Rover, before going out to shoot again. Fishing was always fly-fishing, casting on Ewan's seven miles of the river Don, which almost encircled Brux, and he was a skilled fisherman, seemingly able to pull a salmon out of the river at a moment's notice. Evenings might be spent in the "cosy room," a wooden conservatory built on the south side of Brux Lodge, where Ewan kept his books and rods and tackle. After such a day, sleep came easily.

And just on the other side of the river Don from Brux were more children, from the Ardhuncart estate, who would run across the bridge every spring and summer holiday to visit Ewan and Patty. They were welcomed wholeheartedly—"we used to do everything with Ewan and Patty, everything," one of them remembered—although sometimes the adventuring could be a bit alarming. When she was ten or twelve years old, one of the Ardhuncart children was helping Ewan round up the sheep. He said, "You drive the Land Rover down the hill and I'll push the sheep round," but forgot to mention that the brake wasn't working! Fortunately, she had the presence of mind to turn so that it came to a natural stop, but if she hadn't, "I'd have ended up in the river!" Patty was just as exploratory but in a more comfortable way. She made raspberry vinegar cordial, which was a delicious novelty drink, and at dinner she served the first bell pepper the children had ever seen. But then, she was an excellent cook who delighted in pleasing people with her food. Although William and Ewan's close relationship had cooled, they still visited each other, and when her in-laws came to Brux for dinner, Patty made William's favorite salmon caviar, a fiddly, tiresome dish to prepare, since it involves separating the salmon roe from the skein, the membrane they are held in, by hand, a few at a time. Patience and caring seemed to be automatic for her: to the children who knew her, she was "just the cosiest, nicest person in the world."

Meanwhile, by 1962, Dr. Robert Stoller had led a group of sexologists, including the late Dr. Richard Green, to establish the first gender identity research clinic at the University of California, Los Angeles (UCLA). Their purpose was to prevent or cure people from being gay, lesbian, bi and trans. The idea spread, and similar clinics were opened in New York and Toronto, all seeking to suppress versions of sex, sexuality and gender that did not match their heteronormative, cisgendered standard. A range of "treatments" was on offer, including aversion therapy, electroconvulsive therapy, psychotherapy and frontal lobotomies, typically using the "ice pick" method of entry through the eye socket to detach the frontal lobe of the brain. Gender identity clinics justified these extreme measures by portraying trans people as horrifically sick, the malignant outcome of "permissive" values and weak parenting.

Getting adequate, supportive medical care became difficult for US trans people, even for those who could afford to pay directly for treatment. The US had no free national health provision and private insurance companies would not pay for endocrinology and reconstructive surgery. At least in the UK, there was the NHS, Lennox Broster, Harold Gillies and a handful of other sympathetic clinicians. But that was changing. The old guard was reaching retirement age and being replaced by clinicians who were interested in, and influenced by, the new American approach. One NHS consultant in particular was as determined as John Money to make a name for himself in this emergent field: Dr. John Randell.

Randell was appointed to Charing Cross Hospital as a physician for psychological medicine in 1950, while Lennox Broster was still treating trans people there. But Randell had a quite different idea of treatment, which he set out in the thesis he wrote for a medical doctorate, "Cross Dressing and the Desire to Change Sex."[27] How he got it past the examiners we shall never know, for it is academically deplorable. A section titled "History and Anthropology" muddles its references to Greek myth, ignores contemporary scholarship and trails off into a scrapbook of newspaper anecdotes. His literature review simply asserts the new view that trans people have "psychosexual homosexuality," "falling mid-way between perversion and fetishism," as "the gratification of early anal-erotic tendencies." He claims that clinicians who view being trans as a natural developmental diversity have been fooled by their cunning patients, who have implanted "such a belief into the psychiatrist's mind," like "the Indian rope trick." And as far as the law is concerned, Randell warns trans people that the police might associate cross-dressing with soliciting, and arrest and prosecute them. As well as psychopathologizing his patients, Randell also criminalizes them.

In particular, Randell's thesis makes a distinction between recreational cross-dressers and trans people. "Transvestitism," as he called it, did not necessarily mean that the cross-dresser was homosexual, although "trans-sexualists" definitely were: he said they had a psychotic, delusional, chronic, morbid form of homosexual transvestitism. Heterosexual cross-dressers—"transvestites"—won his sympathy and he advocated HRT and psychotherapy as a means of releasing their tension and saving them from degenerating into "trans-sexualists." For Randell, "trans-sexualists" were frauds and masqueraders who set out to hoodwink unwary clinicians. He viewed them with distaste, especially trans men.

At this point, it is relevant to know that Randell was himself a highly secretive cross-dresser, keeping a flat near Charing Cross Hospital to which he would invite selected clinical colleagues and junior doctors, to serve them cocktails while dressed *en femme*. In any other field of medicine, this private life would have been irrelevant. But throughout his thesis, and in his medical practice, Randell obviously projected his own anxieties onto his patients. What should have been a nonjudgmental therapeutic relationship was intensely colored by Randell's own closeted life, which he kept away from his home, wife, daughter, and many intimate friends. At the same time, in his clinical role he ruled trans patients with a rod of iron, giving or withholding medical care at whim. He was able to do this because there were no medical or legal restrictions on his actions. "Gender identity" was not a clinical specialty in the UK, and so there was no medical Royal College to agree terminology, diagnostic criteria, care pathways, clinical standards, outcome measures or regulatory frameworks. Randell could simply do as he pleased.

When Lennox Broster retired, the patients who came seeking endocrinology and surgery from him were redirected to John Randell. In this way he garnered seventy-seven patients for his thesis. But his sloppy, chaotic research produced a mass of contradictory data. What is clear is that he supported surgery for only a very few trans women and not at all for trans men. In particular, he said that "no cases received plastic surgery for the construction of a vagina and it was made clear to these individuals that they were not to be made into women but were merely to be made into castrated males." Since the NHS provided vaginal reconstructive surgery, this brutality would seem incomprehensible, were it not for his next sentence: "They were warned against attempts to marry." Randell's central anxiety was that "normal" people might be taken in by "deviants" masquerading as "real women."

New medical climates emerge gradually, over time, and are reported and discussed on the professional grapevine before they get into publication. As a doctor with a personal interest at stake, Ewan would have been aware of these developments. Of course, his birth certificate had been corrected in happier times, and initially, the US's psychopathologization of trans people, and its gradual transfer to British medicine, played no part in his life until, on December 30, 1965, Ewan's brother, William, died.

In 1962, William's wife, Cecilia, had persuaded the head of the National Trust for Scotland to take on Craigievar Castle, and the family still had rooms there. But anesthetic failure during a minor surgical procedure had left William with a level of intellectual impairment, and caring for him at Craigievar had become difficult.

Ewan's medical partner, Dr. Manson, advised that William should be moved to an Edinburgh nursing home for the end stages of his life, and he died there happily, surrounded by nuns, whom he had always loved, and secure in the knowledge that the castle would be preserved for posterity. But now there would be no eccentric but hospitable lord to greet visitors at the castle door with the traditional ceremony of bread and salt, as William used to do, or at dinner to toast "the King over the water" in memory of Bonnie Prince Charlie, the romantic figure who had tried and failed to reclaim the Scots crown from England.

His father, the Auld Laird, had left William only a life interest in Craigievar. If William died without a male heir, the Auld Laird's will said, the estates should be enjoyed by Ewan's uncle Lionel until his death, and then passed on to Lionel's son, John. William had no male children. Lionel had died three years earlier, in 1962. The new heir, according to the Auld Laird's will, was Ewan's cousin John.

Ewan had been at the heart of the syndicate that put Craigievar into the National Trust, and he knew very well that one of the motivations for that had been to keep it from John, who was a complete stranger to the place, its business and the needs of its communities. In the same vein, much of the farmland had been sold to its tenant farmers, and Ewan had been instrumental in ensuring that families who had farmed the land for years were now able to own it. One such family remembers talking to Ewan about their wish to buy their farm, and Ewan telling them what price to bid to get it, a tip-off that spoke more to enduring ties than strict legality. To put Craigievar into the National Trust, Ewan had had to surrender many items that carried personal memories and meant a great deal to him, but he had been gracious and generous at every step. Now Cousin John would expect to inherit the remainder of the estates of Craigievar and Fintray, together with the family jewels and family portraits. But it was not the loss of material goods that troubled Ewan: he knew that a far worse cataclysm was waiting in store. Meanwhile, he had his brother's funeral to attend to.

Honoring the family tradition, William's body was laid out with due ceremony at Craigievar, and on January 3, 1966, the Bishop of Aberdeen said a requiem Mass for him at St. Mary's Catholic Cathedral. As well as William's family members, an impressive roll call of dignitaries attended the funeral, including the Earl of Haddo, the Earl of Dalhousie, Knight President of the Honourable Society of Knights of the Round Table, and representatives of the Institute of Advanced Motorists (William had been their president) and of the Gordon Highlanders. William's tenants carried his coffin, both at the cathedral and for his interment at the quiet parish church, which nestles in the secluded countryside of Leochel-Cushnie. Ewan provided a memorial made from Brux stone, carved simply with the symbol of the cross, which united their religious differences, and whether by accident or design, oriented to face south, toward the Druidic, unvanquished sun.

There were obituaries in all the local, regional and national newspapers, and they all recalled William's remarkable career in aviation, the numerous awards he had gained and his deep commitment to Gaelic culture. But they also speculated on the future of his titles. Like his father, William had been both the Baron Sempill and the Baronet of Craigievar. But while the barony could proceed down the female line, to William's daughter Anne, the baronetcy could only pass to a male heir. What's more, because it was subject to primogeniture, the baronetcy *had* to be inherited by the next male in line. It wasn't possible to transfer the baronetcy to another family member or to relinquish it. The most that could be done was to leave it in abeyance, so that it lay dormant on the Rolls of the Baronetcy, until the next male in succession claimed it, when the title was reactivated.

Clearly, since Ewan was legally male, he should automatically have been the next male heir. But the Auld Laird had never considered such a thing. It would be completely outside his experience, and had Ewan suggested it, he would probably have been laughed at or cut off. Consequently, in his will the Auld Laird had made a provision only for descent through William, and after him, Cousin John.

William had done nothing to change that situation. As head of the family, he had been in a perfect position to explain to his uncle Lionel that the legal route of succession had changed after Ewan's birth certificate had been corrected in 1952. This would have renegotiated Cousin John's expectations and supported Ewan. But it was Ewan who spent time sorting out William's business, not the other way round. While Ewan and Cecilia were managing the transfer of Craigievar, William had to be dragged to the table to do his part. Business, estates and legal matters were simply not on his horizon. There had also been a cooling of relations between William and "Bruxie," as he always called Ewan. Partly, perhaps, this was to do with Ewan not giving William advance warning that he was correcting his birth certificate; partly to do with William's increasingly obsessive Catholicism and Ewan's dedication to Presbyterianism; and partly, perhaps, because Ewan had had to see the estates he loved mismanaged and finally handed over to the National Trust. Ewan had hoped to live at Craigievar himself, and it must have been a painful loss.

So, although Ewan was the next male heir and expected to succeed to the baronetcy as Sir Ewan Forbes of Craigievar, there were press reports that "the claim might be challenged by Dr. Ewan's cousin, Capt. John Forbes-Sempill, a film producer who owns a large house in Newton Stewart, Wigtownshire."[28] Who was he, this Cousin John, and why were William, Cecilia and Ewan so concerned about him taking over Craigievar?

In family terms, John Alexander Cumnock Forbes-Sempill was the son of the Auld Laird's younger brother Lionel, a vice-admiral who was the only one of the Auld Laird's brothers to survive World War II. After an undistinguished education at Stowe School, John was sent to the Royal Military Academy at Sandhurst, rather than following his father's footsteps into the navy. After four years in the Seaforth Highlanders, he left with the rank of captain and began a new life as an actor-producer in London. His career in entertainment was mixed. In 1951, a kind reviewer described him as "deserving a helping hand,"[29] but a year later, he was both producer and actor in a play at St. Martin's Theatre that closed after the first night since, as he explained to the syndicate that backed the play, "In view of the terrible write-up we had in the press there is nothing else we can do."[30] Nevertheless, he persevered, and in 1965, John was the director of the Garrick Theatre, living on Mallord Street in Chelsea, in the heart of Swinging Sixties London. He had also become involved in film and was trying to make a comedy about a family raising two lion cubs in their home in Scotland, using his own house in Galloway as the set: that project was another flop.

Everything about him was antithetical to the Craigievar family. It was not just the traditional supposed rivalry between Lowlands and Highlands Scots, nor was it that he was metropolitan to their rural—William and Cecilia knew London as well as John did, and as a noted sculptor, Cecilia had her gallery, Dunbar Hay, in Mayfair. The problem was that because he had never visited Craigievar or the family, he knew nothing about the estate or its people. Nor did it seem likely that he would be able to learn, since every business he started independently seemed to end in failure: the inheritance would hardly be in safe hands. Then, too, there was a family story about him deliberately setting fire to his house for the insurance money and getting away with it. And another speculating that he and the army had parted company as a result of "conduct unbecoming to a gentleman." And another about the quantities of alcohol he consumed and the company he kept. His sudden arrival at the funeral of a relative he had never known or cared about seemed the height of indiscretion and bad manners.

Ewan knew that there was only one way in which John could make good on a claim to the Craigievar title and estate—he would have to prove that Ewan was female. If such a claim was successful, it would destroy Ewan's and Patty's lives. Rather than man and wife, they would be regarded as lesbians who had made a perjured marriage. They would be subject not only to social opprobrium and the full force of a hostile press, but also to a prison sentence of two years each. This was the catastrophe Ewan had been fear-ing, and now it had arrived. John's legal representative had told the press that "he falls heir to substantial property, including the estates of Craigievar and Fintray." And privately, John had approached Ewan's family solicitors and asked them to arrange a meeting: he was making a move for the inheritance on the grounds that Ewan wasn't a "real man."

Ewan had just buried his brother, and now he had the press on his doorstep again, perhaps about to treat him with the same contemptuous cruelty they had visited on Michael Dillon, Christine Jorgensen and Roberta Cowell.

With no choice, Ewan agreed to John's request and asked his solicitor, Harry Forbes from Stronachs, the family's solicitors in Aberdeen, to attend but not to be present in the actual meeting. Ewan and John met at a hotel in Alford on January 5, 1966, and John told him that he felt he ought to put in a claim for the baronetcy since his late father, Lionel, had arranged that that should be done.

Subsequent events show that Ewan bought him off. He had reconciled himself to losing Craigievar to the National Trust as a means of saving it from John. The tenant farmers he had known from childhood were safe in their properties, and he had his own lovely estate at Brux. John told Ewan that he was unsure whether he should follow his father's wishes and claim the baronetcy, implying that Ewan could make him change his mind with sufficient inducement. After their discussion, Ewan said, he believed that John was going to withdraw his claim, and it is clear that the subject of that discussion was the Craigievar estate. Downstairs, Harry Forbes was waiting for them with papers to sign: Ewan relinquished the Craigievar and Fintray estates, still a very substantial holding even after the depredations of war and time, to persuade John to withdraw his claim to the baronetcy.

John had told both Ewan and Harry Forbes that he had decided to withdraw his claim. Really, though, it seems saying so was just a ploy to get as much as he could. That afternoon, John's solicitor, Baird Matthews, contacted Harry Forbes to say that whatever he might believe to the contrary, John was still going ahead with his claim to the baronetcy. His agreements had turned out to be lies, and Ewan and Patty were suddenly faced with ruin.

The rock that Ewan could stand on, though, was his corrected birth certificate. It was true that anyone who checked the birth register entry would find him listed as "Elisabeth," with an "F" under the column marked "Sex." But they would also find a link to the Register of Corrected Entries, directing that "Ewan" should be substituted for "Elisabeth" and "M" for "F," and the authoritative statement that: "The above corrections are made under the direction and by the written authority of the sheriff (dated 21st August 1952) in consequences of the Deposition of the Person to whose birth the said entry relates."[31] The medical evidence that had been provided to support Ewan's corrected birth certificate was confidential. His adolescent journeys round Europe with Gwendolen were a thing of the past, and it was over twenty years since his mother had died. John had not been seen or heard of until he turned up at the funeral, and he had no way of accessing any details of Ewan's past life. Ewan and Patty could breathe safely: the decision that he was legally and medically male was signed, sealed and delivered. But quite unknown to Ewan, so, too, was a fateful letter.

5

MARGARET'S FATEFUL LETTER

When eight-year-old Ewan and fifteen-year-old Margaret stood patiently waiting to unveil the new war memorial at Fintray, Margaret was already an old hand at public engagements. As an eight-year-old herself, she had laid the foundation stone of Fintray Public Hall, to be built on land donated by her parents. Her father made a speech, and spreading the concrete with a silver trowel inscribed with her name, Margaret declared the foundation stone "well and truly laid."[1] Seven years older than Ewan, she was very much the big sister and daughter of the house. She, too, was taught by a nanny and a governess in the same airy nursery at the top of Craigievar Castle as William and Ewan, before leaving for Queen Margaret's School when she was six. While toddler Ewan was paddling himself round the room in his upturned turtle shell, young Margaret was soldiering up 102 steps between bedroom and bathroom, for the school had been evacuated from Scarborough during World War I and moved to temporary premises at the Atholl Palace Hotel in Pitlochry. Life at Craigievar, with its many steps, will have stood her in good stead.

After Queen Margaret's (where she got in trouble for being "unruly" and climbing on the school's roofs), Margaret was sent to finishing school in Brussels and then, in 1924, when she was eighteen, she "came out," and was presented to the King and Queen as a debutante at the palace. The subsequent round of garden parties and events included one held for Margaret by Gwendolen and the Auld Laird at their Kensington home.

A major purpose of the London Season was to pair off debutantes with promising young men, and its expected consequence was the announcement of engagements: its elaborate ceremonies were all about upper-class matchmaking. But no announcement resulted for Margaret, and consequently, in the Victorian tradition, she was sent to India, where eligible British brides were in short supply and she might be snapped up. It was a degrading period for women: although votes for all women had been achieved in New Zealand in 1893, and in the US in 1920, it did not happen in the UK until 1928, and until then, women had no independent social status. When Margaret attended the Aboyne Games, like all the other women there she was described only in terms of her name and frock, "the Hon. Margaret Forbes-Sempill, who was wearing green chiffon, beaded."[2] The expectation was that both her name and her style of dress would change when she married. Women were required to take their husband's name and give up their own, to wear their hair up, not hanging down freely, and to adopt sober, matronly clothes and appearance. But Margaret had other ideas. She resisted all of these social pressures and returned from India unmarried.

Instead, at the age of twenty-four, Margaret opened a Shetland pony stud, consistently taking prizes at shows, although a family story says she sometimes boosted her chances by "improving" the color of her ponies' hooves. When horses and ponies are being judged on their "turnout"—that is, the beauty of their appearance—good markings and color contrasts can give them a competitive edge: Margaret, it is said, used to paint her ponies' hooves black to give a stronger contrast and make them stand out from the rest. This paint would be removed after the show, surprising visitors to the stud, who expected to see a black-hooved pony.

Like her brother William, Margaret was also a keen motorist, enjoying watching motor-car racing at the world's first purpose-built motor-racing circuit, constructed at Brooklands, Surrey, in 1907. Perhaps it was her love of speed that led to an unfortunate car accident in 1930, which caused her to lose her sight. She was in the hospital, first in London and then at Ellenden nursing

Margaret with her Shetland ponies

home in Kent, for four months, before her vision began to return, and she spent several months more convalescing with a friend in Hampshire. Five years later, Margaret was still wearing spectacles, unless she was posing for a photograph for the press as part of her social duties: one was accompanying Lord Carnegie to see the Fry's Chocolate train when it visited Aberdeen.

The Fry's chocolate company had sent a train on a massive three-thousand-mile tour of the UK, carrying exhibitions of their factory and products, including the cocoa tins that Robert Falcon Scott had taken on his Antarctic exhibition. Visitors to the exhibition were given bars of Fry's chocolate, while the entrance money was donated to a local charity. Margaret and Lord Carnegie's job was to provide a newsworthy photograph and a little story of excited approval to boost attendance, which they duly did.[3] Events like this formed Margaret's life, together with her pony stud and a round of social gatherings: a Guards funeral in Chelsea, a garden party at Fintray, cricket at Lord's, sales of works at the Public Hall, whose foundation stone she had laid, and of course the regular Highland gatherings at Aboyne, Braemar and Lonach. But she longed for more, for the kind of adventures that William had, and for a long time, including while she was watching the cricket at Lord's (where she was described as wearing "a warm coat of yellow angora over her pale robin's egg blue frock") she must have been thinking about the possibilities of joining the Women's Auxiliary Territorial Service.[4]

In December 1938, Margaret took the plunge and became company commander of the 14th Aberdeenshire Company of the Women's Auxiliary Territorial Service, which was affiliated to the 6/7th Gordon Highlanders infantry regiment. Members of the ATS, as it became known, received two-thirds of the pay of male soldiers and performed administrative, noncombatant duties: drivers, telephonists, postal workers, clerks, storekeepers, cooks and munitions inspectors. On February 6, 1939, Margaret reported for the new recruits' intensive training course, "six days hard" at the ATS School of Instruction at the Duke of York's Headquarters in Chelsea. Ewan had come south with her, but it was to lead the Dancers of Don at the Queen's Hall for the Celts and Scots nights organized by the famously innovative dancer Margaret Morris: he had been happy managing William's estate, was looking forward to entering medical school and had no desire to be a fighter.

Eight months later, Britain was at war and Ewan was in medical school making his own contribution to the war effort. The forty-eight RAF companies that had been part of the ATS had been separated out to form the Women's Auxiliary Air Force (WAAF), and Margaret ended her war as a wing officer, just one rank below William. She had been mentioned in dispatches, and the US had awarded her the Bronze Star medal for "valuable services in connection with the war." We do not know what that work was, for it was given the vague title of "liaison services" and Margaret did not discuss it with her family. It is a designation sometimes given to intelligence services, and Margaret certainly fit the profile of the women who did that work: impeccable family background, courageous, resourceful, strong, determined and successful. And whatever the task was, it was clearly risky, since she was invalided out of the military in 1945. Perhaps the family spy story should have been about her.

Just as Ewan was graduating from medical school, Margaret returned to civilian life and her horse breeding, but now with a medal and a new sense of achievement. She was in time to carry Gwendolen's ashes with Ewan on the short, somber walk to St. Meden's. Now they were both orphans, and perhaps, like Ewan, Margaret felt the need for a partner and a home of her own.

Joan Wright had been part of Margaret's social circle since before the war. She had been in a production of the operetta *Cinderella* in 1935, with relatives of Margaret, and they had both been at the 1938 Aboyne Ball, though in different parties. They joined the ATS together, in 1938. Joan had become company commander of the 15th Banffshire Company, affiliated to the 6th Gordon Highlanders infantry regiment just two weeks before Margaret got her appointment. But the war took them in different directions, as Margaret moved into the WAAF and then worked with the US. So it was not until after the war that they met up again, at Margaret's aunt's house in Aberdeen, in September 1953. They fell in love and became partners both in business and in life.

Seventy years ago, lesbians lived discreetly to the point of being secretive. Unlike gay men, in the UK, lesbians had escaped being turned into criminals. Parliament had tried to criminalize them in 1921, but the attempt had been defeated in the House of Lords since, as the Earl of Desart told the House, "You are going to tell the whole world there is such an offense, to bring it to the notice of women who have never heard of it, never thought of it, never dreamed of it. I think that is a very great mischief."[5] Women were supposed to be sexually inert until "awakened" by a man, and the Lords wanted to keep it that way. But by never speaking of them, lesbians were made culturally invisible, so much so that, as the lesbian author Val McDermid puts it, when she was growing up in rural Scotland in the 1960s, "the word lesbian was in our vocabulary but it was a kind of fabled beast like unicorns. You heard about them but you never met one."[6] Margaret was subject to another kind of invisibility as well: an acceptance and dismissal of lesbian couples that was peculiar to the upper classes. It was not uncommon for aristocratic women to live with their female "chum" and attract little adverse attention: these "friendships" were felt to be an extension of the crushes and pashes of girls' boarding school, and while it was financially foolish of them not to catch a man and bear his heirs while they could, if they refused to see sense, then that was up to them. It was these kinds of invisibility, and these kinds of preconceptions about women's sexuality and social function, that meant that Margaret was assumed to be heterosexual, automatically expected to marry, and sent to India to find a husband. She was very fortunate. Many lesbians found such pressures intolerable and gave in to them, entering unhappy marriages purely for the sake of social convention. But just as with William and Ewan, Gwendolen recognized the unique needs of each of her children, and after the India trip, Margaret had been free to go her own way.

Although Joan always maintained her own home at Bridgend, Inverkeithny, near Huntly in Aberdeenshire, she and Margaret lived together permanently at Druminnor Castle, about twenty miles farther south, toward Alford. Using the money she had inherited from her mother and whatever savings she had accrued, Margaret bought Druminnor in 1954, just as Ewan was preparing to step back from his medical practice and devote himself full-time to Brux. The castle had been the stronghold of the chiefs of Clan Forbes for over five hundred years, until it was sold in 1770, and with her purchase, Margaret returned it into the family, which was a source of reasonable pride. However, her program of restoration was very controversial. After demolishing the nineteenth-century structure and stripping the medieval house, Margaret discovered that by doing so she had disqualified herself from getting a grant from the Historic Buildings Council. So she sacked her architect and "drew up her own plans and, with some historical and archaeological advice (which she did not always follow), and acting as her own architect, contracts manager, clerk of works, and sometimes labourer, saw the work through to a successful conclusion."[7] It was a remarkable achievement, but the result was more of a conversion than a renovation and, lovely though it was, it drew sharp intakes of breath from the architectural and historical cognoscenti. But like her brothers, Margaret followed her own path, with the same family determination and energy.

At the same time as restoring Druminnor, Margaret and Joan ran their Fintray pony stud, showing and winning all over the country. Margaret bred garrons, the big-footed, strong-boned, quietly intelligent Highland ponies used for carrying game on moorland shoots, whether two deer slung across their saddle or grouse in a pair of pannier baskets. Their temperament is so calm that they are trained to be led only by head collar, without a bit, and allowed to pick their own way to some extent. But although they are only between 13.2 and 14.2 hands high, they are giants to a small child. When Margaret on one occasion was moving them from one field to another, she told her tiny nieces to stand in a row to corral them in, but since they were even more scared of the garrons than of their aunt's notoriously sharp temper, their nerve gave way, and they fled! Margaret's ponies were part of the family's continued friendship with the royal family, for when the Queen arrived at Balmoral, her first port of call was its Highland pony stud, and she named every foal. In the past, some of them were sired by one of Margaret's stallions, probably prizewinning Callum Og: horses, dogs and a love of Aberdeenshire country life were enduring meeting points for members of both families.

A prizewinning photo taken in 1963 at the North of Scotland gun-dog trials, held on the royal moors near Balmoral Castle, shows the Queen Mother stepping out gaily with her companions, Margaret and Joan, carrying matching cromachs, the tall shepherds' crooks traditionally used for country walking in Scotland. Another photograph shows Margaret with HRH Queen Elizabeth at the 1965 gun-dog trials, when Margaret was president of the North of Scotland Gun Dog Association. She looks happier there than two years earlier with the Queen Mother, perhaps less taken

Left to Right, Joan, Margaret and the Queen Mother in 1963

off guard by the photographer than in the other, "candid" shot, or perhaps happy at being about to move into Druminnor at last, or perhaps, simply, because she was just pleased to be out on the moors, doing her presidential work, with her royal colleague.

Work at Druminnor ended in 1965, the same year that William died. There had been endless delays due to dry rot and burst pipes, during which, Margaret said, "I went to live with my friend at Inverkeithny." The newspaper reporting the story knew that "the friend with whom she is meanwhile staying is Miss Joan Wright, her enthusiastic partner in the Fintray pony stud," but following the convention of the time, it made no mention of Margaret and Joan's personal relationship.[8] Had they been married, it would have been reported as a matter of course, but same-sex marriage would not be legal in the UK for another fifty years. In 1965, lesbians and gay men suffered emotionally by having the most important person in their lives, the one they loved beyond everyone else and who returned that love, demoted in the social scale to the level of friend. Of course, in lesbian and gay circles, "friend" would be given invisible quotation marks by being said with a certain inflection and look, denoting a shared understanding of the inadequacy of the term while at the same time promoting it to its rightful place of intimacy. But once in heterosexual society, your partner became just your friend, not the equivalent of your host's husband or wife. It was a kind of general, perpetual humiliation.

There had always been sibling rivalry, and Margaret felt animosity toward Ewan. Although it was customary for aristocratic children to attend boarding school from a young age, perhaps she resented being sent away from home when she was six years old and blamed the new baby Ewan for it. Certainly, as they were growing up, she was envious of the close tie between William and Ewan: "She was hurt because she was the one that was the outsider," Ewan said, "because my brother and I got on very well."[9] Then, in adult life, for reasons we do not know, William and Margaret had quarreled further: Ewan said, "She had in fact done something to him that was not quite fair, and he had forbidden her his house."[10] Further, Margaret always deadnamed and misgendered Ewan, calling him "Betty" and "she," seemingly unable to come to terms with his being male. In her eyes, Ewan was female, and his relationship with Patty was the same as hers with Joan, but everyone accepted Ewan and Patty as man and wife and gave them the social distinction that was denied to Margaret and Joan. Perhaps this was the cause of her hostility. Another reason might have been the political tension between lesbian and trans communities. Some lesbians viewed heterosexual trans men as traitors to the ideal of "woman-identified-woman": confusing sex, gender and sexuality, they insisted that trans men who had female partners were simply lesbians who were ashamed of their sexuality.

After their mother's death there had been a rapprochement between Ewan and Margaret. Margaret had invited Ewan to lunch at Little Fintray, supposedly to divide some remaining possessions of their mother's. But when Ewan arrived, Margaret was entertaining a woman guest and told Ewan that since there wasn't really anything to do, she and her friend (or "friend") were going to the theater. Then she presented him with a huge bill. Ewan had stayed at Little Fintray for his one weekend off every month while he was at medical school and Margaret was on military service, and the unexpected bill was for the time he had spent there. It must have been all the more startling for Ewan, because when he had been injured as a passenger in a car accident, Margaret had taken good care of him and been very kind. Now, though, instead of a straightforward discussion, Margaret had created this curiously underhanded scenario. It was a spiteful, manipulative thing to do, presumably designed by Margaret to humiliate Ewan in front of her friend, and as he was leaving, Ewan told her cook-housekeeper, in his Doric, "Your boardinghouse is ower dear, I'll never be back."[11] After that, Margaret and he saw each other only at weddings and funerals.

When William died, therefore, there had been a long-standing estrangement between Margaret and Ewan, bordering on hostility. They were both present at all the ceremonies, at Craigievar, where William was laid out; at his requiem Mass at St. Mary's Cathedral; and at the interment at Leochel-Cushnie cemetery. Their brother's death did not bridge the gap between them, however, and perhaps this was obvious to Cousin John, who turned up at William's funeral on January 3, 1966, the first time the family ever saw him. Certainly, when Ewan saw the front page of the *Aberdeen Press and Journal* the following day, he'd have known that Margaret and John were up to something. Their reporter quoted Margaret as saying that because John was challenging Ewan for the Forbes of Craigievar baronetcy, it would "go to the court of baronetage through the office of the Lord Lyon" since "this is always done when any succession is not absolutely direct."[12] This was dreadfully disloyal to her family, but Margaret had always refused to acknowledge Ewan as a man.

Life for trans people was changing for the worse. It wasn't just isolated centers like the new, abusive regimes being run by Stoller in the US and Randell in the UK: the larger LGBTI world was shifting. In 1957, the *American Journal of Psychotherapy* had published an article by male cross-dresser Virginia Prince called "Homosexuality, Transvestism and Transsexualism: Reflections on Their

Etiology and Differentiation." Prince carefully distinguished het-erosexual male cross-dressers from gay men and from "transsexu-als" and created a new, separatist community for "transvestites" with a privately circulated newsletter, *Transvestia*.

In 1961, subscribers to *Transvestia* came together to form a pri-vate club in Los Angeles, which evolved into a national organi-zation called the Foundation for Full Personality Expression. As gender historians Dave King and Richard Ekins point out, "FPE was clearly aimed at those cross-dressers who, like [Virginia] Prince (at that time), were heterosexual and married: homosexu-als and transsexuals [*sic*] were not admitted."[13] The idea was that members should pastiche a stereotyped hyper-femininity that ran more or less diametrically opposite to everything that second-wave feminism's emergent "women's liberation" movement stood for:

> Prince wags her fingers at readers and tells them: "if you are going to appear in society as a woman, don't just be a woman, be a lady," and "it is the best in womanhood that the FP seeks to emulate, not the common. Be the LADY in the crowd if you are going to be a woman at all, not the scrubwoman or a clerk. It is the beauty, delicacy, grace, loveliness, charm and freedom of expression of the feminine world that you are seeking to experience and enjoy, so "live it up"—be as pretty, charming and graceful as you can."[14]

A branch of FPE was opened in the UK by Alice Purnell in 1966, which she developed into the Beaumont Society, with a similar separatist focus on heterosexual male cross-dressers.

This shift in the LGBTI world was accompanied by fragmen-tation. Gay men were strongly focused on decriminalizing them-selves, partly achieving that in the UK through 1967's Sexual Offences Act. In 1969, the US National Organization for Women evicted its lesbian members for "having male psyches, being male identified, and bringing 'male energy' into women's space,"[15] while in the same year, the Stonewall Inn "riot" in New York City her-alded a new sense of "gay pride."[16] US women's groups such as

New York Radical Women and Radicalesbians articulated separatist radical lesbian feminist standpoints, excluding heterosexual women, gay men, trans men and trans women, all of whom were labeled as instruments of "the patriarchy." In parallel, the Black Power movement supported the development of a distinctive movement of radical black women, epitomized by the National Black Feminist Organization founded in New York in 1973. Mainstream lesbian life had been advertised in the 1968 British film *The Killing of Sister George*, which provided on-screen, for all to see, the phone number of the popular lesbian Gateways Club in London. By 1970, the UK Gay Liberation Front had formed, splintering further as many lesbians left GLF to set up separatist lesbian feminist collectives.[17] Bisexual people continued to live their discreet lives, loving whom they wished, disregarding the heterosexed binary of male and female. The idea of a common LGBTI purpose did not survive these new sociopolitical movements, which either excluded or ignored trans people: the most important influence on their lives was pseudo-medicine's separation of intersex from being trans, which had redefined them as floridly psychotic.

The hoary issue of sex tests for female athletes had reemerged in 1966, with a front-page article in *The Observer* and a documentary called *Sex Change?* on BBC television. As *The Times* reported the BBC documentary, it made a clear distinction between intersex conditions and "a purely psychological disorder called transsexualism . . . most sufferers were highly disturbed."[18] Everyone wanted to "cure" trans people, just as earlier in the decade everyone had wanted to "cure" gay men and lesbians, using the same methods and generally ascribing the same etiologies in a fruitless, circular, "nature-nurture" binary debate. This was potentially explosive for Ewan.

In the US, a wealthy Louisiana trans man named Reed Erickson had done what he could to improve trans people's lives, setting up the Erickson Educational Foundation to support social understanding and healthcare services. Reed had created and funded the Harry Benjamin Foundation in 1964 to support a non-psychopathological etiology for trans people, and in 1966, it had funded the first surgical support for trans people at Johns Hopkins Hospital. That news might have reassured Ewan that not everyone thought trans people were mentally ill. But the medical world was rocked to its foundations by two very particular cases.

"Agnes" (we do not know her real name) had followed the well-trodden path of extensive self-medication with estrogen. Like many trans people, she did not reveal her self-medication when, in 1959, she presented herself to UCLA sexologist Robert Stoller as inter-sex, rather than as trans. This gave her the best chance of accessing the medical treatment she needed and avoided her being treated as delusional. And unusually, Agnes had begun her self-medication at twelve years old, using estrogen that had been prescribed for her mother, so she had none of the visible effects of a male puberty. The history she provided followed the typical patient narrative that had been established by Krafft-Ebing and used by Lili Elbe and Christine Jorgensen, including its required refusal of homosexuality. Accordingly, Agnes was accepted by Stoller and UCLA as a unique example of spontaneous pubertal feminization and was fêted internationally by leading sexologists. This meant that in 1959 she was granted the endocrinology and surgery that US doctors often denied other trans people. Further, UCLA's renowned sociologist Harold Garfinkel made Agnes the subject of extensive study, in a seventy-page chapter in his landmark work, *Studies in Ethnomethodology*.[19]

It was a remarkable case because medical opinion had accepted that a spontaneous change of sex could take place. Instead of just knowing she was female, Agnes had demonstrated that the body would instinctively become female to match the mind. The case seemed to make sense of the trans experience, to justify doctors supporting trans people with appropriate medication and surgery, and it provided a strong argument against medical opinion that believed being trans was a mental illness. In fact, Agnes of course had simply made an inspired, tactical use of the limited affordances provided by US medicine, presenting with a narrative that would provide access to the treatment she needed. What was unusual about her case was that, like Ewan, she had been able to access hormone therapy at a much earlier age than most trans people, who typically had to wait until they were adults, after going through the wrong puberty, before they could self-medicate.

Then, in 1966, when Ewan was dealing with the aftermath of William's death, Agnes startled the medical community by revealing that she was trans and had self-medicated with estrogen prescribed to her mother. This was a major embarrassment for Stoller and Garfinkel, both of whom had interrogated Agnes for many hours. Stoller was obliged to retract his findings publicly, and Garfinkel had to tack an apologetic appendix onto his book. Agnes had shown that pseudo-medicine's distinction between intersex and trans was nonsensical, and this was not welcome news to psychiatrists. It almost seemed like retaliation when, two years later, in 1968, "transsexualism" was created as a separate heading in the *Index Medicus*, the authoritative annual bibliography of clinical studies published by the American Medical Association. It formalized the categorization of trans people as psychiatrically disturbed, separating them from intersex conditions and signposting their new treatment as mental health patients.

But exactly what should that treatment be? John Money had been working on an answer. In his notorious case, known as "John/Joan," a seven-month-old baby boy named David Reimer was accidentally given a penectomy (removal of the penis) during a minor surgical procedure. Money advised David's parents that he should be raised as a girl, with surgical and hormonal support to change his anatomy, and that this should be kept secret from him. The boy had a twin brother, Brian, who could be used as a "control" against which David's "gender" could be judged. Here was a chance to show what Money meant by "gender identity" and how he could push a boy through the "gender gate" to be happy as a girl, with appropriate behavioral conditioning. In the reports he published, Money described what he viewed as a successful gender role:

> Although the girl had been the dominant twin in infancy, by the
> time the children were four years old there was no mistaking which

twin was the girl and which the boy. At five, the little girl already preferred dresses to pants, enjoyed wearing her hair-ribbons, bracelets and frilly blouses, and loved being her daddy's little sweetheart. . . . Dolls and a doll carriage headed her Christmas list when she was five and . . . quite unlike her brother, the girl was neat and dainty, experimented happily with styles for long hair, and often tried to help in the kitchen.[20]

His description reflects all the female stereotypes debunked a decade earlier by Betty Friedan's *Feminine Mystique*. "She" has made an appropriate attachment to her father, which will ensure a heterosexual future; is being prepared for the kitchen and child-care; and is compliant with feminine dress and adornment. Every threat of the so-called sexual revolution was neutralized. There was no male or female sex, just masculine and feminine gender, and that was infinitely malleable. Nurture, not nature, decided everything. Trans people, therefore, had simply been badly nurtured and with proper psychiatric "help" could be "cured," or, in incurably psychotic cases, managed with endocrinology and surgery, according to individual clinicians' preferences. Whatever the "cure," being trans had been "proved" to be a mental illness.

It was not until thirty years later, in 1997, that the truth came out. David had been deeply unhappy and distressed and had been forced by his parents to feign "female" behavior when Money visited.[21] When he finally learned his medical history from his parents, he immediately reiterated his male sex, changing his name and social identity to correspond with his biology. Money had manipulated the results of his experiment. The stresses of a lifetime of medical abuse to which he had been subject were so great that in 2004, David Reimer died by suicide.

When Ewan had corrected his birth certificate and married, being trans had been an intersex condition and he was not regarded as having any kind of psychosis. But if he was now identified as being trans, as John maintained, then he was in danger of being reclassified as a floridly psychotic lesbian. His profession

and connections might protect him from being detained for forc-
ible psychiatric treatment, but not from his and Patty's prosecution
for perjury, or from them being crucified by the media. The press
would have a field day with them. Trying to position himself within
this new environment, Ewan must have thanked heaven he had
been able to buy off John with the Craigievar and Fintray estates,
and thanked heaven, too, that there was no evidence in existence
that could identify him as trans. It looked like a precarious position, but it was still a safe one.

He had no idea that, from William's funeral onward, Margaret
and John had been plotting against him.

Margaret was in debt to the tune of £3,000 (£47,500 or $62,000
in today's value). Where Ewan had invested his inheritance from
Gwendolen in becoming a doctor and then buying an estate, both
of which provided him with an income, Margaret had spent her
inheritance on buying Druminnor. The cost of restoration had
been heavy, and although she had opened it to the public, adding
a little museum of Highland and Scottish antiquities as an extra
attraction, she could expect only a small income from that source.
Then, too, horse breeding is a notoriously uncertain business, as
likely to lose money as it is to make it. John told Margaret that if
she supported his claim to the Forbes of Craigievar baronetcy, he
would pay her debts. He asked her to write him a letter.

Ewan had no inkling of these negotiations between Margaret and John, or that John had engaged a solicitor who had had a
meeting with Margaret and was writing formally to her with questions about Ewan. All he knew was that after he had signed over
the estate to John, Baird Matthews, John's solicitor, had told Ewan's
solicitor that John still intended to put in a claim for the baronetcy.
But he had no way of knowing whether that was just hot air, and
anyway, there was no material evidence that Ewan wasn't the next
male heir: his birth certificate was male and his medical records
from Europe had disappeared long ago. However, Baird Matthews
had informed the registrar of the baronetage that John would be
making a claim for the Forbes of Craigievar title. Following that,

and completely without Ewan's knowledge, Mr. Matthews had vis-ited Margaret on February 25 to get her to make good on her side of the bargain she had struck with John. Subsequently, Margaret had received a letter from Matthews asking her questions about the family tree and saying in particular:

> We were interested to gather that you had some information regarding Dr. Ewan Forbes-Sempill in connection with his having been brought up as a girl and we shall be pleased to have any infor-mation you can give us in this connection with as much detail as possible to help us in our claim.[22]

On March 4, Margaret received another letter, asking her to respond quickly. Margaret was in the middle of moving into Druminnor, and so it was not until March 8 that she asked Joan Wright to write a letter at her dictation. We do not have the full let-ter, but from the parts that remain, we can see that Margaret said everything that John might have hoped for:

Druminnor Castle,
Rhynie,
Aberdeenshire

March 8th 1966

Dear Mr Matthews
    Thank you so much for your letters JMM/ER.
    I understood that a claim had been lodged on John's behalf with the Registrar of Baronetage immediately after Lord Sempill's death. I hope that the following information is all that you require, and you will see that I have made three cor-rections on the family tree which you enclosed.
    I always regarded Dr Ewan as my sister and I feel quite sure there was never any doubt as to her sex.
    After all I was seven years older than her and when my mother died in 1944 she never said anything about a possible

change. As a small child, she was very delicate but after her middle teens she became quite strong and healthy.

She went through the phase (as I did myself and so many girls do) of wanting to be a boy. She went to parties, dances, etc., and was presented at Court in 1929 or 1930. She had her periods regularly just the same as any other girl. (Miss Deal would confirm this. I give you her address later.)

That will show her on whose side I am on.

From 1939 till the end of 1944 I saw very little of her, as she was studying medicine in Aberdeen and I was stationed in the south of England. I was invalided out of the Service in 1945 and my sister used to spend almost every week-end with me at Little Fintray which was my home. She stayed with Tibby Cramb i.e. Mrs Maurice Cramb.

A year or two after I came out of the Service my sister got the Practice at Alford. I went to see her in her house there when she first moved in, but after that she cut herself off from all her relations and friends. This made everybody very sad and we could not understand it. Then the Bombshell! I did not know a thing until my sister-in-law Lady Sempill told me. Apparently Dr Ewan had rung Craigievar to tell Lord Sempill that she had changed her sex and as he was away spoke to my sister-in-law. Just fancy—I her only sister had to be told by a relation by marriage.

So up to 1946–47 (I am not quite sure of the year) I saw her most week-ends, and we were as usual good friends, since then I could count the times that I have spoken to her on my fingers.

Miss Wright has written this letter as I have talked hence its being so disjointed. We have kept a copy.

Yours sincerely
Margaret Forbes-Sempill[23]

Blissfully unaware, Ewan continued to farm at Brux and worry about the title. If John had not entered the picture, he might have let it lie dormant, for he had already dropped his title of "the Honorable" and never responded to requests for information from directories of the peerage. Certainly, if he could have, he would have given the title to John. The title of "Doctor," which he had earned, was the one Ewan valued, just as he loved his own exquisite estate of Brux more than the vast lands of Craigievar. But it is not possible to divert the line of a baronetcy. And although John would automatically inherit the title on Ewan's death, he would not wait for it because, John petulantly told the family, "Daddy always promised me a title." The press had already reported that the Lord Lyon, Sir Thomas Innes, who lived near Craigievar and was a friend of Cecilia's, might be called on to give an opinion on the correct line of succession. By spring, John and his solicitor began talking about a contest, possibly before the registrar of the baronetage.

Wanting only to live his peaceful life at Brux with Patty, Ewan was caught between a rock and a hard place. If he did not claim it, then it would look as though he believed he had no right to inherit a male-line primogeniture title. It would be tantamount to stating that he was not the next heir because he was not a man. But the thought of the grueling adversarial process of the law, the exposure to the media that would provide and the sheer humiliation of having to prove who he was were huge disincentives. Finally, at the last minute before the six-month deadline, after months of anxiety and indecision, Ewan put in a counterclaim for the baronetcy. It was the first indication that he might be prepared to stand and fight.

Like every other claimant, John had provided a family tree and birth, death, marriage and divorce certificates for three generations to substantiate his claim to the title. That included Ewan's corrected birth certificate, showing him to be male and preceding John in the succession, and so the registrar of the baronetage informed John that the secretary of state would not accept his claim "in the present circumstances." Consequently, on August 21, John served a summons on Ewan, to take him to court to prove that Ewan "is now and has all along been of the female sex in the physical, anatomical, physiological and genetic meanings of that term."

It was a nightmare for Ewan. He had given John the estate and family possessions, and had done his best to give him the title, by allowing John's solicitors to inquire whether it could be transferred to him, given that it would in any event be John's in the fullness of time. However, male-line primogeniture titles are not allowed to be treated in that way. Now he asked John at least to agree to the legal contest being held in private. Ewan's solicitor, Herbert Haldane, an Edinburgh solicitor with greater expertise in difficult areas of the law than the family solicitor Harry Forbes, had managed to get a special dispensation for it to be heard in summary trial, away from the public eye. After weeks of negotiations, John refused. He had decided not only to try to take the title but also to do his best to publicly humiliate Ewan in the process.

Time and again Ewan must have repeated to himself that his birth certificate was safely corrected and there was no evidence extant to show he was or ever had been female. No matter what the medical viewpoint had become, he and his beloved Patty were safe. He will have gone over and over those boundaries in his mind, endlessly checking for any breaches that might make him and Patty vulnerable, as weeks of waiting and fruitless negotiations stretched into months. And so, when he took a day off from the harvest in October to go and sort out family silver with Margaret and his widowed sister-in-law, Cecilia, the news he got must have been utterly devastating.

Ewan left the meeting early to go back to driving the combine harvester at Brux, and when they were alone together, Margaret told Cecilia about the letter she had written for John seven months earlier. Cecilia, who was very well disposed toward Ewan, immediately informed him, and the bottom dropped out of his world.

Cecilia had told Ewan that Margaret "had given certain written testimony," which she now regretted, because Margaret "would really have liked to be friends" with Ewan. Ewan rang Margaret up and said, simply, "Would you like to come over and discuss this?" It seems like a remarkably patient response, but from childhood, Margaret had been given to tantrums, and Gwendolen had told both Ewan and William that they must give in to her, just as they did to their father. Ewan said that he and William were "brought up on a policy of appeasement," and they were both instructed that as far as their father and Margaret were concerned, "You must never cross them."[24] Gwendolen was right: Margaret had taken full revenge on Ewan for whatever slights she imagined she had suffered: "That will show her on whose side I am on," she had said angrily in her letter to John.

On Monday, October 17, Margaret dined at Brux with Ewan and Patty, and they explained both Ewan's medical circumstances and the implications of the letter she had written. It was as though for the first time it dawned on Margaret what she had done. She stayed there for hours trying to make sense of the various medical documents that Ewan took her through, but she just became more bewildered. When she got home at four o'clock the next morning, she told Joan that they were "all Greek and Chinese" to her. Margaret told Ewan that she was very sorry for having written the letter but that it was done and she could not take it back. To Joan she said simply, "I don't go back on anything I have said," standing by her statement about Ewan, but at the same time saying that she was terribly sorry for Patty, and, "I can't bear this thing to go on because I am so sorry for her."[25] At last she understood that she was helping to destroy Patty's life as well as Ewan's, sentencing her to imprisonment for a perjured marriage, disgracing her in court and shaming her in public.

Perhaps it also dawned on Margaret that as a key witness and Ewan's sister, she, too, would be in the public eye, and it was impossible that her relationship with Joan would not attract the attention of the press as well. The growing visibility of lesbians meant that they would no longer be able to protect their privacy under the guise of business partners and friends. The same self-interest that had made her write her letter to John was making her reconsider her convictions about Ewan.

On October 18, obviously feeling in need of legal support, Ewan told his solicitor, Herbert Haldane, that Margaret had expressed a wish for reconciliation and asked his advice. Haldane rang Margaret, who confirmed that "she had made a statement which she very much regretted, but she felt that what she had said she had said and she could not withdraw." But at the same time, she told Haldane, "When Brux walked out of my life I thought I had lost a sister but I am by no means sure now she is not my brother."[26] It was a telling comment. Her previous deliberate deadnaming and misgendering of Ewan was certainly part of "the rift" between them, and calling him "Brux," like everyone else, recognized both his lairdship and his maleness. Within their traditional family structure, a brother was more than just a male sibling: he carried the responsibility for protecting and providing for his sister's well-being enduringly, as an automatic duty. A one-off payment from John was one thing; ongoing material support from a brother who was a successful local landowner and businessman was quite another.

At the same time, Margaret informed Haldane that she was shortly to see John, and it is difficult not to wonder whether she was setting up a bidding war for her evidence. Yes, John had the letter, and yes, she would not retract it. But it would be the easiest thing in the world to stand up in court and say that she had not been aware of the full facts of the matter when she wrote it, that she had written in haste due to the pressure from John's solicitors to reply, and that anyway, John had paid her to say what she had said. John's case would be gone.

We do not know precisely when, but sometime in the next few days, Margaret met John and his solicitor at the Station Hotel in Aberdeen. She told them that she had reconciled with Ewan and that they were "on speaking terms with quite a happy relationship existing between them."[27] Doubtless she also told them that Haldane had arranged for her to dine with Ewan again, on October 28, and that Ewan had given her permission to talk to Dr. Manson, who was his GP, who would confirm Ewan's medical status as male. Now Margaret had leverage, and she used it to persuade John that any court proceedings must be heard in private. She was very effective. Only a week after Margaret's reconciliation with Ewan at

Brux, on Monday, October 24, John caved in. In a letter from his lawyer to Ewan's solicitor, John agreed to conditions for a summary trial, which would be held in camera before a judge. His two conditions were: first, that Ewan would agree to a medical examination by John's medical experts; and second, that Ewan would pay all the costs of the legal proceedings, John's as well as his own. John had sold the Craigievar estate to the Eagle Star insurance company and was now a very wealthy man, but he would not give an inch.

Ewan knew that the medical examination was going to be a problematic hurdle for him, and John's demand that Ewan pay all the costs was a deliberately contemptuous insult. But at least he now had Margaret on his side. Even though she couldn't take back her letter from John, she could say in court that she had been completely wrong about its contents, misled by her parents, wholly mistaken at the time she wrote it, coached in what to say by John's lawyer and desperately in need of the money John paid for it. Every shred of its credibility could be destroyed and John revealed as artful, vindictive and manipulative. Ewan had some breathing space: he could hope for the best.

On Tuesday, October 25, Margaret told Joan that she was dining at Brux that Friday, and seeing Dr. Manson, who would explain to her everything about Ewan, and they said goodbye to each other, expecting to meet that weekend. On Thursday, October 27, Margaret gave Ewan "a very sincere apology" and their reconciliation was complete.[28] What a relief: with Margaret's testimony now supporting him in court, Ewan had little to fear from John. But on the night of Friday, October 28, only three miles away from home, driving down the narrow road from Druminnor to Brux in her Land Rover, Margaret collided with a car and a lorry. She died instantly.

6

THE MEDICAL EXAMINATION

When the ambulance reached Margaret's Land Rover, they found it so thoroughly crushed that they had to cut it apart to reach her. But even this was delayed, for her dogs had survived the accident and were protecting her fiercely. The Royal Society for the Prevention of Cruelty to Animals had to be called out to sedate them before anything else could be done.

Ewan's former medical partner Dr. Manson attended the accident and pronounced Margaret dead. He, too, had been expected at Brux that evening, and perhaps he saw the ambulance on its way and followed it to help, for in those days there were no paramedics. Ambulance staff were given a basic training in first aid but were otherwise regarded as manual laborers whose job was simply to transport acutely ill or injured patients to a hospital. Wullie Manson was Ewan's friend, confidant and shooting companion, as well as his medical partner, and after pronouncing death, he will have driven the four miles to Brux to break the news to Ewan and Patty. He had been expecting to see Margaret that evening to explain that Ewan was male, and he knew the legal implications for Ewan of Margaret's death, as well as the natural grief the news would bring.

The place where Margaret died was an accident black spot, a Z bend on a T-junction crossing a narrow bridge, and consequently the lorry driver who killed her was simply fined £16 (present-day value £240 or $327) for dangerous driving. The local press printed a front-page story, "Queen's Friend Killed," but Margaret merited only two sentences in the national press. Margaret's will was also only two simple sentences, scribbled on a piece of notepaper from Champneys Spa in Hertfordshire. It read: "I leave everything I possess to Joan Mary Wright Inverkeithny by Huntly, Aberdeenshire. This cancels any previous wills."[1] Joan herself must have been devastated by Margaret's death. She had said goodbye to Margaret on the Tuesday and expected to see her that weekend, with great news about her reconciliation with Ewan. We do not know how she got the news of Margaret's death, but it will have been a terrible blow, and her anguish will have been exacerbated by the social conventions that named her simply "friend," not "partner" or "wife," and so accorded her limited sympathy. Poignantly, Joan held the estate and the castle in trust for Margaret and for Margaret's heirs.[2] Now that she was alone, she cherished Margaret's memory by completing the restoration and moving into Druminnor Castle, reopening it to the public on weekends, just as Margaret had intended.

Margaret's death benefited John. Ewan's male birth certificate meant he was legally the next heir to the Forbes of Craigievar baronetcy, and the Standing Committee of the Privy Council, which adjudicated such inheritances, would certainly have found in Ewan's favor. But the law regards a letter from a sibling as a reliable source of evidence until proven otherwise, and Margaret had set out her clear and firm understanding that Ewan was and always had been female. She gave John precisely the power he wanted. Now, instead of simply being accepted as male, Ewan would have to prove himself male in order to inherit the baronetcy. And John, of course, would do everything he could to argue that Ewan was female.

In less than a year, Ewan had lost both his brother and his sister, and in addition to the grief of these bereavements, he had the problems they had bequeathed him. William had done nothing to change the idea set out in the Auld Laird's will that John was next in line for the Craigievar baronetcy: his head was so in the clouds about anything other than his aircraft and Celticism that it probably never occurred to him to ensure that Ewan's right to inherit wasn't challenged. And where William had done nothing, Margaret had done too much: between them, his siblings had pushed Ewan into catastrophe.

Ewan was once again on a downward spiral. Nine months earlier, he had believed he was safe, having given the Craigievar estates to John and done his best to relinquish the baronetcy. Then the ground began collapsing beneath his feet with the contest for the title and the news of Margaret's letter. But Ewan had scrambled his way back up, reconciled with Margaret, brought her onto his side and reestablished a new, friendly footing. Now her death threw him back into the hole he'd just climbed out of.

In Britain, the pseudo-medical portrayal of trans people was growing more alarming. According to Charing Cross psychiatrist Clifford Allen's 1962 *A Textbook of Psychosexual Disorders*, trans people were narcissists with an unhappy childhood and a castration complex—"pitiable problems," who masqueraded as the opposite sex and ended up as "mutilated" men if, like Christine Jorgensen, they were given access to surgical support. He was very definite that being trans had nothing to do with intersex conditions, and his mantra was that "the aim should be not to make the *normal* body fit the *abnormal* psyche but vice versa": trans people were floridly psychotic and must be cured of their psychosis.[3] It was directly opposed to the rational analysis of Harry Benjamin's 1966 *The Transsexual Phenomenon*, which set out a process for treating trans people according to the dictates of scientific medicine. Benjamin gave a voice to trans people themselves by including selected autobiographies in his book, and he argued that the scientific medical pathway was endocrinology and elective surgery, just as for other intersex conditions: let the body fit the mind. On that basis, Benjamin argued, birth certificates should be corrected in the same way as those of intersex babies, since "the only difference between a wrong sex-diagnosis at birth and (inborn) transsexualism" was "the time element, that is to say, how soon after birth either fact is discovered and amply verified."[4] This kind of correction was precisely what Ewan and other UK trans people had done in the past, and it provided strong support for Ewan's position.

Scientific researchers like Benjamin recognized that they worked with uncertainty, and accordingly they presented their results modestly and provisionally. But pseudo-medicine has no room for doubt. Although Clifford Allen was clear that he was writing only about "my own clinical impression," he presented his impressions as if they were an absolute truth. In a similar way, a new book from the US, Richard Green and John Money's *Transsexualism and Sex Reassignment*, was about to declare trans people definitively psychotic.

The contents of *Transsexualism and Sex Reassignment*, published in 1969, had been discussed at medical conferences several years earlier and will have already been generally known in the relevant medical communities. Reed Erickson funded the publication of the book, presumably feeling that treatment on any grounds was better than no treatment at all, and Harry Benjamin wrote an introduction, for, after all, the book had come out of the foundation named after him. It was his swan song before he retired completely, and in it he set out his aim for the trans medicine community of the future: "to try to promote scientific objectivity, open-mindedness and—a bit of compassion."[5]

But the book's co-editors, Richard Green and John Money, "honored" Harry Benjamin by burying him. Both viewed trans people as floridly psychotic, while supporting "sex change" operations on the grounds that some patients were so psychotic as to be incurable. Their book put the medical care of trans people into the hands of psychiatrists who believed that trans people were mentally ill, while being self-congratulatory about their compassion in providing endocrinology and surgery to a select few patients. First they tried to "cure" trans people with aversion therapy and psychotherapy. If that didn't work, then those patients who met the doctor's personal, unaccountable, but absolute criteria, might get the scientific medical treatment they needed. Imagine diabetes being defined as mental illness resulting from moral degeneracy with treatment denied to all but the repentant and "deserving" few.

To make matters worse, public interest in trans men was growing. Christine Jorgensen and Roberta Cowell had refocused media publicity on trans women, especially since pseudo-medicine's category error linked trans women with male homosexuality, and the decriminalization of gay men was a hot topic at the time. This popularity was reflected by Green and Money's book, which had focused predominantly on women, whom they called "male transsexuals." But everyone working in the medical field knew that trans men, who were referred to as "female transsexuals," continued to be as present as ever, even if they were now less visible in the popular press. As one chapter in Green and Money's book put it rather dryly, "The female transsexual does, in fact, exist."[6] Then the popular gaze suddenly shifted back to trans men. Concerns about Mark Weston reemerged, as well as those about other trans man athletes such as the Czech Zdeněk Koubek, who had formerly won in women's athletics. These were entangled with anxieties about intersex women athletes, which seemed to be justified when, in August 1966, five gold-medal-winning women athletes withdrew from the European Athletic Championships, supposedly to avoid being obliged to have the newly obligatory "sex test."[7] And in September, a Sunday scandal sheet gave a full page to a story about a trans man who had worked as a female secretary before disappearing and reappearing as her "brother" and going into partnership with the former employer.[8] When Ewan's solicitor was arranging the medical examination John had demanded, the media view of trans people was emphatically on masquerade, mental illness, and monstrosity.

In this climate, the thought of the kind of media storm John might be able to create must have been terrifying.

The next step in the legal negotiations was to agree who the medical examiners would be. It was a matter of finding clinicians who had the expertise and seniority to make authoritative statements, who were available and who were willing to carry out the examination. Finally, on November 25, 1966, Ewan's and John's solicitors agreed that only one doctor would examine Ewan: Professor Strong, from the University of Edinburgh's department of medicine at the Western General Hospital, in the northwest of the city.

Professor Strong was an endocrinologist, and as well as carrying out Ewan's examination, he agreed to take blood and skin samples, and a buccal smear, a swab from inside Ewan's cheek. Biological scientist Dr. Patricia Jacobs, from the Medical Research Council laboratory at the hospital, would be present at Ewan's examination to authenticate the samples taken, which she would later analyze. The letter of instruction was very clear that only Professor Strong and Dr. Jacobs would be involved in Ewan's examination, and that it would "not involve anesthesia or any other surgery except with the express permission" of Ewan.[9]

Professor John Strong was distinguished in his field, very well connected, a strict Calvinist who valued upright behavior, and a person of strong habits, traveling north from Edinburgh to the Highlands in Sutherland to shoot each year. In other circumstances, he and Ewan might well have been friends. But their relationship was going to be that of doctor and patient, Strong's knowing gaze examining and judging Ewan's objectified body in a context Ewan knew was adversarial, even if Strong believed it was a "neutral" clinical analysis. What was Strong looking for?

When Ewan left his general practice in 1955, medical science recognized three main diversities of sex that were apparent at birth.[10] One was called "male pseudohermaphroditism," in which male hormones are released while the baby is in the womb but fail to operate effectively. Typically, although the person has the common male pattern of XY chromosomes, they also have external genitalia that look female. However, they are likely to have only a very short vagina, while internally they are likely to have undescended testes. The second recognized condition was "female pseudohermaphroditism," in which the person had ovaries and the common female pattern of XX chromosomes but had been subject to male hormones while in the womb. This could produce an enlarged clitoris that looked like a penis but didn't have a urethra, and might result in little breast development, no menstruation and increased body hair development. A third possibility was "hermaphroditism," in which the person's physical development included both ovaries and testes, sometimes fused together as an "ovo-testis."

Since then, although there had been many advances in producing more detailed diagnoses for an increasing range of variations of sex, there was still a mistaken but general view that the common XX and XY chromosome patterns were the best indicators of biological sex. The "sex test" controversially used by athletics included a swab taken from the inside of the cheek and was used to establish whether a competitor's chromosomes were the frequent male pattern of XY or the frequent female pattern of XX. But even then, this view was a popular belief, not a scientific fact. Using chromosome tests in sports was controversial simply because although many men have XY chromosomes, not all do, and although many women have XX chromosomes, that is not universal. These were the broad parameters that Ewan knew Strong would be using.

From the start, however, something felt wrong with the arrangements. Ewan was anxious about privacy and had asked for it to be carried out in private consulting rooms, but Strong had responded that he didn't have any. This was the first oddity, since professors in university hospitals were able to command most of its facilities, and even if Strong had no private practice himself, he certainly had colleagues who would have loaned him their rooms. In any event, Professor Court Brown, who was also at Edinburgh and who had been involved in the negotiations to find appropriate examiners, provided one of the private wards allocated to his clinical team. Accordingly, Ewan had to present himself to Strong at the General Western Hospital, and he asked his solicitor in advance to check the privacy of the examining room to make sure he did not have to go through the general part of the hospital. Fortunately, the "one-man ward" provided by Court Brown meant that Ewan could avoid the public.

A Saturday had been chosen for the examination, when the hospital would be quieter, and on November 26, 1966, Ewan arrived at the appointed place to see Professor Strong and Dr. Jacobs as agreed. To his shock, seven people were waiting for him in the examination room, including Strong's assistant, Dr. Price, a junior doctor working his way to a consultant post, with an interest in the way in which chromosome variations affect human beings. Professor Strong was of the old school, and as far as he was concerned, his junior was as much a part of his personal accoutrements as his stethoscope: where he went, Price went to do his bidding. Every junior doctor of that period knew the unwritten rule that whatever your boss said, you agreed with; whatever question he asked, you gave a positive answer; and irrespective of the difficulties you might be in, you never dared to disturb him, even though he will have told you to get in touch with him if you needed any help. Senior hospital physicians really did rule like gods in those days, and someone as distinguished as the professor at a leading medical school was positively transcendent. Ewan noted Price's presence, in defiance of the written legal agreement that said only Strong and Jacobs would be there, and banked the information for future use. We do not know who the other four people in the room were, but they may well have been staff preparing it for the examination, or other students of Strong's he had invited along to watch the examination as part of their education. The idea that patients had to give their permission for students to observe their intimate examinations was at least a generation away, for the "medical model" still positioned patients as puppets, not as autonomous human beings. But whether of their own volition or at Ewan's insistence, the seven people were reduced to three—Strong, Jacobs and Price—for what was to be a three-hour examination.

When Professor Strong asked Ewan to provide a urine sample, and Ewan returned a few minutes later saying that he had been unable to do so, Strong put it down to nervousness making him unable to urinate, something, he said, that "is so common I really don't take much notice of it."[11] He had wanted the sample to analyze it for steroid hormones, to see whether male hormones (androgens) or female hormones (estrogens) predominated. But Ewan was not going to give away any more information than he had to.

Learning to take a patient history is a fundamental part of medical training, and both Strong and Ewan will have taken hundreds in their time. It follows a routine process, beginning with recording the patient's name, date of birth, address and other personal details, proceeding to the reason they are there and the history associated with that, asking for their past medical and surgical histories, checking on any medications they may be taking or allergies they may have, and moving into their social, occupational and family histories. Nowadays the questions generally include smoking, alcohol consumption and recreational drug use, but in the 1960s, the first two were not really regarded as being dangerous and the third was largely unknown.

But this was not a general patient history, aimed at identifying a common medical problem. Professor Strong's job was to report on Ewan's sex, and as a leading endocrinologist in the field of intersex, he will have known and used the most up-to-date practices in his field. This will have included the Money-Primrose interview schedule used for trans people and, punctilious as he was in all his actions, Strong will doubtless have felt obliged to ask Ewan the remarkably intrusive questions it comprised.[12] As well as childhood illnesses, Ewan will have been asked about developmental issues such as toilet training, bed-wetting, tantrums, phobias, obsessions, stealing, delinquency, nail-biting, thumb-sucking, head banging, hair twisting, hallucinations, delusions, sports and game playing. Then questioning will have moved on to sex history: masturbation and masturbation fantasies, erotic and romantic daydreams, dating, petting, and lovemaking, menstruation, breast development, erotic zones, erotic stimulations and orgasm. Strong said that his prime task was to "deal in anatomical and scientific and measurable terms," and so he probably left out the usual questions about sexual deviance, cross-dressing, dreams and nightmares, fetishism and body image. Nor would he have used the so-called oblique inquiry technique, where the patient is required to play games: your three wishes, who would you want with you on a desert island, what would you do with $100,000 or £100,000, what would you do if you had only ten years to live, what would you do if you were invisible, and so on.

Ewan will have known what was coming and will have prepared for it. He was expert at deflecting and defending, at being helpfully vague, self-deprecatingly forgetful, and politely regretful at not having the answers people wanted. The answers he gave Strong will have been the information he wanted Strong to hear. But then came the physical examination, the part that was Strong's particular forte. After having his weight and height taken, Ewan had to strip naked and lie on the examination bed to be palpated, percussed and probed.

The process for conducting a physical examination is as well laid out as the process for taking a patient history, and Strong will have had to hand all the usual equipment, including a tape measure, reflex hammer, stethoscope, flashlight, lubricating jelly and rectal gloves. The process aims to reduce the number of shifts of position by the patient to the minimum and begins with the patient sitting, to examine the head, neck and torso, and then lying down to reexamine the breasts and heart, and to examine the rest of the body. Unlike other men, Ewan will have been subjected to the humiliation of putting his feet in stirrups for his genital examination, and almost certainly at that point his rectal examination will have taken place. Every part of him will have been judged, for the purpose of a physical examination is to look for "abnormality" and question the patient about it. So Professor Strong noted that Ewan had "a fresh complexion" and "a marked recession of the forehead hair" as well as "a history of shaving," "a vigorous growth of grey hair on the chest" and "a vigorous growth also on the pubis and the upper thighs."[13] No part of him was left unsurveyed.

There were two events that must have seemed completely insignificant to Professor Strong at the time, but which were to come home to haunt him. First Ewan pointed out two swellings in his groin to both Strong and Dr. Price. As part of giving his history, he had already said that fifteen years earlier Professor Cawadias thought there could be testes at some stage of descent, and the implication was that the swellings might be them. Strong seemed already to have made his mind up about Ewan, for he "did not seem to bother very much with this," Ewan said. Instead, "he put Dr. Price onto it, and Dr. Price examined it, and I showed him two swellings, one inguinal and one femoral which is slightly lower, and I don't know what he said, he went across the room and mumbled something to Professor Strong."[14] Both Strong and Price were to regret not paying more attention to Ewan's apparently naive concern.

It was Dr. Price's job to take blood and skin samples from Ewan. It is clear from the letter of agreement, which precluded any anesthetic being given without specific consent, that Ewan expected the few cells that were necessary for laboratory examination to be scraped off after a numbing preparation had been applied to the area. Perhaps it was the tense atmosphere in the examination room that caused things to go wrong. Doctors are taught as a matter of course to examine from the right side of the bed: no one knows exactly why or how this tradition arose, although there may be some clinical justification for it, but it is deeply ingrained into every doctor's practice. Professor Strong was in just that position when he was taking the buccal smear from Ewan's mouth and so it will have been a surprise to both of them when Dr. Price approached the bed from the left. While Ewan's mouth was being held open for the smear to be taken, Dr. Price jabbed Ewan in the arm with a local anesthetic. Ewan made no complaint at the time, but he was to use the incident to great effect later.

He was glad when the examination came to an end and he could leave the hospital and Edinburgh and travel home. But someone on John's side had tipped off the press, so that although Ewan said that "a careful check was made on the security for leakage or information," nonetheless he "was pestered by the Press after that visit." Ewan had been set up. Unsurprisingly, as Ewan's solicitor put it, "the one thing my client was determined not to do under any circumstances was go back to the Western General Hospital."[15]

All Ewan and Patty could do was wait for Professor Strong's report and wonder what his conclusion would be. Strong would have to wait for the laboratory results of the buccal smear and the blood and skin tests to arrive before he could put his findings together, which he did during the Christmas break, finalizing his report on December 30,

1966. It was exactly a year after William's death had precipitated the whole situation. The report did not reach Brux until January 5, 1967, and it said precisely what Ewan and Patty feared most.

Strong had made every examination possible, short of surgery, including a rectal examination, but he had been unable to find any trace of testes. The two swellings in his groin pointed out so hopefully by Ewan were just varicose veins. The report said that Ewan's breast development, nipples and areolae "more resembled the female pattern than the male."[16] His external genitalia were a virilized clitoris—a phallus, as it is properly called—which was "greatly enlarged in terms of what one would expect in the normal situation for a clitoris, but if it was regarded as a penis it could only be regarded as abnormally small."[17] The urethra was behind the phallus, and behind that was a vaginal opening, which Strong said was "not examined any further than noting the existence of the opening."

The conclusion Strong reached was simple. His report read, "In anatomical terms, examination indicates that Dr. Forbes-Sempill is a female,"[18] and Strong diagnosed "a moderate degree of congenital adrenal hyperplasia [CAH],"[19] a variant of the condition that had earlier been called "female pseudohermaphroditism." CAH can produce an enlarged clitoris that looks like a small penis but doesn't have a urethra, and it may result in little breast development, increased body hair development, and no menstruation, although ovaries are still present. In other words, having no access to Ewan's medical history of long-term dosage with testosterone, Strong interpreted him as a woman who had been subject to masculinizing hormones while in the womb. Attached to the main report was a note from Dr. Jacobs that read, "The results of both sex chromatin and chromosome investigation show Dr. Forbes-Sempill to have two x chromosomes and therefore genetically to be a normal female."[20]

It was game, set, and match to John. Ewan was done for.

7

AN AUDACIOUS DEFENSE

The first major turning point in Ewan's life had been his refusal of family duty in favor of correcting his birth certificate so that he could marry Patty. Now he faced his second turning point. Both he and William had been brought up to appease the Auld Laird's black moods and Margaret's sudden tempers, and perhaps inevitably, Ewan's first response to John had been to try to appease him. But as soon as he understood exactly what he was up against and what was at stake, Ewan began to fight.

He had met Cousin John twice: once at William's burial, when John kept rudely whispering to William's widow, Cecilia, and a second time at Alford, when Ewan had handed over the Craigievar and Fintray estates in return for John not disputing the baronetcy. John must have thought Ewan was a pushover. But he had vastly underestimated his opponent.

Ewan now knew without any doubt that John was willing to destroy him and Patty for the sake of a title. He also knew that there was only one way out of the predicament they had been put in. He had to reverse Strong and Jacobs's decision and be declared indisputably male. He set about pursuing that, careless of the cost to himself.

Ewan's first move was to visit William's family doctor in London, Dr. Stuart Hensman, who recommended that he consult Professor Paul Polani, at the world-renowned Guy's Hospital. Polani was the most distinguished pediatric geneticist of his day and a leading expert on intersex conditions. An Italian national, he had been interned as an enemy alien on the Isle of Man during World War II, but on his release, Polani joined Guy's. He established an internationally famous pediatric genetic research program, became the first Prince Philip Professor of Paediatric Research, and effectively created the new subject of medical genetics in the UK. Polani discovered the genetic base of asymptomatic intersex conditions such as Turner syndrome, did groundbreaking research into Down's syndrome and established the existence of chromosomal mosaicism, in which one part of the body contains XX cells and another XY cells. Brilliant and compassionate, he was known to his colleagues as "a kind, gentle and selfless person with extraordinary intelligence and vision and a steadfast and generous nature."[1] During his wartime internment, Polani had been camp doctor to the other detainees, and perhaps he and Ewan bonded over their common experience of managing the health of prisoners of war. Variations of sex development was too specialist a subject to have been explored in any depth at medical school, and patients experiencing it were infrequent in a family doctor's professional experience. Now, though, Ewan was in the right place to learn all there was to know about the subject and to examine a wide range of examples of gonadal tissues. We know that he explained his circumstances to Professor Polani, since Polani gave Ewan a referral to a colleague of his, Dr. Peter Bishop, for help with his court case. However, Bishop was not available because he had already been consulted by John's side. But it was on this visit that Ewan either collected or discovered how to acquire the material he required for the audacious plan he had formed. This is the story he told the court.[2]

Ewan said that in September 1966, before he knew about Margaret's letter, one of Patty's nephews had an undescended testicle removed, and a biopsy showed it to be precancerous. This had concerned Ewan because when he had seen Professor Cawadias fifteen years earlier, Cawadias had agreed it was possible that Ewan might have testicular tissue somewhere in his anatomy. It was usual for clinicians to acknowledge that possibility, partly to support their patients and partly to reflect the complexity of genetics and variations of sex development, about which little could be certain. Cawadias had given Ewan a short course of high-dose testosterone to see if it stimulated testicular growth or descent, which it did not.

As well, Ewan said, "I had a scare about malignancy in 1959 when I had a ruptured tendon which they thought was malignant at the time and proved not to be so but nevertheless it leaves this question very much in one's mind." He was claiming to have a good reason for believing the lump might be cancerous. These concerns, Ewan said, led him to point out the swelling in his groin to Professor Strong at the time of the medical examination. Although Strong was certain the swelling was just varicose veins, Ewan was nevertheless anxious because "it could have been due to a tumor which could again have been a malignant thing."

Finally, his concern about his health increased on January 5, 1967, when he read Professor Strong's diagnosis of him as a female with congenital adrenal hyperplasia (CAH). Now, Ewan said, he "was extremely worried at the thought of having adrenal hyperplasia because this is a condition from which one may become gravely ill and die."

Having set the scene, Ewan launched his bombshell. In mid-January 1967, after reading Strong's report, Ewan said that he had a severe attack of bronchitis. A weak chest was something he was prone to, and this time he was really quite ill. Suddenly, during a particularly bad coughing fit, the swelling in his groin grew and, astonishingly, a testicle descended. It lay there, "quite evident."

This was terribly disquieting, Ewan said, and he felt there was no time to waste. Immediately, on January 19, he performed a biopsy on himself, making a three-inch incision in his inguinal region, where the scrotum usually sits, and cutting off a part of the lump. Ewan sent this tissue sample to Dr. Hensman, who was going to forward it to a pathologist friend for a private analysis. Ewan then put a large piece of sticking plaster over the incision in his groin, which meant that no one else could see it.

Five days later, on January 24, he went to Sheffield Medical School to see Mr. Jack Dewhurst, a gynecologist and an authority on intersex conditions. Dewhurst was the first of three experts Ewan recruited to give evidence on his side in court. At their meeting, Ewan explained how the testis had descended and that he had taken a specimen. He regretted that Dewhurst would be unable to examine that area because the wound was so recent and sore.

Of course, it was a scientific impossibility for such a thing to happen to a fifty-four-year-old man with Ewan's medical history. He had obviously acquired a sample of testicular tissue after his visit to Polani and used it to manufacture the evidence he needed for his audacious plan. But all anyone knew about his medical history was what Ewan told them, and he told them what suited his purposes best.

Unfortunately, the colleague of Dr. Hensman who was going to do the analysis was taken ill with a heart attack. Consequently, the specimen was unexamined and lost, and perhaps this really was the case, or perhaps the tissue Ewan had obtained was not of the right kind to substantiate his story. Either way, Ewan said that he had to start again. So, on March 3, 1967, he did a second biopsy in exactly the same place:

> Early in the afternoon immediately after lunch in fact and I put it in a plastic box, the kind of thing one gets medical samples sent in, and I took it, I sealed it up and addressed it to the Pathology Lecturer at Foresterhill in Aberdeen, and I posted it myself.

Ewan had enlisted the help of Dr. Wullie Manson. Manson was an "easy" doctor, immensely popular as someone who didn't take life too seriously and wouldn't castigate his patients if, like him, they enjoyed their whisky and cigarettes. With his agreement, the tissue sample was sent to Aberdeen's pathology department under Dr. Manson's name, even though he had never seen it, much less taken it. Ewan said that he needed a practicing doctor to request the analysis, though in fact, since he was still on the medical register, he was perfectly entitled to make the request himself.

But Wullie Manson's help was crucial in authenticating Ewan's testis. On March 28, a third tissue sample was taken, this time by Dr. Manson, with Reverend Reid, the minister from the kirk where Ewan was an elder, present as a witness. Of course, in practice, it was impossible for Reid to see precisely what Dr. Manson was doing: he was simply in the room, "present while Dr. Manson removed a piece of tissue from Dr. Forbes-Sempill's groin."

At the medical examination, Ewan had claimed to be too nervous to produce a urine sample for Professor Strong. But having seen Strong's report, he said, and being anxious at the possibility of having CAH, "I approached Mr. Phillip who is the Senior Lecturer in Surgery in Aberdeen who granted one of my original medical certificates, and I talked to him about this business." Mr. Phillip said he would carry out a urine test to determine whether CAH was likely, and so a few days after the third biopsy, Ewan "went up to the minister's house and passed a urine sample in his presence, and he took it to Dr. Klopper." Whether Reverend Reid actually watched Ewan pee into a urine-collection pot, whether Ewan handed him that same pot or a substitute, or whether Ewan had carefully self-administered enough testosterone to make sure the urine contained the right quantity of androgens, we do not know. And it does not really matter. Having refused a urine sample to John's side, he was bringing one to support his own position and claiming he was only doing so because of Strong's report. Whatever John had done would be turned against him.

Now that Ewan had created the appearance of completely independent medical evidence, authenticated by a minister, he was ready to present himself to the other clinicians he was calling in his defense. He traveled south again, across the English border, to Newcastle upon Tyne.

On April 6, 1967, Ewan was examined by Professor Martin Roth, who was then head of the department of psychological medicine at the University of Newcastle upon Tyne. Roth was the most eminent psychiatrist of his day, consulted by the World Health Organization, part of the Ministry of Health's advisory committee on mental health and the first president of the Royal College of Psychiatrists, which he was instrumental in forming. And Roth was a scientist, championing biological psychiatry's use of pharmaceuticals to improve mental health, and rigorously empirical in his approach to medicine. He was, so to speak, the heavyweight titleholder of his profession. Ewan approached him carefully, mentioning the existence of a lump but not sharing his idea that it might be a testis. During the examination, Ewan recounted to Roth his story of a European tour when he was a child, seeing doctors whose records were by that point lost, for purposes about which he himself had never been clear. But his early life matched the official typical patient narrative, set out by Krafft-Ebing, and he submitted to the infamous Terman-Miles test, which used a series of exercises, such as word association, inkblots, emotional responses and questions about personal interests, to determine whether men were effeminate. To pseudo-medicine, "effeminate" meant being gay and earmarked for "cure" or prison. Consequently, the purpose of the test was disguised from those taking it, since "subjects who know what the test is intended to measure are able to influence their scores so greatly as to invalidate them entirely."[3] But of course, as a clinician, Ewan was aware of its purpose and gave the answers that supported his case. Roth said that they were too rushed to do the test properly and asked Ewan to have it repeated in Aberdeen.

On the same day, Ewan was also examined by another distinguished member of the University of Newcastle upon Tyne's medical school, Professor Armstrong. As well as being an expert on intersex conditions, Armstrong was also the regional dean of postgraduate medical education, positioned as a very senior member of the profession, knowing and influencing medical practice nationally. Again, Ewan was circumspect in the history he gave, and as he strolled back through the university's peaceful quadrangle, and under its iconic golden stone and scarlet brick battlemented arches, he must have felt that he had done a good day's work.

Two weeks later, both Roth and Armstrong got the results from Ewan's biopsy. The material that had been taken to Aberdeen Medical School for examination was unequivocally testicular, definitely part of a testis. If the evidence could be believed, Ewan had just made medical history as the only known case of a trans man with an otherwise invisible testicle spontaneously appearing at the advanced age of fifty-four years old.

Meanwhile, Ewan had made arrangements for the Terman-Miles test to be completed as Professor Roth had advised. He was leaving nothing to chance. In early May, Mrs. Cordiner, the principal psychologist with the North-Eastern Regional Hospital Board for Scotland, carried out a series of tests on Ewan "with a view to assessing the degree of masculinity or femininity in his personality orientation." She selected 450 questions from the Terman-Miles test; ran the Minnesota Multiphasic Personality Inventory, with its 566 items that have to be answered true or false; and carried out an object relations test, in which Ewan was shown seven "pretty vague" pictures and had to "make up a story about the pictures," Mrs. Cordiner said. Doubtless Ewan had done his background research prior to seeing Mrs. Cordiner and knew precisely what to say and do.

Ewan had gotten all his powerful supporters lined up, just as he had when he corrected his birth certificate, and he was ready to do battle in court. Part of the legal process is what is known as "disclosure," in which each side reveals to the other the evidence that they are going to rely on in court. Ewan's "inventory of productions," as it is known, included photographs of him taken as a child with his ponies and one of him as a young man in lederhosen with his sixteen-bore and gun dog Bran; the reports from his biopsy and urine samples; and nine medical articles, including two long scientific articles, one by Mr. Dewhurst about a man with both ovarian and testicular tissue, and one from the University of Hawaii, by Professor Milton Diamond, about the way in which biological sex develops and presents.[4] He was definitely outgunning John, whose own inventory was mainly all the birth, death, marriage and divorce certificates he had had to produce to make his claim for the baronetcy, plus two medical reports; Margaret's letter; a short feature article from the *British Medical Journal* about the sex of the women athletes who had recently withdrawn from the European Games; and two legal excerpts, one from Manitoba and the other about "Hermaphrodites and the Law."[5] Where John had four medical experts, Ewan countered with eight.

We know that on Monday, May 15, 1967, John, Ewan and their lawyers and witnesses assembled together for the start of a four-day hearing before Lord Jack Hunter. But we do not know precisely where the trial took place. Since it was being heard in the Court of Session, Scotland's Supreme Court, it would ordinarily have taken place there, in the august buildings whose rounded Roman arches and massive columns frown across Parliament Square to St. Giles' Cathedral, high up in Edinburgh Old Town. But Ewan had bargained for a hearing outside the public eye: he had submitted to the medical examination purely to get that privacy, and he was not going to let it go. The records of the case say that it was heard in Lord Hunter's chambers, that is, in the capacious suite of offices where he and his various officials spent their time when not in court. Such a location would have ample facilities for witnesses to wait and for the hearing to be carried out, for it was not uncommon for judges to hear cases in chambers rather than in open court, especially where privacy was required. But the *Glasgow Herald* said that "the most that could be learned was that the judge and his clerk heard the case not even in Parliament House but in a solicitor's office," suggesting that an even greater secrecy shrouded Ewan's hearing.[6] Since John must have felt that he had the upper hand, perhaps Ewan had been able to negotiate for the hearing to take place in the offices of his own solicitor, Haldane & McLaren. If so, not only would that have given him the advantage of home turf, but it would also have resonated happily with him, for Archie Haldane's book *The Drove Roads of Scotland* was one of Ewan's favorites.

Whichever the location was, on Monday, May 15, 1967, the process opened. This was not a trial with a jury, but a hearing in which "a proof" would be taken by Lord Hunter himself. John had put in a "petition," as it was called, to prove that Ewan was and always had been female. Ewan's task was to prove that petition untrue.

Whichever side presented the best proof, in Lord Hunter's judgment, would win.

At the start of the proceedings, Lord Hunter would have checked with his officials that all the entrances were secured and that there was no risk of intrusion from the press or public. Then the process was simple. After being sworn in, each witness was examined. John's witnesses would first be examined by John's lawyer, William Grieve, QC, and then cross-examined by Ewan's lawyer, Charles Jauncey, QC.[7] The reverse was to be the case for Ewan's witnesses. Examination was by simple question and answer, a dialogue between lawyer and witness, with the occasional interjection from Lord Hunter if he wanted clarification on any point. They argued for four days, from Monday to Thursday, while both lawyers subjected all the evidence to the most rigorous scrutiny and cross-examination.

John himself appeared only very briefly, at the end of the first day, and did himself no favors. The short replies he gave to Ewan's QC sounded truculently defensive.

> Q: On the death of the Second-Named Petitioner [Ewan], you will become the baronet in any event?
> A: That is correct, yes.
> Q: But you seek to become the baronet during your second cousin's life?
> A: That is right.
> Q: And you raised an Action to that effect last year?
> A: I did.
> Q: So there will be no doubt about it, there is no question of any inheritance or any money dependent upon the result of this Action?
> A: No.

It was clear that John was acting purely out of ego and vanity. At the same time, though, it was a remarkable opportunity to discuss the ways in which medicine and the law thought about the sex of individuals. Since Roman times, UK law had recognized only two sexes, male and female, and insisted that everyone must be categorized as one or the other. But medicine had always known that "male" and "female" were ends of a spectrum, with a range of intersex conditions between them. Constrained by the law's artificial demand for a purely dimorphic citizenry, medicine saw its job as being to work out which category, male or female, would be most comfortable for the lives of people with variations of sex characteristics. How could that best be done?

The usual way was to use the "balance sheet" method, which Professor Cawadias had exemplified in his 1934 book *Hermaphroditos*. As he put it, "For each individual a sheet is filled in, one column comprising the male features, the other the female features," and according to which set of features predominates, the individual should be regarded as male or female. But as well as this reductive approach, obviously based on crude stereotyping, Cawadias was a strong supporter of what he called "the pragmatic sex": "that indicated by the will of the patient." He was clear that "the sex that brings most happiness and the best adaptation is surely the true sex."[8] He recognized a tension between the scientific need to classify and categorize and the individual's moral and democratic right to autonomy. At the heart of his analysis, Cawadias posed the ethical question of compassion: What do we owe to each other?

It was this ethical dimension that shaped the responses given in court by medical experts. Scientific medicine rarely does well in an adversarial setting, since by its very nature it is focused on uncertainty and open to possibility, interested in expanding debate, not closing it down. But it is usually good at compassion, at thinking about and acting in the best interests of patients. Then, too, the possibilities for conflict were limited, since the most senior medical authorities in court already knew one another. Although they had been placed on opposite sides now, Professor Strong, Dr. Jacobs, Mr. Dewhurst, Professor Roth and Professor Armstrong shared the same broad field of inquiry, were familiar with one another's research, and had collaborated with one another in the past. They were not going to abandon their mutual respect to score points in court; that would be professionally unethical and academically stultifying.

As to the less elevated clinicians, Dr. MacLean and Dr. Price on John's side would follow the lead of Professor Strong; it would have been the end of their careers to do anything else. On Ewan's side, Dr. Stalker, Dr. Shivas and Dr. Manson were his "ain fowk," Aberdeen graduates of a similar vintage to Ewan himself, while Mrs. Cordiner and Dr. Klopper were both employed by the university. Medicine of the day was clannish as well as autocratic, and provided his demands were not too extreme, they would support whatever Ewan claimed. The key was in sticking to the precise detail of what they could definitely swear to in court and never going beyond that boundary.

Ewan had provided enough evidence to make his incredible story almost believable. Whether he got his medical sample of a testis from Polani, or from a supplier Polani had alerted him to, and whether he did so himself or through an intermediary such as Wullie Manson didn't matter. Every doctor knew that such samples were easy to acquire. To their medical eye, Ewan's story of self-biopsies was unlikely at best. The medical reports recorded only two scars for what were claimed to be three incisions, and no one could self-administer two cuts in exactly the same place on one of the most difficult areas of the body to reach. Similarly, they knew that Dr. Manson could easily manage the supposed biopsy witnessed by Reverend Reid, whether by Ewan temporarily implanting tissue for Dr. Manson to excavate, or simply by putting Reid out of line of sight at the crucial moment and using sleight of hand.

And what every doctor could be sure of was that a testicle had not magically descended in a fifty-four-year-old as the result of testosterone administered sixteen years earlier by Professor Cawadias. It was as incredible as the "spontaneous feminization" of Agnes that had been reported by Robert Stoller in 1963 and which he was now busy retracting. Like Agnes, Ewan was trans and had been lucky enough to get access to HRT before puberty: nothing else made scientific sense.

But unlike Agnes, Ewan was not going to spill the beans. He had his story, and he was sticking to it. The *BMJ* article that John had brought to court supported the new pseudo-medicine in which trans people were delusional, extreme masqueraders who would "go to great lengths" to "assume the appearance of the opposite sex."[9] It argued that the balance sheet for determining sex should focus almost solely on "genetic sex," simply dividing people by whether they had XX (female) or XY (male) chromosomes. This would provide "a useful screening procedure" for athletics, without bothering about factors such as gonads (testes or ovaries), hormones (levels of testosterone or estrogen) or psychology (masculine or feminine "outlook"). Everyone who didn't fit this simple standard could be ignored, and since Ewan had XX chromosomes, its system would classify him as female. Without his miraculous testis, Ewan would have stood no chance.

It would be another twenty years before DNA profiling became authorized for use in the UK legal system, and so there was no way of proving that the testis sample was not his. But every medical expert was on their guard, and they all danced very carefully around the question of the testicle's provenance.

Professor Strong was first into the witness box on that Monday morning in May, ready to be examined by John's lawyer first and then cross-examined by Ewan's lawyer. Strong's team had carried out a very thorough physical examination, and he confirmed that his report had found Ewan to be female, and possibly a case of CAH. He was magisterial and precise in his answers, politely explaining medical terms with which lawyers were not familiar and being professionally exact at every point. He was asked about his report on Ewan's medical examination:

Q: In the last paragraph on that page you say that there was no evidence of testes found in the labia or in the region of the inguinal canal and you found nothing further following on a rectal examination. Did you conduct a purposeful search to see if you could find any evidence of testes?

A: Yes, I did rather, because by this time the likelihood, or one of the likelihoods was that we were dealing with a case of the testicular feminization syndrome. In this condition the testes are often found lying in the inguinal canal, that is to say the passage through the abdominal wall, which opens immediately above the groin, and we searched this rather carefully because we were anxious to see whether or not we could feel an organ of this type.

Q: And you found nothing?

A: Found nothing.

Doctors learn to speak in restrained understatements, so that to describe something as "rather helpful" is high praise, while a "rather disappointing" could indicate disaster. When Strong said "we searched this rather carefully," he meant, "we examined it minutely and extensively, using every possible technique, checking and cross-checking again, beyond all conceivable doubt." There had been no testis. Accordingly, when asked whether he would now stick to his original diagnosis of CAH, he replied, "Not at all; if the testes had been found, this diagnosis would be untenable." It was very much "if" rather than "since," for without saying so, Strong was clearly implying that the reason he hadn't found Ewan's testis was because it had never existed. Still, *if* the testis was to be believed, then the only conclusion available was that Ewan was a "true hermaphrodite."

Even so, the chromosome test was another major problem: Ewan had the XX chromosomes, typical in women. This was John's second major proof that Ewan's sex was female. But after lunch on the Monday afternoon, John's second expert witness, Dr. Jacobs, destroyed that certainty. At thirty-two years old, she was the youngest person in the courtroom, but she was one of the scientists who had pioneered the development of chromosomal studies, and she had been leading that field for ten years, at the same time as being a permanent member of the Medical Research Council. Dr. Jacobs was clear and authoritative. Asked if she could exclude the possibility that Ewan had "a Y chromosome somewhere," she replied:

A: No, you cannot exclude this, you can only talk about
the cells you have examined, and you can never exclude
in any individual, normal or abnormal, the presence of
another cell line with different chromosomes which you
are not in a position to examine, so you can only talk
about the cells looked at.

The phenomenon of "mosaicism," she said, meant that one part
of a person's body might have XY cells and another have XX cells,
and so it was impossible to know whether Ewan had a Y chromosome without examining every cell in his body.

Second, Dr. Jacobs confirmed that even if every cell in Ewan's
body could be examined, and no XY cell was found, that did not
mean that an XY cell had never existed. The circumstance known
as translocation could cause XY cells to be absorbed by XX cells,
and if that happened while the baby was in the womb, it would
never be evident or demonstrable. Her point was that absence of
evidence was not evidence of absence: just because no XY chromosome had been found, that did not mean that none existed,
then or in the past. Finally, Dr. Jacobs said, it was a moot point
as to whether a Y chromosome was needed to produce a testis.
That was "an area of great doubt at the moment," since "we have
no information one way or the other." The closer the scientific evidence was examined, the greater the uncertainty. John's senior
medical witnesses had destroyed the basis of his claim that Ewan
was female.

Dr. Jacobs was followed briefly by Dr. Price, who had been the
third person at Ewan's medical examination, the doctor who had
injected him with anesthetic. Nervously, he distanced himself from
the proceedings as far as possible:

A: I did not do any work on the samples which were taken.
Q: What part did you play?
A: I took the samples of blood and skin, and I was pres-
ent while Professor Strong obtained Dr. Forbes-Sempill's

history and carried out his examination, and I corroborated certain points which Professor Strong established.

Professor Strong had agreed that *if* the testis sample came from Ewan, then he would have to be classified as a "true hermaphrodite," and so of course, Dr. Price did exactly the same. He was followed by Dr. MacLean, a pathologist, who said, "I have had an opportunity of examining certain specimens which were given to me, said to be associated with Dr. Forbes-Sempill." He was distancing himself from the evidence and his reserved way of answering was for a good reason.

Q: Was it one portion of tissue you examined or two portions in Specimen 1?

A: In Specimen 1 two small portions of tissue.

Q: Did both consist of immature testis?

A: That is correct.

Q: And in Specimen 2, what did that consist of?

A: There seems to be a certain confusion about this, what I understood was the real specimen was a portion of ductus deferens, but attached to one of the slides there was a portion, probably a third, of a mature testis.

The portion of mature testis was explained away as having come from a different person and being there as "merely a control for a stain reaction." Nevertheless, its presence was confusing, and it showed both how easy it was to obtain such samples and how simple it was for medical evidence to be contaminated. Asked, "What sort of a person would you expect them [the specimen donor] to be?" Dr. MacLean replied, "I could not tell that; it is consistent with the possibility that it may have been derived from a person with two X chromosomes; I could not establish that merely from examination of the tissue." "May," "possibility," "could have": MacLean would not commit himself to anything on the basis of such strangely presented evidence.

On the second day, Tuesday, May 16, 1967, Ewan's colleagues from the University of Aberdeen took the witness stand, and attention focused again on the pathology reports for the testis. It looked like a straightforward story. Two samples had been sent to them for analysis, the first posted by Ewan using Dr. Manson's name, and the second delivered by hand by Reverend Reid. They had been examined by two very senior pathologists, Dr. Stalker and Dr. Shivas, and an obstetrics researcher, Dr. Klopper. The court had their reports, confirming that the slides of the tissue samples they had examined microscopically were certainly testicular. But they were equally cautious in their responses. Under questioning, it rapidly became clear that it was impossible for anyone to swear that the tissue had come from Ewan.

The problem was that there was no secure chain of custody, nothing to prove that the samples that Ewan and Wullie Manson said they had taken were the same as the samples that had been examined. Indeed, in court, Dr. Klopper would not even confirm that the slides held in evidence were the ones about which he had written his report: he would say only that they "resemble closely the ones I had prepared from the specimens. Without examining them under a microscope I could not presume to say they were exactly the same as my originals." As Dr. Stalker explained the process of receiving tissue samples, preparing slides from them and examining them for report, it became obvious that there were endless opportunities for introducing new or different material. The sample that Ewan claimed to have taken himself and posted under Dr. Manson's name had been received at the pathology laboratory's desk, unpacked and handed to a technician, who pigeonholed it for a junior pathologist, who began the complicated, multistage preparation process. The best that anyone could say was that the first set of tissue samples that Ewan had sent to Aberdeen Medical School had been labeled with his name. It was clear in court that no one could say how many people's hands the tissue samples had passed through or whose hands they were.

Reverend Reid confirmed in court that he had personally taken the second tissue sample to Aberdeen University's pathology laboratory. But Dr. Klopper would only say, warily, that the specimen "was handed to me by a gentleman in clerical garb whom I was told was the Reverend Reid." Nevertheless, Dr. Klopper prepared the specimen personally, and it seemed as if there was a secure chain of custody for that set of slides. But then Dr. Klopper went to the United States and they were transferred to Dr. Stalker, by persons unknown and without any record of process. And by the time the slides came to be examined in Edinburgh, by John's pathologist Dr. MacLean, they had been through a bewildering game of pass the parcel. After Dr. Klopper had left the country, Dr. Stalker had passed them to Dr. Shivas, who had taken them to Edinburgh and passed them to Professor Strong, from whom they had somehow found their way to Dr. MacLean. Somewhere in all this hand-to-handing, someone had changed the original slides, for when Dr. MacLean received them, as he had said in court, they had attached to them an additional portion of testis that was not a sample sent in by Ewan. Since there was no secure chain of evidence, no one knew who had attached it.

All of Ewan's colleagues in court on that Tuesday morning spoke cautiously. Professional friendship went only so far, and they would not perjure themselves. They limited their evidence to the tissue samples they had examined and refused to swear to their provenance. The best they would say was that the tissue was human (though not necessarily from the same person) rather than animal. But they all agreed that *if* the tissue samples had come from Ewan (always "if"), then he was definitely a hermaphrodite.

Dr. Manson was next up, and Ewan's lawyers were keen to make sure that if the hearing was influenced by crude stereotyping, then it would be in Ewan's favor. Professor Strong had already answered questions about Ewan's hairline, his upper leg hair, his pubic hair, his physique, the relative size of his hips and shoulders and the color of his complexion, and he had said simply that Ewan's appearance was "in keeping with a virilized female in the same way as it is with a male." Dr. Manson, who had known Ewan since 1952, was asked whether he had "come to any view as to what his sex appeared to you to be":

A: Yes, I think so, to my mind I consider him as a male. To me he has always appeared to be a male, yes.

Q: Can you elaborate that a little, in what respect did he appear to you to be male?

A: I thought generally when I was Assistant to Dr. Forbes-Sempill, and latterly, our conversation has always been as male to male, and that his interests to my mind are wholly male. I shot with him, and we have walked up in very hilly rough country, and to my mind his stamina on the hill was beyond any female, and all his interests and pursuits and the way he followed them were to me male.

Dr. Manson then went on to confirm Ewan's ability to muck out farm stock, drive a combine harvester, lift bales and carry food to his hill cattle. That done, questions turned to the biopsy. Manson was cagey in his answers, following the same lines as the other clinicians in giving simple descriptions without drawing any inferences or conclusions. Ewan had asked him to "take a small biopsy from a mass in the left groin and give this to the Reverend Reid to take in to Dr. Klopper." It was, Dr. Manson said, "a small rounded mass about the size of a small walnut" that "could have been a gland or it could have been perhaps an undescended testicle." Just above the incision that he made was "a mark of an incision, a recently healed incision." He put the tissue sample in a specimen jar and gave it straight to Reverend Reid.

John's lawyers cast doubt on Dr. Manson's honesty, making much of the fact that he had allowed Ewan to send in the first sample under his name without seeing it or even knowing what was in the accompanying letter. They were clearly implying that he couldn't be trusted. Then they went on the attack about Ewan's appearance. Dr. Manson had joined Ewan's practice in December 1951, almost a year before he corrected his birth certificate, and questions focused on that.

Q: Locally, the Doctor was a woman doctor. Is that not right?

A: Yes and no, I think if I can put it that way, I don't think generally the patients looked on Dr. Forbes-Sempill at that time as a woman doctor, you know, completely as one would compare with a woman doctor elsewhere.

Q: Did she dress as a woman?

A: No, mostly in a suit or in the kilt.
BY THE COURT [i.e., Lord Hunter]

Q: What do you mean by a suit?

A: I beg your pardon, sorry, in a gent's suit or in the kilt with a kilt jacket.
CROSS-EXAMINATION CONTINUED

Q: Would it be fair to say that she was a woman who appeared to have certain masculine interests?

A: To my mind, dressed in the kilt, a pair of legs in the kilt, it did not look like a feminine person below the kilt, a pair of legs, it looked to me like a good man in a kilt.

Questions continued in this vein, pushing Dr. Manson to identify Ewan as "one of those persons who although women, appear to have certain masculine interests and certain masculine attributes," apparently trying to imply that Ewan was really a lesbian, and then asking directly, "Did Dr. Forbes-Sempill ever in your experience wear women's clothes?" But Wullie Manson wouldn't be shaken. As far as he was concerned, Ewan was male. No one asked, and Dr. Manson didn't volunteer any comment about the anomaly of two scars from three biopsies.

Of course, the authenticity of Dr. Manson's biopsy depended on Reverend Reid being there to witness it. But when Reid was asked, it became clear that he was not a reliable witness:

Q: Did you attend Dr. Manson's surgery in Alford on the 28th March 1967?

A: Yes.

Q: What was the purpose of your visit?

A: The purpose of my visit was to be present while Dr. Man-
    son removed a piece of tissue from Dr. Forbes-Sempill's
    groin.

Q: Did you see Dr. Manson perform this operation?

A: Yes, I was present.

Q: Would you describe the area of the body whence the tis-
    sue was removed?

A: It was in the groin.

Q: Which groin?

A: I am not sure which groin.

He was present in the room but, perhaps, like the majority of
laypeople who find themselves in surgical settings, he flinched
from looking at the scalpel cutting into flesh. Most likely, though,
he had no line of vision: Dr. Manson's body will have got in the way
of Reid seeing anything much of the procedure.

Everything was uncertain. Mrs. Cordiner reported that the
Terman-Miles and other tests of psychological orientation she had
used on Ewan to show "the degree of masculinity or femininity in
his personality orientation" confirmed that he was masculine. But
this was a matter of degree, not an unequivocal "male or female."
Indeed, such an answer was not possible, for as Mrs. Cordiner
pointed out, her tests "have nothing to do with determining sex, it
is purely attitudes and interest and ways of thinking." Although it
wasn't a terminology available to her, she was saying that she could
comment on Ewan's gender, but not on his sex. She could, however,
comment on her clients' sexuality, for the tests were intended to
expose people who were gay. In the case of Ewan, "he gave responses
that showed a fairly close, affectionate, perhaps dependent relationship for a member of the opposite sex." This was followed up:

Q: Would you have expected to get the same result as you
    did from Dr. Forbes-Sempill from a masculine partner in
    a Lesbian relationship?

A: No, I think I would have expected more conflict, because this person would be physiologically and physically female, and I think there would have been a great deal more conflict and disturbance in the series than there were in his, his were a fairly normal masculine series suggesting a fairly positive affectionate relationship.

Ewan had managed to get through pseudo-medicine's most pernicious stereotyping.

Wednesday, the third day of the hearing, was given over to Ewan's senior medical experts. Much of what they said simply confirmed what Professor Strong and Dr. Jacobs had already explained. Chromosomes were not a reliable indicator of sex, and not everyone was born absolutely male or female. An article Ewan entered into evidence, written by his medical expert Mr. Dewhurst, had described a married man who had XX chromosomes and both ovarian and testicular tissue, which made it clear that the law's demand that everyone be labeled "man" or "woman" was scientific nonsense. Medicine's way of managing the disconnect between the law and the science was the balance sheet, but every expert had a different balance sheet, listing different items and weighting them differently. Scientific medical opinion agreed on one point only: that the self-declared "psychological sex" of intersex people, including trans people, should be decisive in their assignment as male or female.

There was scientific consensus about this. The second article that Ewan had brought to court was by Milton Diamond, from *The Quarterly Review of Biology*. In twenty-eight pages of carefully referenced argument, it exposed the fallacies of John Money's belief that people are born without a sense of their sex and that sex is "imprinted" by proper parenting. Diamond's point, echoed by all the senior medical experts in court that day, was that people are autonomous individuals, aware of their sex, and fully capable of finding the best way for themselves to live, provided the opportunity to do so is not removed from them. Ethically, therefore, "the patient's social circumstances, sexual identification and personal wishes have to be allowed to decide the issue." Scientific medicine upheld the individual's democratic right to self-determination and personal autonomy.

Professor Martin Roth gave the most extensive and authoritative evidence. He was the only clinician with substantial experience of working with trans people, and he was explicit that they were "intersexual personalities" and that irrespective of all other considerations, "an underlying constitutional basis" determines "psychological intersex." Roth was politely skeptical of Ewan's account of his life: having treated trans men, Roth was aware that Ewan's physiology was exactly what one would expect from long-term use of high-dose testosterone, and he said, "There is a trans-sexual phenomenon here." At the same time, like all the other clinicians, he agreed that since there also appeared to be a testis in the case, there could be "hermaphroditism in the physical sense."

On Thursday, May 18, 1967, Ewan took the stand all morning and into the afternoon. His voice in the court transcript is quite different from that of everyone else. Where his Aberdeen Medical School colleagues had been obviously nervous, and the senior clinical experts reserved, precise and authoritative, Ewan's voice sounds confident, cheerful and obliging. Adopting a tone that was benign and only too eager to be helpful and clear up what he positioned as a series of unfortunate misunderstandings, he set about decimating John's case.

Ewan confirmed details of his career, his general practice and his estate and agreed that he had tried to renounce the baronetcy so that there would be "no fuss and bother," since he and his wife simply wanted to live "undisturbed and peacefully at Brux." Previously, as a doctor, he had worked with quiet dedication to his community, and now, as a married man, he wished to live with the same dedication to his wife, his farm and the kirk of which he was an elder. A placid, tranquil life was all he wished for. But that had been disturbed by John's summons the previous August, and so now, out of a sense of duty and fair-mindedness, Ewan was attending court to help settle the matter. He had neatly taken the moral high ground.

The main issue, of course, was his incredible testis. John's QC focused straight on it when he began his cross-examination, and Ewan immediately defended his position:

Q: You were examined by Professor Strong on the 26th November 1966?

A: Yes.

Q: That was following an agreement which had been reached between your solicitors and the solicitors acting for the First Petitioner [John]?

A: Yes, that is correct.

Q: At that time you were aware of a swelling in your groin?

A: I thought that there was something, in fact there were two places there were swellings, and I indicated those to Professor Strong and Dr. Price.

Q: You did bring those to their attention?

A: I did, yes, but they did not seem to think very much about it.

Q: But Professor Strong I think told us, did he not, that he had conducted a pretty extensive search in that area to see if he could find any indication of any swelling?

A: What actually happened I think in this particular region is that Professor Strong did conduct a very thorough examination in many ways, but he did not seem to bother very much with this, he put Dr. Price on to it, and Dr. Price examined it, and I showed him two swellings, one inguinal and one femoral, which is slightly lower, and I don't know what he said, he went across the room and mumbled something to Professor Strong, but I gathered that they could not be certain of interpreting the findings.

In this first step of his defense, Ewan said that he wasn't himself certain what the swellings were, so that like everyone else, he was reliant on John's expert, Professor Strong. But Professor Strong had "put Dr. Price on to it" rather than doing the examination himself, indicating that whatever Strong had said, it did not come from firsthand knowledge. Then, Price and Strong had "mumbled something" together—hardly a professional-sounding co-consultation—and Ewan had gotten the impression that they were uncertain what the swellings were. Ewan was eroding the certainty of Strong's written report into vagueness and inattentiveness. Now he was ready for his second step.

Q: You were very interested in this examination because at this point of time this was the only examination to which you I think were going to submit. Is that not so?

A: The examination was granted by me in return for having a summary trial instead of a trial in open Court, so I had no choice in the matter, I had to submit myself to this examination or else we would have had the case in open Court, which would have been very unpleasant for not only my wife and myself but all my relations, whom I considered very much as well.

Q: This was the agreement which was reached?

A: Yes.

Q: On behalf of your cousin that this particular form of procedure would be adopted?

A: Yes.

Q: Provided you were prepared to agree to submit to medical examination by doctors agreed on both by you and on behalf of your cousin?

A: Yes, the agreement was not quite . . .

Q: Is that not right?

A: The agreement was not quite carried out, because we were led to understand there would be only two doctors who I would be seen by, Professor Strong and Dr. Jacobs.

Ewan has diverted questioning away from the swelling and the authenticity of his testis and on to the legalities of his examination. In particular, he has indicated to John's QC, for whom this seems to be new information, that he was coerced into the medical examination, so that "I had no choice in the matter." Ewan is suggesting that in effect, he was blackmailed into the examination by the threat of an open court and its attendant publicity, with the implication that John's medical experts were complicit in this intimidation. His voice trails off, inviting John's QC to find out what Ewan seems reluctant to say. Watching him walk into the trap he has set, Ewan takes his third step:

Q: Was Dr. Price's name not mentioned?

A: Dr. Price's name was not mentioned.

Q: If you look at the Petition which was jointly adjusted do you see in Paragraph 6 "Thereafter by agreement between the Petitioners . . . the Second Petitioner underwent medical examination on 20th November 1966, by Professor Strong accompanied by Dr. Price"?

A: Yes, it says this after it happened, but before it happened I was not told Dr. Price would be there, and I did at the time mention it to Mr. Haldane because I felt we had not quite had a square deal for a joint agreement.

Ewan's point was that Dr. Price's name had been added to the legal proceedings *after* the medical examination. Before it, the agreement was that "there would be only two doctors who I would be seen by, Professor Strong and Dr. Jacobs." And although he tried his best, John's QC couldn't get over the fact that the strict word of a legal agreement had been breached and then covered up later. The best he could do was to ask Ewan why that mattered. This was just what Ewan had been waiting for.

Q: Are you taking objection to having been examined by Dr. Price in any way?

A: Yes, I do.

Q: Why?

A: I don't think his examination was a good one, and he

also did damage to my arm, and I had a loss of sensation for three months in my thumb and first finger [from the clumsiness of Price's injection].

Q: Did you tell those people who are acting for you about this?

A: I did, I also showed my hand to Mr. Phillip the surgeon in Aberdeen, but we decided that there were so many difficulties that rather than make more, I would not make a fuss about it, but since this arose I think I am quite justified in saying something. Moreover, it says in our agreement that no anesthesia will be allowed except by the express wish of Dr. Forbes-Sempill. What occurred in the MRC Unit when I was lying on the couch bed, Professor Strong was at my right side taking buccal smears, that is scrapings inside the mouth, Dr. Price was on my left side, and while I was having my mouth held open and this was going on he jabbed me in here and injected a local anesthetic which caused the subsequent trouble.

Q: Did you tell those who are instructing you about this at the time?

A: I informed Mr. Haldane about it when there was no return of sensation in my hand after two or three days, and he informed Professor Strong, and I could have taken action about it, but I am not the kind of person who likes to take action against my colleagues.

It was a masterly display of disarming meekness, his devastating accusations against Strong and Price seemingly forced out of him by cross-examination. With apparent generosity, Ewan said he had not taken action against them because he was not that kind of person: nevertheless, he was clearly signaling that Professor Strong lacked moral integrity and that Dr. Price was professionally incompetent. Of course he hadn't complained. He had been saving up these two breaches of the legal agreement, Price's presence and his use of anesthetic, for just this moment. He was downgrading the professionalism of John's medical experts to zero.

What could Strong and Price do? Their use of anesthetic while examining Ewan had broken a legal agreement, so that they were already professionally compromised, saved only by Ewan's magnanimity from a legal charge of assault and a hearing for professional misconduct before the General Medical Council. They were like two snipe taken with both barrels. It must have been a terrible moment for the upright but autocratic Professor Strong. But after Ewan's revelation, Strong's testimony was tainted. The best John's QC could do was immediately to instruct a court officer to telephone Dr. Price to check whether he really had injected Ewan with anesthetic: a little later, that was confirmed, and both John and his lawyers immediately denied all prior knowledge of it, although, "It is now accepted that Dr. Price in fact did so."

John's QC moved on to his next target: Margaret's letter. Ewan was ready for him.

Ewan's immediate family were all dead at this point, and he could present the past just as he wished. He had already explained that because his parents were prudish Victorians who refused to speak about intimate matters, he knew very little about his childhood and adolescent medical history, and there were no medical records to challenge his pretended ignorance. Armstrong, Dewhurst and Roth would have understood perfectly the significance of the treatment Ewan got on his youthful European tour, but they had no evidence to refute his story and anyway were supporting him. So, under cross-examination, the story Ewan told was that his medical tour of Europe with Gwendolen was not to avoid him having a female puberty but because he was unable to menstruate, and all the various medications he was given were ineffective in bringing on menstruation. It was a simple, highly effective mirror image of the truth. Instead of menstruating, Ewan said, he began to have "erections and emissions" when he was about sixteen, but he was too embarrassed to mention them to anyone, least of all to his parents. In other words, just like Agnes's "spontaneous feminization,"

Ewan claimed a spontaneous masculinization, which produced chest hair and obliged him to shave.

John's QC turned to the most damning assertion in Margaret's letter, and Ewan met it head on:

Q: To come back to the other passage which you have been asked about already, which is on page 2 in the fourth paragraph, where it is said, "She had her periods regularly just the same as any other girl." I think you say that is untrue?

A: This is quite untrue.

Q: What I am puzzled about is why on earth should your sister say that if it is untrue and she had no knowledge of it, say so specifically?

A: I think I know why she said it, but I think the reason is unpleasant. I don't know whether you want to hear it.
BY THE COURT [i.e., Lord Hunter]

Q: We may as well know.

A: May I explain I feel in a way it is irrelevant, and I would rather not say it, but if it must come out then I will say it. My sister died in a motor accident in October this last year, and she was in fact in financial straits, and she left £9,000 and apparently her total debt was £12,000. I cannot vouch for these figures, but I have seen them on paper.

Ewan recounted the events of the previous autumn, in which Margaret had told Cecilia what she had done, Cecilia had informed Ewan, and Ewan had begun the reconciliation with Margaret that ended with her death. Then he began a skillful denouement:

Q: What I think you are suggesting is that for an oblique motive your sister put this paragraph in her letter to Mr. Matthews which she knew was totally untrue?

A: I say this again because she is dead and she is not here, she cannot defend herself, but I think that it would only be fair to say that she was ignorant of the facts, because as I have told you, there were facts kept from her because my parents did not consider that she would be able as a bright young thing to keep things to herself, and I think that one should take that into consideration.

It was an admirable courtroom tactic, positioning Ewan as a protective brother who would not hear anything said against his dead sister, no matter how silly she might have been. Under close cross-examination, Ewan regretfully explained other motivations for Margaret. She was hurt because Ewan and William got on very well, but William had forbidden her his house because "she had in fact done something to him that was not quite fair"; she was angry at Ewan for reregistering his birth; and she was aggrieved because she had heard about the reregistration from their sister-in-law, Cecilia, not from Ewan himself. Finally, John's QC put the question bluntly:

Q: I want to be clear about this. Do you say your sister wrote the paragraph about you having your periods regularly because she hoped to get some money out of your cousin John or because she honestly believed that that might have been true or for some other reason or for none of those reasons?

A: She just said to me in my own house, and I think my wife was present at the time, that "I am very disillusioned now, but I did believe in John and he said he would provide for me."

In the best melodramatic tradition, poor, silly, jealous, ignorant Margaret had been corrupted by designing, unscrupulous, villainous John, but she had made a deathbed reconciliation with her much-wronged but honorably generous brother Ewan.

Ewan had easy answers to everything else. He had waited to correct his birth certificate until after his mother's death, in case it upset her, and then until he had found help in the shape of Professor Cawadias. He had endured this wait by dedicating himself to his work: he "was totally absorbed in my medical practice, and I dressed, as you know, in male attire, and my patients all regarded me as a male practitioner, and that was just my life, I lived to serve my community." Marriage was, of course, a natural motive for reregistration but it was only a secondary one. As Ewan put it, "I had lots of patience, I could thole [tolerate] things, but they sometimes were intolerable, and I can tell you quite straight that whenever the opportunity presented itself, I would have done this in any case." It was a heartfelt statement, breaking through his courtroom manner and echoing the words of countless other trans people who had suffered in similar silence until a possibility of resolution became available.

Asked about names, he said that no one ever called him Elisabeth. He was Benjie to his mother and girlfriends, Forbes-Sempill to his lecturers, Wink to his fellow students and the Doctor or Brux to everyone else. Asked if he ever got any letters "addressed to the Hon. Miss," he replied with a dry disdain for his questioner's lack of etiquette, "No, the Hon. E.; they would never have been addressed to the Hon. Miss in any case, that would have been quite incorrect." Questioned about his entries in *Debrett's*, and the updating forms they sent regularly to aristocracy, Ewan said with a fine indifference, "I filled them in once for the change of name and marriage, and beyond that I am afraid I never do anything about it." Cross-examined about the role he took in the Dancers of Don, he said simply that he always danced as a man.

Then, just as it seemed his ordeal was over, Margaret's letter was put before him again. On one of the pages she had attached to the main letter, she had referred to a Dr. Innes as the family's doctor and it seemed that she had claimed his authority for declaring Ewan female and suggested that Ewan had discussed his reregistration with him. But Innes had died three years previously, and Ewan not only took him in his stride but walked right over him. Yes, Ewan knew Dr. Innes very well and thought him "a very nice man indeed," but he had never discussed any medical needs with him. Instead, he discussed any problems with an old friend, Mr. Gordon Bruce, whom he had first met in 1928, years before Dr. Innes came on the scene. Older than Ewan, "Brucie," as Ewan always called him, was also a keen shooter and expert fisherman, and it was he whom Ewan consulted, not only about his varicose veins but also about his intention to reregister. Casually, Ewan mentioned that Mr. Gordon Bruce "was also the Queen's surgeon and who has recently retired from practice, and I was in consultation with him recently." The implication was obvious. Bruce's position meant that he would be familiar with intersex conditions, since establishing the sex of royal babies was a crucial part of ensuring the succession to the throne. Ewan's sex had a sort of surrogate royal approval, therefore, and what was good enough for the Crown should be good enough for the Court of Session.

It seemed as if the worst of the courtroom ordeal was over. But then Patty was called to the stand.

As a doctor who was used to maintaining a clinical distance between feelings and physiology, Ewan had at least some professional defenses against this incessant assault. But when Patty was called to the stand, she had none. In the most horrifically abusive episode of the trial, she was questioned aggressively about the minutiae of her and Ewan's sex life.

First she was required to confirm that she had had sex with another man before marrying Ewan. In 1967, sex before marriage was still frowned on. The contraceptive pill was only available via the NHS for married women, and elective termination of pregnancy was still illegal. The bruising implication, therefore, was that Patty had "loose morals." Equally offensive were the implications that Patty's sexual experience proved she wasn't a lesbian and that she knew how "normal" men had sex. Following that line of inquiry, in a series of questions that were so medically and legally irrelevant that they can only have been designed deliberately to humiliate her, Patty was required to describe precisely how she and Ewan had sex.

Both medicine and the law knew that there were many intersex men whose genital conformation was different from the mainstream textbook appearance. As well as these natural variations in sex characteristics, two world wars and further conflict in Korea and Vietnam meant that there were numerous men whose war wounds had given them, too, a strongly individual genital anatomy. That is still the case today, especially in conflict zones like Afghanistan, where enemy tactics such as improvised explosive devices are designed specifically to mutilate rather than kill, as a means of demoralization, distraction and tying up resources. Such injuries do not change servicepeople's legal identity or medical status as male or female: they were and are nobody's business but the veteran's own. Thus, for four days, every medical expert had been at pains to point out that genitalia were not a reliable indicator of sex. What's more, the lawyers and judge knew there was no legal precedent as to how heterosexual adults were required to have sex with each other. What consenting adults did in bed was their own private concern, everywhere in the land . . . apart from in Lord Hunter's courtroom in Edinburgh on the afternoon of Thursday, May 18, 1967.

The questioning was horrific. Patty was first of all required to confirm that Ewan had a phallus, which he placed "in my vagina," and that it had "a natural erection and climax," during which there was an emission. Further cross-examination demanded that she say, specifically, that the "emission" came "from directly behind the phallic organ." At least, in that courtroom, "emission" would be understood as semen: the sexual ignorance of the judge and John's lawyers precluded the possibility that it was female ejaculate. But the questioning was an appalling violation for Patty, demeaning and humiliating, and devastating for Ewan to have to sit by helplessly and watch. Then, for utterly incomprehensible reasons, Lord Hunter decided to add abusively prurient questions of his own:

> BY THE COURT
> Q: Perhaps at this stage I might ask you this, can you describe in your own words what effect intercourse has so far as you are concerned?

A: Complete satisfaction.

Q: Can you elaborate, I am thinking of the physical effects on you if you can describe them?

A: I can honestly say a normal complete reaction and satisfaction.

Q: I take it you know what I mean by orgasm, do you?

A: Yes.

Q: Can you say whether or not you experience that during intercourse?

A: Yes, I do.

Q: On all occasions or on some?

A: On all occasions.

Q: Can you give me some indication of the frequency with which you have had intercourse over the years approximately?

A: Over the years sometimes twice a week, sometimes less, according to physical fatigue and different circumstances, indisposition.

Hunter's interrogation was so legally and medically irrelevant as to seem intentionally punitive.

Psychologically, such experiences make people feel "in exile from themselves," isolated, and bereaved.[10] But at least Ewan and Patty could now go back home to Brux, where the placid Don formed a kind of moat round their hills and moors, back to their peaceful wide-horned Highland cattle and sturdy Hampshire sheep, and the enduring natural rhythms of cropping, growth and reaping. There, they might perhaps be able to refind themselves after the alienating disorientation of Edinburgh, its sequestration of their lives and their degrading objectification in the Court of Session. Still, even back at Brux, they were left waiting in suspense for a judgment that might destroy their lives.

8

THE JUDGE'S DILEMMA

After leaving Edinburgh, Ewan and Patty had to wait another eight months while the judge, Lord Hunter, came to a decision. They had been living through three years of constant anxiety since William died and John turned up at the funeral. Hogmanay, the Scots' joyful celebration of New Year, had been turned into a time of dread: John's antagonism in 1966, Professor Strong's damning report identifying Ewan as female in 1967, and now another long, anxious wait until New Year 1968 for Hunter's legal opinion. What took the judge so long?

Lord Hunter was the same age as Ewan and a keen fisherman: in other circumstances they, too, might well have been friends. But Ewan had faced Hunter with a perplexing situation. He could find no firm ground. The UK's most senior medical experts had overturned the law's dogma that everybody must be male or female, since science knew that simply wasn't true. Clinicians from both sides had said, in effect, that the law was not keeping pace with scientific knowledge and social change. John's own medical experts had destroyed the basis of his claim that Ewan was female, leaving him without a leg to stand on. Then, too, the case raised grave procedural doubts. The absence of a secure chain of custody for the tissue slides and the refusal of the doctors who had examined them to swear to anything about their provenance were deeply disturbing. And as a close listener, Hunter will have noticed the doubt implied by Ewan's testis being discussed with the conditional "if" in statements from both sides.

Wherever he had looked for clarity, Hunter found confusion. Urine samples had been taken, and they were "very much consistent with the normal male or post-menopausal female," but just as with the tissue samples, no one seemed sure when they had been taken, and again, there was no secure chain of custody to prove they were Ewan's. Questions about Ewan's sex life before he met Patty didn't help Hunter either. Asked if he had "ever had any sexual feelings towards a man," he said he hadn't but agreed that before he married, he had sexual intercourse with several women, all of whom had subsequently married. By the standards of the day, a woman who married couldn't possibly be a lesbian; since his former girlfriends had all married, they couldn't have been lesbians or believed Ewan to be female. The court's naivety supported Ewan's case. But Professor Roth was asked whether "the psychological orientation of Dr. Forbes-Sempill is to be compared with that of the active partner in a Lesbian relationship?" and Roth explained that it wasn't, since lesbians "do not wish to achieve a change of identity." The ignorance of the 1960s assumed that lesbian couples imitated the roles traditionally assigned to heterosexual couples, one masculine and active, as a husband was supposed to be, and the other feminine and passive like a wife.

Unsparingly and in grueling detail Ewan's physiology had been anatomized in court. The size of his phallus, the location of the urethra behind it, and his vaginal opening had all been subjects of discussion. The length of his perineum (the distance between the anus and the next opening) had been brought into evidence because in those days, medicine believed that men had a longer anogenital distance than women. In fact, it is widely variable for everyone. Similarly, Dr. Price had said that it was possible for Ewan "to urinate in the standing position, possible but difficult," reflecting the general cultural belief that only men could urinate standing up, although of course, with practice any woman can easily do so.[1]

But perhaps one of most difficult aspects of the case for Hunter was the dissonance between its trivial motive and its profound implications. John's only apparent motive for starting the case was impatient vanity, wanting the Forbes of Craigievar baronetcy immediately, rather than waiting to succeed. Certainly the contrast between this frivolous purpose and its potentially devastating consequences had brought Ewan's medical colleagues to his support. Ewan was a respected member of their profession, urbane, cosmopolitan, a pillar of the local community, a "good chap" and "one of us." The idea that his life could be devastated for such a piffling matter was preposterous. If Ewan stated a testis had descended, therefore, then they would not declare it had not, and they would limit their evidence accordingly. But for Lord Hunter, as the instrument of Scotland's supreme civil court, the baronetcy's male primogeniture status was of overwhelming significance.

The law surrounding male-line primogeniture was so old that it had been lost in time, impossible to separate from the fabric of rule and government. When William the Conqueror had instituted it after the Norman Conquest in 1066, his intention had been to ensure that the UK lands he appropriated and gifted to his barons could never be removed from them and that they in turn would provide him with a continuous, unbreakable lineage of obligation. Over centuries, primogeniture had fossilized into a part of the hazy ideas surrounding royal prerogative, something as separate from statutory law as it was from logic and reason. Now it continued to decide not only title, estate and entitlement, but its archaic conventions also wrapped up billions of pounds and the right to govern by sitting in the House of Lords. Most significantly, the "male preference" form of primogeniture determined the right to be monarch: the current Queen of the United Kingdom and Commonwealth rules only because her father left no living brothers and no deceased brothers with surviving legitimate descendants.

King Edward VIII's abdication to marry Wallis Simpson had produced a constitutional crisis thirty years earlier. Now, to his consternation, Lord Hunter was being asked to decide on a case that could have similarly resounding constitutional implications. Whether Ewan was considered to be trans or intersex was irrelevant. The most senior medical opinion made no distinction between them, and legally they both presented the same problem. If Ewan, as a child wrongly assigned as female at birth, could inherit a male primogeniture title, then succession to the Crown and other primogeniture hereditary titles was no longer secure. Producing a child who was assigned as a boy at birth would not automatically be a guarantee of the next male primogeniture successor: whether king, duke, marquess, earl, viscount, baron or baronet, they might find that their psychological sex was female, and transition. Or an older sibling who had been assigned as female at birth might have a male psychological sex and so claim the throne or title instead. Male primogeniture, which was supposed to bring stability to the British kingdom by protecting the undisturbed succession to the Crown, would be destabilized. Lord Hunter's decision was not just about succession to one baronetcy: it was about the authority, continuity and supremacy of the whole British establishment.

The medical evidence had left no doubt that, scientifically, humanity occupied a broad spectrum of female, intersex and male. All of the experts on both sides made it clear that individual self-declaration was the only valid basis for determining sex. Balance sheets for categorizing people as male or female were just a rule of thumb, scientifically unreliable and all differing from one another. Lord Hunter had a golden opportunity to make new law and support equality for all trans and intersex people. He knew that countless trans people had already had their birth certificates corrected without any ill effects on society. The 1956 decision in the case of X, which had refused legal recognition to a trans woman, was simply one case in a junior court and based on low-level medical expertise. Hunter had the opportunity to make what lawyers call a "broad decision," a judgment that provides guidance for future similar contexts, shaping the legal landscape by making general rules that influence government policymaking. A broad decision would have found immediately in Ewan's favor and signaled to the government that it was time to support trans and intersex equality. Such a move would have made the UK the most culturally advanced society in the world. Instead, Lord Hunter began to prepare a narrowly draconian decision.

Meanwhile, elsewhere in the UK and US, two other significant events were being set in motion. Hunter's was not the only verdict waiting to be given on the relationship between trans people and aristocratic inheritance. On the same day that Ewan and Patty went to court, May 15, 1967, the Honorable Arthur Corbett, the son and heir of the Lord Rowallan, filed a petition for divorce from April Ashley, a trans woman. In sharp contrast to Ewan and Patty, April and Arthur had been very public figures since April's publication of her autobiography in the *News of the World* in 1962 and their widely reported marriage a year later. Now their relationship had broken down, April had filed for financial support and Arthur had retaliated by petitioning for divorce. Knowing about these events, perhaps Hunter realized that here was a second opportunity for the law to deal with the knotty matters of trans people's sex and its effects on hereditary titles, and perhaps he let that affect his own decision.

Simultaneously, a medical conference was being planned that would form a turning point in trans history. In the US, young psychiatrist Dr Richard Green was busy organizing the US/UK transatlantic First International Symposium on Gender Identity, planned to take place in London in July 1969. These three events— Hunter's decision, April's case and the symposium's purposes— were to combine into a perfect storm, with horrific consequences for trans people. First came the symposium.

During a one-year internship at the Maudsley Hospital in London, Richard Green had become close friends with John Randell, and the symposium was a way of consolidating both their friendship and their professional positions. Even today, with the benefit of email and internet bookings, international medical and academic conferences are planned two years in advance. At a period when communication was limited to written mail and telephone calls, things took longer. By 1966, everyone interested in trans medicine will have heard of plans for the symposium, and the names of its proposed key speakers, and thus its direction of travel, will have been general knowledge in those professional circles. Ewan will have been well aware of the symposium's determination to support pseudo-medicine's abuse of trans people, and that insider knowledge was perhaps a factor pushing him into fabricating his testis.

First Green and Randell had to get financing, for international conferences are expensive affairs and the bodies that funded scientific medical research would be unlikely to support the new pseudo-medicine. Any independent scientific scrutiny would dismiss its assertion that trans people were mentally ill as unresearched, unevidenced and invalid. Instead, the conference organizers represented their purpose as being to help trans people and got funding from two nonmedical, nonscientific charities. UK funding was provided by the Albany Trust, which had been set up in 1958 to provide expert professional support to sexual minorities, notably contributing to the Homosexual Law Reform Society's campaign to decriminalize gay men. From the US, Reed Erickson both underwrote the symposium and attended it, though he was not invited to speak.

The Gender Identity Symposium took place at the Piccadilly Hotel in London, on the weekend of July 26–27, 1969. Close enough to the aristocratic district of Mayfair to have some borrowed respectability, the hotel was also convenient to Soho's sex shops, strip clubs and LGT bars, and even closer to Piccadilly Circus, then the center of London's illegal drugs trade. Ironically, the Piccadilly Hotel was the former site of a concert hall infamous for a thirty-five-year continuous run of blackface minstrel shows, in which African Americans had been constantly lampooned as laughable masqueraders of a white elite. Similarly, the symposium was about to deride trans people as inadequate masqueraders of cis men and women.

John Money, Richard Green and John Randell were all committed to the idea that being trans was a psychiatric disorder that they knew best how to manage. Randell's doctoral thesis, Money's invention of a "gender identity gate" and his "research" into David

Reimer, and Green's experience at UCLA's gender identity clinic were about to coalesce into an Anglo-American axis that would dominate and decide the direction of trans healthcare.

Many other clinicians were treating trans people quite differently. Like Lennox Broster, who had just retired, Professors Roth and Armstrong at the University of Newcastle upon Tyne viewed being trans as a form of intersex. So did private medicine at Harley Street, and working from this basis, it offered one consultation with a psychiatrist to establish patients' competence to give informed consent, followed by admission for reconstructive surgery two days later. But under the guise of a neutral inquiry into the best treatment of trans people, Money and Green intended to crown Randell as the indisputable head of UK trans healthcare, make his gender identity clinic (GIC) into the authoritative, specialist center for NHS trans medicine, and consolidate their shared views into a new power base.

They needed a stalking-horse, and startlingly, Professor Jack Dewhurst, who had appeared on Ewan's side fourteen months earlier and been clear that being trans was not a mental illness, took on the role of chairman of the symposium. Perhaps the incredible narrative about Ewan's testicle had caused him to doubt his clinical convictions, or perhaps he was so politically naive that he believed the symposium was genuinely about impartial scientific inquiry. But as his later book *Royal Confinements* demonstrated, Dewhurst was deeply interested in the monarchy, and it is possible that he had decided to support pseudo-medicine to protect succession to the throne.[2] Whatever his motives, Dewhurst opened the symposium by describing trans people as confused. "Confusion in the patient's mind," he said, was paralleled by clinical uncertainty about treatment. Should trans people be treated "by getting the patient to accept their true anatomical sex" or by endocrinology and elective surgery? And were there any criteria for prescribing HRT and reconstructive surgery to patients other than, "Whether I like them, whether they seem to fit well into a new sex?" Still more significantly, Dewhurst raised questions about when to "recommend registration into the other sex" and "the legal position of the surgeon who undertakes sex-reassignment surgery of this kind."[3] He was signaling that medicine's rules about trans healthcare and the correction of trans people's birth certificates were about to be rewritten.

It was Money, Green and Randell's symposium, and they had decided whom to invite to speak and the order of speaking. Following the well-trodden route of takeovers everywhere, the opposition was to have its say first, so that it could appear to be listened to, then be dismissed, and the new order established. To obliterate dissenting voices, only the papers given by the new order were published and circulated after the conference, as though no other views had ever existed.[4] This was not a scientific meeting, dedicated to intellectual inquiry, but a political event, determined to create a London GIC operating to the same dogmas as those at UCLA and at Johns Hopkins Hospital. It was an exercise in power, control and propaganda.

First, neutralize the opposition. Dr. Peter Scott was from the Maudsley Hospital, the oldest psychiatric hospital in the world, and his voice had to be heard. Working from examples of competitive reproduction in other species, such as chaffinches and empid flies, Scott concluded that trans people had an underlying personality disorder that made them submissive and unable to compete. Frustrated by this lack of dominance, they wished to "change sex," but this same passivity meant that sensible general psychiatrists and even family doctors could make them "settle down very nicely without surgery." Accordingly, Scott said, "I don't believe transsexualism is a disease at all," and was against setting up a London GIC since, "I'm just a little bit scared that if you were to set up a clinic for transsexualists, the jolly thing would be used." He was rapidly slapped down by John Money, who asked, "[Does] he thinks that all the people in London who go insane, go insane because they have a Maudsley Hospital to go to?"

Other opposing voices came from the audience. Endocrinologist Joseph Adler was controversial in all sorts of ways, not least because his teamwork with the recently retired Mr. Lennox Broster had successfully provided endocrinology and surgery to trans people for thirty years. This was not what the symposium wished to hear, and although, to the chairman's obvious exasperation, Adler frequently interrupted proceedings, his views and long-term experience were not included in the symposium's published proceedings. Virginia Prince (founder of the Foundation for Full Personality Expression and the newsletter *Transvestia*) and Reed Erickson, who partially funded the conference, were both in the audience, and they were treated more or less politely when they asked a question or expressed an opinion, but their views, too, were ignored and unreported. Trans people were objects for discussion, deluded masqueraders at best, to be told who and what they were, and in no way experts on their own lives.

The new London GIC aimed to group trans people with "all the problems of psycho-sexual disorder, including the sex-offender disorders." It was direct psychopathologization and indirect criminalization by association. Making the London GIC's operation identical to UCLA's and Johns Hopkins's offered opportunities for international research into the etiology of being trans. Such research, in collaboration with biological scientists, might have been able to find a way of identifying and ending the "disease" while the child was in the womb, permanently eradicating trans people. At the same time, an international consensus on the psychiatric status and care of trans people would protect clinicians from litigation by patients.

Dr. Fred Oremland from California gave a paper on managing risk in US private practice, and it was clear that business expansion was important to many of the symposium's attendees. In the UK, the Sexual Offences Act had decriminalized sex between consenting male adults in private in 1967; just before the symposium met, Germany and Canada had announced similar decriminalization; and the American Law Institute had recommended that these measures be implemented in the US. The need for gay men to seek psychiatric help as an alternative to imprisonment was evaporating, but a new marketplace would open up if trans people were firmly reclassified as mentally ill. The murmur at the news that "a Morocco surgeon" was offering his services for £1,500 (now about £25,000 or $34,000), including airfare, seemed as much envy as censure.

The speakers had no scientific or historical perspective. They agreed that the majority of postoperative trans people just melted back into society, but they viewed this as a loss of research data from long-term follow-up, not as an indicator of their robust mental health and well-being. There was no consistency or logic to the various views expressed. Although they had no data to support it, the opinion was that a cross-dressing parent had no discernible negative effect on their children. However, the view was that a "transsexual" parent had to divorce before they could access HRT and surgery, apparently because the legal status of trans people was unknown now that they had been redefined as mentally ill masqueraders. Trans people were infantilized. They were positioned as putting themselves in danger by their irrational behavior and needing to be saved from themselves by a "cure" if possible, or if not, carefully controlled.

But a trans ally provided a dissenting voice. Margaret Branch, a social worker from Guy's Hospital, where Ewan had visited Professor Polani, described her NHS work with trans people and the support she gave them. She openly admired "the transsexual's courage" in coping with circumstances that were, at best, extremely difficult and was proud to be part of a team that made their transition as easy as possible. Her work included helping them to organize new documentation, such as insurance cards, medical cards, driving licenses, passports and income-tax returns, and ensuring that degree certificates were reissued in new names and that universities with single-sex colleges relocated their names and records appropriately. She visited families to help manage their issues and anxieties, and during transition she ensured patients had access to the Ministry of Labour's training schemes, helping them into a new occupation if that was what they wished. It was a glimpse into a world of friendship and support that was soon to vanish, for when John Randell took the stage, he described a quite different regime for the London GIC he intended to establish.

Although Randell's paper was based on his thesis, his views had changed. He now believed that reconstructive surgery was appropriate for some patients, and he set out stringent criteria for their selection. These had nothing to do with science. Although he dutifully listed the kinds of personality tests, physical examinations and interview schedules that Money and Green advocated, Randell had two key criteria for access to healthcare. The first was "conformity to social mores," so that trans people "should not bring to themselves publicity, or notoriety, nor to the surgeons who assist them." The second was that trans patients must never waver in their intention to have surgery, since it was "not for vacillating or changing, or those who switch." Both of these criteria had to be met consistently over time, so that Randell could "watch over a period of six to twelve months, and for some of them much longer, for any evidence of vacillation of purpose, of deviation from reasonable social standards."

Randell's criteria echoed the distinction between private and public lives that had underpinned the UK's partial decriminalization of gay male sex in 1967. It had pushed gay men into the closet, forcing them to live a double life, since public displays of affection were still criminalized.[5] Similarly, trans people were required to be both invisible and silent if they were to gain treatment from Randell. Part of that silencing was Randell's third criteria: that his patients must accept that they would never be their real sex. Women had to accept that "they will remain castrated males, and that they will not be made into women." They must contribute to their own subordination by agreeing that they could only ever be masqueraders.

The NHS ideal of equal access to healthcare was lost. Randell would provide surgery only for people between the ages of twenty-one and forty-eight, without "defective intelligence," and they had to tread a narrow line in consultations: they must not be timid or shy, but they must not be assertive either. If married, they must divorce;

they must not have any mental health problems and they must not be sexually explorative. At the new London GIC, subsequently set up at Charing Cross Hospital, NHS treatment was not a right but a privilege, to be won through an endurance test that lasted as long as Randell wished it to. Medical science was not involved. Pseudo-medicine required only the ability to jump through Randell's personal, subjective hoops, especially "the ability to pass, and pass over a protracted period without exciting remark."

There is no record of conversations between Randell and Virginia Prince, but it must have been disorienting for him to see Prince in the audience and addressed as "madam" by Professor Dewhurst. Randell's own cross-dressing was so highly closeted that his close friend Richard Green knew nothing about it until thirty years later, after Randell had died.[6] Randell filled the symposium with warnings about the dangers of police arresting male cross-dressers for importuning, or for creating a public nuisance, or for behavior likely to cause a breach of the peace. It would be impossible not to sympathize with what was obviously Randell's deep personal fear of cross-dressing in public, were it not for the ruthless way he projected it onto his patients and held them in thrall to his own anxieties. It was as if Randell was controlling himself through controlling them, denying his own being by denying theirs.

One effect of this projection was for him to make a clear separation between cross-dressers and trans people. Randell viewed cross-dressers as "usually superior" to other people, and he happily and sympathetically prescribed them HRT. But he was highly agitated by the terrifying fantasy that trans people might be "a transvestite who's perhaps verging on thinking, playing with the idea of surgery." This was his justification for treating patients harshly. Instead of the supportive regime that Margaret Branch operated at Guy's Hospital, Randell said, "If the police are interested, if their family are affronted, if they lose their job, this is their responsibility, not mine." All of those circumstances would stop patients from getting medical treatment because, as Randell put it, "they should be ladylike and conform," that is, be obedient, silent and submissive.

The symposium had nothing to do with medical science. It was just a haphazard collection of opinion, prejudice and anecdote in which anything went. A former pupil of Harold Gillies said that Roberta Cowell had "awful male legs" and felt that should be a criterion for refusing treatment. Everyone professed their ignorance about the etiology of being trans, but apart from Margaret Branch (who was a social worker and so didn't count), everyone agreed it was a mental illness. Randell's great strengths were his certainty and his close connection with Money and Green. Together they instituted the new regime in which being trans was no longer a physical intersex condition but a mental illness.

If you had asked them, Money, Randell and Green would have been astonished and outraged at being thought cruel or inhuman. Money saw himself as a liberating influence, a champion of sexual revolution and 1960s counterculture, a kind of Timothy Leary of sex. He had a charismatic television personality and in real life was affable and charming. Randell was well-known to his colleagues as a clubbable bon viveur, and some of his patients thought of him as a father. He saw his job as to give patients a sharp shock of reality, to be icily implacable in making them face life's harshness by making their care pathway an assault course that only the fittest survived. Green, younger than both and their professional junior, hero-worshipped them. Money was one of his life mentors, and Randell was like an older brother to him: whatever they did, Green wanted to do as well. All three saw themselves as the good guys, people who dedicated themselves to helping trans people. At the symposium they betrayed no sense of their complicity in destroying trans people's lives and autonomy. There was a very evident gap between them and trans allies such as Margaret Branch, who were always supporting, never misgendering or disrespecting trans people, willing to challenge authority in the name of equality. The majority of the doctors present either laughed at their trans patients or spoke of them patronizingly as lesser human beings: the colonial mindset was constantly evident.

This casual colonial cruelty is evidenced by tape recordings of the symposium, which form a counter-memory to its published proceedings. The printed record offers a public face of concern, positioning Money, Randell and Green as caring doctors and rigorous scientists. But the symposium's voices, their tone and emphasis, and their often-sneering dismissal of their trans patients tell a different story. All colonial masks shelter a heart of darkness, and theirs was a self-serving, subjective, unevidenced judgmentalism, formed by partiality and bias, which refused individuality and autonomy. Like all eugenicists, they saw themselves as working for the best interests of society by segregating and controlling its undesirable members, so that neither they nor their peers saw them as monsters, in spite of the monstrous things they did. The new medical regime for trans people that they engineered through the symposium was the foundation of the abjection and social exclusion of trans people for the next thirty years.

Of course, Lord Hunter was as aware of this direction as Ewan was. And like Professor Dewhurst, he understood fully the implications of his judgment for male primogeniture succession. The route he took was to make the narrowest decision possible, one that limited itself rigidly to the facts of Ewan's case and deliberately avoided creating any new general principles. The opinion he gave was explicitly punitive. His view was that "persons who are actually born are either male or female," pointedly ignoring thousands of years of cultural record and all the modern scientific evidence that said exactly the opposite.[7] Defying the UK's most senior medical and scientific opinion, Hunter created his own balance sheet for determining sex: gonads, apparent sex, psychological sex and chromosomal sex, with chromosomes being "the least valuable of the available criteria." Using these criteria, Hunter said, "An hermaphrodite should be assigned to one sex or the other according to the sexual characteristics which are found in that person to prevail or predominate."

Human suffering was irrelevant. Hunter was explicit that his approach "may result in deep human unhappiness and misery," but he believed that "with a very few unfortunate exceptions, [it] probably works well enough." It was a callous dismissal of intersex people but, irrespective of anything science might say, Hunter was clear that the law "must in my opinion attempt to draw a firm line, which leaves males on one side and females on the other." In particular, trans people were to be kept out of the equation. Hunter was explicit that anything he said was not in their support and that his opinion must not:

> leave a possible loophole for those suffering from sexual aberrations or deviations, such as certain trans-sexuals, who may have the strongest motives or drives to pass, legally or illegally, from one side of the sexual spectrum to the other, and who, in the event of success in achieving the social sex of their desire, might bring disastrous consequences not only upon themselves but upon others in the society in which they live.

Since there had been no "disastrous consequences" so far, Hunter can only have been referring to the destabilization of male primogeniture and the constitutional crisis that might be precipitated if succession to aristocratic or royal title was no longer certain. That specter had been raised once by Dr. Michael Dillon, and it was being raised again by Dr. Ewan Forbes.

Where did this leave Ewan? Although he was a callous bigot, Hunter was no fool. He knew that Ewan had misled the court with his trumped-up testis, and he castigated the Aberdeen Medical School pathologists who had assisted him, for "a degree of secretiveness in the taking of certain biopsies which might have resulted in evidence of facts of a most important and material character being left in doubt." And he singled Ewan out for particular censure. Everyone else who had given evidence had done so as briefly and formally as possible. Only Ewan had been at his ease, giving a breezy account of the testicle's appearance and a blithe description of self-biopsy after lunch, with convenient absences of knowledge, elaborate name-dropping and a strategically failing memory. His mention of sending the biopsy in "a plastic box, the kind of thing one gets medical samples sent in" seemed a deliberate taunt, for why would he have such a thing, twelve years after leaving medical practice? Hunter's rebuke was oblique, but when he described "an age when one regularly sees perjury committed in a manner which can only be described as light-hearted," it can only have been Ewan who was meant.

As far as the rest of the evidence was concerned, Hunter dismissed Margaret's letter entirely. It was "based on hearsay or even double hearsay, and quite possibly on information that was meant to be misleading," written when "her state of mind at the material time was confused" and when she clearly felt "something approaching resentment or pique" toward Ewan. Then he returned to Ewan. Since John's medical experts had been unable to disprove Ewan's story about the testis, it had to be accepted into evidence, as did the possibility that Ewan might have had ovarian tissue somewhere in his body. More important than this hypothetical gonadal ambiguity, though, was Ewan's sexually functional phallus.

> Judged purely by appearance, the external genitalia are predominantly female, but, judged by function, they are predominantly male. . . . The fact that in sexual intercourse the Second Petitioner is, despite his physical handicaps, able to penetrate with his phallus the vagina of his wife and to function mechanically as a male, to the satisfaction both of himself and his partner and to the point of orgasm and emission, is in my opinion of greater importance than the predominantly female external appearance of the genitalia.

It was also important, Hunter believed, that a man was unlikely to find sex with Ewan satisfying. Ewan looked more or less typically male, Hunter said, and Dr. Manson's testimony as to his manly occupations and his stamina walking up hills corroborated that.

But the decisive factor was that Ewan's psychological sex was male. Scots law has the idea of an "adminicle," something that proves the existence of an item that is itself not available for scrutiny. Chromosomes were useless as evidence for someone's sex. In the absence of decisive scientific proof, therefore, psychological sex was the adminicle that proved "real" sex. Accordingly, Hunter said, in the case of *Forbes v. Forbes*, he had decided that Ewan was "a true hermaphrodite in whom male sexual characteristics predominate."

Ewan had not been declared female, and that must have been a huge relief to him and Patty. But they were not out of the woods yet. There had been considerable discussion in court about just what "a true hermaphrodite" meant. For Dr. Jacobs it had meant Ewan was "neither a boy or a girl," but for Dr. Klopper it had meant Ewan was "both rather than neither." Professor Roth, meanwhile, said authoritatively that it meant Ewan was either male or female as decided by his self-declaration. What's more, Hunter's judgment sounded like an oxymoron: How could a "true hermaphrodite" have predominantly "male sexual characteristics"? And what did all of this mean for the primogeniture inheritance of the Forbes of Craigievar baronetcy?

Trading on these confusions, John kicked the legal ball back into play. Ewan had defeated John's attempt to prove he was female, but he had not yet gained the title at the heart of John's challenge. Because his was an unprecedented case, it was not known whether a "true hermaphrodite in whom male sexual characteristics predominate" was man enough to meet the requirements of male primogeniture. Matters were not helped by the vagueness surrounding the basis of primogeniture itself. Accordingly, John felt that there was still a chance that he might grab the title he wanted so desperately. He continued his challenge, and the correct line of Scots aristocratic inheritance of the Forbes of Craigievar baronetcy went for determination to the Lord Lyon, the authority on all matters of inheritance, together with the Lord Advocate, the senior Scots legal authority, and the Home Secretary, keeper of the Rolls of the Baronetcy. Ewan and Patty had to wait through another long year for their fate to be decided.

9

A PERFECT STORM

Both Ewan and Patty must have felt deeply concerned about what another decision might mean for their marriage. Ewan's corrected birth certificate had not stopped the law from allowing John to take action against him, and although he had avoided being declared female, there was no guarantee that the law would allow him male primogeniture inheritance. If Ewan was not found to be the next male heir, would that mean his and Patty's marriage was perjured? They continued to carry out the daily and seasonal round of tasks that were required of all farmers, but the possibility of a further abusive court hearing, with prison waiting for them at the finish, must have been an agony.

While Ewan's case was in process in Scotland, another case was unfolding in England: April Ashley and Arthur Corbett's highly publicized relationship. Ewan and Patty will certainly have read about April and Arthur in the press, after she was outed by the *Sunday People* and retaliated by serializing her biography in their competitor tabloid, the *News of the World*, from April to June 1962. But they could never have guessed how directly their lives would impact hers.

April was born in 1935, the year when William became the 19th Lord Sempill and Ewan began to manage the Craigievar estates. But instead of a castle, April was born in what she called "a dockland slum" in Liverpool, and instead of an attentive, resourceful Gwendolen, April's mother used to pick her up by the ankles "and bang my head on the ground like a workman with a pneumatic drill" or "hit me until I was black and blue."[1] Her affectionate father was either at sea or drunk, and money was short, so like all her clothes, the wooden clogs April wore were hand-me-downs from older siblings. At the same time, she was a slight, fragile child, born with "a severe calcium deficiency" that required weekly hospital visits, and she was bullied by other children, who nicknamed her "Sissy."[2] But in spite of her deprivation and abuse, April was absolutely clear that she was a girl, not the boy it said on her birth certificate.

From the time she was three, strangers asked April's mother if she was a boy or a girl, and at school, although she was "constantly taunted for being like a girl," she very definitely "wanted to be one," having "long conversations with God each night, asking him to make me wake up normal, wake up a girl."[3] Like Christine Jorgensen, by the time she left school at fifteen years old, she had no facial or pubic hair, her voice hadn't broken and she was still very undersized for her age. Her life experience followed the typical patient narrative set out by Krafft-Ebing and exemplified by Lili Elbe, Christine Jorgensen, Michael Dillon and Ewan.

In her biography, April described her failed attempts to "be like a man" by joining the Royal Navy and the journey that took her to London, where she said she met Albert Einstein in a Soho café and he asked her, "Are you a boy or a girl?"[4] Then April learned of the existence of Le Carrousel, a Paris nightclub famous for its male and female impersonators. When she was twenty-one, in 1956, just as Ewan was settling into full-time farming at Brux, April had moved to Paris and, using "Toni" as her stage name, was starting a new job at Le Carrousel. Now she knew where to get medical support, could pay for regular estrogen injections and began saving up for reconstructive surgery. Four years later, in 1960, April traveled to Casablanca for a vaginoplasty from Dr. Georges Burou: she was his ninth patient, and something of a guinea pig. Perhaps Burou's lack of experience explains the heavy postoperative bleeding April described in her biography, but other medical details were less explicable. She was given no effective pain control, so that postoperatively she felt "as if branding irons were being vigorously applied to the middle part of my body"; her hair fell out; and she became temporarily blind.[5] None of these were expected consequences of vaginoplasty, nor did the procedure mean that, postoperatively, patients no longer need to take estrogen, as April said she was told.[6]

When April returned to London, she became a fashion model, her work including photo shoots for *Vogue* by famous photographers such as Lord Snowdon and David Bailey. She was very much at the center of the King's Road set that dominated "Swinging London" and the galas and parties that accompanied its rich, famous and aristocratic members. Then, in November 1960, April was invited to lunch by a man who called himself Frank, but who was really the Honorable Arthur Corbett, son and heir of the Lord Rowallan.

Although they, too, came from Scotland, the Corbett family did not have the antiquity or distinction of the Forbes-Sempill family. Arthur's grandfather Archie was a London property developer who became a member of Parliament for the Liberal Party. He had married into the Polson family, co-owners of the wealthy corn and flour merchants Brown & Polson, and his mother-in-law had bought the couple the sixty-thousand-acre Rowallan estate in Ayrshire, just over the border from England, in the Scottish Lowlands. In 1911, in recognition of his political services and philanthropy, Archie was enrolled in the peerage, taking the title of 1st Baron Rowallan. Where the heritage and connections of Ewan's Highland family went back many centuries, Arthur's family title and estate were only fifty years old. Arthur's father, the 2nd Baron Rowallan, had a distinguished career, sitting in the House of Lords, becoming chair of the family firm of Brown & Polson and heading up the Boy Scout movement in the UK as Chief Scout for fourteen years. When Arthur met April, Lord Rowallan was midway through his appointment as governor of Tasmania and was looking forward to a quiet retirement.

Arthur became obsessed with April. He divorced his wife and left his four children in order to be with her, and in 1963, Arthur and April married in Gibraltar. It was not a success. As April put it in her raffish way, "Arthur wanted me on a pedestal, not on a bar-stool. My inability to remain on either thing was the cause of many rows between us."[7] Less than four years after they married, Arthur filed for divorce on the grounds that at the time of their marriage, April was "a person of the male sex." Unlike Ewan, April had not corrected her birth certificate, which still identified her as male. Quite why this was is unexplained: perhaps Dr. Burou had not been willing to provide the necessary letter to take to Somerset House, the central registry where such corrections were made, or perhaps Somerset House had not found his medical opinion acceptable. But at that time, some trans people didn't correct their birth certificate, partly because it was an additional expense, partly because it was inconvenient and partly because they had no idea of the impor-tance that would eventually be attached to it. As people in the UK are not required to produce a birth certificate in order to marry, its absence had been no impediment to April going through a mar-riage ceremony with Arthur. But certainly, without a corrected birth certificate, April's marriage was not legal, and at first it was a mystery why Arthur went to the trouble and expense of starting divorce proceedings. In the eyes of the law, their "marriage" was void from the start, and April was simply his perjured, same-sex "wife," which is to say, no wife at all. He could have just walked away from the relationship without April having any legal recourse.

April and Arthur ended up in court because she started legal proceedings against him. Their relationship had broken down, Arthur had not kept his promise to sign over a villa in Marbella to April, and as a badly judged ploy to force his hand, April's solicitor, Terrence Walton, advised her to sue Arthur for financial support. April was perhaps unaware of how foolish such an action was, for fallacies such as the idea of a common-law marriage and confu-sion about the relation between a marriage ceremony and a legal marriage were as prevalent then as they are now. Terrence Wal-ton, who suggested the strategy and encouraged April to follow it, must certainly have known that financial support was payable only in the case of a legal marriage. April and Arthur's marriage was not lawful, and her solicitor was putting April in a perilous position, exposed and fraught with legal danger. Arthur made the obvious riposte that he was not liable for financial support because they had never been legally married. But instead of doing this by simply ignoring April's action or sending a "cease and desist" letter, Arthur chose a particularly cruel course of action. On May 15, 1967 (the same day Ewan's court case began), Arthur filed a petition for divorce on the grounds that April was and always had been male. It was a mirror image of Cousin John's attack on Ewan. April's case was scheduled to be heard in the High Court by Lord Justice Roger Ormrod in November 1969.

In London in May 1968, therefore, as spring was breaking at Brux, Arthur's lawyers were putting April through the same traumatizing process of medical anatomization as John had inflicted on Ewan. Just as John had tried to prove Ewan was female in the Scottish Court of Session, so Arthur was taking April to the English High Court to prove that she was male.

April's life was public property in a way that Ewan's had never been. Ewan and his family were well-known in their local community and among their own private circle of friends, but they were not in the wider public eye like April. As a successful dancer, model and actor, she had mingled in international circles with the rich and famous, and her career was dependent on publicity. But there was an edge to April's career and image that other successful female models and actresses didn't have. Their shared work area was all about projecting stereotyped images of hyper-femininity, beauty and elegance in a socially approved masquerade, which everyone knew was public performance, not private identity. Indeed, discussing the gap between public image and private life was a mainstay of their publicity, sold to lifestyle magazines and newspaper columns in the *True Story* tradition as "intimate glimpses" of privileged lives. But like Christine Jorgensen, April's public image carried a political tension. Other women performers could exaggerate their appearance and mannerisms without adverse comment, but if trans women did the same, public prejudice would consign them to the world of burlesque and drag. The nature of this popular prejudice, its readiness to pounce and its reductive illogicality had been demonstrated in full at Ewan's trial: What were his legs like? Did he dress like a lesbian? What about his hairline and his hobbies? The colonial *Systema Naturae* was never far below the surface, poised to measure, categorize and condemn. Although April had enjoyed hearing Arthur describe her as the next Lady Rowallan, at the same time she had to defend herself from a constant, casually transphobic trickle of curiosity and insults from people who knew her public story. However bad that got, though, it was nothing to what she was to meet in court.

Nevertheless, April had many reasons to be hopeful of success. Gender fluidity was everywhere in London's Swinging Sixties. Michael Fish was selling men's dresses from his shop in Mayfair, where David Bowie famously bought five, to wear on his 1970 US tour.[8] Mick Jagger and James Fox cross-dressed in the cult 1970 film *Performance*, and Ray Davies's 1970 hit song for the Kinks, "Lola," explicitly celebrated gender ambiguity. April's social circle included people like Sir Michael Duff, Lord Lieutenant of Caernarvonshire, whom she knew liked "to dress up as Queen Mary and pay surprise visits in a royal car."[9] And Ormrod was part of this bohemian circle, so that April recalled a friend of hers, Joan Foa, saying to her:

> "If only we could get Roger Ormrod to be judge. I know him. He'd surely understand." When the letter arrived saying that the case was indeed to be heard before Ormrod we hugged each other and danced round the kitchen. "I know it's going to be all right now," she said.[10]

But Joan was mistaken. There were three factors that neither she nor April had taken into account. The first was April's birth certificate, still identifying her as male. The second was that the First International Symposium on Gender Identity had just finished its recategorization of trans people as mentally ill. And the third was Ormrod's public homophobia.

Ormrod was an unusual lawyer, having qualified in medicine and practiced in the Royal Army Medical Corps during World War II, before moving his career to law. While a barrister he had also been a part-time lecturer in forensic medicine, his work naturally spanning the medicolegal disciplines, and as a judge, he had professional experience of trans cases. He had already heard a case similar to April's, *Talbot v. Talbot* in February 1967, when he had simply declared the marriage void on the grounds that the trans man husband had no legal evidence that he was male.[11] Since April had not corrected her birth certificate, she had no legal evidence that she was female, and Ormrod could have applied exactly the same judgment to April and Arthur's case. But Ormrod knew that Ewan's case had just raised the fraught constitutional matter of primogeniture. And although Ormrod's experience of medicine was limited, he knew enough to recognize that Ewan had hoodwinked the Scottish Court of Session. In the English High Court, Ormrod planned to outmaneuver that judgment, settle the legal status of UK trans people permanently and end the constitutional crisis. To do this, Ormrod would pretend that Ewan's summary trial had never happened. His masquerade of amnesia effectively allowed him to try Ewan again by proxy. He could revisit Hunter's decision and use April as whipping girl not only for Ewan but for all trans people.

The most grotesque aspect of April's case was the cover-up of Ewan's case. His summary trial had taken place in camera, in an unknown location. Hunter had decided that it was not in the public interest to record the case in the usual legal records, since, he claimed, it was not relevant to the status of any other person. Additionally, Ewan's sister-in-law, Cecilia, had used her influence on his behalf to rein in the press. Cecil King, chairman of the tabloid group the International Publishing Corporation, owned an estate at Cushnie that marched with Craigievar, so he and Cecilia were neighbors. At her request, he effectively stopped reportage of Ewan's case. These were some of the means by which Ewan's case was hidden.

Consequently, knowledge of Ewan's summary trial was limited

to specialist medical and legal inner circles. A long article in the *Medico-Legal Journal*, simply indexed as "Transsexualism," had discussed it and quoted from Lord Hunter's opinion,[12] but without naming Ewan or the case. Ormrod himself was subsequently to refer somewhat sneeringly to "one case in Scotland which I think arose in connexion with succession to a title or chieftainship" and to discuss Hunter's decision with a colleague who referred to it as "rumoured, no more."[13] A cloak of secrecy had been drawn over Ewan, so much so that although three of the medical experts in April's case had given evidence in Ewan's case, they were told they could not reveal its existence. Even more bizarrely, before they entered court, Ormrod showed the proceedings of Ewan's hearing to April and Terrence Walton and told them that they could not refer to it, that it had been removed from the public eye and that everyone who knew about it had been sworn to secrecy.

Nothing could have been more irregular. By agreeing that he would not present information that might be in his client's interest, April's solicitor was being complicit in a breach of ethical conduct. It is true that since Ewan's case was decided under Scots law, it did not set a precedent for England and Wales. But it was the first legal case in the UK to determine a person's sex for the purposes of marriage, consummation of marriage and inheritance of title and property. What's more, it had been decided by a more senior court than the one presided over by Ormrod. On any showing, the judgment in Ewan's case should have been persuasive on the issues in April's case, and at the very least the court proceedings should have been made freely available to both sides.

The only records that exist for the seventeen days of *Corbett v. Corbett* are Ormrod's report, his subsequent discussions of it and April's memoirs. None of them explain how Ormrod enforced his ban on references to Ewan's hidden case, but it is clear that somehow he operated what is now termed a super-injunction, a privacy so powerful that it bars all mention of the case's existence. Ewan's falsification of his testis was not at issue: what Ormrod was really hiding was the scientific consensus in favor of Ewan, that being

trans was a biological variation of sex characteristics, a form of
intersex, and that self-declaration of their "psychological sex" was
the only valid criteria for deciding trans people's legal sex.

By concealing this absolutely crucial legal precedent, based on
scientific medicine and made in a British court senior to his own,
Ormrod was able to proceed on the basis that April's was "a case
of first impression," the first judgment of its kind ever made. Consequently, Ormrod's decision "shaped the developing law relating
to transsexualism in its own jurisdiction and in others": it became
a "super-precedent," cited in other countries, deciding the fate
of trans people not only in the UK but across the world.[14] And
it solved the constitutional crisis about male primogeniture that
Ewan's case had raised.

Every step of Ormrod's actions demonstrates this intention.
Instead of simply declaring April and Arthur's marriage void, as he
had two years earlier in *Talbot v. Talbot*, or dismissing it as a waste
of the court's time, or prosecuting both April and Arthur for perjury, he carefully mirrored the lengthy process used in Ewan's case.
Ormrod began by appointing two independent medical inspectors
to examine April in advance of the hearing, both very senior in
their field. On May 22, 1968, while Ewan and Patty were still waiting anxiously for the Home Secretary's decision, April's "sexual
organs" were examined at private consulting rooms in Wimpole
Street, London, by Mr. Leslie Williams, a founding member of the
Royal College of Obstetricians and Gynaecologists, and Miss Josephine Barnes (subsequently Dame Josephine Barnes and the first
woman president of the British Medical Association).[15] They wrote
a terse report. Referring to April in quotation marks as "her," they
said that her breasts were "well developed though the nipples are
of the masculine type" and April's voice was "rather low pitched."[16]
Their examination showed no uterus or ovaries, and they recommended that the court should contact Dr. Burou, in Casablanca,
for "a report on what exactly was done at the operation."

In particular, their report described April's vagina as no different from any other. It was "of ample size to admit a normal and

erect penis," its walls were "skin covered and moist" and there was "no impediment on 'her' part to sexual intercourse." This was an important legal point in deciding the validity of a marriage. A prior legal decision had determined that a woman who had been born with a foreshortened vagina and had it extended by vagino-plasty had been able to consummate her marriage and that the marriage was therefore valid.[17] Ewan's ability to penetrate Patty's vagina had been a deciding factor in Hunter's decision five months earlier. This first report from Barnes and Williams indicated that April was equally capable of conventional sexual consummation.

But that was not the direction of travel Ormrod wished for, and he made Barnes and Williams revisit their conclusions and pro-duce a more damning report. At his request, six weeks later they submitted a supplementary report, which cast April in a different light. Now she had "an artificial vagina," a term used to make it distinct from a "normal vagina." But still, in spite of the pressure from Ormrod, the only difference they could find between April's vagina and every other woman's vagina was that April's appeared to be moistened by sweat glands rather than by mucoid secretions.

April's real vagina was to disconcert Lord Justice Ormrod as much as Ewan's fake testicle had perplexed Lord Hunter. Mean-while, though, Barnes and Williams had recommended a chro-mosome test, which was carried out at Cambridge University by Professor Hayhoe, who reported, on October 31, 1968, "that all the cells which he examined were of the male type." Like the medi-cal experts in Ewan's case, he knew that did not mean all of April's body was made up of XY cells. Mosaicism and translocation meant he could speak only to the cells he had examined, and he was aware that such "sex tests" were inherently unreliable. And in spite of Hayhoe's report, April's case was that she was intersex and had had reconstructive surgery and hormone therapy to correct a congeni-tal physical condition. Her understanding was the same as Ewan's and that of a whole generation: being trans was a variation of sex development, another form of biological diversity, which doctors had the medical and surgical know-how to support.

Countering that, though, was the international symposium and the press conference that followed it, which had been set up deliberately to redefine trans people. In addition, Lord Hunter had spoken out against "certain trans-sexuals" who "bring disastrous consequences not only upon themselves but upon others in the society in which they live."[18] Ormrod was about to elaborate on both themes.

April had retained Professor Armstrong and Professor Roth, who had given evidence to support Ewan, as well as a Professor Mills. But Professor Dewhurst, who had previously supported Ewan's case, was now testifying on Arthur's side, against April, and he was joined by Dr. John Randell and a Professor Dent. The involvement of Professors Armstrong, Roth and Dewhurst meant that although they had been sworn to secrecy about Ewan's case, both sides were well aware of the arguments involved: that chromosomes were irrelevant, and psychological sex was the determining factor for legal sex. But they knew that Ewan's evidence of a testis was suspect in the extreme and that medical viewpoints had just been redefined at the international symposium. Summing up the symposium's findings as its chair, Dewhurst had spoken strongly against clinicians continuing to provide letters of authentication to enable trans people to correct their birth certificates. He said that if they were "certifying that a mistake was originally made, it would be my view that we could not certify that; I could not, at any rate," although "some may feel otherwise." Dewhurst, a close friend and collaborator with Randell, had abandoned his former support for scientific medicine and gone over to pseudo-medicine. This division between medical science and pseudo-medicine would be at the heart of a trial that Dewhurst found so upsetting that he never again worked with trans people.

April was subjected to a series of degrading physical examinations that nowadays would contravene the European Union's Charter of Fundamental Rights. Like Ewan, her body ceased to be her own and she became Homo nullius, a nonperson, reduced to an object to be weighed and measured. Dewhurst "performed the three-finger test, which is the standard method of determining whether the vagina can accommodate a normal-sized penis," and her head was X-rayed to see if it had "male characteristics." April's shoulders were half an inch wider than her hips, which was taken as a sign of masculinity, while pseudo-medicine's colonial anteced- ents asserted themselves in a discussion about her absence of facial hair, like "the races of the world that do not have hairy faces, Ori- entals, Mongols, Red Indians."[19] She had been Orientalized, turned into a mysterious, inhuman creature, made exotic and fascinating while also being classified as dangerous and repulsive. Put simply, like Ewan, she had been dehumanized, assaulted and humiliated. The implication of the brutal processes to which first Ewan and then April were submitted was that they had no identity until they were given one by a cis elite. And April was very aware of this. As she later put it, the question was not so much "who was I?" as "more alarm- ingly, *what* was I?" She had been turned from a person into a thing.[20]

Just as April was entering her own personal hell, Ewan was finally able to leave his. After three years of misery, on Decem- ber 4, 1968, the front page of the local *Aberdeen Press and Journal* announced, "Sir Ewan Gets the Verdict." The Home Secretary had announced his decision that Ewan should be entered on the Rolls of the Baronetcy as the 11th Baronet Forbes of Craigievar.[21]

Ewan had supplied the *Press and Journal* with a statement from his lawyers and a photograph of himself: one way of trying to mini- mize publicity is to brief just one newspaper, so that the public inter- est of transparency has been served, while declining to engage with the rest of the media. The statement listed each of the public steps in Ewan's painful path: William's death; Cousin John's claim that he was the next male heir; Ewan's effort to settle the dispute using a summary procedure in the Court of Session; the court's decision in Ewan's favor; John's continued opposition to him; and the lengthy consultation between the Home Secretary, James Callaghan, and the Lord Advocate. But it said nothing of the private pain Ewan had endured: trying to appease John by handing over the estates of Craigievar and Fintray; his betrayal by his own sister, and his grief at her death; the humiliating violation of the medical examination; his dread at reading Strong's report denouncing him as female; the desperation that led him to falsify medical evidence; and the horror of witnessing Lord Hunter's questioning of Patty in court.

The press photograph shows Ewan at home, dressed in his usual kilt, checked jacket, shirt and tie, standing by his fireplace at Brux. He is portlier now, at fifty-six, than he was when he could squeeze out of Craigievar Castle windows to run away from unwelcome guests, and his hair has receded a little more than in the photograph taken twenty-five years earlier with Bran, his Labrador. One hand is on the fireplace, while the other has its thumb firmly hooked into his broad leather belt. Eventually he will bend to the task of being a baronet and replace his plain belt with a ceremonial one, its large buckle, cast in solid silver, showing a raised ornament of leaves and thistles encircling an engraved knight and bear, who stand on either side of a shield emblazoned with three muzzled bears' heads, surmounted by a helmet where the Craigievar cock stands, its sharp eye epitomizing Ewan's one-word motto: WATCH.

Technically, two factors seem to have weighed in making the judgment in his favor. The first was that Hunter's judgment had decided that, if there was testicular tissue present, it might not be impossible for Ewan to father children. This meant that male-line primogeniture succession could, theoretically, proceed to a son of Ewan's. The second factor was particular to the Forbes of Craigievar baronetcy, which, most unusually, could be inherited by "heirs and assigns whatsoever."[22] The "and assigns whatsoever" implies that descent might not necessarily be to the usual male born in wedlock: unlike every other primogeniture title, it could be argued that Ewan did not have to be unambiguously male to inherit this particular baronetcy.

The official process had been a referral to the Lord Advocate, the senior legal authority in Scotland, for advice to be given to the Home Secretary, James Callaghan, whose decision it was whether Ewan should be entered on the Rolls of the Baronetcy. But it is frankly unlikely that a decision that would affect primogeniture inheritance, and thus the security of succession to the throne, would be left to a Labour Home Secretary. These were serious matters of state, especially given the unusual nature of the baronetcy's terms of succession, and consequently it will have been discussed at the highest level. It is likely that the prime minister, Harold Wilson, discussed it at his weekly, confidential, unminuted meeting with the Queen, since it bore so directly on succession to the Crown. Perhaps the Queen knew better than anyone the irrelevance of sex to the ability to do a good job, whether as monarch, aristocrat, doctor or farmer: certainly, Ewan was confirmed as heir to the Forbes of Craigievar baronetcy, and the Court of Lyon began to matriculate his new arms.

Once again, there were few reports of the case. Cecil King had resigned from the International Publishing Corporation after an astonishing incident: he had tried to organize a coup against the Labour government and had written a grandiose front-page editorial in the *Daily Mirror*—"Enough Is Enough," it read—to support it.[23] But his influence still seems to have been felt, for there was none of the fuss about Ewan that was made when he corrected his birth certificate and when William died. However, the *Glasgow Herald* picked up the *Press and Journal*'s report a day later and recorded that "Dr. Forbes-Sempill is now 11th Baronet of Forbes."[24] Then, a day later, it ran another news report, "Disquiet over Forbes-Sempill case secrecy," expressing considerable concern about the "exceptional and disquieting circumstances in which the case was heard."[25] Was Ewan's case a proper use of Section 10 of the Administration of Justice (Scotland) Act 1933, and if it was, why was there no record of the case's progress? Was it proper to employ a judge at public expense to decide a purely private matter? And why was the judgment never issued to the press? Although no answers were ever given to these questions, it was these two reports that, years later, my former history teacher was to find and send me, showing me where and when the hidden case of Ewan Forbes had been heard, and leading to its disclosure.

Less than a year after Ewan's final verdict, and two and a half years after Arthur filed for divorce, on November 11, 1969, April put on her black velvet maxi coat and fox-fur hat to enter the High Court on London's Strand, "a Victorian Gothic masterpiece designed to reduce to the size of a mouse anyone who sets foot in it," she said.[26] When the judge came into the deep, pitlike court, she was disconcerted by his response to her: he "never once looked me straight in the eye but glanced furtively in my direction and mumbled his references to me as if they were distasteful to him."[27] It is a look and response that every trans person has experienced from someone who knows their medical background and has difficulty with it, and it did not bode well for April. Almost immediately things went from bad to worse. Arthur gave his evidence first, and the story he told was as Victorian and Gothic as the building they were in. It was a dreadful tale of terrifying temptation and his slow slide into an abyss of immorality.

Arthur's salacious story began with "a desire to dress up in female clothes" "from a comparatively early age," something that he presented as despicable and degenerate, but which he had done "in the presence of his wife on a few occasions."[28] But his dark desires had moved him beyond the socially safe boundaries of marriage, and he had "dressed as a woman four or five times a year, keeping it from his wife." Little by little:

> his interest in transvestism increased; at first it was mainly literary, attracting him to pornographic bookshops, but gradually he began to make contact with people of similar tendencies. . . . This led to homosexual behaviour with numerous men, stopping short of anal intercourse. As time went on he became more and more involved in the society of sexual deviants, and interested in sexual deviations of all kinds. In this world he became familiar with its ramifications and its personalities, among whom he heard of Toni/April as a female impersonator at the Carrousel, which he described as "the Mecca of every female impersonator in the world."[29]

Arthur's supposed decline, in what Ormrod called "this essentially pathetic, but almost incredible story" concluded with his meeting April. He claimed to see her not as a person but as a real-ization of his cross-dressing fantasies. He said: "This was so much more than I could ever hope to be. The reality was far greater than my fantasy." For Arthur, April was a mythical beast that "far out-stripped any fantasy for myself," and he made their marriage into a pursuit of unreal desire.

It was a clever, devastating ploy. As April said:

Suddenly I realised what he was doing. So did my medical and legal advisers. Arthur was emphatically presenting himself as a deviate, in vivid detail, some of which was new even to me. For example, I had not realised the extent of his homosexual experiences. By adopting this confessional approach, by posing as the pervert since struck by contrition, by casting a pall of sulphurous depravity and transgression over our entire relationship, he was able to convey the impression that our marriage was no more than a squalid prank, some deliberate mockery of moral society perpetrated by a couple of queers for their own twisted amusement. By implication, I too was a deviate, and no more than a deviate. He appeared to be apolo-gising in court and sympathy was forthcoming. I was not apologis-ing for being myself and sympathy wasn't forthcoming.

It was the first turning-point of a case which was now revealed as something quite different from an objective consideration of my status for marriage purposes. I now had to defend myself against an all-purpose stigma of indecency, against the prevailing opinion, led by Arthur's testimony, that our marriage was a shameful joke because I was myself a shameful joke.[30]

Arthur was using the hack writer's "sin, suffer, repent" trope from populist *True Story*-type magazines and extending it into soft-porn mock-horror. In so doing, he was also presenting April as a version of Gore Vidal's malicious, transphobic novel *Myra Breck-inridge*, which had been a literary sensation in 1968, selling over two million copies in the US. It was April who had fascinated him and entrapped him with her wily oriental spell. Like Vidal's Breck-inridge, she was a ruthlessly manipulative gold digger who used a corrupt sexuality and surgically distorted body to exploit other people's weaknesses. The novel's popularity meant that this became an instantly acceptable discourse: trans women were manipulative masqueraders, psychotic self-mutilators and psychopathic abusers of all who took up with them.

With a newfound confidence from the support given to him at the international symposium, Randell gave a typically brutal verdict on April. Always misgendering his patients as a matter of principle, Randell will have referred to April as "he" and as "the operated transsexual," emphasizing that April was not and must not be considered to be a woman. "He" was and always would be a man and must not seek to marry another man. Ormrod accepted both Randell's diagnosis that April was "properly classified as a male homosexual transsexualist" and Dewhurst's new view that "the description 'a castrated male' would be correct."[31] There was little that April's advocates, Professors Armstrong and Roth, could say to turn this tide. They gave the same evidence that they had given in Ewan's case: that April was intersex and pointed out that she certainly couldn't live in society as a man. But Ormrod was not interested. Partway through the trial he "suddenly asked if it were necessary to continue wasting the tax-payer's money" by listening to the evidence in full, and "grumpily agreed to go on" only after representations from both sides.[32] He had made up his mind about his verdict and the only questions left for him were how to justify it, and how to make it unassailable.

Part of April's problem was her obvious beauty. As a model, she embodied a popular female ideal, and in Ormrod's eyes, this seems to have turned her into a kind of Siren, someone irresistible but deathly dangerous. If, as Ormrod believed, April was "really" a man, then any man's relationship with her could only be homosexual: she was tempting men like Arthur (and, by extension, Ormrod himself), only to corrupt them. To prove this fundamentally homophobic point, Ormrod put a great deal of effort into disauthenticating April's vagina.

Under pressure from Ormrod, the court inspectors had made a distinction between a "normal vagina" and April's "artificial vagina." Ormrod made this separation greater by describing it as "a so-called artificial vagina." He claimed that "without the qualification so-called . . . the association of ideas connected with these words or phrases are so powerful that they tend to cloud clear thinking." Just the thought of April's vagina could overwhelm him. But the "clear thinking" Ormrod laid claim to was chop logic. He called April's vagina "a cavity which opened on to the perineum" and said, "I do not think that sexual intercourse using the completely artificial cavity constructed by Dr. Burou, can possibly be described . . . as 'ordinary and complete intercourse' or as *vera copula* of the natural." But in fact, every vagina is a cavity that opens onto the perineum: if April's was not an "ordinary" and "natural" vagina, what could it be? And if heterosexual, penile penetration of it did not constitute *vera copula*, or "true union," then what did it constitute?

Ormrod's answer to this puzzle was grotesque and perplexing. Just as with Ewan, one of the measurements that had been taken from April had been the length of her perineum, her anogenital distance, since the fallacy persisted that this was distinctively different between men and women. Accordingly, Ormrod said, "When such a cavity has been constructed in a male, the difference between sexual intercourse using it, and anal or intra-crural intercourse is, in my judgment, to be measured in centimeters." Whatever was he thinking? Every vagina is "a matter of centimeters" from every anus, while intra-crural intercourse, placing the penis between a partner's thighs and using friction from them to achieve orgasm, doesn't involve either vagina or anus. And yet this was a qualified doctor, a member of the Royal College of Physicians, registered to practice by the General Medical Council, supposedly delivering a professional opinion.

Rather than making a definitive, scientific statement, Ormrod seemed to be slipping into soft-porn fantasy, as if he was imagining April as "really" male but intercourse with her as a permissible mistake, homophobically excusing Arthur (and by extension himself) from being gay for finding her physically desirable. For Ormrod, April's anxiously ambiguous vagina legitimized an accidental slip into sodomy, in the same way that some heterosexual men use the idea of an "accidental slip" from the vagina to legitimize nonconsensual anal intercourse with women partners.[33] Ormrod turned April into a piece of pornography, objectifying and degrading her, with a similar crude salaciousness to that which Hunter had visited on Patty.

Having disposed of April's vagina, Ormrod dispensed with the rest of her body. In spite of her successful modeling career, she was only "passing as a woman more or less successfully." She was wholly artificial, a "pastiche of femininity" and the more you saw her, the more April's "voice, manner, gestures and attitude became increasingly reminiscent of the accomplished female impersonator." It was a viciously personal attack, and Ormrod made his final judgment in the baldest of terms: that April "is not, and was not, a woman at the date of the ceremony of marriage, but was, at all times, male. The marriage is, accordingly, void."

This was bad enough. But at this point Ormrod had achieved only half of his purpose. Defining April as male was devastating for her, but he wanted his judgment to be devastating for all trans people. He achieved this by taking two steps.

The first step was to rewrite the balance sheet that Hunter had created for Forbes. Hunter had used four items for determining sex: psychological sex, gonads, apparent sex and chromosomal sex, with chromosomes being the least valuable criterion and psychological sex the most significant. Ormrod's new balance sheet had just three criteria: chromosomes, external genitalia and gonads, with chromosomes the most important instead of the least important item. He threw out "apparent sex" and "psychological sex" altogether. By "external genitalia," he meant genitalia observed at birth, thus disqualifying April and all other trans people who had had reconstructive surgery or whose genitalia had been modified through HRT. It caused a furor in medical circles, not least because Harry

Benjamin's balance sheet had nine items and Robert Stoller's six. Howard Jones, from Johns Hopkins GIC, objected to the removal of "psychological sex," and one of April's medical experts, Professor Mills, wrote in protest to *The Lancet*, saying that in April's case, an "artificial vagina was constructed in an intersex patient."[34] But Ormrod was being deliberately reductive, intentionally supporting pseudo-medicine by invalidating psychological sex.

Ormrod's second step was to create an argument that looked solid and indisputable. In fact, it was wholly insubstantial and hollow, but Ormrod's brilliance lay in spinning a rhetorical edifice that concealed this, a device sometimes called a "marshmallow." Since Ormrod's marshmallow disenfranchised a generation of trans people, it is worth seeing how he spun it.

His main tactic was to use the terms "natural" and "ordinary" to give the sense that everyone knew and agreed with what he said.[35] Then, with a neat sleight of hand, he deployed the category error conflating sex, gender and sexuality. Ormrod said that it was a matter of "natural and ordinary" fact that everyone's biological constitution was fixed at birth, and since April had been identified as male at birth, that must be her "true sex." Thus, she was a man. As a man, she could not marry another man, and the only relationship she could have had with Arthur was a homosexual one. Accordingly, the marriage was void.

Thirty years later, an Australian judge exposed Ormrod's logical fallacy. He had treated gender as identical to sex. By equating "biological constitution at birth" with "true sex," Ormrod had excluded all consideration of social and psychological matters. And he had made this equation "by way of definition: no reason is given for excluding them . . . nothing has been said to support it. No relevant principle or policy is advanced. No authorities are cited to show, for example, that it is consistent with other legal principles."[36] Simply, it had been a circular argument based on the idea that at birth everyone is unchangeably male or female. Psychosocial factors were ignored: this was an argument based purely on "nature," without any taint of nurture. What's more, it was a particularly narrow "nature," in which intersex was to be discounted once again. It ran counter to the most senior medical opinion in the UK. Ormrod rode roughshod over Professors Roth and Armstrong, rejecting their scientific expertise in favor of Randell's pseudo-medicine. Now Ormrod had defined all trans people as naturally psychotic, mentally deficient in some irredeemable way, masqueraders without any legal right to marry.

When they were in court, Professor Mills had said to April, "There is a great deal of snobbery in this case," and she had taken it to mean simply the "subtle association between Arthur, Arthur's counsel and the bench, the subconscious intransigence and hauteur of educated gentlemen," an implicit upper-class snobbery that positioned her as an outsider.[37] But when Ormrod gave a lecture on *Corbett* to the Medico-Legal Society two years later, he provided a different insight. He opened by saying that the law was largely indifferent to sex, except that "it could be crucially important where succession to a title is concerned."[38] It was at this talk that Ewan's case was discussed, and it is evident that April's instinct was right. Privilege and entitlement were at work, and Ormrod had solved the constitutional problem Cousin John's malice had created. Male primogeniture inheritance was now safe from the fantasized menace of trans people.

April was devastated, in a state of shock that slowly fell into depression. She kept a professional appointment, a late-night television chat-show appearance with Malcolm X, John Lennon and Yoko Ono, and then booked herself into a health farm to try to recover. She felt, she said, as though she was "on a helter-skelter, going down very fast in an agony of despair and panic," unable to sleep and finding it intolerable to meet other people, while at the same time feeling intense loneliness.[39] When she did eventually go back into society, she found a new level of transphobia from strangers: "Some poked me in the breasts to see if they were real, or pulled my hair to see if it was false. . . . They acted as if they had a perfect right to humiliate me in this way, as if my past meant that I surrendered all rights to the basic courtesies."[40]

Ormrod's damning judgment and its sensationalized news coverage ushered in a new era of trans-misogyny. Now, "in the public imagination, trans people would always be trans women (so that trans men became invisible) and trans women would always be, in the judge's terms, 'a pastiche of femininity,' a sort of piss-elegant drag-queen, a kind of figure of fun."[41] The media had used April to create a brilliantly precise image of being trans, a dystopian ideal that was beautiful and cursed, celebrated and shameful, that was to haunt trans women from then onward.

On the face of it, Ewan won and April lost. But there are no winners in these kinds of battles. When Craigievar Castle had been passed to the National Trust for Scotland seven years earlier, Ewan had paid the bulk of the costs of the transfer, draining his capital. When William died, Ewan had tried to buy off John from claiming the baronetcy by handing over the land and assets from the Craigievar and Fintray estates, which would otherwise have gone to Ewan. What's more, by threatening to hold his legal dispute in public, John had blackmailed Ewan into paying for both of their legal costs, so that by the time Ewan was awarded the title, he was in poor financial straits.

But far worse than that, he had been forced to sacrifice the thing that, after Patty, he prized most. He and his colleagues knew that he had falsified medical evidence in a court of law, and that this amounted to gross professional misconduct. It did not matter to Ewan that he had gotten away with it. His own sense of honor obliged him to deregister himself with the General Medical Council, to relinquish the only title that he had ever wanted. From 1970 onward, after the long fight he had gone through to earn that cherished status, officially Ewan was no longer "the Doctor."

PART THREE

10

OUTLAWED

Ewan's case and its backlash on April Ashley marked the end of first-wave trans activism. For eighty years, trans people had followed Krafft-Ebing's typical patient narrative and law of the sexual homologous development to gain the medical treatment and corrected birth certificate they needed to live equally. It was a restrictive discourse, but it was better than the desperation of no treatment at all, or the violence of a custodial sentence for being "degenerate," or confinement in a mental hospital as "diseased."

After Ewan and April, everything changed. Ewan's case shaped April's fate: she was the whipping girl used to save male primogeniture from being tainted by trans people. In its turn, the repercussions from April's case affected other trans people, including Ewan, who must have been disturbed by the verdict, which was reported in detail by the press.[1] Like other UK trans people whose birth certificates had been corrected, he will have breathed a sigh of relief at having avoided the new pseudo-medicine, while at the same time feeling terrified at what might happen next. Would they now be rooted out, put through Ormrod's balance sheet to decide their sex, and, like April, be mauled by the press? Silently, the trans world divided into two, those with corrected birth certificates who had melted indistinguishably into the general population, and those without. The have-nots were about to become the focus of an invisible eugenics project.

After the trial, April had told the press that the only difference the outcome made to her was that she was unable to marry and that was a matter of indifference to her. She believed that for every other purpose, she would be treated equally with every other woman. But as soon as Ormrod's verdict was given, preparations began to enter a new bill into Parliament: the Nullity of Marriage Act. Discussion in the House of Lords showed that its purpose was to ensure that trans people could never again marry, on the grounds that they were always the sex assigned at birth.[2] Gay men had been only partially decriminalized three years earlier, the new Gay Liberation Front was organizing highly visible protests against continuing inequality, and supported by the MP Leo Abse, the Homosexual Law Reform Society was considering taking up the case of trans marriage.[3] Part of the Nullity of Marriage Act's intention was to ensure marriage could take place only between a man and a woman, and the sex test it applied was Ormrod's balance sheet.

This absorption of Ormrod's decision into statutory law made it both pervasive and invisible. It permeated officialdom, so that without any formal direction being given, trans people's birth certificates were no longer corrected. After the verdict, April's solicitor Peter Madok had said, "If April was sent to prison or to a hospital, she would be classified as female," but as trans people were to learn, that was not the case.[4] Slowly and untraceably, they began to be stripped of their civil liberties. As Edwina Currie, MP, was later to comment, "This change in the law did not involve any vote in the House of Commons" or indeed any public discussion.[5]

In his discussion of the processes through which the Holocaust was enacted, the human rights lawyer Philippe Sands comments that for many atrocities, there was "no big smoking gun," no signed statements or speeches, just a quiet bureaucratic process that proceeded systematically to corral and destroy Jewish people.[6] A similar kind of process operated for UK trans people. In the absence of formal written policies, bureaucrats developed a shared, implicit set of principles and values, perhaps transmitted as verbal advice from one department to another, forming an implicitly agreed approach that gradually and imperceptibly set trans people outside the law and the usual rule of democracy. Sometimes this process can be seen by an absence, a gap where a provision for trans people was intended to be made but in the end never took place. One such example is in the committee stages of the Sex Discrimination Bill, where, on April 24, 1975, there was clear agreement that it should cover "cases of sex change":

> Mr. Lane: A thought crossed my mind, and I should like to mention it merely for an assurance that the Government either have thought about it or will think about it. Are they sure that the Bill, either here or elsewhere, adequately and clearly covers the cases of sex change, which we read about occasionally and which we should hate to be overlooked in such a comprehensive Bill?
>
> Dr. Summerskill: We considered this. Clearly people who have legally changed sex will be covered by the Bill, under whatever sex they have legally changed to. Clause 5 goes out of its way to provide key definitions for the purposes of the Bill, and it provides that sex discrimination means discrimination falling within Clause 1 or 2— that is, discrimination against a woman or a man. The point that the Hon. Gentleman raised is covered.[7]

But somehow that was overlooked, and although the Sex Discrimination Act 1975 was intended to include and protect trans people, it did not.

The amnesia Ormrod had constructed about Ewan's case was spreading. The simple fact that a generation of trans people had lived unproblematically and enjoyed equality with every other UK citizen became universally forgotten. Somehow, through routes that remain unmapped, and by decisions that remain unrecorded, trans people were placed outside the law. Their only recourse was to embrace their psychopathologization and accept that they were mentally ill. Then, on production of a letter from a psychiatrist, limited civil documentation could be obtained, such as driving licenses, employment cards and passports showing a new sex and name, and bank accounts and utility bills could be similarly updated. But unlike most other Westernized countries, the UK has no formal document of civil identity, and so the birth certificate stands as proxy, required as proof by employers and officials across the country. Since birth certificates could no longer be corrected, trans people's private lives were instantly exposed by a natal sex and name that was not theirs. Interactions with officialdom became humiliating, an institutionalized intrusion of privacy. And driving licenses were secretly coded so that their serial number indicated the natal sex, telling the police and other officials "in the know" that the holder was trans, promoting discrimination against them. Social-security documentation similarly revealed the former name and natal sex of trans people. Individual officials at labor exchanges and job centers decided whether to publicly humiliate a trans applicant by calling out their original sex marker ("Mr." or "Miss") and former name to the rest of the waiting room, or using it to address them on official business. A custodial sentence meant being sent to the wrong-sex prison, where trans women faced the certainty of being raped, not least because after Ormrod's refusal of April's vagina, the law did not count it as rape. There had been no general announcement, no public speeches, no new formal government position. Outlawing trans people was an exercise in scrupulous meanness by a gray bureaucracy, a deathly but quietly dull removal of liberties by unclear, uncertain, indistinct means: backdoor dealings and bad-faith democracy that turned a blind eye and denied culpability.

Ewan's case had been spirited away into secrecy, and so there was no way of working from it to see how and why its medical opinion and senior legal precedent had used different criteria from those created for April's case. Instead, Ormrod's judgment, supported by transphobic media reportage, became a universal truth, an enduring pattern of ideas that transferred itself from one context to another. Crucially, combined with the new medical classification, it became the reason why trans people were not competent to enjoy equality.

These were the events that were unfolding around Ewan as he tried to recover his equilibrium. But he would never recover completely. His experiences had been traumatic and protracted, and like others who lived through such disaster, he experienced the symptoms of what we now call "complex posttraumatic stress disorder" or PTSD. He became more easily upset or offended, found it hard to trust people, and became hypervigilant, always on the lookout for betrayal or trouble. It made him difficult to live with or work for. He would sit at the top of the hill at Brux and watch his staff through binoculars to make sure they were doing as they were told, and he would be angry if they were even a few minutes late for work. Partly, he took refuge in formality, insisting on being called "Sir Ewan" by his staff, lecturing them on their behavior, and refusing to give them a good reference if they had displeased him. Patty did what she could to make up for this, waiting for him to leave and then going out to staff working round the house with sweets and cigarettes: she would never do it if Ewan was there, for better than anyone, she understood what Ewan had endured and why he was so easily upset.

His medical career over, Ewan did not bother to remove his British Medical Association members' badge from the front of his Lancia coupe when he sold it in 1972. He put on his peaked cap and shorts and drove the combine harvester as he always had before. He invited friends to his walk-up shoots at Brux, and they returned the compliment on their estates. He maintained his relationships with his nieces, but now it was easier for them to get into his bad books for an imagined slight, and harder to get out of them.

To the people of Alford, he was now simply "Sir Ewan," and his business was nobody's but his own. If the guides showing round visitors at Craigievar Castle were asked about Ewan, they were instructed to say only that this was his family home. A second inquiry from an inquisitive visitor would be met with a blank stare, and if they persisted, they would be taken back to reception, their entry fee refunded and sent on their way. The National Trust for Scotland still maintained a close relationship with the family, and when the tourist season was over, in early winter, Ewan would visit Craigievar, a fire would be made in the Great Hall, and he would sit in one of the enormous chairs in front of it, reading from the family library and surrounded by family heirlooms. When the afternoon drew into darkness, and the fire was embers, he would leave what had been his home for so many years and go over to the mains for bacon and eggs with Mr. and Mrs. Booth, the keepers who still lived there.[8]

This sense of community had always sustained Ewan, and it was part of the reason why he loved being the local doctor. Now having surrendered his registration, he sought equivalent professional and personal community elsewhere. In 1969, he became a justice of the peace, a magistrate presiding over a local court and sentencing the accused. He did not need any legal qualification, for JPs are advised on points of law by a qualified legal advisor, but he was an integral part of local life, dealing with cases such as motoring offenses, shoplifting, theft and breach of the peace. Having been ordained as an elder at Kildrummy Kirk in April 1965, Ewan immersed himself still deeper in his religion, supporting the church financially, attending each Sunday, and becoming superintendent of Kildrummy Sunday School, where he taught the local children.

Patty seems to have been less harmed by the events. Her temperament had always been calm, and she had always known her own heart. Growing up in the isolation of Glen Rinnes had given her resilience and independence of mind, so that she had married Ewan even though her family had not approved of marriage to someone with such a different life and background. The size of her family meant that as the seventh child, she was distant from the elder children apart from her sister Ella, and she was content for them to live their lives while she lived hers. It might seem that she was isolated at Brux, but its remoteness was nothing in comparison with the Mitchells' farmhouse, and while the northern aspect of Brux Lodge made it colder than other places, it was still a considerable improvement on life in a damp valley under the shadow of Ben Rinnes. Patty was content with her lot, and where Ewan was now occasionally "nippet"—curt in manner—Patty was warm and accessible, with nothing about her to make people feel she wasn't part of everybody's life: approachable, welcoming and friendly.

She made an enormous difference and was a great consolation and support to Ewan, as their friends all knew.

But Patty, too, was getting older and stouter. She no longer accompanied Ewan on his shoots: four or five hours of walking on trackless hills, wading through waist-high heather in full leaf, stem and bloom was now too much for her. She would drive up occasionally in the Land Rover, but for the most part, she stayed on the banks of the Don, fly-fishing. Both she and Ewan loved to fish: Ewan called it "a healing balm," and perhaps he told her stories of when the Craigievar gamekeeper, Henry Smith, used to tie a rope round him and hold him, to prevent him from falling into the Don when he was casting his fly with more ambition than wisdom. Of course, they fell out like any other couple that has been together for thirty years. Ewan would speak to Patty too abruptly and she would retaliate by standing at the back door and smoking—something Ewan hated—in angry puffs, referring to him acerbically as "the wee mannie" until peace was restored again.

Meanwhile, across the UK, trans people were trying to make sense of their new outsiderdom. Exiled, terrified and uncomprehending, they began to seek community by organizing as support groups. This was the start of second-wave trans activism, a range of national and local groups through which trans people could find mutual support. Some turned to the Beaumont Society, founded by Alice Purnell in 1966, as the UK branch of Virginia Prince's US organization for cross-dressers, while others found support in the Gay Liberation Front, another US-inspired group, notable for its vibrant activism. But the event that landmarked second-wave trans activism, setting out its agendas and tensions for the next two decades, was the First National TV TS Conference, *Transvestism and Transsexualism in Modern Society*, jointly organized by Leeds University TV/TS Group, Leeds Gay Liberation Front and the Beaumont Society. Held at the university from March 15–17, 1974, this was second-wave activism's first concerted attempt to map its new medical and legal landscapes.

At this time, there was an information vacuum. It was unclear what the criteria for reconstructive surgery were, although married people with children and "the transsexual who, for physical reasons like great height or bulk, could not make the change socially with any ease" were probably out of luck.[9] No one knew for sure whether driving licenses or birth certificates could be corrected now, but they did know that employers sacked trans people over "the fact, that dressed as a woman, it is a man who is using the female loo, and this they just cannot take." This lavatorial anxiety was to become an enduring trope for transphobia. A proposal to compile a list of trans-sympathetic clinicians was vetoed as "a breach of medical etiquette" that would "incur the wrath of the medical profession," but attendees from the Transsexual Action Organization (TAO), another US group that had spread to the UK, went ahead and compiled a list anyway. Such a list was vital to trans people but of little import to cross-dressers, and the dispute exemplified rapidly opening divisions in LGBTI communities. The conference report included calls for a separate organization for "transsexuals," assertions that "those who call themselves transvestite will not mix with those who call themselves transsexuals," and fears that "homosexuals" would be "both embarrassing and detrimental" to the Beaumont Society. By 1976, a clear and distinct group in the Beaumont Society wanted to exclude gay men, trans people and any cross-dressers whom it viewed as "too masculine."[10]

The new realities were as grim as the new politics. TAO produced a nine-page survival guide for trans people, warning them that while "we need the help of medicine to be able to live happily in the sex we feel we are," many doctors "consider transsexuals to be mentally ill and, as a result, many transsexuals find themselves in mental institutions."[11] To avoid this, TAO advised using the sympathetic doctors, psychiatrists and surgeons on their list and, after trans people had completed their healthcare, separating themselves from their former life by moving to a new location, preferably the anonymity of a city. Once there, secrecy and paranoia were essential strategies: "put as little in writing about your history as possible"; "if you have to name schools omit 'Girls' or 'Boys' ";

and never let your employer find out that you are trans. Survival meant avoiding jobs with medical examinations, compulsory pension schemes, superannuation, life insurance or where you might have to use changing rooms. Danger was inevitable, self-isolation was necessary and social acceptability was nil.

In 1977, a trans man named Edwynn White, who had not moved away from home, was recognized as having attended a local school as a girl. His fellow employees began to gossip and to ask, "What was she doing in the men's toilets?" so that their employer, British Sugar Corporation Ltd., dismissed Edwynn.[12] Aggrieved, he went to an industrial tribunal, which found against him on the grounds that he was female, he had been dishonest during his interview, and created "an embarrassing situation with an element of deception." Because trans people had not been covered by the Sex Discrimination Act, this judgment provided the guiding principle for all such employment disputes. By 1988, the Institute of Personnel Management was advising its members that instantly dismissing employees who were trans was not only legal, it would remove any risk of future customers or staff being offended by their existence.[13]

Meanwhile, in the rest of the world, *Corbett* began to take on the status of a super-precedent. This meant that instead of examining Ormrod's argument, courts simply applied his new judgment and his balance sheet. In the US, it was used by the New York Supreme Court in 1971, the Ohio's Stark County Probate Court in 1987, the Texas Court of Appeals in 1991, Kansas Court of Appeals in 2001 and Florida District Court of Appeal in 2004.[14] It was persuasive in New Zealand in 1975, in South Africa in 1976, in Canada in 1984 and in Australia in 1988.[15] Ormrod's pseudo-medical sex test became the kind of pervasive knowledge that French philosopher Pierre Bourdieu calls "doxa," something that we already and always know. In spite of everything science said against it, in the collective mind, chromosomes and external genitalia became the definitive test of "true sex" in its "ordinary and common" sense.

Trans people started to lose the few political friends they had. Radical feminist Andrea Dworkin had advocated for trans people at the start of the 1970s, as having "the right to survival on his/her own terms,"[16] and the Campaign for Homosexual Equality produced a four-page booklet advocating "reasonable discussion of the subject without the present hysteria that surrounds it."[17] But they were the exception rather than the rule, and their views were being eroded by a minority group in the women's liberation movement: second-wave trans activism was meeting second-wave feminism, and the sexual politics were not always amicable.

Although 1960s feminist writers had been crucial in mobilizing the women's movement, their work was beginning to feel intellectually naive. Betty Friedan's description in *The Feminist Mystique* of "the homosexuality that is spreading like a murky smog over the American scene"[18] was explicitly homophobic, while Germaine Greer's assertion in *The Female Eunuch* that "that most virile of creatures, the buck negro, has very little body hair at all," had begun to feel like racism.[19] New feminist critiques were emerging, with a range of ideological positions. Socialist feminism utilized the Marxist perspective that disadvantage was based on economic inequality, while radical feminism viewed women's disadvantage as an inevitable biological construction by a male patriarchy, a very different idea from twenty-first-century feminist scholarship's understanding of patriarchy.[20] Black feminism focused on the relationships between race and sex that were eventually to be formulated as "intersectionality," and although liberal feminism sought equality for everyone, it had not yet begun to work out how such inclusiveness could be achieved.

By the late 1970s, these ideological lines had begun to harden and splinter into smaller groups. In particular, radical feminism's focus on patriarchy had become very visible. It posited a binary male-female society in which all men were automatically more privileged than all women: a universal male primogeniture. Separatist radical lesbian feminist communities were created specifically to avoid being part of this patriarchal hegemony. They worked with, bought from, and sheltered only women, and in the US, their members could travel across the whole country while living only within their network. Like all intentional communities, it was a utopian movement, but like many such minority communities, whether self-identified by political or religious beliefs, they gave to others the respect they demanded for themselves. Many separatist radical lesbian feminists felt deeply shocked, therefore, when a virulent attack was launched against trans people, in their name, by Janice Raymond.

Janice Raymond's *The Transsexual Empire*, first published in the US in 1979 and in the UK a year later, was an extended conspiracy theory asserting that male doctors were creating a race of artificial women to replace "real women." This was a popular theme in contemporary science fiction films, such as *The Stepford Wives*, *Invasion of the Body Snatchers*, and *Invaders from Mars*.[21] But Raymond's pornographically violent work represented itself as serious scholarship, claiming that all trans women were rapists because they had penetrated "women's spaces."[22] A similar accusation of sexual violence was made against African Americans in D. W. Griffith's infamous 1915 film, *Birth of a Nation*, and against Jewish people in the German 1940 film *Jud Süss*. Raymond's work followed this path of vilifying minority groups to assuage tribal anxiety. But as well as this generalized transphobia, Raymond made a personal attack on one trans woman in particular, Sandy Stone, a sound recordist at the all-women Olivia recording studios in Washington DC, and herself a separatist lesbian radical feminist. Always referring to her as "he," Raymond said that Sandy Stone had become an important part of Olivia not because she was talented but from her "masculine behavior" and "male privilege": she was an instrument of the patriarchy, usurping "women's space" with the intention of disrupting feminist politics.

Raymond's position was based on Ormrod's judgment, which by then had been applied in the US. With no attempt at academic critique, Raymond repeated the "natural and ordinary" fact that everyone's "biological constitution at birth" was their "true sex." Like Ormrod, too, Raymond collapsed sex and gender together, so that all men had "masculine energy" and their behavior was predestined to be patriarchal. They had been born with a male privilege that permeated their lives and determined their existence unchangeably. It was a fundamentalist, anti-intellectual point of view, as absurd in its way as John Money's swinging "gender gate," which fenced off "normal" men and women from LGBTI people. Of course, Raymond was unaware of the irony of her stance. She knew nothing of Ewan's case, the problems it had created around primogeniture and the way Ormrod had solved them with his balance sheet. Without realizing it, Raymond was repeating arguments designed specifically to protect male-line primogeniture, the most literally embodied, exclusive, visible and material expression of male sociopolitical dominance. She was doing the patriarchy's work for it.

The Transsexual Empire has been compared with the infamous anti-Semitic text The Protocols of the Elders of Zion as an example of sustained hate propaganda, and unsurprisingly, only a very few separatist lesbian radical feminists supported Raymond's viewpoint.[23] Still fewer supported Raymond's hate campaign against Sandy Stone, but it takes only a few to do lasting damage. In spite of the wider support she had, Sandy Stone left Olivia.

Perhaps the majority of feminists realized that, as a critical review pointed out, it was Janice Raymond who was dividing feminist communities, not trans people, and that her so-called empire comprised a tiny number of socially excluded people who had great difficulty accessing medical support and who were struggling for identity and sometimes for existence.[24] But the harm had been done, and Raymond's hate rhetoric encouraged exclusion, justified prejudice and legitimized violence.

Increasingly now, trans people were being made powerless, as a series of cis elites appropriated their lives and explained them back to them in negative terms. Pseudo-medicine, the law and now sexual politics were engaged in what might be termed "cisplaining," an appropriation and representation of trans lives that was to become increasingly prevalent in the 1980s. Nowhere was cisplaining more evident than in gender identity clinics.

The largest in the UK was John Randell's, at NHS Charing Cross

Hospital, and there were two routes into it. The easy way was by a referral from a charity such as the Albany Trust, which would take you to Charing Cross GIC directly. But if you didn't know that and went via your GP, you were almost guaranteed to be referred for aversion therapy, since many GPs knew little or nothing about trans healthcare. If you were lucky, aversion therapy would be at a psychiatric outpatients' facility, which was easy to escape from: you could stop attending as soon as the realization dawned that you were being abused, not helped. Unfortunately, the grooming inherent in such abusive relationships meant many people didn't escape. And if you were unluckier you would be detained in a locked ward from which escape was impossible. No public record was kept, and so the number of trans people who sought care, attended GICs or were subjected to aversion therapy is unknown.

Patients attended John Randell's GIC for six-monthly appointments for an indeterminate period of years. To get access to healthcare, they learned to comply with anything he demanded. Attending in 1971 after a referral from the Albany Trust, a trans woman named Valerie told me, "If you were totally submissive and did exactly what he said, then you were all right or mostly all right; there was no room for any argument."[25] Randell demanded that by her next appointment she had to be "working in a full-time job as a female": when Valerie asked what she should do about employment documents that showed her as male, he responded, "That's your problem, you sort it out." He gave her the sense that he was omnipotent and "could check up on [her]," and so for the first time in her life, Valerie began to work illegally, in the black economy. After six-monthly appointments for two and a half years, she was referred for surgery and told she was a "star patient." Other patients were not so lucky, and Valerie recalled one trans woman who had been attending for seven years but had still not been granted the surgical referral she required. Some patients were rejected altogether as unsuitable for treatment, either because they were not obedient enough, or, if they were trans women, because they didn't meet Randell's personal criteria for being "a lady." Such judgments were an obvious projection onto his patients of Randell's own anxiously closeted cross-dressing.

Randell's criteria for access to healthcare were that a patient must be single or divorced, able to support themselves financially, not be in trouble with the police and be "accepted socially" through "more than average skill in male and female impersonation."[26] He seems rarely to have used the tests he cited in his presentation at the First International Symposium. Instead, patients like Valerie were subjected to systematic gaslighting: coerced into believing they were mentally ill, groomed into compliance with Randell's demands and blackmailed by Randell's constant reminders that he had complete control over their access to essential medicines and surgeries. There was no exploration and discussion of Valerie's or other patients' feelings or options, only a constant reminder that to "waver," as Randell called any such exploration, would be to end access to care.

There could be no therapeutic relationship under such circumstances. Instead, Valerie and Randell's other patients experienced traumatic bonding, a version of so-called Stockholm syndrome, in which a person in an extended, entrapped, abusive relationship becomes dependent on, identifies with, and may defend their abuser. As Valerie put it, "even if a dog gets beaten by its master, it does eventually come to think the world of that master," and "whatever kind of monster he was, we would have had to play ball" because "in those days, you weren't given choices."

These kinds of draconian regimes were supported by the International Symposium on Gender Identity, which continued to meet annually. In 1977, it produced a consensus statement, which it persuaded the World Health Organization to adopt: being trans was now officially "sexual deviation centred around fixed beliefs that the overt bodily sex is wrong."[27] By 1979, symposium members had reorganized into the Harry Benjamin International Gender Dysphoria Association (HBIGDA) and agreed a general clinical pathway, which it termed *Standards of Care*. But as their emphatic categorization of "gender dysphoria" as a mental illness indicated, these were not medically or scientifically objective standards designed to support trans people's autonomy. They did not operate to the four key ethical principles of scientific medicine—autonomy, non-maleficence, beneficence, and justice—through which medical practice is regulated, nor did they meet the scientific tests of validity and reliability.[28] Rather, they "were designed to protect professionals who prescribed hormones or performed surgery from legal, ethical, or moral scrutiny and liability."[29] Their purpose was to avoid accountability. Effectively, they were a set of restrictive business practices created by a cartel of GICs and clinicians and shaped to their interests.[30]

In her landmark history of US trans experience, Joanne Meyerowitz sees HBIGDA's Standards as "liberal doctors" neutralizing "the long-standing threat by the doctors who opposed sex-change surgery."[31] It is true that they offered a measure of security for trans healthcare, but they did so by creating and perpetuating a system based on psychiatric abuse. HBIGDA's pseudo-medicine viewed being trans as a mental disorder, defined by a "wish to be rid of one's own genitals and to live as a member of the other sex." Although it was accepted that some men might not wish for reconstructive genital surgery, this was because of the surgical limitations of phalloplasty, not patient choice. Irrespective of what it might do to sexual sensation, women were automatically supposed to want full genital surgery, just as men were expected to want hysterectomies. Complying with these expectations was the only route through which trans people could access healthcare. Any patient who suggested an alternative would be "wavering" or "uncertain" and excluded from the program. HBIGDA set out an agenda for no-choice surgery, a compulsory sterilization of trans people that endured for over thirty years.

A suggestion that a trans person might be on the committee producing the Standards was voted down, and trans people had no voice in their healthcare. Now GICs became a version of the secure residential homes, tellingly known as "colonies," in which, a decade earlier, people who had been defined as "mentally defective" had been confined and in many countries subjected to enforced sterilization. But GICs were not so much a physical space as a temporal one, a location where trans people were "warehoused,"[32] kept in limbo until they were deemed "ready" for the treatment they desperately needed. The *Standards* set minimum times, effectively two years of psychiatric interviews before HRT was prescribed, and another year of living in the person's proper sex (termed the "Real-Life Test") before becoming eligible for reconstructive surgery. But there was no maximum waiting time. GICs could warehouse trans people interminably, with patients whom doctors found "unconvincing" being sentenced to endless "unreadiness." They would enter suspended time, "waiting, staying, delaying, enduring, persisting, repeating, maintaining, preserving and remaining," in an endless nightmare that became "arduous, boring, and mundane, or simply unbearable."[33]

GICs had absolute power and it was entirely up to them whom they treated. The *Standards* were inconsistent. In one paragraph, patients with schizophrenia were excluded from treatment, but a few paragraphs later, treatment could be given to anyone who "can be reasonably expected to be habilitated or rehabilitated," including people with "the diagnosis of schizophrenia."[34] Doctors could do as they pleased. HBIGDA's final business triumph was to get their diagnostic criteria for "transsexualism" included in the third edition of the American Psychiatric Association's (APA) *Diagnostic and Statistical Manual of Mental Disorders* (DSM-III),[35] the medical taxonomy against which US psychiatrists claim payment from private health-insurance companies. According to Professor Richard Green, who drafted the DSM-III entry on "transsexualism"[36] and was one of the six authors of the *Standards*, the removal of homosexuality from the DSM had left a financial gap, which badly affected the income of APA members. When it was proposed to fill that gap with "transsexualism," Richard told me, "They went, 'High five! Let's do it!' "[37] One piece of pseudo-medical psychiatric abuse was replaced by another for the financial benefit of doctors.

Now it was open season on trans people, and the media cashed in. Transploitation horror films such as *Dr. Jekyll and Sister Hyde*, *Dressed to Kill* and *The Silence of the Lambs* presented trans people as violently insane murderers.[38] Pop sociology such as Liz Hodgkinson's *Bodyshock* patronized, cisplained and titillated.[39] The popular press maintained its unremitting output of shock-horror stories about trans women: "Sex-Change 'Man' Gets a Divorce from Her Wife"; "Sex-Change for a TV Music Man"; "Oh Sister! Sex-Change Secret of a Monk"; "My Husband, the Sex-Change Para"; and "Plea for Sex-Change Vicar" were just a few 1970s headlines.[40] In the UK, John Randell's book *Sexual Variations* set out his vision of a GIC that would "breed out of our inheritance those with psychopathic and adverse genetic propensities . . . some form of eugenics, in fact."[41] In the US, John Money's mass-market book *Sexual Signatures* popularized his pseudo-medical fantasies and boasted about his success with David Reimer, the little boy who was accidentally given a penectomy and was raised as a girl.[42]

Trans activists fought back as well as they could. In 1973, four trans women activists used BBC public-access programming to produce an hour-long television discussion about trans rights.[43] Four years later, a trans woman named Renée Richards made history by bringing a successful challenge to her exclusion from the US Women's Open Tennis Championships, and she later produced both a book and film based on her legal triumph.[44] In 1980, a primetime BBC documentary exposed John Randell's brutal treatment of trans woman Julia Grant at her regular Charing Cross GIC appointment, shocking both viewers and the press.[45] They heard him bullying, infantilizing and threatening Julia: even the right-wing *Daily Telegraph* newspaper was outraged by the "entirely unsympathetic psychiatrist" who "appeared to wield absolute power over her" and "the extraordinary attitude of the medical profession."[46] Judy Cousins formed SHAFT, the Self Help Association for Transsexuals, which produced an authoritative thirty-page guide to help members negotiate brutal medical and legal environments, providing a realpolitik of accommodation, which was crucial to survival. By contrast, the Transsexual Action Group (TAG), developed a socialist feminist critique of trans people's positioning by society, seeking to frame an ideology focused on active resistance and social change.

Meanwhile, a trans man named Mark Rees, anonymizing himself as "Nicholas Mason," had published a stirring article in the

Journal of Medical Ethics.[47] A direct, frank description of the verbal abuse he had experienced, his psychopathologization and dismissal from the Women's Royal Naval Service, and his eventual access to endocrinological and surgical support led to his main theme: "The greatest problem was, and still is, the refusal of the Registrar General to permit amendment of my birth certificate."[48] In 1986, Mark took the UK government to the European Court of Human Rights (ECHR), arguing that by refusing to correct his birth certificate, the government had breached the European Convention, which protected the "right to respect for private and family life," and the "right to marry." He lost. The UK government argued that the purpose of birth certificates was to establish "the connections of families for purposes related to succession, legitimate descent and distribution of property" and the court reiterated that twice in its judgment.[49] Any attempt to provide Mark with the privacy associated with normal human dignity would require "detailed legislation" and might affect "the interests of others."[50] Ewan's hidden case and the issue of primogeniture ran all through the proceedings, but neither the ECHR nor Mark knew that case law from a senior UK court, endorsed by the Home Secretary, already existed and would have supported his action. Instead, the court decided against Mark, on the grounds that it was in the remit of the UK government to regulate this matter itself.

Of course Ewan knew about Mark's case, for it was all over the media. Certainly he looked for forgiveness for his perjury in court, which to a devout Presbyterian was like lying in the face of God. He told his sister-in-law, Cecilia, that on occasion, he fell to his knees in the fields to pray for his soul: she did not know the desperate measures he had taken and politely inquired whether he ever prayed for anyone else as well. At other times he found comfort in history, which was one of his passions. It was a source of satisfaction to him that Brux was one of the oldest locations in Forbes family history, and he would happily point out the very rock where, in 775 CE, his legendary ancestor O'Conchar Forbhasach had killed the bear that appeared on the family arms. The same bear appeared on Ewan's new coat of arms, which named him not only Sir Ewan Forbes of Craigievar but also Baron of Brux, making the arms specific to him alone, a tiny detail that he enjoyed. Visitors would be taken to the Laird's Cave, and Ewan would tell them the story of a Jacobite ancestor, on the run from the King's troops, who was lying low there and meanwhile building a drystone wall, the self-same one, Ewan said, they could still see, bordering the Quaker burial ground. When the Redcoats caught up with him, they mistook him for a workman and asked, "Is the laird at home?" to which he replied with careful equivocation, "He was when I was having my breakfast." His pursuers left unsatisfied.

Both Ewan and Patty were becoming frailer. In 1976, after Ewan had recovered from a stroke that paralyzed his left side, they moved a couple of hundred yards from Brux Lodge to a Scandinavian timber-built two-story chalet on the bank of the river Don. The ostensible reason was that it was easier to manage, but family and friends knew the real story. Patty had heard heavy footsteps and glimpsed a tall figure in the hallway at Brux Lodge. She went to investigate and saw a monk there. Outside, another monk was walking along the riverbank. The Don corridor had housed a number of small early Christian hermitages, and it was clear to her that these were ghosts from the past, come to reclaim the place that had formerly been theirs. Patty told Ewan that she wouldn't go into the lodge again and immediately decamped to the chalet, leaving Ewan with no choice but to follow.

It was there that Ewan wrote his memoir, *The Aul' Days*, published by the University of Aberdeen Press in 1984. It is a gently entertaining collection of after-dinner stories, strongly evocative of his childhood days and his passions for shooting, fishing, medicine, farming and friendship. Most significantly, though, it is Ewan telling his own story, representing himself in his own terms, radically refusing to be defined by anyone else. As far as Ewan was concerned, he was a boy who grew into a man: at no point does he make any mention of his medical history or of the court case that had been so carefully hidden away.

11

ANOTHER AUDACIOUS DEFENSE

In his declining years, Ewan was happiest when he was immersed in his local community. The neighbors who had welcomed the lonely child into their homes had long since died, but their children and grandchildren lived on: Ewan had delivered many of them when he was a doctor, attended their childhood illnesses and given awards to them for their Highland dancing, whether at the Lonach Gathering or the many competitions he had organized. He knew them, knew their histories, who had married whom, their triumphs and losses, the texture and fabric of their lives. And they knew him, whether as "the Doctor" or as "Brux" or as "Sir Ewan," for he, too, was knitted into the community's warp and weft. They viewed his court case and the press sensationalism surrounding it as simply "a very bad time for him," the kind of private personal devastation that anyone might experience, a tightening of the lips at the world's cruelty, and a gazing away, rather than a subject for gossip. Theirs was the familiar, everyday Ewan, who lived in much the same way as they did. Everyone knew that his Land Rover had slipped into the river Don when the bank gave way at Brux: similar events happened to every farmer, and the local garage at Alford pulled it out and repaired it like every other vehicle. A local woman named Betty Reach fell into friendly chat with Ewan when she bumped into him at the Alford newsagent's. She told him she'd just bought a copy of *The Aul' Days*, and, gesturing to the walking stick he was carrying, Ewan said, "Well, that's guid, but I'm in the bad books at hame the day!" He had been carrying out the ashes from the fire, slipped on the way out and tipped them on the floor, dust and ash everywhere, a muscle pulled, and Patty not best pleased.

Ewan was frailer now. Writing a reference for one of his staff, he spoke of the "great help" they had been to him "during my final years of farming, when I have suffered much ill-health and have not been able to look after things in a personal way."[1] Tending cattle and driving farm machinery had become too much for him now he was in his seventies, even after his remarkable recovery from his stroke. Leaving the estate work to younger men, Ewan focused on his role as an elder at Kildrummy Kirk, giving much of his time to supporting the many elderly people in its congregation. His help was much needed: the 1980s in the UK was a period of Thatcherism, an extreme right-wing retrenchment of social welfare expressed as the state's systematic attrition of health and social services, and a decline in employment and the economy. Local bus routes were being shut down, and local shops were closing, both very damaging to rural communities. Ewan understood these problems of ordinary people. His neighbors knew that he kept a simple house himself at Brux, much like their own, and unlike the summer visitors, he lived alongside them all year round. People were fond of him and liked him popping by, perhaps bringing the gift of a game bird or a rabbit for the pot. His favorite visiting spot was one of the Craigievar estate's gamekeepers' cottages, high up on the Kirk Hill, above Leochel-Cushnie, where Auld Sir Wullie and Ewan's brother, William, were at rest. The simple stone-built cottage, now owned by his favorite niece, was the last tiny piece of the vast estate he had known in his childhood. Ewan would take his Land Rover up the forest track to visit her in its tranquil seclusion and gaze over the land stretching into the distance that he had turned over to Cousin John and John had then sold.

In 1985, Ewan wrote a short piece about Craigievar Castle for a compendium called *Tales from Scottish Lairds*.[2] It reads like a reconciliation piece, as if he is trying to resolve his losses—his lost peace of mind, his lost privacy, his loss of the estate and castle—by recollection. Now, Craigievar was "a dream castle," that "allows the imagination to indulge itself," with a "fairy tale appearance" and towers that "shot straight up into the sky." But it was inhabited by ghosts, both those that made "a tremendous tramping about and clanking of arms" outside when he was a little boy and the footsteps on the stairs he heard distinctly when a young man and mistook for his mother's. Loss and pain are deflected onto the family legend of the Covenanters' curse, that if "descendants failed to support the Kirk of Scotland and the Covenant, the lands would surely be taken from them," and onto William, who "embraced the Roman Catholic religion" and caused the curse to come true. "The story ends here," he said, "like the blowing out of the candle."

Although Ewan no longer danced, he still loved the Highland tradition, and, encouraged by the success of *The Aul' Days*, in 1989 he published *The Dancers of Don*, a memoir of his dance company, the people in it and the places they had danced. It was a kind of love letter to all the partners and companions of his past, before he married Patty and settled down. He cataloged the dancers, their various attributes, their notable performances and the people who helped the company. Like *The Aul' Days*, it is interspersed with gentle jokes, often against himself, as well as touching stories, and it is here that he recalls the silver cigarette case that the Auld Laird had won for Highland dancing in 1884, and which, shortly before his death, he gave to Ewan, who "felt as if I was owned as a worthy descendant, and was proud of it."[3] He had finally made peace with the gruff father who had refused to pay for him to attend medical school, and ironically, he had grown to resemble him in some respects. Like his father, Ewan had become a stickler for the proprieties. As well as forbidding anything but fly-fishing on his side of the Don, on Ewan's shoots, keepers and beaters sat and ate separately from the "guns," the guests invited to shoot. This was the snobbish custom of an earlier generation, which his brother, William, had discarded when he was laird.

In his new book, too, Ewan continued to reject every identification of him apart from his own. When he quotes newspaper reports about the Dancers of Don, he always revised his own name to Ewan and his pronouns to male ones. He repudiated the pseudo-medical idea that sex assigned at birth was final, and trans people were masqueraders. Instead, he insisted on his self-identification, not in a "before and after," or a "then and now" way, but as something lifelong and indelible. It is a stark contrast to the reigning media narrative of "sex change": Ewan created a kind of counter-memory, substituting his gaze of autonomy for the official histories in a radical repositioning of the self that was years ahead of its time.

In the UK, the US, Europe, Canada, New Zealand, Australia, Hong Kong, and South Africa, the clear message of the previous twenty years had been that a world without trans people would have been a better one. Legally excluded, their lives appropriated and turned into freakish entertainment by the media, sterilizing surgery a compulsory part of the patient pathway, patient choice removed, unvoiced and unrecorded, no one knows how many trans people were treated in this way or how many died en route.[4] There was no support forthcoming from lesbian and gay communities in the UK, partly because they, too, were under attack. In 1988, Margaret Thatcher's infamous "Section 28" had forbidden "the teaching in any maintained school of the acceptability of homosexuality as a pretended family relationship." It shocked lesbian and gay communities and prompted their formation of a new lobbying group, Stonewall. Gay men and lesbians were being subjected to the same trope of masquerade that trans people had endured for two decades.

Trans activism was changing, too. Some second-wave support groups continued, but they were joined now by a new, third wave of legal activists. In 1989, the Council of Europe's recommendation on the "condition of transsexuals" had called for a comprehensive restoration of their civil liberties, including rectifying entries in "the register of births," protecting "the person's private life" and ending "discrimination in the enjoyment of fundamental rights and freedoms."[5] A new collective of trans activists formed, called Press for Change (PFC), aiming to "achieve equal civil rights and liberties for all transsexual and transgendered people in the United

Kingdom through legislation and social change."[6] Its leading figure rapidly became legal expert Stephen Whittle, and by July 1993, PFC had a stable group of ten activists, all unpaid, working when they were free from professional and family commitments and paying all their own costs: a low-cost, high-energy, deep-commitment agenda for policy-oriented direct action.

Similar developments were taking place in the US. In 1992, trans lawyer Phyllis Frye had organized an International Conference on Transgender Law and Employment Policy, and a year later, Cheryl Chase founded the Intersex Society of North America to lobby against intersex genital mutilation (IGM). But in particular, US third-wave trans activism focused on unpicking the language, concepts and histories of trans identities, by drawing on feminist scholarship. Activist and author Leslie Feinberg began to disentangle the collapsed categories of sex, gender and sexuality, writing about "an oppression that, as yet, has no commonly agreed name" in *Transgender Liberation*.[7] This work was given impetus by the horrific rape and murder in Humboldt, Nebraska, of a trans man named Brandon Teena in 1993. In 1994, Kate Bornstein's landmark work, *Gender Outlaw*, part confessional, part cultural critique and part performance, debunked the idea of trans as a disease or a masquerade and popularized the ideas of gender fluidity and a nonbinary identity. In both the US and the UK, trans people and their allies were beginning to find a new, distinctive voice.

A crucial difference between the UK and the US was the European Union. It provided an externality that the US didn't have, a location from which to look back at the UK and evaluate how far it was meeting its aspirations for social justice. And if there were serious lapses of conduct in the UK government, then its citizens could go to the EU not just for an opinion but for a legally binding decision. First Mark Rees and then the model and actress Caroline Cossey had used this route,[8] and while the ECHR had found against them, their cases had advanced the debate considerably. This European dimension was to be crucial for the case of *P v. S and Cornwall County Council*, whose events took place from 1991 to 1996. It was the first time anywhere in the world that a legal decision prevented discrimination because someone was trans, and although the legal team at the time did not know it, it was the first successful challenge to the backlash from Ewan's trial.

The woman we know only as "P" grew up in an English industrial town, playing on its spoil heaps and canal banks, part of a working-class community. It was an utterly different childhood from Ewan's at Craigievar and Fintray except for one thing: they were both trans. Unlike Ewan, P had no access to support of any kind. Stunned when she was seven by the shocked realization that her body wasn't going to change as she had expected, P knew, as an absolute truth, that she couldn't go on living as she was. With a child's matter-of-fact finality, she comforted herself with the thought that she would just automatically die. Still alive a year later, P fell into a profound, numbing depression and retreated from the world into her imagination, a wistful, solitary child whose gaze sometimes seemed to be looking into another world a million miles away.

Perhaps her imagination was her salvation. She found her way to university, part of the UK's experiment in funding working-class children, and in the library there she was at last able to put a name to her conundrum. She was intersex, and now knew she could get medical help and support. It seemed as if a doorway to light and life had suddenly opened. P went to her university GP, who referred her to the hospital for what P assumed would be the start of the long endocrinological and surgical process she had read about. Tragically, she had no idea that the textbooks she had consulted were from the 1960s, and that then, in the 1970s, trans people had been reclassified from intersex to floridly psychotic. The "help" she found at the hospital was not endocrinology but psychiatry, not hormone therapy but aversion therapy. Mercifully, she was at an outpatients' facility: P left, changed address and didn't return.

Now she knew the dangers, and she laid her plans accordingly. P knew she had to bide her time, manage the devastating emotional complexities of being classed as trans in a transphobic world, wait until she could find a better route: she had to survive until she could find a way to live.

By 1989, she had made a career for herself as a senior manager in a major university, and she was looking carefully for healthcare support. Once bitten, twice shy. She had discovered a local support group and met a community of trans people who had explained her best chances of success. Avoid Charing Cross GIC at all costs; pay privately for all your healthcare; present yourself in this way; always say this, never say that; hope to stay alive in the process. Expect to lose your friends, expect to lose your family, expect to have to sell your house, change your job, move somewhere you are unknown. If you are married, the doctors will make you divorce before they will treat you, and if you have children, expect never to see them again. Don't expect understanding or sympathy from anyone: if you are a member of a church, expect the congregation to expel you; if you are a member of a club, expect to be barred; if you play sports, expect to be banned. Never get in trouble with the police; never tell anyone about your past; think before you say anything. Make yourself invisible, and if you see trouble coming up the street toward you, get out of the way or take a beating or worse. You are safe in your own home or in the homes of trans friends but not traveling between the two. You are safe in the local lesbian and gay club, but if you end up floating in the canal at the back, be sure the police won't investigate. Now you are on your own and outside society and you are not even a statistic.

It was austerely practical advice, and cautiously, P began to pick her way across this hazardous landscape. By any standards, she was highly qualified and very good at her job, and this, she felt, would be her saving grace. She attended a private clinic in London, paid for a private prescription for HRT and then waited for her hair to grow and for her HRT to take effect.

Then, P had what looked like a lucky break. A colleague had recently become principal of a college in Cornwall; he was looking for a senior manager, and he invited P to apply. S, as he is known, wanted P to reengineer a college department from being wholly reliant on government funding to trading commercially in a competitive marketplace. Although she had no wish to move to Cornwall permanently, P realized that a short-term contract would provide a break from her immediate milieu and provide useful experience for a permanent job elsewhere. On April 1, 1991, she took up the post.

It was a huge success. In just twelve months, the department's budget deficit was reduced by 80 percent, its profile raised with a range of prestigious new programs, and its staff trained in business management and quality assurance. In April 1992, S asked P to extend her contract for another year, with a much-improved employment package, and P accepted S's offer, explaining that she was in the process of transitioning and that an additional year would be the maximum she would wish to commit to. S was supportive, and there was no suggestion that P's job was in jeopardy, but later on S said that the news had been a "bombshell that hit me."

Although P's new contract had not arrived by June, she continued to work in good faith. But S's attitude had hardened, and by mid-September bullying began in earnest. S set P three tasks that were academically impossible, including writing and validating a new degree program in twelve weeks. Then, humiliatingly, P was told to report to her deputy, who was now in charge, and when P returned to her office, she found it emptied and her staff told to deny her access to the files. How was she to complete the three tasks she had been set? Happily, P had applied for another job, with an employer who had no objection to her being trans, and had gotten it, subject to references. She was devastated when the job offer was withdrawn because S had given her a bad reference. It began to seem as if he intended to destroy her. Now, P "felt completely trapped, entirely in S's power and quite at his mercy," subject to "conduct designed to degrade and humiliate."[9]

In November, S forbade P from contacting her staff, from attending meetings with them and from entering the college and her department without his express permission. Her staff were instructed to tell inquirers that P no longer worked there, and on one occasion she was obliged to wait in a car park for several hours before S gave her permission to enter. She was in a spatial limbo, present and absent, visible and invisible, located and dislocated. Isolated in the car park, she was neither at the college nor not there, suspended in a temporal lacuna, warehoused, while literally all around her, the work she had initiated carried on. At the end of December 1993, she was made redundant, unemployed for the first time in her life.

P's local employment office offered her lifetime disability benefit if she would agree never to apply for a job again; otherwise, they had an opening for selling encyclopedias door to door. Grimly, P started applying for jobs. In her own specialist sector, she would be treated like everyone else until interviewers, working through her CV, suddenly telegraphed their shocked recognition of her from her professional profile. Twenty interviews and three months later, P was starting her career again from scratch, in a different part of the country, just about managing to scrape by, not destroyed, still alive and, what's more, ready to fight back.

She found her way to Madeleine Rees and Ramby de Mello, a solicitor and a barrister who were deeply committed to human rights. P learned that she was up against the so-called equal misery argument. UK law demanded equal treatment in employment, and if an employer's policy was to dismiss both trans men and trans women, or both lesbians and gay men, that was considered to be equal treatment. They were equally dismissed. For P to show that she had been discriminated against, the law said, she needed a "third-party comparator," that is, she would have to find a trans man in the same circumstances whom S had treated more favorably than she had been treated. Without such a person, S could simply say that it was his policy to dismiss both trans men and trans women and so he had not discriminated against P. That was the equal misery argument, and it was deemed that there was no way of challenging it: put simply, it was legal to discriminate so long as you were consistent.

But like Ewan, P was an audacious and inventive thinker, and like him, she refused to buy into the conventional trans narratives of masquerade and psychosis. Brushing aside decades of case law, she put a new argument to Madeleine and Ramby. P said that she did not need a third-party comparator, a trans man who had been treated more favorably than she had. When S had believed P was male, he treated her in one way, appreciative of her work and offering her an enhanced contract. When S discovered P was female, he treated her quite differently, threatening to bully her out of her job and then dismissing her. P was her own third-party comparator, she said.[10]

Without knowing it, P had exposed the legal limbo to which Ormrod had consigned trans people: the logical gap between de facto and de jure, what someone is as a matter of practical common sense and what they are as a matter of law. Her point was that for all social purposes she was female, irrespective of what her legal status might be, and that in defining her in any other way, the law was an ass. While this argument would not fly technically in a court of law, it opened up a novel view of sex discrimination, one based on the way we see the world and live within it, rather than on abstract administrative definitions. It was enough to persuade the Equal Opportunities Commission to fund the cost of legal action.

On July 28, 1993, an industrial tribunal granted P anonymity, a precedent that was to be used time and again in future trans legal cases. It was a formal recognition that a medical condition can cause social prejudice to an individual that might stop them from seeking legal redress. Anonymity was crucial to P's well-being, for the tabloid press was routinely outing and vilifying trans people, as a "sex swap shocker,"[11] a "sex swap secret"[12] and a "sex-swap sham."[13] On November 17, 1993, an industrial tribunal in Truro found in her favor, referring the case to the European Court of Justice (ECJ) on the grounds that the EU's Equal Treatment Directive might provide the protection that UK equality legislation denied trans people. The law moves slowly, and so it was over a year later, on March 21, 1995, that P and her legal team sat in the ECJ, where their senior lawyer, Helena Kennedy, QC, was about to battle for trans equality.

Ewan knew nothing of these events. During his last few years,

his life had become harder. Money, always difficult after the depredations made by Cousin John, was tighter, UK farming had
become less profitable, and his increasing age meant that he had
to employ more staff. At the same time, he felt obliged to meet his
social obligations as a family member and a host to the visitors
who arrived during the summer season, sighing with relief when
they had departed and he and Patty could return to their usual
frugal diet of porridge and a rabbit for the pot. He had to sell off
some of Brux's land, but fortunately the family at Ardhuncart, on
the other side of the river, was happy to buy the strip that faced
their estate. Kindly friends, and careful of Ewan's sensitivities, they
agreed that he should continue to farm it and take the income from
it, so that no one would know he was in financial difficulties. Physically, Ewan was weaker. He now needed a gun-carrier when he
went shooting, and a close friend was happy to supply that need.
As they walked, he would talk about his family, about history and
about the heritage he was part of, grounding himself in the distant past—and his companion would be careful to keep to those
subjects for, as she put it, what had happened to him was both
unthinkable and unspeakable.[14]

Ewan now had it firmly fixed in his mind that the loss of Craigievar, which precipitated all of his losses, was due to the Covenanters'
curse, and he had become eccentrically anti-Catholic. A few years
earlier, in 1984, his sister-in-law, Cecilia, had died, and in family
tradition, she had been laid out in Craigievar Castle for a Catholic
Mass. Ewan objected strongly to these arrangements and insisted
that the castle should be exorcised afterward. It became an idée fixe
for him, as the historian Ian Mitchell Davidson records, describing
one of Ewan's last public appearances:

> He was invited to take the salute when the Lonach pipe band came
> to beat the retreat at the castle. The invited guests included local
> landowners, dressed in their old family kilts, farmers with red faces
> and tight-fitting tweed jackets and a scattering of oil executives
> from Aberdeen in pinstripes. It was a fine, colourful affair.

We retired to the Great Hall where the fire was crackling and Sir Ewan, who now walked with the aid of two sticks, was placed on the wing-backed tartan armchair beside it. We all crowded in and Sir Ewan was asked to give a short address. He struggled to his feet and, in his ancient Forbes tartan kilt, thanked those there for attending and for the care the Trust took of the castle. Then he lamented the change in family fortunes, blaming this on the move from staunch Protestantism to Catholicism. His voice was raised and his fist thumped the table. He had had the Kirk minister exorcise that Catholic funeral mass, he told us. The oil executives looked bewildered, but for me it was a window into 300 years of history, to the Covenanters and the arrival of the Marquis of Montrose at Bridge of Alford, ready to do battle.[15]

Late one night in September 1991, a few months after P had begun her disastrous new post at Cornwall, the phone rang at the home of Henry Smith, the former Craigievar gamekeeper who had been much loved by Ewan's family. It was Patty, saying that Ewan had fallen out of bed and she couldn't get him back in again. Henry was in his late seventies then, and so his son, Frank, said that he would go up and help. At the Brux chalet, Ewan's increasing frailty was obvious from the stairlift that had been fitted, and upstairs Frank found him in a very poor way. He went to pick him up "and he was like a bag of water, with fluid retention": it was clear that he was failing fast.[16] Perhaps the fall had been the result of a mini heart attack, or perhaps the fall prompted a major episode: either way, Ewan was taken to Aberdeen Royal Infirmary, where he had a stroke while he was hospitalized. Mercifully for a man who had led such an active life, the weak chest that had suggested his audacious defense in court came to his aid: he contracted pneumonia, "the old man's friend," as it was called, and died in the late afternoon of September 12, 1991, at the age of seventy-nine.

Although he had been unwell for some time, the suddenness of his death took everyone by surprise, and so Ewan's funeral was a quiet affair, attended just by Patty and their solicitor, Smithy.

Instead of the usual family internment, Ewan had requested a cremation, with his ashes scattered on Coillebhar Hill at Brux, the estate's most beautiful spot, whose name shared its etymology with Craigievar. But at noon on October 15, 1991, friends and relations joined Patty at the little rural Kildrummy Kirk: it stands alone on the hillside, its bow end crowned by a bell cote, the stone deeply grooved by generations of bell-ringers hauling its external rope to call the Donside faithful to spiritual comfort. Inside, light floods through two Gothic tracery windows in the east wall, which frame the pulpit, with simple wooden pews clustering around it, and on the north wall is a medieval memorial to the third Laird of Brux. The service of thanksgiving to celebrate the life of "Dr. the Hon. Sir Ewan Forbes, Bart of Craigievar," as it named him on the order of service, was being held in the kirk he and his ancestors had loved.[17]

The congregation was shocked when Cousin John joined them. Without knowing the details, Ewan's friends knew how John had suddenly appeared, poisoned Ewan's life and disappeared again. Why was he there? they wondered. Perhaps he wanted to make sure Ewan really was dead and that he could have the title.

Three hymns, three readings, two prayers, a benediction and a tribute to Ewan formed the simple service. Intentionally or not, they spoke to the ordeal Ewan had gone through, with Psalm 138's "Though I walk in the midst of trouble, thou wilt revive me," St. John's "In my father's house are many mansions," and Revelation's "He that overcometh shall inherit all things." The tribute was given by Henry Duncan, the session clerk, who had known Ewan for nearly fifty years. It rehearsed his childhood at Craigievar and Fintray, his time abroad as a young man, his life as a doctor skiing to his patients, his leadership of the Dancers of Don, his marriage, his shift to farming, his Doric recitals and his ordination as an elder. Everyone knew that Ewan had become more "nippet" with age, and they will have appreciated the tact with which Henry said that Ewan "was ready to give of his wisdom and advice which, though sometimes controversial, was always appreciated." Generous, caring, damaged and dogmatic—he always had to have the last word—he was nevertheless their friend, neighbor, doctor, host and entertainer: as Henry put it, "Within each of us who were privileged to meet and know him, there will remain a warm and glowing affection for him which needs no written word and which will live on in all our memories."[18]

Ewan had left everything to Patty. It was little enough: not quite £40,000 in savings (£75,000 or $103,000 at today's values) and another £8,500 from the sale of his car, furniture and other effects (£16,000 or $22,500). And the Brux estate was valued at £286,000 (£500,000 or $686,000), although nine years later it fetched £1 million, even in the dilapidated state it had been allowed to fall into. Still, there was enough for Patty to retire to sheltered accommodation at nearby Aberlour, where she had family.

With Ewan's death, John had the title and nothing more. He had frittered away the money from the Craigievar and Fintray estates that Ewan had given over to him and was a photojournalist for *Horse & Hound* magazine. He might call himself Sir John Forbes of Craigievar, but he had no connection with the place, the people or the practice of lairdship: if he saw it as a victory, it was a hollow one. Just over four years later, the existence of Ewan's hidden case began to emerge.

In her residential home in Aberlour, a calming, caring presence among its elderly residents as she had always been in Ewan's life, Patty would certainly have seen and heard the various news reports following the progress of P. In December 1995, eight months after the ECJ hearing, the advocate general gave an opinion in favor of P. Reviewing the arguments, he said:

> One fact, however, is not just possible, but certain: P would not have been dismissed if she had remained a man. So how can it be claimed that discrimination on grounds of sex was not involved? How can it be denied that the cause of discrimination was precisely, and solely, sex?[19]

He spoke, too, about the absolute moral values that should underpin laws, "the true essence of that fundamental and inalien-

able value that is equality . . . what is at stake is a universal fundamental value, indelibly etched in modern legal traditions and in the
constitutions of the more advanced countries: *the irrelevance of a
person's sex with regard to the rules regulating relations in society.*"[20]

It was a moving, resonant statement, a breath of fresh air from
Europe, which might herald a new life for trans people. But it
would be another four months before the ECJ gave its final verdict. Meanwhile, P teamed up with another trans woman, G, to
challenge in the High Court the government's refusal to correct
their birth certificates. Since birth certificates had been corrected
in the past without any known problems arising, it seemed reasonable and logical that they should be corrected in the present. But
in court, the government claimed that there were no cases "where
a person was correctly entered by reference to biological sex at the
time of birth but where the register was later annotated because of
gender reassignment surgery,"[21] and the court dismissed the corrected birth certificates of Michael Dillon, Roberta Cowell and
other trans people as "irrelevant."

The High Court's judgment was inexplicable from every viewpoint except one: that for reasons unknown, the UK government
was obsessively, fanatically protective of birth certificates to the
extent that now it would say and do anything to prevent their correction by trans people. Something had happened between the
1950s, when they were corrected as a matter of course, and 1996,
when P and G went to court. Clearly, the government knew what
that something was, since it had all the records and had made the
new rules, but it was a secret it was not going to share.

That evening, though, a remarkable series of events began to
unfold. April Ashley's solicitor Terrence Walton rang my colleague
Madeleine Rees and told her of a mysterious case that had ended the
correction of birth certificates for trans people, because "there are
some interests that it is more important to protect than the rights
of individuals." Everyone who knew about it had been sworn to
secrecy, and all records of it had been removed from the public eye.
This was Ewan's hidden case. If such a case really existed, it would be

important for the legal actions my colleagues and I were bringing to advance trans human rights, and accordingly, I started looking for it, increasingly puzzled at finding it nowhere recorded. I was even more puzzled when I found it *did* exist, but two successive Lord Advocates refused to release any information about it to my colleague, Dr. Lynne Jones, MP. It took another two years for the government to be persuaded to let its skeleton out of the closet and many more before the full implications of Ewan's legacy were understood.

In blissful ignorance of Ewan and his hidden case, trans activists plodded on and received their reward on May 1, 1996: P won her case and regained employment rights for trans people in the whole of Europe. It was the first time anywhere in the world that case law prevented discrimination because someone was trans. As a European decision, it could be cited persuasively on other continents, opening the door to progress internationally as well as nationally. It had been worded carefully so that if it won, it could be used to extend rights to other minority groups and, most immediately, it helped to end the automatic dishonorable discharge of lesbians and gay men from the armed forces. In effect, P's case had rewritten human-rights law, and suddenly trans equality was headline news in the press and on radio and television everywhere. Keen to protect the hard-won anonymity that had kept her safe for the last three years, P gave only one interview, to the *Independent*, which had agreed to publish her personal statement, in her own voice, alongside its interview report.[22] It was accompanied by the sole photograph taken of her: P is in a three-quarter portrait view, standing, turned away from the camera, wearing a dark business suit, her gaze on the book she holds, an upright, slender professional woman with bobbed, slightly wavy blond hair, absorbed in her work, while beyond her, through the window of her home, a red double-decker bus goes by.

P's victory protected trans people who worked in the public sector, and a year later it was extended to the private sector by a court case that exposed the shocking treatment of another trans woman. R was employed as a rides' technician at Chessington World of

Adventures theme park, where, after she revealed her planned transition to her employers, fellow employees subjected her to severe, prolonged harassment. Some of it was exhausting, such as incessant theft of her tools; some humiliating, such as leaving used tampons on her workbench; some vandalism, such as defacing her property with lipstick; some sinister, such as leaving a replica coffin inscribed with her name and the letters "RIP" on her workbench; some violent, such as taping razor blades to her car door handles so her hands would be lacerated; some deeply menacing, such as taking bets on who could be first to cause her serious injury, force her to resign or have her dismissed; and some permanently damaging—employees' ostracism of R meant she had to do heavy lifting unassisted, causing joint damage that led to her spending the rest of her life in a wheelchair. R's situation was made far worse by her GIC, which insisted that she had to stay in work in order to complete her Real-Life Test as a precondition of access to essential healthcare. She endured almost three years of this treatment before suffering a severely disabling injury when working alone, which made it impossible for her to do her job: consequently, R was dismissed by Chessington World of Adventures in 1994.

Like P, it was not that R's treatment was unusual: it was, after all, state-legitimized bullying, a kind of specific persecution that the law deemed appropriate treatment for trans people. What was unusual in both P's and R's cases was that they found the inner reserves, the courage and endurance, to hold their ground against overwhelming odds and stand up for justice. Using P's case as a precedent, R took Chessington World of Adventures to court, and an Employment Appeal Tribunal found in her favor on June 27, 1997. Now trans people had the same employment protection as cis people in both public and private sectors.

Third-wave trans activism was gaining momentum. Labour member of Parliament Dr. Lynne Jones and I had co-founded the Parliamentary Forum on Gender Identity, and its first meeting had been held in June 1994: trans community leaders, lawyers and doctors meeting with government departments and parliamentarians to advance trans equality.[23] Working from new medical evidence,[24] in February 1995, forum members had produced *Transsexualism: The Current Medical Viewpoint*, shifting being trans from a mental illness to having a "biologically-based, multifactorial etiology" and asserting that "medically, there is no reason why people receiving treatment or who have received treatment for transsexualism should be given any lesser legal status than that of any other person."[25] It was published on the internet by Cyberia, the world's first internet café, which had opened in London six months earlier, as perhaps the first UK trans activist resource on the World Wide Web.

Then, in 1997, Professor Milton Diamond exposed the flawed research that had supported pseudo-medicine. An anatomist and reproductive biologist, Diamond could never make scientific sense of Money's John/Joan case, and he had spent his own money advertising to try to find the child who had been treated in this way. Eventually, he found him, David Reimer, the boy whose accidental penectomy and "reassignment" by John Money had led to long-term tragic outcomes.[26]

The medical world was changing. In 1997, the Gender Identity Research and Education Society was formed to educate the world at large about trans issues.[27] In the same year, following a Parliamentary Forum report on the provision of healthcare for trans people,[28] a group of trans activists, known as A, D and G, successfully went to court and won the right for trans people to have their healthcare provided by the NHS, like all other patients in the UK.[29] But the law seemed to be erratic. In 1997, the ECHR found against the right of a trans man, X, to be entered as "father" on the birth certificate of the donor-conceived child of his partner, Y, on the grounds that X was "not prevented in any way from acting as Z's father in the social sense": he could masquerade as Z's father, but he would be given no legal recognition.[30] When Kristina Sheffield and Rachel Horsham took the UK to the ECHR in 1998 for the same right to correct their birth certificates that Mark Rees and Caroline Cossey had sought, they lost, too, by eleven votes to nine.[31] The judgment had more dissenting opinions from individual judges than ever before, but UK trans people were still left in a legal limbo. At the same time, though, the Parliamentary Forum was collaborating with the UK government to produce its *Guide to Sex Discrimination (Gender Reassignment) Regulations*, to take forward the new laws protecting trans people's employment,[32] together with a comprehensive, interdepartmental action plan to improve trans equality in every area of government.[33] Part of the government seemed to be working for trans equality and another part working against it: it didn't seem to make logical sense.

Unaware of Ewan's hidden case, it seemed as if a negative public profile was to blame for lack of legal progress. When P was going to her industrial tribunal in 1993, Sally Vincent in the *Guardian* had pilloried trans women as part of "a grotesque limbo of dirty-joke freakhood," one of the "lost boys" who, in spite of "the chop," can "never become women" and have made themselves "disenfranchised, ostracised, mocked and despised."[34] Three years later, in the same newspaper, Suzanne Moore mocked P's victory, which had won trans people employment rights in the armed services, as "an army of transsexuals, marching in their sling-backs, what a terrifying thought that is."[35] In the tabloids, a surgeon who operated on the Queen Mother was described as "a secret transsexual hiding female breasts,"[36] and the continued employment of a police officer was crudely headlined as "No-Nobby Bobby Keeps Jobby."[37] In the cinema, Neil Jordan billed his transphobic film *The Crying Game* as "the shock sleeper hit to top them all." It legitimized violence and disgust, expressed as literal vomiting, at the thought of being attracted to a trans person, a trope that became stock humor for other directors, and that fueled the idea of a "trans panic defense" excusing cis violence against trans people.[38] The film won a BAFTA, one Academy Award out of six Oscar nominations and an accolade from the British Film Institute.

Television marginalized trans people in a more patronizing way. A BBC docusoap, *Paddington Green*, included trans woman sex worker Jackie McAuliffe as a regular character, using the docusoap tropes of confessional and morality tale; although an Israeli woman named Dana International won the 1998 Eurovision contest, the media ensured that the audience's focus was as much on her trans history as it was on her singing;[39] and the long-running soap *Coronation Street* ran wedding plans for its fictitious trans woman (played by a cis woman) to marry, headlined by *What's on TV* as "Indecent Proposal?"[40] Whether as jeering press or condescending television, trans people were located in the UK mind as entertaining oddities, their trans identity the most notable part of their lives. It was a depressing counterpoint to medical and legal progress.

In the US, meanwhile, shock waves went through the LGBTI communities in 1991 at the news that a trans woman had been ejected from the women-only Michigan Womyn's Music Festival. It fragmented views both in the festival itself and among LGBTI activists, and highlighted issues of trans exclusion, which were repeated at the 1993 March on Washington for Lesbian, Gay and Bi Equal Rights, and the 1994 commemoration of the twenty-fifth anniversary of the Stonewall riots: both excluded trans people. Riki Wilchins founded the ironically named Transexual Menace, which gained media attention by holding peaceful vigils outside courts where anti-transgender crimes were being tried. On November 8, 1996, an alliance that included the National Gay and Lesbian Task Force, the Intersex Society of North America, and the Transexual Menace, picketed the American Psychiatric Association as a common enemy of LGBTI human rights.

But the US's state-devolved legal system meant it was harder to make country-wide legal change there than in the UK, especially since there was no equivalent of the EU to hear appeals. Consequently, when President Bill Clinton reauthorized the Hate Crimes Statistics Act on July 4, 1996, it included race, religion, sexual orientation and ethnicity, but once again excluded trans people. However, the US excelled at scholarship. In 1990, philosopher Judith Butler argued that gender was simply the product of repeated acts, which "congeal over time to produce the appearance of substance, or a natural sort of being."[41] She called this congealed appearance of reality "performativity," actions and words that have validity only in their own discourse. Change the discourse and you could change the world. Ideas like these coalesced at the University of Iowa's Queer Studies Conference in 1994, bringing together scholars researching the complex relationships between gender, power and sexual violence. A new stream of feminist analysis, founded in Black feminism, drew attention to "intersectionality," the idea that individuals and groups may stand at a series of crossing points between race, class, gender and sexuality, which determine their exclusion. Sex and gender were parts of a network of power relations, and the idea that people could be homogenized as "women," all equally disadvantaged in comparison to "men," was obviously naive. What did the life of Prime Minister Margaret Thatcher have in common with that of a seven-year-old girl sewing in a sweatshop? And how could the Queen be less privileged than the male street person sleeping outside Buckingham Palace?

These new viewpoints encouraged legal action in the UK. Liz Bellinger was seeking to have her marriage of twenty years legally recognized, and two more trans women, Christine Goodwin and another trans woman known as "I," had appealed to the ECHR. Both had suffered because they would not humiliate themselves by presenting their birth certificates for civil identification purposes. "I" had been turned down for a training course, a student loan, and a job that required her to present her birth certificate, and Christine had been unable to apply for life insurance, for a mortgage or for the government's winter fuel allowance. They asked for the right to respect for their private and family lives, the right to marry, the prohibition of discrimination against them, and the same legal protections as everyone else.

But before either of their cases was decided, an Australian court made a remarkable judgment. In 2001, giving his decision in *re Kevin*, Judge Chisholm exposed the false basis of Ormrod's decision in *Corbett v. Corbett*, which had removed equality from a generation of trans people. Chisholm showed how Ormrod used a circular argument to equate "biological constitution at birth" with "true sex," excluding all consideration of the social and psychological matters that are equally relevant in determining whether some-one is male or female. Ormrod had gone against senior medical authority in excluding these factors and had presented no reason-ing, evidence, principle or policy to support their exclusion. Orm-rod's balance sheet, used worldwide to exclude trans people, was finally exposed as the sham it had always been. This was a big help to the Bellinger and Goodwin cases.

And there was a fatal chink in the UK government's armor. In the aftermath of P's case, the Parliamentary Forum had helped to produce the official *Report of the Inter-Departmental Working Group on Transsexual People*, which had proposed "full legal rec-ognition of the new gender, subject to certain criteria and proce-dures." But the government had shelved the report, and European judges were concerned to find that "no steps whatsoever have been or . . . were intended to be taken to carry this matter forward."[42] The UK government would not implement its own recommendations and, accordingly, it was time for the ECHR to step in.[43] On July 11, 2002, Christine and "I" won their case. Almost immediately, the government issued guidance that being trans "is *not* a mental ill-ness" and announced its intention to create a Gender Recognition Act (GRA) to restore trans equality.[44]

There was instant opposition from two lobbies. One lobby wor-ried that trans people's use of single-sex spaces such as toilets and changing rooms might threaten cis people. But the Home Office's extensive inquiries found "no instances where this has proved a problem."[45] The second lobby was fundamentalist religious groups that viewed trans people as a violation of God's law. Fundamental-ism's negative world view defines itself by what it opposes, claiming exclusive knowledge of an inarguable truth. It has no room for the "humanistic reception" of mainstream religions or their ecumen-ism and interreligious dialogues that seek commonality through the spirit of different sacred texts. Instead, fundamentalism focuses on the literal word, lifting verses out of context and clinging to them as "proof texts" for a dogmatic belief in their rightness and everyone else's wrongness. They found trans people "incompatible with God's will as revealed in Scripture and in creation," protested against the GRA and advocated for aversion therapy to make trans people repent and "reorient their lifestyle in accordance with biblical principles and orthodox church teaching."[46] Their bigotry inspired the Sibyls, an interdenominational safe space where trans people could worship,[47] and the development of a "transgendered theology,"[48] with the character of liberation theology, release from insufferable oppression by direct action.

Patty witnessed only some of these events. She saw P, and R, and A, D and G, and Christine Goodwin and "I" winning their various battles in the European and domestic courts, and perhaps she felt reassured and vindicated that she and Ewan had been right in their personal fight for trans equality. But she will also have known from that terrible, years-long battle that there are no victors in such conflicts: those who win do so at a personal cost.

Patty could remember the good times, the practice in Alford, their wedding and the farm at Brux. She was just Aunt Patty to her nieces, kind, warm and thoughtful: Ewan's pet name for her had been "bella te," "beautiful you," and hers for him, "little one," both a gently teasing reminder of their height difference and an expression of the protectiveness she felt toward him. Their evenings had been spent together comfortably, Ewan with his glass of whisky and Patty with her crème de menthe, reading, watching television or listening to music or the radio. Theirs had been a love match and a simple life, complicated only by John's ruthless pursuit of the Craigievar baronetcy. When her friends and relatives visited, bringing the new generation of children, she could tell them stories of that past: buying her clothes off the big maroon van from Jimmy Birse's general stores in Alford, which did the rounds of the hill farms and cottages (she did not care about expensive fashions); the special milk bottles they had had at Brux with Ewan's new aristocratic crest on them (a good businessman, he had an eye for the prestige market); the children who, like them, had come to visit, had helped with "the coos and the caafies," had herded sheep, and gone shooting with their uncle Ewan. And she could tell them about their uncle Ewan being born in a castle, skiing through snowstorms to see sick patients, Ewan the crack shot and expert fisherman, the talented dancer, good doctor, successful farmer, kind neighbor, and lively minded, interesting and generous host: her Ewan, the man she had loved, chided and protected in a marriage four decades long, and to whom she had always been "my wonderful wife." Patty died on February 17, 2002.

12

EWAN'S LEGACY

Trans equality should have been simple after 2002. Legally, Ormrod's balance sheet had been overturned and trans discrimination should have gone with it. Medically, since being trans was no longer a mental illness, it could only be a usual variation of natural human diversity. The government could have accepted that everyone is entitled to equality and extended the male-female binary with a third civil category. Natal birth certificates could have been corrected. The UK could have been an equal society. None of those common-sense steps were taken.

Hidden away, neutralizing every attempt at legal and social reform, was the legacy of Ewan's case. Trans activists knew that male primogeniture was a sticking point for trans equality, that it represented the "interests that it is more important to protect than the rights of individuals," as Terrence Walton had put it, and that Ewan's case had been hidden away to prevent it from being used to challenge that status quo. But it wasn't until 2013 that the full force of that legacy began to be felt.

Celebrating the sixtieth anniversary of her succession to the throne, Queen Elizabeth II modernized the monarchy by replacing male-preference primogeniture with absolute primogeniture. She had become Queen only because her father had left no male descendants eligible to become King. From then on, though, the eldest child would become the next monarch, whether female or male. It was not an easy task, since constitutionally, all of the Commonwealth countries that recognize the Queen as their head of state, such as Canada and Australia, had to give their assent. But it was popular: the Queen had "struck a historic blow for women's rights," as the *New York Times* put it.[1] Consequently, the Succession to the Crown Act was passed in April 2013, establishing that "the gender of a person born after 28 October 2011 does not give that person, or that person's descendants, precedence over any other person (whenever born)." Two hundred British aristocrats had signed a letter to the *Daily Telegraph* asking for the same abolition of male primogeniture for their titles, since "if gender equality can be granted to the Royal Family, it is only logical and just that it be granted to all families. . . . There should not be gender discrimination in Britain, full stop."[2] Accordingly, in 2013, the Equalities (Titles) Bill was entered in the House of Lords to extend the Queen's reform to all hereditary titles.[3]

It met strong resistance. A small, influential clique of peers wrecked the new legislation. They said a title was personal property, part of the amorphous tradition called "Royal Prerogative," and thus a matter for the Crown to deal with, not Parliament. Even if it was a matter for Parliament, it was too difficult to do, for some titles were linked to ancient legislation that could be altered only by a Private Act of Parliament or the involvement of European law. And then there were the complexities of Scottish clan chieftainships, which were a separate matter from other titles, while being historically intertwined with them, not to mention Irish titles, and individuals who held three different titles from these three different parts of the UK. The bill failed.

Suddenly, Ewan's unfortunate legacy appeared in a new light. It wasn't only royal male primogeniture that had precipitated the social ostracism, legal exclusion and compulsory sterilization of trans people that comprised trans eugenics, but also the self-interest of a particular political group. I started to follow the progress of the primogeniture legislation and began to wonder exactly what had happened in Ewan's case. I dug out the five hundred pages of Ewan's court transcript from storage and began to examine its role in trans history.

Another bill to abolish male primogeniture was entered for the 2015 Parliament, and the same clique killed that one, too. Like a cat-and-mouse cartoon, it was revived in 2016 and it was killed again. Revived again in 2017, it was killed again. In 2018, it was renamed and entered in the House of Commons, but the government objected that it was up to the House of Lords to sort it out and refused to debate the matter. In its latest incarnation, the 2020 Hereditary Peerages and Baronetcies (Equality of Inheritance) Bill is still waiting for a date for debate.[4]

The clique defending male primogeniture was flouting the principles of a century of UK equalities legislation: the Representation of the People Acts of 1918 and 1928, which provided women's suffrage; the Equal Pay Act in 1970; the Sex Discrimination Act in 1975; and the Equality Act 2010. Its justification of protecting an undisturbed royal succession that brought stability to the nation could no longer hide its real self-interest.

This repeated refusal to support equal inheritance of titles had the character of what depth psychologists, who concern themselves with the unconscious mind, call a "cultural complex," a simplistic, self-validating ideology, with knee-jerk emotional reactions that override fact and reason. Cultural complexes "are recurring, repetitive, and expressive of the same emotional and ideological content over and over again" with "a remarkable capacity—like a virus replicating—not only to repeat itself but also to make sure that whatever happens in the world fits into its pre-existing point of view."[5] As Lord David Pannick, QC, said, "The peerage cannot claim to be exempt from the basic principles of fairness that govern the rest of society."[6] Nevertheless, they were determined to do just that. The intensity of feeling and deeply rooted sense of entitlement driving them brought into historical focus the defensive anxiety that had used *Corbett v. Corbett* to manufacture trans eugenics. After all, male primogeniture had ridden roughshod over women for a thousand years; it wouldn't hesitate to do the same to April Ashley and a generation of trans people. Ewan knew these people, and he knew that unless he was declared definitively male, he, too,

would be ridden over. When Cousin John pushed him into conflict, Ewan knew that fighting for his right to belong in the primogeniture elite was the same as fighting for his and Patty's lives.

Watching the new Daughters' Rights movement search for
equality underlined for me how anachronistic male primogeniture
is in the twenty-first century. It makes women into insignificant
objects for circulation between men, their value limited by their
ability to produce male heirs. In this way, it reifies heterosexuality: male primogeniture is implicitly homophobic. Perpetuating
the idea of aristogenesis, male primogeniture posits that the best
and brightest men will inevitably produce more of the same: it is
instinctively eugenic. Politically, it is a very particular version of
what Judith Butler terms "homosociality," a network of male relationships designed specifically to exclude women from power and
influence, forcing sisters and daughters to live as acknowledged
inferiors. All of this creates the delusion of a "real woman": someone who accepts their inferiority and fulfills their only useful purpose—producing male heirs.

Cultural complexes are overwhelming to those who exist within
them, distorting their rational perceptions with emotional anxieties. In the lived realities of a morally conscious world there is
obviously no real reason why women can't occupy the same social
status or do the same jobs as men. Ewan knew this, and his life
demonstrated how empty primogeniture is. As a trans man, he
could carry the Forbes of Craigievar baronetcy equally as well
as a cis man, and since correction of his birth certificate did not
change him in any biological way, he could have done the same
if he had remained legally female—except that he would not have
been allowed to. His hidden case demonstrated what the European
courts recognized in P's case in 1996: the irrelevance of a person's
sex with regard to social responsibilities.

But seven years of women's thwarted attempts to end male primogeniture gave form to the invisible obstacle that kept getting
in the way of UK trans equality. As failure followed failure, I was
reading legislation, medical standards and media productions in

the light of Ewan's legacy. Its influence was particularly evident in the Gender Recognition Act (GRA) 2004.

The GRA recycled a failed private member's bill from 1995, written by April Ashley's solicitor, Terrence Walton, and entered in Parliament by Alex Carlile, MP.[7] It had been strongly criticized at the time for requiring trans people to be sterilized and giving them only limited rights and civil status via a "recognition certificate."[8] Reprising this failed bill, the GRA created a Gender Recognition Panel, which could issue a Gender Recognition Certificate to a trans person who produced medical evidence from two doctors that they had "gender dysphoria" and had "lived in the acquired gender throughout the period of two years." Panel and applicant never met: an anonymous bureaucracy decided trans people's lives. One doctor had to be a psychiatrist, and the expectation was that the other would be a surgeon, unless there were medical reasons why surgery—that is, sterilization—could not take place. As Lord Filkin put it in debate, "In cases where the person has not had surgery we would expect the panel not to treat that as prima facie evidence that there was doubt, but at least to question why surgery had not taken place."[9] This medical evidence was deemed crucial, since the panel's role was to gatekeep against people seeking to change legal sex "on a whim."[10] Of course, people often make life-changing decisions on a whim, such as marrying or conceiving children, but there is nothing whimsical about being trans. Trans people had to make a statutory declaration saying, "I intend to live full time as a male/female [delete as appropriate] until death," the overlapping redundancies of "to live," "full time" and "until death" indicating deep anxiety about trans people's social existence.[11] To prevent same-sex marriage, married trans people were required to divorce, thus ensuring that, as the House of Lords debate put it with unintended irony, "marriage is not collapsing."[12]

Instead of restoring trans people's equality, the GRA subjected them to multiple exclusions and disclosures. Trans people are excluded from rights to parenthood, inheritance of property, state benefits, competing in sports, marriage in church and, of course, inheritance of male primogeniture title. Their birth-assigned sex is used for so-called gender-specific offenses and must be disclosed at the request of courts, at the wish of the police, for social security and pension services, and at any other time the secretary of state sees fit.

The "masquerade" trope of "before and after" is prominent. For a moment in the act, it seems that is about to end. The GRA says, "If the acquired gender is the male gender, the person's sex becomes that of a man and, if it is the female gender, the person's sex becomes that of a woman."[13] It seems as if sex and gender must be the same thing, and like Ewan, trans people are who they know themselves to be. But although "sex" and "gender" are used interchangeably elsewhere in the GRA, in practice the government set out to separate them into a "real sex" and an "acquired gender." It did this through the birth certificate.

The natal birth certificate is not corrected, but kept as a permanent record. However, an additional faux birth certificate is issued, not in the person's sex but in their "acquired gender." Its logic is obvious: trans people are masquerading as real people, just as their faux birth certificates are masquerading as real ones. To underline this, from 2004 to 2011, faux birth certificates had one column less than real, natal birth certificates, making them instantly identifiable. That was rectified after intensive lobbying from trans communities, but it is still easy for any curious amateur genealogist or administrator to breach a trans person's privacy and discover their confidential medical history. Although the ECHR ruling in *Goodwin v. United Kingdom* guaranteed respect for private life, the personal histories of UK trans people are still unprotected from intrusion, invasion and violation. Perhaps more clearly than any other single factor, the absence of confidentiality, dignity and respect for private life epitomizes trans second-class citizenship in the UK.

Read against male primogeniture's cultural complex, it was suddenly obvious why the GRA separated trans people's "acquired gender" from their "real sex." When Ewan's generation corrected their birth certificates, doing so had no material impact on society at large. As Roberta Cowell discovered, negative consequences were limited to the individual, who might be outed and vilified by the press. But if someone assigned female at birth (as Ewan was) could make that correction and disturb the expected line of male inheritance, then within the tribalistic primogeniture cultural complex, the social consequences were dire, disastrous, apocalyptic. That extreme knee-jerk fantasy was pivotal, for the peers who experienced it were not bystanders but legislators, part of the framework of government, influential in their political parties, possessed of huge social capital, influence and connection.

Examining how medicine had responded to the legislation, I could see that it had a choice of working round the GRA or going with its ultra-right flow. US practice was still strongly influential on the UK, and its impulse had been to continue psychopathologizing trans people. In 2010, the World Professional Association for Transgender Healthcare (WPATH) declared its opposition to surgery or sterilization as requirements to change legal gender, and in 2018, it called for complete decoupling of medical requirements from legal processes for gender recognition.[14] But although its influential US-based *Standards of Care*, produced in 2012, recognized that being trans was "a matter of diversity, not pathology," trans people's pathway to endocrinology and elective surgery was still through mental health assessments carried out by psychiatrists. At the same time, psychiatry was extending its reach. Trans people who didn't require either endocrinology or surgery could now be "validated" by a psychiatrist, and intersex people, newly described degradingly as "Disorders of Sex Development," could claim "a subtype of gender dysphoria" if the surgeons who had operated on them as babies had assigned them to the wrong sex.[15] Coming ten years after the UK had recognized that being trans was not a mental illness, this extensive psychopathologization was a disturbing anachronism.

Psychiatry's inappropriate engagement with trans people was especially obvious in the American Psychiatric Association's new list of registered mental illnesses, DSM-5. It said that "gender nonconformity is not in itself a mental disorder," but it was included in DSM-5 "to get insurance coverage for the medical treatments."[16] Clearly, responsibility for care could have been passed from psychiatry to endocrinology and been equally eligible for US private health-insurance coverage. Instead, people without any mental illness were compelled to be treated by psychiatrists and to have mental health assessments. To a critical eye, APA's claim to trans advocacy was entirely self-serving.

In 2012, I had expressed similar concerns to the NHS about its first draft of a national service specification for gender identity services, which espoused a blanket policy of compulsory psychiatric referral.[17] With discussion and wider consultation, however, by 2014, the NHS had accepted that reconstructive surgery should be a matter of patient choice.[18] After almost half a century, the NHS policy of no-choice surgery and enforced sterilization had come to an end. But when the final specification for adult care was produced in 2018, it had to work uncomfortably round the GRA's separation of "real sex" and "acquired gender." It said:

> The term used to describe a discrepancy between birth-assigned sex and gender identity is gender incongruence; this term is preferable to the formerly used terms of gender identity disorder and transsexualism. Gender incongruence is frequently, but not universally, accompanied by the symptom of gender dysphoria.
>
> Gender dysphoria is not, in itself, a mental health condition.[19]

Here, "gender identity" is concerned with "gender incongruence," which may have "gender dysphoria" as a symptom. The aim is apparently to treat gender incongruence to remove gender dysphoria. Since gender dysphoria is not a mental health condition, its treatment is physiological, using endocrinology and/or reconstructive surgery, plus a range of physical therapies. In this reading, "gender" has taken on an anatomical identity and become medically indistinguishable from "sex." The clinical interventions are the same as for intersex conditions, so that "gender incongruence" has become a synonym for "intersex."

Awkwardly, though, the specification requires the renamed "gender dysphoria clinics" to have "expertise in mental healthcare needs that are specific to individuals with gender dysphoria." Since these apparently are not the general mental health needs that attend anyone undergoing life-changing healthcare—anxiety, depression, stress—what could they be? And why does an associated NHS circular to family doctors require diagnosis "by a health professional who specialises in gender dysphoria and has general clinical competence in diagnosis and treatment of mental or emotional disorders"?[20] This can only describe a psychiatrist, but since being trans is not a mental illness, they can have nothing to diagnose. And why is trans healthcare still located in NHS mental health trusts instead of in ordinary district general hospitals? None of this is rational. It is the NHS trying to make the best of a legal system that will not grant trans people equality, but which cannot reasonably explain why they must remain second-class citizens. The law was not keeping pace with social change.

By now there was a new, fourth wave of activists with a different life experience and set of expectations. They had grown up with globally interactive social media and a vocabulary in which "trans" was now an umbrella term for people who require medical support such as HRT, and trans* denoted those who required no medical intervention. Many of them identified as nonbinary, refusing the idea of "transition" from one sex to its opposite. NHS care from childhood onward was available, including hormone "blockers," prescribed after the start of puberty to delay its development and buy time for decision-making, while the charity Mermaids provided a national support community for trans kids and their parents. Fourth-wave activists set to work with YouTube, Facebook, Twitter, Snapchat, Instagram, blogs, vlogs and the rest of social media to build community, mobilize action and share ideas. This new generation expected to be able to make their own decisions about their own lives, and it was puzzling to them that a certificate might be needed to authenticate their bodies, and even more bizarre that the certificate would reduce their civil liberties.

In particular, the new activists were familiar with postfeminist and postcolonial literatures.[21] No respectable academic now believed in the old "nature or nurture" division, or the mind-body split of trans people having the brain of one binary sex and the body of the other. Instead, life was now understood as intersubjective: people live in a collective landscape formed by the experiences of others as well as by their own experiences. The experiencing self is the total bodily organism, mind and body, operating as a corporeal, material, sentient, sensuous whole. As Judith Butler put it, "Human bodies are not experienced without recourse to some ideality, some frame for experience itself. . . . This is as true for the experience of one's own body as it is for experiencing another."[22] Humans are constantly porous to an intertwined biological, social and psychological world, which is itself continually shifting and adjusting, whether it is the world of people, of flora and fauna, or of climate and terrain. In this fluid world, human variations are as inevitable as natural selection. Consequently, the division of humans into binary categories of man and woman was an obvious act of political power, quite separate from the reality of the world. Gender, race and class were all understood as historical products of patriarchy, colonialism and capitalism, and neither "sex" nor "gender" were irrevocably identifiable at birth, but might change over time.

In addition, the idea of patriarchy that had dominated 1970s radical feminism had long been critiqued as too blunt to explain complex social injustices, since it was "universalizing, homogenizing and essentializing of women's (and men's) experience."[23] The AIDS crisis had mobilized a new, non-separatist, "queer" critique, that "did not organise itself around identity categories but which instead took aim at the overarching social structures that marginalised the disease and its victims."[24] This supported a growing political awareness that power was decentered and that injustice and inequality were "intersectional," operating through combinations of race, age, disability, income, religion, sexuality and education, as well as sex and gender.

Bringing these new ideas together, in 2007 in the US, Julia Serano published *Whipping Girl*. Incisive and accessible, it defined a pervasive trans-misogyny that excluded trans men whose "expressions of maleness or masculinity are not targeted for ridicule—to do so would require one to question masculinity itself."[25] Trans-misogyny, Serano said:

> hyperfeminizes us by accompanying stories about trans women with pictures of us putting on makeup, dresses, and high-heeled shoes in an attempt to highlight the supposed "frivolous" nature of our femaleness, or by portraying trans women as having derogatory feminine-associated character traits such as being weak, confused, passive, or mousy.

At the same time it hypersexualizes trans women, positioning them as sex workers or sexual deceivers or sexual predators, belittling them and implying that "women as a whole have no worth beyond their ability to be sexualized."[26]

Trans-misogyny was fueled by a "cissexual gender entitlement" in which cis people "consider themselves to be the ultimate arbiters of which people are allowed to call themselves women and men." This inevitably leads to "cissexism," "the belief that transsexuals' identified genders are inferior to, or less authentic than, those of cissexuals."[27] Serano demanded that "gender-anxious cissexuals must begin to admit that the issues they have with our transsexual bodies stem directly from their own insecurities, from their fear of having their own genders and sexualities be brought into question." Complaints by a past generation of feminists, such as Germaine Greer, that trans women didn't ask cis women's permission to "belong to their sex," Serano said, expressed a "severe sense of gender entitlement."[28]

At the same time, though, the "masquerade" trope was still being peddled by film and television. The idea that Ewan wasn't a "real man" had been Cousin John's sole argument for taking him to court and the reigning idea in the backlash that followed. The

GRA had institutionalized it to protect male primogeniture—I could find no other rational explanation for such irrational legislation—and the media exploited it. Hayley Cropper, the stock "trans character" played by a cis actress in the UK's longest-running soap, *Coronation Street*, epitomized the masquerade motif. Faced with terminal cancer, she chose assisted suicide because "she was fearful that if she was too heavily sedated, she might become muddled, forget who she was—worse, become who she was," her natal identity of "Harold."[29] Shown in Australia, Canada, South Africa, New Zealand and the US, *Coronation Street*'s message was that even when trans people were not obviously monsters, they had monsters within them, Harold as a Mr. Hyde to Hayley's Dr. Jekyll: better they should be killed.

The US soap *Orange Is the New Black* gave a more positive view of its stock "trans character," Sophia Burset, played by trans woman Laverne Cox. But social hygiene still raised its head. Sophia is securely locked away in prison, part of a deviant, criminalized community, safe from contaminating "normal" people. It looked as if Amazon might do better in 2014 with its much-heralded *Transparent*. When the dramedy appeared, though, it was overshadowed by the double political gaffe of misgendering and "transface" (after "blackface"), with Maura, its stock "trans character" being played by cis man Jeffrey Tambor, but no cis parts being played by trans actors. Writer and producer Joey Soloway apologized fully, instituting a "Transfirmative Action Program" by employing trans people to act trans characters as well as write and shoot subsequent series.[30] But the fourth season was eclipsed by allegations of sexual misconduct by Tambor on set, which seemed to confirm all the worst representations of trans women as "really" being men, posing as women in order to wreak sexual violence. The series has moments of brilliance, especially in its acknowledgment of trans people's persecution in the Holocaust. However, like the UK's BBC2 sitcom *Boy Meets Girl*, in which all the most ignorantly offensive questions that trans women could be asked were trotted out as "entertainment," *Transparent* couldn't release itself from the "masquerade" trope of "before and after" or from a pervasive trans-misogyny. Both were lessons in the difficulties of realizing good intentions.

Against this cultural background, in 2014, US academics Susan Stryker and Paisley Currah launched the *Transgender Studies Quarterly* as the journal of record for the newly emergent academic field of transgender studies. Crossing disciplinary boundaries, the *TSQ* focused on trans people "as subjects of knowledge as well as objects of knowledge," who could "articulate critical knowledge from embodied positions that would otherwise be rendered pathological, marginal, invisible."[31] It rapidly provided fresh, original voices and understandings that spoke to a new generation of trans people.

Meanwhile, more transface was playing in the cinema in *The Danish Girl*, with Eddie Redmayne portraying first-wave trans activist Lili Elbe. As critic Rani Baker pointed out, "The structure, the beats, the emphasis on certain images" evoked "crossdresser erotica,"[32] a soft-porn exercise in simpering prettiness. The serious issue of trans people being forcibly detained in mental institutions was presented as a comic episode. It would be another two years before the stark poetry of Daniela Varga's performance in *A Fantastic Woman* (2017) recorded the abuse of power and the casual violence to which trans people are subject, and asserted her and their right to equality, self-definition and self-determination.

Again, this incessant media humiliation of trans people was something Ewan had recognized and done his best to avoid, correcting his birth certificate as discreetly as possible, driving his Land Rover over the hills to avoid journalists, holding his wedding in the greatest privacy, even allowing his degrading medical examination as a quid pro quo for a court hearing in private. He rejected what is now called "cis entitlement": cis people feeling they can and should sit in judgment on the lives of trans people. But Ewan's life in the period of trans equality up to 1970, and P's life in the subsequent period of trans eugenics, were ancient history to fourth-wave trans activists. To them, the kind of personally intrusive questions that had been usual in the past were "like so decades ago."[33]

It was startling to everyone, therefore, when in parallel with new, more sympathetic ideas, an aggressively transphobic movement suddenly emerged in 2013.

At that point, I was just starting to unpack the full significance of male primogeniture for trans people's lives. It was clear that something kept excluding trans people from social equality and from the same medical protections as everyone else. I knew that for all other UK citizens, the Mental Capacity Act 2005, the Mental Health Act 2007, and their attendant Deprivation of Liberty Safeguards regulated interactions with psychiatrists, protecting autonomy and the right to informed consent. But GICs still forced trans people into lengthy psychiatric interviews, effectively violating all of those legal protections. No one seemed to know why this was. The General Medical Council, which regulated the medical profession, refused to act or even to comment on trans people being placed outside the rules for psychiatric intervention that protect the rest of the population.[34] And when Caroline Lucas from the Green Party[35] and Liberal Democrat peer Joyce Gould[36] raised questions in Parliament, asking why trans people were obliged to undergo two years of psychiatric assessment even though being trans was not a mental illness, the government had no convincing answer. But the Scottish Transgender Alliance had published a major research study in which 62 percent of respondents said they had experienced intrusive and inappropriate questioning from clinicians at GICs. Because these gatekeepers were essential to accessing medicines and surgeries, patients knew they had no choice but to endure the abuse.[37]

However, private healthcare had always been an option for those who could afford it. Consequently there was widespread concern in the UK trans community when clinicians from NHS Charing Cross GIC wrongly accused private provider Dr. Richard Curtis, a trans man and former GP, of professional misconduct.[38] They had made similar accusations in the past about another popular

private provider, who had subsequently retired: as Liberal Democrat councilor Sarah Brown put it, "The doctors who seem to end
up in front of the GMC seem to be those ones who are generally
well regarded by trans people and who have a reputation for helping us when nobody else will."[39] She launched #TransDocFail and
received over two thousand tweets on the first day from trans people describing institutionalized abuse within the NHS:

> Doctor told me gay trans men don't exist. I am one. And this guy
> gives interviews in the press.
>
> My voice therapist wanted my old name. I think she wanted to
> refer to [oldname]'s voice. Kept talking about how "real women"
> speak.
>
> At a psychiatric assessment: "you can do what you want to your
> body, but you'll always know you're not *really* a woman."
>
> Got told off by CHx for not presenting as feminine enough
> when wearing jeans the Dr. was female and also wearing jeans.[40]

Jane Fae in the *Guardian* and Charlie Hallam in the *New Statesman* analyzed the tweets in feature articles.[41] They gave examples
of doctors laughing at patients during appointments, denying that
their condition existed and saying that they were "too ugly to merit
treatment." Subjected to a reign of fear, patients were "cowed into
silence" in case vindictive clinicians denied them essential medical
care. GICs were "slow, controlling and unsympathetic," and trans
patients were left in no doubt that their "multiple appointments
with psychiatrists" were "to assess the mental health and sanity of
those seeking treatment."

Giving detailed evidence to a major inquiry into the standards
of the British press, the group Trans Media Watch had reported
"horrific and humiliating treatment," "intrusive and mocking press
attention" and "degrading and exploitative coverage."[42] This was
immediately demonstrated by the media backlash to Fae's and Hallam's articles. Three days after they were published, the weekend
broadsheet the *Observer* printed a long, angry diatribe by popular

columnist Julie Burchill describing trans women as "a bunch of dicks in chicks' clothing," "screaming mimis" who had had their "nuts taken off (see what I did there?) by endless decades in academia," "bed-wetters in bad wigs" who had their "cock cut off and then plead special privileges as women," "shims, shemales," who "cut their dicks off and be more feminist than me."[43]

As trans activist Roz Kaveney commented, "Once you decide that some people's lives are not real, it becomes OK to abuse them."[44] A group of cis women commentators was forming, all treating trans people with what media critic Lili Loofbourow calls the disdain of "the male glance," which "looks, assumes, and moves on" and "feeds an inchoate, almost erotic hunger to know without attending, to omnisciently not-attend, to reject without taking the trouble of the analytical labor."[45] These were the so-called trans-exclusionary radical feminists (terfs),[46] a group that included Germaine Greer, who contributed to grossly offensive descriptions of trans women in a notorious 2015 interview: "Just because you lop off your d**k and then wear a dress doesn't make you a woman. I've asked my doctor to give me long ears and liver spots and I'm going to wear a brown coat but that won't turn me into a f*****g cocker spaniel."[47] In 2006, the Yogyakarta Principles had established international ethical and legal standards relating to sexual orientation and gender identity,[48] in 2013, the United Nations had identified trans and intersex people as marginalized groups that required special protection.[49] In 2014, Amnesty International had condemned their lack of legal recognition,[50] and the European Union had condemned their psychopathologization.[51] But neither Germaine Greer nor the rest of the terf lobby seemed to be aware of the historical inequities that had prompted these major position statements.

Commenting in the *Guardian*, Lucy Mangan pointed to the illogicality of terf trans-misogyny: the absence of comment about trans men, whom the terfs presumably viewed as female and would oblige to use women-only spaces; the problematics of viewing trans women as occupying male privilege when "the thing that usually brings privilege has brought you nothing but grief"; and the "hundreds of infinitely more pressing issues" of social injustice eclipsed by this attack on trans people.[52] Terfs aimed to exclude trans people from the equality and autonomy enjoyed by other free citizens, and in particular, to exclude trans women from recognition as "real women." They positioned themselves as secular fundamentalists, cultish and doctrinaire like the right-wing fundamentalist religious groups that had opposed the GRA a decade earlier, validating their views with the tag of "radical feminism," using 1960s slogans as "proof texts" and recycling views and values that had been discredited a generation earlier.

Feminist academics expressed general concerns about "right-wing populist claims and new nationalisms, often interwoven with influence from the religious right," which were "linked to attacks particularly on the reproductive rights of women and are threatening to the legitimacy of LGBTQI+ communities."[53] In fact, as Mark Gevisser points out in his book *The Pink Line*, terf ideology is "led by American Christian conservatives." Their "constant message" is that supporting trans equality was "voting to allow transgender women into the women's bathroom. Women are not safe; girls are not safe; your family members are not safe."[54] Ideologically, their campaign reprised the homophobic "predatory males" slur formerly used against gay men. It was the spiritual inheritor of the transphobic Anglo-American axis formed in 1970 by Money, Green and Randell at their International Symposium in London:

the conservative Evangelical movement, having been "on a losing streak across America" with its "tired hymn sheet on the perils of homosexuality failing hard against the 'love is love' mantra" of the marriage equality movement, had found a new way of fighting the culture wars: against transgender rights. And now, in a "surreal" transfer, some British feminists were importing from across the water an argument hatched by right-wing American fundamentalists.[55]

Now, though, the terf campaign was being disseminated globally by the digital revolution, and attacking trans people had become "the ideological clearing house for cooperation among all conservative Christians, including Russian Orthodox ones in Eastern Europe and Evangelical ones in the Americas." As Mark Gevisser puts it, terfs "telescoped all the issues against which social conservatives fought, from birth control through abortion and gay marriage to sexuality education" into its attack on trans people, setting ideas of "traditional values" and "natural order" against those of "modernity" to create a moral panic in which trans people were the new "scapegoats or bogeymen."[56]

Part of the difficulty of opposing this new transphobia was that by now, the term "gender" had come to mean different things in different contexts. To the person in the street, "gender" and "sex" were the same thing, interchangeable on countless forms and documents. In contrast, for cultural theorists, "gender" was a complex, fruitful, multiple-meaning, inherently fluid state from which biological, political, social, psychological and philosophical meanings and identities emerged. Meanwhile, medicine continued to use "gender" as a clinical diagnosis, its language wobbling between deviation, disorder and dysphoria. However, as the GRA demonstrated, the law used "gender" to continue the inequality and second-class citizenship that were Ewan's unwilling legacy.

Trying to bring some clarity to these issues, in 2016, Parliament's new Women and Equalities Select Committee published a major report on transgender equality, calling for both the Gender Recognition Act and the Equality Act to be updated, requiring "a root-and-branch review" of an NHS that was still "letting down trans people," and proposing an "X" option for passports like that being used successfully in Australia.[57] Its recommendations became part of an LGBT Action Plan, which included a public consultation on reform of the GRA to introduce the self-declaration system used successfully in Ireland, Argentina, Belgium, Brazil, Colombia, Denmark, Malta, Norway, Pakistan, and Portugal.

Terf ideology had by then cemented its Anglo-American identity. A new far-right administration had taken power in the US, under President Donald Trump, with a new isolationism, driven by a fear of difference, expressed as xenophobia, white supremacism and belligerent self-aggrandizement. It was epitomized by Trump's tweet: "if Turkey does anything that I, in my great and unmatched wisdom, consider to be off limits, I will totally destroy and obliterate the Economy of Turkey (I've done before!)."[58] Ultra-conservatism found sympathizers in far-right fundamentalist Christian groups and in terf groups, and trans people rapidly became a target for Trump's administration. Advances made under the Barack Obama presidency were reversed, with a "bathroom ban" on trans people in some states, trans people banned from the armed services, removal of guidance that protected trans students and plans to remove healthcare for trans people.[59]

In the UK, Prime Minister Boris Johnson echoed Trump's isolationism. Where Trump pledged to build a wall between Mexico and the US in order to "Make America Great Again," Johnson promised to make Britain "the greatest place on earth" and to remove the UK from the European Union, no matter what the economic or social cost. Both nations seemed gripped by a crisis of identity, grappling to find something distinctively "American" or "British" in societies that were multiethnic, multilingual, and multifaith. Ironically, the permeability to new influences, cultures, ideas and people that historically defined both the UK and the US was being denied in a politics of intolerance. It was as if the colonial eye was reasserting its violent gaze in a swaggering insularity toward other nations and a new narrow-mindedness toward its own citizens. This supported the terf moral panic about trans people, especially its misogynistic ideal of a "real woman." It was uncomfortably reminiscent of the *Systema Naturae* that had fueled the slave trade, denied women equality, criminalized gay men and ultimately driven the Holocaust. The quality of compromise and acceptance that was supposed to embody "Britishness" and the US's claim to "liberty and justice for all" had vanished.

As contemporary sociologists recorded, in 2018, the UK government's public consultation on GRA reform became a terf rallying point:

Leading up to the consultation, multiple campaign organisations were founded to specifically resist self-determination as the mechanism by which birth certificate sex marker can be changed. Organisations including A Woman's Place UK (WPUK), Fair Play For Women (FPFW), Mayday4Women, We Need To Talk and the Lesbian Rights Alliance held meetings across the UK, building a new trans-exclusionary feminist movement that also rapidly expanded online through digital platforms, such as Twitter and the Mumsnet "feminist chat" message board.[60]

This latest terf campaign propagated moral panic by manufacturing doubt, turning both the present and the past into a blur, so that nothing is quite certain, and fact, reason and memory become impossible to grasp. It was demonstrated on *Woman's Hour*, a cornerstone of BBC Radio's weekday light entertainment since 1946. The program on October 2018, was devoted to a discussion about the proposed reform of the GRA to introduce a system of self-determination like those operating successfully in other countries.[61] A lengthy, expensive process involving intrusive medical reports would be replaced by a simple administrative process in line with international human rights guidance. At the start of *Woman's Hour*, listeners heard a solicitor explain to the presenter that use of single-sex space was regulated by the Equality Act 2010, not the GRA. They then heard the program discuss at length whether and how reforming the GRA would jeopardize single-sex space. Finally, listeners heard the presenter's surprise when the same solicitor told them again that this fantasized relationship between the GRA and single-sex space was wholly incorrect. It seemed impossible that the program's researchers were unable to establish this simple legal fact before *Woman's Hour* was broadcast and felt like an object lesson in how "false news" is propagated.

Some terf attacks were direct and encouraged by the media. In a 2018 television "debate," independent television company Channel 4 promoted intimidation, encouraging terfs in the studio audience to shout "penis, penis, penis" whenever trans women on the debating panel spoke.[62] Its orchestrated bullying suggested that a new level of violence was replacing reasonable discussion.

Watching these events unfold as I was writing about Ewan, I saw the press and internet filled with misconceptions about the trans experience. Recognizing why Ewan's case had been hidden was easy, for recent history was full of cover-ups and their victims.[63] Understanding them was simply a matter of asking, "Cui bono?"—Who benefits? But making sense of terf transphobia was more difficult.

A key misconception was that there had suddenly been a huge explosion in young women wishing to transition. This was built on two other misconceptions: first, that formerly it was people assigned as male at birth who wanted to transition; and second, that transition was always to an opposite sex. In reality, there are hardly any numerical data about trans people. Until very recently, they were not included in the medical record and even now data are not collected in a way that is consistent enough to make valid comparisons between groups or countries. Historically, in Ewan's generation it was assumed that trans people were all trans men, with trans women a rarity. Then, in 1970, April's publicity had made trans men invisible, so that trans people were assumed to be mainly women who were "really" floridly psychotic gay men. The law and medicine excluded a nonbinary life, so that we have no idea how many nonbinary people there would have been, had they been allowed to exist. However, statistically, it makes sense that a usual human diversity should be present across the board, and socially, it is reasonable that all young people should feel equally empowered to decide who they are, however they were assigned at birth. The "sudden explosion" meant only that trans boys now felt more empowered and that consequently the public was taking more notice of them. A similar "sudden explosion" had taken place in Black, Asian, and minority ethnic (BAME) trans people, who had previously been unnoticed in the UK because they had been additionally disempowered and silenced by institutionalized racism.

A further misconception was a new piece of pseudo-medicine, "rapid onset of gender dysphoria," supposedly a form of "social contagion" in which "multiple or even all members of a friend group . . . became transgender-identified at the same time."[64] The historical echoes go back even further here, to the criminalizing of gay men as diseased and degenerate, and the idea of "the predatory homosexual," which was used to oppose their decriminalization. It was "a deliberate attempt to weaponize scientific-sounding language to dismiss mounting empirical evidence of the benefits of transition," manufactured by "parents from transantagonistic websites," in "an attempt to circumvent existing research demonstrating the importance of gender affirmation."[65] Unfortunately, the idea of "rapid onset gender dysphoria" was picked up, supported, and publicized by influential commentator J. K. Rowling.[66] However, in reality, gay, lesbian and trans young people make friends with each other because they are gay, lesbian or trans, not the other way round, just as they group together for countless other reasons.

But some parents have never been happy with having LGBTI children, and there have always been clinicians willing to provide preventative "cures," from Krafft-Ebing onward. The problem is not with trans children but with the toxic dynamics created by parents who can't accept their children for who they are.

Terf misconceptions are often interwoven with moving narratives of personal distress from people who have suffered violence and sexual assault. Unsurprisingly, their common psychological defense is to exclude trans women from women's bathrooms and changing rooms to prevent violence against women, but in reality, if anyone, trans or cis, male, female or nonbinary, wants to walk into a women-only space to assault women, they can do so. Having a gender identity certificate, however acquired, makes such assault neither more or less possible and certainly not less illegal. What is happening here is the psychotherapeutic coping strategy of transference: feelings about their abuser being transferred onto trans people, a survivor's attempt to deal with trauma. With unfortunate irony, distressed people who are unaware of the traumatic history of the trans experience are perpetuating a cycle of abuse. Terf attacks and the media coverage that supports them force many trans people to reexperience their powerlessness, their abuse and the institutionalized humiliation of their second-class citizenship.

Historically, the position seems to have substituted trans-misogyny for second-wave feminism's homophobic anxiety about lesbians, critiqued forty years ago in Adrienne Rich's "Compulsory Heterosexuality and Lesbian Existence."[67] Rich described the erasure and distortion of lesbian lives caused by the politics of feminist heterosexuality, at a point of alt-right political growth much like today's. Compulsory cisgenderism seems to have replaced compulsory heterosexuality as a new beachhead for intolerance. And disturbingly, terf insistence that trans people are too dangerous to be treated equally echoes the Jim Crow laws that legalized US racial segregation on the grounds that African Americans were not "fit to be free" like white people. These two currents of intolerance met at Speakers' Corner in Hyde Park, London, where on August 31, 2020, terf activists "mocked and shouted at Black Lives Matter protesters," who were marching against police brutality.[68] It made apparent "transphobic feminism's increasingly close association with reactionary ethnonationalism."[69]

Transference exaggerates emotions and negative transference may express itself as violent fantasy. As sociologist Sally Hines indicates, terf fantasy is about reimposing a male-female binary on trans people and policing it by reference to their genitalia.[70] People who might be expected to oppose body-shaming about, for example, pregnancy, breastfeeding, rape, abortion, sex, sexuality, race, religious practices, disability, weight, age, muscularity and height began to propagate "crotch-shaming," focusing on trans women in a kind of virtual upskirting. This misogynistic fantasy of genital correctness ignores trans men, intersex people and armed forces personnel with genital injuries from the improvised explosive devices used in conflict zones such as Afghanistan. It also ignores the impossible question of how such a measure could be policed.

Moral panics spread easily at times of social anxiety. Disseminated by what columnist Gaby Hinsliff terms "the roiling cesspit of social media" as the Covid-19 pandemic spread, more people were drawn into this terf fantasy.[71] Even the UK government fell prey, replacing its planned reform of the GRA with proposals to reduce trans equality by introducing:

> the "protection" of single-sex spaces (erroneously implying that the GRA has or would have interplay with who may use them); "maintaining the proper checks and balances in the system" (implying a gatekeeping model for trans adults' autonomy); and "protecting" under 18s from "decisions they could make," raising serious concerns regarding the already highly constrained ability of trans people under 18 to access medical care related to gender, but also an implicit threat to bodily autonomy for all young people.[72]

These kinds of antagonism and misinformation dismayed liberal feminists such as the famous lawyer and writer Helena Kennedy, who won P's case in the European courts:

> I greatly regret that the transgender issue has divided some women. For any of us who have worked with those transgender people who have been raped and abused, sacked from employment or rejected by family and friends, who have lived from childhood with the emotional pain of having the wrong identity, we know these are questions of human rights and compassion.[73]

But human rights and compassion seemed in short supply for trans people in both the US and the UK. In May 2020, the US Department of Education administration issued a letter requiring schools to ban trans students from participating in school sports, and in July 2020, Trump finalized "the extensive rollback of health care discrimination rules, to eliminate the protections for transgender people experiencing discrimination in health care settings."[74] But at the time of writing, the new president is Joe Biden, who supported the career of the first trans state senator, Sarah

McBride. On November 20, 2020, the International Transgender Day of Remembrance, commemorating those trans people lost to transphobic violence, Biden tweeted:

> To transgender and gender-nonconforming people across America and around the world: from the moment I am sworn in as president, know that my administration will see you, listen to you, and fight for not only your safety but also the dignity and justice you have been denied.[75]

In any event, Trump was unable to carry out his ongoing proposals to remove trans people's protection from discrimination by homeless shelters and federally funded housing services before leaving office in January 2021, and President Biden remains committed to restoring and advancing trans equality in the US.

In the UK, a new terf attack focused on trans children's healthcare. NHS care had fallen badly behind for children and adolescents: in 2020, there was a twenty-seven-to-twenty-eight-month waiting list for a first appointment at one of the two NHS gender identity clinics (both with the same provider), which have to cope with the whole country's needs. That delay in care is exacerbated by a long diagnostic process, which continues to be psychologically based, before a child can see an endocrinologist and get access to medical treatment. Since 1998, the approved medical pathway has been to provide hormone "blockers" for children (young people under the age of sixteen), after they have reached Tanner Stage 2 of puberty, when they are persistently and consistently aware that they have been assigned the wrong sex.[76] Not until they are sixteen years old, when they are legally "adolescents" rather than "children," will they be considered for cross-sex hormones. However, the time lag in gaining appointments combined with the lengthy diagnostic process means that parents and children now face the same concern that Gwendolen and Ewan faced: that treatment will not be timely enough to avoid the trauma of going through the wrong puberty.

But these are not the concerns of the terf lobby. Rather, they oppose affirmative treatment for young people, advocating instead a range of aversion therapies based on the idea that children and adolescents are not competent to make such decisions about their future. For trans and gender-diverse feminists, "these 'debates' are waged on our lives and bodies, as well as those of our friends, colleagues, and loved ones."[77]

Most recently, matters came to a head with a judicial review of UK child and adolescent gender services.[78] But this was not because they were violating legal waiting times and thus causing unnecessary suffering to children and parents. Rather, it was actuated by complaints by two people, a twenty-three-year-old who began taking puberty blockers when she was sixteen but then started "detransitioning" in her early twenties, and the mother of a sixteen-year-old who is waiting for treatment. Their shared claim was that children were not capable of giving informed consent to medical treatment. The case, known as *Bell v. Tavistock*, raises the important issues of "regret" and competence to consent.

Regret rates are a matter of fact of medical life. The regret rate for prostate surgery is between 17 percent to 47 percent of patients, for example, but the legal principle of informed consent means that such regret is the responsibility of the patient and it does not invalidate the medical process.[79] This principle of informed consent is so important to individual autonomy that it is applied even where patient choice may result in death, such as choosing not to undergo chemotherapy for cancer treatment, or refusing a blood transfusion for religious reasons. In the case of children and adolescents, it is enshrined in the principle of "Gillick competence," that young people "are presumed to have sufficient capacity to decide on their own medical treatment, unless there's significant evidence to suggest otherwise" and that consequently "children under the age of 16 can consent to their own treatment if they're believed to have enough intelligence, competence and understanding to fully appreciate what's involved in their treatment."[80]

However, in *Bell v. Tavistock*, the court decided that trans children under sixteen are not competent to give consent to the administration of puberty blockers, arguing that it is doubtful that they could understand and weigh the long-term risks and consequences. It further advised that adolescents should be regarded as "cases where the authorisation of the court should be sought prior to commencing the clinical treatment." The two main reasons given by the court for its decision were that "when decision making is 'hot' (i.e. more emotional), under-18-year-olds make less rational decisions than when the responses are made in a colder, less emotional context"; and that the administration of puberty blockers "is, in our view, properly described as experimental treatment." It required firstly, a formal clinical review of the care plans of all trans children and adolescents, irrespective of their age, and then a formal decision by a court before any of them could be prescribed puberty blockers. The question was ignored as to what useful contribution such a court could possibly hope to make where child, parents and doctors all agree on the right course of treatment.

It was a shock that a particular group of children could be identified as so different from all other children that the Gillick principle couldn't apply to them, and surprising that the Court issued clinical guidance without inviting submissions from the many regulators that ensure best medical practice in this area: the National Health Service England; the National Institute for Health and Care Excellence; the Care Quality Commission; the General Medical Council; the World Professional Association for Transgender Health; the Endocrine Society; the Academy of Medical Royal Colleges; the Royal College of Physicians; the Royal College of Paediatrics and Child Health; or the independent Cass Review of gender identity services for children and adolescents, which was announced a fortnight before the *Bell v. Tavistock* hearing. Equally incongruously, a routine inspection by the Department of Health's Care Quality Commission, a month later, found that although pressures from the Tavistock's huge waiting list of 4,600 patients had caused some procedural inadequacies, "staff treated young people with compassion and kindness" and provided "medical treatments that were consistent with good practice."[81] Unsurprisingly, therefore, "feedback from young people and families currently being seen at the service was overwhelmingly positive about the care and support staff had provided."[82] The issue seemed to be NHS economics and transphobia, not good medicine. As the chief executive of the Tavistock put it, "The Gender Identity Development Service has found itself in the middle of a cultural and political battleground."[83]

From a historical perspective, the judgment seemed like a return to 1970 and Lord Ormrod's pseudo-medicine in the April Ashley case, *Corbett v. Corbett*. It collapsed together the two quite separate clinical interventions of puberty blockers and cross-sex hormones, treating the multiple clinical pathways that individualize patient care as if they were a single, monolithic, inexorable route. Its assertion that the administration of puberty blockers represents an "experimental" treatment obviously ignored the medical and scientific definition of what constitutes "experimental treatment," as well as ignoring the long-established, well-authenticated international evidence of their use in the treatment of trans children and adolescents.[84] A blanket decision based on one applicant's regret and another third party's anxiety seemed to be bad law at best, ignoring the hundreds of patients who had benefited from the same treatment, and compromising the care pathways of those who were midway through or waiting for treatment. At the time of this writing, the case has gone to appeal.

But there was a social concern as well as a medical one. The Gillick competence principle was established because another anxious mother, Mrs. Gillick, wanted a court to prevent her daughter, who was under sixteen, from being prescribed the contraceptive pill. Her application was refused on the grounds that the girl could understand the doctor's advice, that she was very likely to begin or continue having sexual intercourse with or without contraception, and that the girl's best interests required the doctor to prescribe contraception, even without parental knowledge or consent. In other words, it is a principle that applies directly to women's reproductive rights and bodily autonomy.

In fact, the applicant in *Bell v. Tavistock*, Keira Bell, was already sixteen years old when she consented to hormone blockers, the point at which UK citizens can legally consent to medical treatment, such as contraception, the "morning after" pill and termination of pregnancy, as well as to sexual activity. All of these are "hot" and "emotional" areas of decision-making, about which the court believed under-eighteen-year-olds make less rational decisions. Positioning Keira Bell as a woman who should have been protected from her own poor decision-making seemed like a gateway to a potential attack on a broader spectrum of women's and girls' rights to make autonomous decisions about their own bodies. Concerns that trans people are being used as stalking-horses for a wider right-wing ideological attack seemed worryingly real.

By 2020, terf websites dedicated to denying the validity and authenticity of trans experience had become well-organized campaigners. The religious "proof-texts" that their evangelical Christian members use to define trans people as morally deficient are bolstered by secular fundamentalists' assertions that trans people are not "real men" or "real women." They assert that being trans is not part of divine or natural design, catastrophize about the effect of trans people on society, and try to popularize inaccurate information about trans lives. So, for example, to try to gain prestige by association for their transphobic views, one terf "false news" strategy claimed that the famous retail store Marks & Spencer no longer allowed trans people to use changing rooms appropriate to their gender but required them to use those related to their birth-assigned sex. In fact, Marks & Spencer have a strongly trans-affirmative policy, including supporting non-binary people's right to choose which changing cubicle they use. Another terf "false news" strategy claimed that "medical evidence" showed that transitioning was likely to lead directly to suicide. Others colonized general websites, including the Facebook forum for listeners to BBC's Radio 4, one of the most popular UK radio channels. Trans community groups continue to do their best to provide reasoned, rational responses to what has developed into a violent propaganda war.

At least some of the immediate devastation of UK trans children's healthcare was remedied by a family court decision in March 2021.[85] Because *Bell v. Tavistock* only removed the capacity to consent from children, it was possible to argue that if the child's wish was supported by their parents, then puberty blockers could be administered without the need for a court decision. The judge found in favor of AB, CD, and XY, the parents and child who brought the case, but it still meant that "trans children without parental support—who are especially vulnerable—will remain disadvantaged" and that there still existed "a profound rolling back of the rights of the child."[86] A century after Ewan's gender-affirmative treatment, today's trans children are forced into the same anxieties that he experienced, with similar dangerous consequences. Getting medical support, which should be automatic, is hardly less difficult for today's parents and children than it was for Gwendolen and Ewan. For this reason, many parents who can afford to do so decline NHS care and opt instead for either a UK private provider, such as Gender GP, or travel to the US for care at Boston Children's Hospital.

In particular, terf campaigning has drawn attention away from the slow but steady forward movement of the larger UK medical community. On September 15, 2020, the British Medical Association voted to support trans and nonbinary people's right to receive healthcare, access settings and gendered spaces, and to gain legal recognition by witnessed, sworn statement, as well as supporting the principle of Gillick competence for children and young people.[87] Two weeks later, the General Medical Council published new guidance on decision-making and consent, which gave similar support to trans people's right to informed consent.[88] Effectively, it means that trans people do not have to be mentally or psychologically tested to make sure that their decisions about their bodies are rational ones. The GMC guidance came into force on November 9, 2020, and it will be interesting to see how it affects the role of psychiatrists in adult gender identity clinics and whether, finally, it might spell the end of the institutionalized psychopathologization of trans people.

However, UK law is not keeping pace with this social change. In what LGBTI lobbying group Stonewall described as "a shocking failure in leadership," Boris Johnson has rowed back from his party's pledge to a thorough reform of the GRA, as recommended by the government's 2018 LGBT Action Plan, and instead "has put forward only minimal administrative changes. . . . They don't go anywhere near far enough toward meaningfully reforming the act to make it easier for all trans people to go about their daily lives."[89] In response, the Women and Equalities Committee launched a public consultation into GRA reform, which is expected to report in 2021. Meanwhile, the GRA continues to undermine the legal status of trans people, epitomized by the issue of parenthood.

It is now commonplace for trans men to give birth, but they are not allowed to be named as the father on their child's birth certificate: indeed, if they are married to a cis woman who gives birth, they are still not allowed to be named as father, but must instead use the term "parent," otherwise reserved for the second female partner in a lesbian relationship. In April 2020, over twenty years after the case of X, Y and Z prevented trans men from being named as father on their children's birth certificates, the Court of Appeal found against a similar application from Freddy McConnell. The difference was that Mr. McConnell had a Gender Recognition Certificate, making it clear that he is legally male, which was not available to X in 1997. The case is now proceeding to the Supreme Court for decision.[90]

Contemporary feminist politics tells us that our way of perceiving bodies is central to political and social transformation, not least because, traditionally, power has been structured to fit the cis-male heterosexuality of a white, able-bodied, elite. Yet ever since Ewan's case, UK law has had difficulty coming to terms with trans bodies. Taking this as my starting point, I asked myself what legal steps were needed to ensure the traumas Ewan and April had undergone are not perpetuated for another generation. If the primogeniture clique's petulant "Daddy promised me a title" was ignored, how might fifty years of trans eugenics be ended?

It seemed that the UK had an imperfect but pragmatic solution ready to hand, which would at least make coherent sense of the conflicted distinctions between legal, medical and social "sex" and "gender." Trans people requiring medical support might simply rejoin intersex people in the category of "sex," and allowing both groups to correct their birth certificates would place them into the Equality Act's protected characteristic of "sex." People who did not require medical support but whose social performance (dress, grooming, name) might be masculine or feminine or androgynous, irrespective of their assigned sex at birth, would fall under the Equality Act's protected characteristic of "gender reassignment." After all, employers have enough dress codes and health-and-safety regulations to meet their needs, and everything else is surely a matter for individual freedom. Coupled with a third, nonbinary option on birth certificates, and a restoration of the gender-free passports that were issued in the 1960s,[91] this would be a first small step forward for society. Of course, separating sex and gender in this way would still be an absurdity, because biology and culture are not as simple as that. But at least it would be a logical absurdity rather than the present illogical one. And it would mean that the clique of aristocrats bent on preserving male primogeniture would be obliged to make a rational defense of their position to a wider public. All of this could form a practical, provisional starting point for developing a more complex equality.

As the French philosopher Luce Irigaray puts it, equal citizenship should be "a function of being born, actually and not abstractly" so that everyone "is, from birth, a full citizen."[92] People are not born equal: the equality that makes everyone "a full citizen" is something that has to be constructed, intersubjectively, collaboratively, in order to arrive at what Irigaray calls "the condition of a true democracy." This means accepting that there is no single truth about what it is to be "man" or "woman" or "intersex" or "trans" or "nonbinary." Rather, their meanings are "locally, culturally, socially and historically specific . . . mutually constituted alongside other categories of social identity."[93] As the advocate general said in P's case twenty-five years earlier, "The law cannot cut itself from society as it actually is."[94] Achieving such a democracy is not just an LGBTI issue, therefore, but one that defines everyone's humanity and urgently affects a future threatened by climate crisis and the global economic downturn created by the Covid-19 pandemic. Trans equality is a yardstick for society's ability to change, for its continued existence or its extinction. Denying trans people's equal humanity is denying everyone's humanity and reducing all our possibilities for future life.

Trans people are still fighting Ewan's battle, rejecting or actively creating vocabularies and categories through which to form and communicate their lives. Like Ewan, many do not think of themselves as trans, while for others an explicit trans identity is crucial, and others still prefer one of the fifty options for describing their gender that Facebook offered from 2014 onward, or a term of their own.[95] Similarly, reconstructive surgery may be crucial for some trans people and unwanted by others. What is important is that trans people should be as free as everyone else to define and live their lives, with the same access as cis people to supportive healthcare, legislation, education and social affirmation. In practice, this means that the only information about themselves that trans people—or anyone—are obliged to give in a social setting is their name and perhaps their pronouns. Any other question about their lives or experience is not just impertinent: it is part of the systemic gendered oppression that forms a major obstacle to true democracy.

Today information, comment, explanation and debate are available from fourth-wave trans activists themselves, on blogs, vlogs, websites, tweets and video posts, internationally accessible, and plentiful enough to need guides like "Top 100 Transgender Blogs and Websites."[96] Although trans confessional is still a popular genre, it no longer follows the *True Story* "sin, suffer, repent" format. Young, new writers position themselves as autonomous, not sinful, see their suffering as the result of public ignorance and intolerance, and have no intention of repenting their life choices.[97]

Instead of defensive apologies, they offer education and explanation in simple guides such as *Transgender 101* and *The ABCs of LGBT+*.[98] Names like Paris Lees, CN Lester, Munroe Bergdorf, Fox and Owl, Rhyannon Styles, Juliet Jacques, Tammy Cravit and Sarah McBride have become well-known as commentators and opinion-makers. They work within an ethos where nonbinary sex and gender fluidity are taken for granted and ignorance about trans lives seems ridiculous and willful.

It's been fifty years since Ewan's case was the tipping point for the removal of trans equality, and twenty-five since P's case began its restoration. Both of them paid the price of personal anguish. Victory is for the generations who come after, not for the people who win it.

PICTURE SOURCES

The cis gaze at images of trans people is rarely neutral. Regrettably, its cultural impulse is still often toward "you would never guess" or "oh yes, you can tell," prurient and patronizing, implicitly destructive of trans people's subjectivity and autonomy. The implication is that this is something worth looking at, someone who is more or less successfully masquerading as a "real person" without actually having that status. Unfortunately, therefore, the purpose of trans images is generally to disauthenticate. With this in mind, all of the images of Ewan that are included here are taken either from those he himself was happy to have published, or those his family approved. However, only one negative survives, a Victorian one of Auld Sir Wullie, William and the Auld Laird outside the door of Craigievar Castle, taken around 1895. The originals of the images of himself that Ewan published in his memoirs, *The Aul' Days* and *The Dancers of Don*, were lost when his publisher went down with the Maxwell empire. Aberdeen University Press as it exists now is a separate entity from the Aberdeen University Press that was part of the Pergamon Group owned by Maxwell, and it has no records remaining from those days. Consequently, eleven of the twelve images reproduced in the text are copies from secondary sources, some from black-and-white photographs, some from print sources, and some from the internet. I am grateful to photographer Sara Hannant (sarahannant.com) for doing the best possible with difficult material, so that we can see Ewan as he saw himself.

1. The Christmas costume party at Fintray Manor: reproduction of a black-and-white image kindly provided by Iain Stoddart.
2. The Flitting: reproduction from *The Aul' Days*, p. 35.
3. Early-nineteenth-century lithograph of Craigievar Castle: reproduction of an engraving kindly provided by Gabriel Forbes-Sempill.
4. The 17th, 19th and 18th Lords Sempill: Auld Sir Wullie, William, and the Auld Laird, from a Victorian negative kindly provided by Gabriel Forbes-Sempill.
5. Ewan's parents outside Craigievar Castle: reproduction from a black-and-white image kindly provided by Gabriel Forbes-Sempill.
6. Ewan at the Lonach: author's photograph of the original from *The Sketch*, August 30, 1933, p. 72.
7. Ewan's picture in his medical student yearbook: author's photograph of the original document at the University of Aberdeen.
8. Ewan with Bran at Brux, September 1952: reproduction from *The Aul' Days*,

p. 56. The name has been changed from the original's "Stolen Day" to "Bran" to reflect the family's memory of Ewan and his dog.

9. Ewan and Patty's wedding: reproduction from *The Aul' Days*, p. 66.
10. Margaret with her Shetland ponies: reproduction from a black-and-white image kindly provided by Gabriel Forbes-Sempill.
11. Joan, Margaret and the Queen Mother in 1963: reproduction of Jim Love's award-winning photograph printed in the *Aberdeen Press and Journal*, December 12, 1963, by kind permission of Aberdeen Journals.

NOTES

Key to Legal Abbreviations

Further useful guides to law reports and to legal abbreviations can be found at the University of Oxford Faculty of Law and the University of Cardiff:

https://www.law.ox.ac.uk/legal-research-and-mooting-skills-programme/law-reports

http://www.legalabbrevs.cardiff.ac.uk

AC	Appeal Cases
All ER	All England Reports
EAT	Employment Appeal Tribunal
ECHR	European Court of Human Rights: Reports of the Judgments and Decision
ECJ	European Court of Justice
EHRR	European Human Rights Reports
EWCA Civ	England and Wales Court of Appeal (Civil Division)
EWHC	England and Wales High Court
EWHC (Fam)	England and Wales High Court (Family Division)
FamCA	Family Court of Australia
Fla. Ct. App	Florida District Court of Appeal
IRLR	Industrial Relations Law Report
Kan.	Kansas Reports
NSWLR	New South Wales Law Reports
N.Y. Sup. Ct.	New York Supreme Court Reports
NZLR	New Zealand Law Reports
Ohio Misc.	Ohio Miscellaneous Reports
RFL	Reports of Family Law (Canada)
SALR	South African Law Reports
SLT (Sh Ct)	Scots Law Times, Sheriff Court Reports
Sol J	Solicitors' Journal

Prologue: Finding Ewan

1 In the UK, until October 28, 1996, unconsented penile penetration of a trans woman's vagina counted only as sexual assault (if it was prosecuted at all—after all, why did she have a vagina if she didn't want a man to use it, was a

general view) and not as rape. It was one of the reasons many women didn't disclose their trans history.

2 Author's note of telephone conversation with Madeleine Rees, February 16, 1996. (Author's private collection.)

3 The Supreme Court (formerly the House of Lords) is the most senior court in England and Wales. Below it is the Court of Appeal, and below that the High Court. At the base of the court structure are two pairs of junior courts: Crown Courts, which are fed by Magistrates' Courts, and County Courts, which are fed by Tribunals.

4 Primogeniture literally means "first born." Male-line primogeniture passes titles and estates solely and wholly through firstborn males, excluding the female line, so that if there is no male heir, the title becomes dormant. This is distinct from male-preference primogeniture systems like the British monarchy, in which succession *preferably* goes through firstborn males. So, Queen Elizabeth II became monarch only because her father left no living brothers who could legitimately inherit the throne, and no deceased brothers with surviving legitimate descendants.

5 Daughters' Rights: Legislation to End Discrimination, https://daughters rights.co.uk.

6 United Nations Population Fund State of the Population 2020, *Against My Will: Defying the Practices That Harm Women and Girls and Undermine Equality* (New York: UNFPA, 2020), 41.

7 "Obituary of Sir Ewan Forbes of Craigievar, Bt," *Daily Telegraph*, October 1, 1991.

8 As I reported to the Parliamentary Forum at the time, Ewan's case wasn't listed in the indexes to the relevant Scottish courts and cases. The Court of Lyon, which deals with Scots titles and coats of arms, nervously told me that they knew about the case, but the room where it was kept was being rewired and I would have to ring again in a week's time. When I did so, they said they had only the most basic details of the case, which did not include the date when it had been heard. I telephoned and wrote to the senior legal authority in Scotland, the Lord Advocate, and to the Register of the Baronetcy at the Home Office in England, but I received no reply from either of them. Neither I nor the Scottish Records Office staff could find any trace of Ewan's hidden case, not in the Minute Book for the Court of Session, where his case had been heard, nor in the indexes for court cases where it should have been listed.

9 Letter from the Principal Clerk of Session at the Court of Session in Edinburgh to Dr. Lynne Jones, MP, August 28, 1996, referred to in a letter from Lord Advocate, Mackay of Drumadoon, to Dr. Lynne Jones, MP, December 10, 1996. (Author's private collection.)

10 Letter from Lord Advocate, Mackay of Drumadoon, to Dr. Lynne Jones, MP, December 10, 1996. (Author's private collection.)

11 In 1987 when British Airways employed its first three female pilots, Kristina, already a decorated military pilot, had taken a job with a small independent Welsh airline. The press made a meal of her, with "before and after" photo-

graphs, demeaning headlines such as "The Officer Who Was a Gentleman," and humiliating cartoons such as one showing an obese woman wearing fishnet stockings and a bow sitting at a dressing table on the flight deck, titled "Girl Pilot Was a Bloke." Turned into a public laughingstock, Kristina found it impossible to get another job.

12 John Ferris, "When Mr. Becomes Ms.—or Wants To! Transvestism and Transsexuals in the Workplace," *Personnel Management*, July 1988, 44–48.

13 Letter from Lord Advocate, Lord Hardie, to Dr. Lynne Jones, MP, December 2, 1997. (Author's private collection.)

14 Letter from Ian Hill, Scottish Record Office, to Captain Kristina Sheffield, December 19, 1997. (Author's private collection.)

1 Childhood

1 Today's visitors to Craigievar Castle will find it a little different from Ewan's day. The main drive is now a footpath, its beech trees depleted, and the hedges and ditches run wild. The rear drive has had its trees felled. The more vivid pink of the castle is achieved by dye rather than by the traditional harling using local granite with a pink tinge. Many of the rooms are closed to visitors, who see a much smaller space than what Ewan lived in.

2 The UK has a complex system of hereditary titles, divided into the five ranks of the peerage (duke, marquess, earl, viscount and baron) and the baronetage. The baronetage, which is quite separate from the peerage, was instituted by King James I in the seventeenth century, but no new baronets have been created since that conferred on Denis Thatcher, the husband of Prime Minister Margaret Thatcher, in 1990. On the face of it, a baron appears to be of little status and a baronet of less, but there are other issues to take into consideration, such as the antiquity of the title and the dignity of the family. An easy comparison could be made with the US's class system, where a range of factors, such as an "old family" (came over with the Pilgrim Fathers), "old money" (families that have been rich for several generations) and "dynasty" (such as the Kennedy or Bush families) decide the sociopolitical pecking order. In the case of Ewan's family, the Sempill barony is a very old one, dating back to 1489, making it particularly venerable, while the baronetcy is similarly very old, dating back to 1630. Ewan's family was distinguished by its service to and friendship with the royal families of Scotland and of the UK, and they upheld a Scots traditional lifestyle, in a way that had a particular prestige associated with it, since it was becoming increasingly uncommon. While not being grand, therefore, Ewan's family was held in high esteem. In practical terms, the barony meant that letters to Ewan's father were addressed to "The Lord Sempill," or to "The Lady Sempill" for his mother, while he and his brother and sister were "The Honourable."

3 *The New Statistical Account of Scotland*, volume VII (Edinburgh: Blackwood, 1845), 88.

4 Court of Session, Scotland, *Report of Proceedings in Summary Trial in Petition John Alexander Cumnock Forbes-Sempill and the Honourable Ewan Forbes-*

Sempill, May 15–18, 1967. Judgment given on December 29, 1967. Available from the National Records of Scotland, reference CS258/1991/P892.

5 In 1999, the House of Lords Act reduced the number of hereditary peers entitled to sit and vote in the House of Lords to ninety-two. The Lord Sempill no longer has a seat.

6 Ewan Forbes, *The Aul' Days* (Aberdeen: Aberdeen University Press, 1984), 20.

7 At the time of this writing, the US leads the world in this field. See, for example, Stephanie Brill and Rachel Pepper, *The Transgender Child: A Handbook for Families and Professionals* (San Francisco: Cleis Press, 2008).

8 Forbes, *The Aul' Days*, 5. Further quotes from Ewan and Gwendolen in this chapter are taken variously from *The Aul' Days*, the transcript of Ewan's hearing, and from family recollections.

9 Richard von Krafft-Ebing, *Psychopathia Sexualis* (Stuttgart, 1886), authorized English adaptation of last revised German edition (New York: Pioneer Publications, 1947), 345.

10 In 1961, the state of Illinois repealed its anti-sodomy laws. In 1967, the UK's Criminal Law Amendment Act decriminalized homosexual acts taking place in private between consenting adults aged twenty-one and over.

11 Michel Foucault, *The History of Sexuality*, volume 1, *An Introduction*, trans. Robert Hurley (London: Penguin, 1978), 55.

12 European commercial and military expansionism from the fifteenth century onward had also imposed colonial legal systems, which criminalized homosexuality in settled and developing nations. See, for example, *Envisioning Global LGBT Human Rights: (Neo)colonialism, Neoliberalism, Resistance and Hope*, edited by Nancy Nicol et al. (London: Human Rights Consortium, 2018).

13 See, for example, Chandak Sengoopta, "Glandular Politics: Experimental Biology, Clinical Medicine, and Homosexual Emancipation in Fin-de-Siècle Central Europe," *Isis* 89, no. 3 (1998): 445–73.

14 Steinach's procedure was simply a partial vasectomy. Tissue rejection meant that Voronoff's implants were ineffective.

15 *The Steinach Film*, Austrian Federal Film Agency, 1932. See Per Södersten, David Crews, Cheryl Logan et al, "Eugen Steinach: The First Neuroendocrinologist," *Endocrinology*, March 2014, 155 (3), pp. 688–702.

16 Robert Beachy, *Gay Berlin: Birthplace of a Modern Identity* (New York: Vintage Books, 2015), 174.

17 Jamshed R. Tata, "One Hundred Years of Hormones," *EMBP Reports* 6, no. 6 (2005): 490–96.

18 National Trust for Scotland, *Craigievar Castle* (Edinburgh: National Trust for Scotland, 2018), 9.

19 Upper-class girls were recommended cold baths, strenuous exercise and other privations to delay menstruation until their "coming out" at seventeen years old, the formal presentation to the monarch at the palace, which launched them into the marriage market.

20 Then, as now, consistency is the key difference between trans children and children who, for a period of time, are exploring their gender role. Children

who are going through a "phase" will eventually lose interest, whereas "over time, parents of transgender children come to recognize that this 'phase" is not changing." See Brill and Pepper, *The Transgender Child*, 16.

21 Gwendolen Sempill, "How Aberdeenshire Can Supply 150 Bags of Cleaned Moss a Week," *Aberdeen Press and Journal*, January 29, 1917.

22 Phyllis Bottome, *The Challenge* (London: Faber & Faber, 1952), 252, 262; Pam Hirsch, *The Constant Liberal: the Life and Work of Phyllis Bottome* (London: Quartet, 2010), 26, 55.

23 Hirsch, *The Constant Liberal*, 178.

24 Forbes, *The Aul' Days*, 50.

25 Hirsch, *The Constant Liberal*, 294.

26 Letter from John Cole, Eton College, to Sir William Forbes, March 28, 1877 (by kind permission of Gabriel Forbes-Sempill).

27 Letter from John Forbes, Master of Sempill, to Sir William Forbes, February 21, 1890 (by kind permission of Gabriel Forbes-Sempill).

28 A ghillie is a "man of the land" who guides and advises fishers, shooters and deerstalkers in Scotland. They combine expertise in those pursuits with expert knowledge of their local flora, fauna and topography and its seasonal changes.

29 Michael Leslie Melville, *The Story of the Lovat Scouts: 1900–1980* (Edinburgh: The Saint Andrew Press, 1981), 17. The detail of the loss of his boots comes from a family story.

30 Forbes, *The Aul' Days*, 5.

31 Rainer Schulze, "Himmler's Crusade Against (Male) Homosexuality and the Continuing Stigmatisation of LGBT People After 1945," in *The Holocaust in History and Memory*, volume 4, *The Pink Triangle: The Long Shadow of the Nazi Persecution of Gay Men*, ed. Rainer Schulz (Colchester: Department of History, University of Essex, 2011), 17–39.

32 Heinz Heger, *The Men with the Pink Triangle* (London: GMP, 1986). First published as *Die Männer mit dem Rosa Winkel* (Hamburg: Merlin-Verlag, 1972).

33 See, for example, Mary Louise Pratt, *Imperial Eyes: Travel Writing and Transculturalism*, 2nd ed. (London: Routledge, 2008); Alix Cooper, *Inventing the Indigenous: Local Knowledge and Natural History in Early Modern Europe* (Cambridge: Cambridge University Press, 2007).

34 Thomas Bendyshe, "The History of Anthropology," *Memoirs of the Anthropological Society of London*, volume 1 (London: Trubner and Co., 1863–64), 397. The quotation appears in an essay written in 1721 by the German scholar Johann Albert Fabricius.

35 See, for example, Stephen J. Gould, *The Mismeasure of Man* (London: W. W. Norton, 1981).

36 The term "orientalism" was popularized by Edward Said, *Orientalism* (London: Routledge & Kegan Paul, 1978). He defines it as "a Western style for dominating, restructuring, and having authority over the Orient" (p. 3), that is, the non-Western world or "occident," marked by the meridian line that supposedly divides the Western Hemisphere from the Eastern Hemisphere.

37 Dorothy Thompson, *I Saw Hitler* (New York: Farrar & Rinehart, 1932).

2 The Medical Student

1 Ewan Forbes, *The Aul' Days* (Aberdeen: Aberdeen University Press, 1984), p. 50.

2 For a discussion of these tensions, see Christopher Andrew, *The Defence of the Realm: The Authorized History of MI5* (London: Penguin Books, 2010).

3 The relationship with Japan was an enduring one: a short piece of newsreel available on YouTube shows William taking Prince Chichibu of Japan for a spin in a two-seater biplane in 1926: see British Pathé, "Stag Lane Aerodrome. Prince Chichibu. Crown Prince of Japan Enjoys His First Actual 'Joy Ride,' " 1926, https://www.britishpathe.com/video/prince-chichibu/query/Chichibu. It is true that William was dogmatic, obstinate, and hyperfocused on flying, as all his family and friends could testify, and that he wrote letters worldwide to promote Britain's new aerospace industry, but none of those things was illegal. Frustrated after five fruitless years of watching him, MI5 decided to "stir him up" by blackening William's reputation to the Greek government, with whom he was in negotiation for a mission similar to those he had taken to Japan and the US. William was incandescent when he found out. The Foreign Office and the Air Ministry were on eggshells over the outcry from William and the scandal MI5 might have precipitated by slandering him: they denied all knowledge of the matter and restored William's reputation with Greece.

4 The Covenanters were Scots who signed the National Covenant in 1638 to confirm their opposition to government involvement in the Presbyterian Church of Scotland. They believed that only God could be the head of the Church of Scotland, whereas the then monarch, Charles I, claimed that the Divine Right of Kings made him head of the Church of Scotland. The so-called Bishops' Wars between Charles I and the Scots ensued, with Sir William Forbes, 1st Baronet of Craigievar, fighting on the side of the Covenanters and swearing that if any future baronets forsook the Presbyterian faith, the lands of Craigievar would be taken from them.

5 The jabot is a decorative clothing accessory consisting of lace or other fabric falling from the throat, usually worn with matching cuffs below the kilt jacket. A *sgian-dubh* is a sheath knife about three inches long, traditionally worn in the right sock with the handle showing, and usually with a decorated hilt, blade or sheath. A sporran is a leather or fur pouch hung on the front of a man's kilt and often highly decorated. They are all items of traditional male Scots dress.

6 Ewan Forbes, *The Dancers of Don* (Aberdeen: Aberdeen University Press, 1989), 35.

7 Court of Session, Scotland, *Report of Proceedings in Summary Trial in Petition John Alexander Cumnock Forbes-Sempill and the Honourable Ewan Forbes-Sempill*, May 15–18, 1967. Judgment given on December 29, 1967. Available from the National Records of Scotland, reference CS258/1991/P892.

8 *Man into Woman: An Authentic Record of a Change of Sex*, edited by Niels Hoyer (Ernst Ludwig Harthern-Jacobson), trans. H. J. Stenning (London: Jar-

rolds, 1933). Although the book is a fictionalization of Lili's life narrative, she died before its publication, and its production was the collaborative work of several people. See Lili Elbe Digital Archive for a publication history: https://www.lilielbe.org/narrative/publicationHistory.html.

9 David Ebershoff, *The Danish Girl* (London: Weidenfeld & Nicolson, 2015), back cover.

10 Richard von Krafft-Ebing, *Psychopathia Sexualis* (Stuttgart, 1886) authorized English adaptation of last revised German edition (New York: Pioneer Publications, 1947), 304–24.

11 Maureen Honey, *Creating Rosie the Riveter* (Amherst: University of Massachusetts Press, 1984), 140. Florence King satirizes the genre in *Confessions of a Failed Southern Lady* as "I Committed Adultery in a Diabetic Coma."

12 Hoyer, *Man into Woman*, 283.

13 Norman Haire, *Everyday Sex Problems* (London: Frederick Muller, 1948), 13.

14 Hoyer, *Man into Woman*, 58–59.

15 Ibid., 59.

16 Ibid., 63–64.

17 In the "Circe" chapter, Leopold Bloom is erotically transformed into "Ruby Cohen" and diagnosed as intersex. See James Joyce, *Ulysses: The Corrected Text* (London: Bodley Head, 1986), 402, 436–37.

18 Hoyer, *Man into Woman*, 64–65.

19 Ibid., 96.

20 Ibid., 71.

21 Ibid., 273.

22 The traditional "biomedical model," which viewed health and disease as a purely biological matter, was displaced at the end of the last century by an approach that recognized that psychological and social factors have an equally significant role to play. This biopsychosocial model of health is now a fundamental part of NHS and UK government policy.

23 David Rorie, *The Book of Aberdeen: Compiled for the 107th Annual Meeting of the British Medical Association* (Aberdeen: BMA, 1939), 4.

24 Churchill didn't pull his punches: he imprisoned his cousin by marriage, Diana Mitford, for three years during the war because MI5 had reported her to be "a public danger at the present time," although she occupied no formal position of power. She had married Fascist leader Sir Oswald Mosley in a secret ceremony at Joseph Goebbels's house, and Adolf Hitler had been a guest of honor at the wedding. William was kept under watch even after his resignation and reminded of that by finding MI5 agents openly searching his office and flat when he returned home after a party. But they still could find no specific, substantive evidence against him, and had there been any, he would certainly have been imprisoned. Frederick Rutland, another distinguished World War I aviator who really was a spy for the Japanese, was interned for two years after Pearl Harbor, and then died by suicide.

25 British Pathé, "Denbigh Eisteddfod," 1939, https://www.britishpathe.com/video/denbigh-eisteddfod.

26 The first International Congress on Sexual Science took place in Berlin in

1921 with three thousand participants, including delegates from Tokyo, Moscow and San Francisco. Subsequent meetings were held in Copenhagen, London, Vienna and Czechoslovakia. See Robert Beachy, *Gay Berlin: Birthplace of a Modern Identity* (New York: Vintage Books, 2015), 184.

27 Karl M. Baer [N. O. Body], *Memoirs of a Man's Maiden Years*, trans. Deborah Simon (1907; Philadelphia: University of Pennsylvania Press, 2006).

28 See Beachy, *Gay Berlin*, 177.

29 Tommy Dickinson, *"Curing Queers": Mental Nurses and Their Patients, 1935–74* (Manchester: Manchester University Press, 2015), 42.

30 Roy Porter, *Madness: A Brief History* (Oxford: Oxford University Press, 2002), 200–04.

31 The "medical firm" approach created a tight-knit team, led by a consultant, which met all of the needs of a particular area of medicine or group of patients. It often involved working long hours and was effectively ended by the European Working Time Directive, implemented at the turn of this century, which replaced it with a "handover" system.

32 Even though Britain did not sterilize people with intellectual impairments, there is evidence that a significant body of psychiatrists would have wished to do so, were it not for political sensitivities. See, for example, Matthew Thomson, "Disability, Psychiatry and Eugenics," in *The Oxford Handbook of the History of Eugenics*, ed. Alison Bashford and Philippa Levine (Oxford: Oxford University Press, 2010), 116–33.

33 Clare R. Tebbutt, "Popular and Medical Understandings of Sex Change in 1930s Britain" (unpublished doctoral thesis, University of Manchester, 2014).

34 L. R. Broster and H. W. C. Vines, *The Adrenal Cortex* (London: H. K. Lewis, 1933), 12. The idea was that women's bodies becoming increasingly male was the product of evolution, which was "naturally" developing them from the lesser, imperfect female form into the perfection of a male body.

35 " 'Woman' Changes Her Sex," *Yorkshire Post and Leeds Intelligencer*, May 29, 1936; "He Was Formerly Woman Athlete," *Portsmouth Evening News*, August 11, 1936.

36 "How Unlike a Woman!", *Daily Mail*, November 18, 1937. In his description of the event in his memoirs, Dillon is uncertain which newspaper it was: he says "the *Daily Mirror*, I think," a faulty attribution copied by biographers Liz Hodgkinson, *From a Girl to a Man* (London: Quartet, 2015), and Pagan Kennedy, *The First Man-Made Man* (New York: Bloomsbury, 2007). For Dillon's misremembered account, see Michael Dillon/Lobzang Jivaka, *Out of the Ordinary: A Life of Gender and Spiritual Transitions*, ed. Jacob Lau and Cameron Partridge (New York: Fordham University Press, 2017), 78.

37 Michael Dillon, *Self: A Study in Ethics and Endocrinology* (London: Heinemann, 1946), 53.

38 A. P. Cawadias, *Hermaphroditos: The Human Intersex* (London: William Heinemann, 1943), viii.

39 Frantz Fanon, *Black Skin, White Masks*, trans. Charles Lam Markmann (London: Pluto Press, 2008), p. 3.

40 Dillon/Jivaka, *Out of the Ordinary*, 218.

41 Ibid., 217.

42 See, for example, Erving Goffman, *Stigma: Notes on the Management of Spoiled Identity* (Englewood Cliffs, NJ: Prentice-Hall, 1963).

3 Marriage

1 "Funeral of Gwendolen Lady Sempill," *Aberdeen Press and Journal*, March 6, 1944.

2 Frank Honigsbaum, *The Division in British Medicine* (London: Kogan Page, 1979), 306.

3 Ewan Forbes, *The Aul' Days* (Aberdeen: Aberdeen University Press, 1984), 88.

4 Ibid., 88.

5 Ibid., 88–89.

6 Author interview with Mrs. Sheena Esson, June 21, 2019.

7 "Clan Banners Will Be Flown at Aboyne," *Aberdeen Press and Journal*, September 3, 1946.

8 Nan Shepherd, *The Living Mountain* (Aberdeen: Aberdeen University Press, 1977), 48.

9 Aline Scott Elliot was the daughter of Colonel Adam Scott Elliot, Queen's Own Cameron Highlanders, who lived at Belhevie Lodge, Whitecairns, Aberdeenshire. Four years older than Ewan, she became a veterinary surgeon in 1942 and lived at Crabadon Manor in Totnes, Devon, with her sister Isabel. She is remembered by her family as a tall, well-built woman with masculine mannerisms. Neither Aline nor Isabel ever married.

10 "Public Notices," *Aberdeen Press and Journal*, September 12, 1952.

11 For example, "Doctor's Birth Re-Registered," *Daily Telegraph*, September 13, 1952; "Exclusive Statement by Dr Ewan Forbes-Sempill," *Aberdeen Press and Journal*, September 15, 1952. The New York Bureau of the United Press reported that Ewan's correction of his birth certificate "has sparked upheaval in one of Scotland's most ancient titled families. Authorities say the change in the records of the country's peerage is unprecedented." United Press, PLA 1008611, New York Bureau, September 14, 1952. (Author's private collection.)

12 "Dr. Ewan Forbes-Sempill Weds His Housekeeper," *Aberdeen Evening Express*, October 11, 1952.

13 Gorecki, "Brux Lodge, Aberdeenshire. December 2008", urbexforums.com: Exploring the Unexplored and the Unknown, February 16, 2009, http://www.urbexforums.com/showthread.php/2991-Brux-Lodge-Aberdeenshire-December-2008. William has signed it as "Craigievar," just as Ewan was known as "Brux."

14 Robert Allen, *There but for the Grace* (London: W. H. Allen, 1954), 81–82.

15 The dirk is the traditional fighting knife carried by Scots warriors. Worn on the belt, it has a pointed, single-edged blade about thirty-six centimeters (fourteen inches) long. It is quite distinct from the *sgian-dubh* worn in the sock and carried in addition to it. The dirk Ewan was presented with was an ornate ceremonial one, not intended for use.

16 D. O. Cauldwell, "Psychopathia Transexualis," *Sexology* 16 (1949): 274–80.

17 Simone de Beauvoir, *The Second Sex*, trans. Constance Borde and Sheila Malovany-Chevallier (London: Vintage, 2011), 429. First published as *La deuxième sexe* (Paris: Éditions Gallimard, 1949).

18 Ibid., 293.

19 Ibid., 432.

20 Ibid., 448.

21 Ibid.

22 See, for example, Tommy Dickinson, *"Curing Queers": Mental Nurses and Their Patients, 1935–74* (Manchester: Manchester University Press, 2015).

23 For discussion about the nature of "affordances," see James J. Gibson, *The Ecological Approach to Visual Perception* (Boston: Houghton Mifflin, 1979).

24 Christine Jorgensen, *Christine Jorgensen: A Personal Autobiography* (New York: Eriksson, 1967), 36–37.

25 Joanne Meyerowitz, *How Sex Changed: A History of Transsexuality in the United States* (Cambridge, MA: Harvard University Press, 2002), 63–64.

26 Jorgensen, *Christine Jorgensen*, 248.

27 Ibid., 224.

28 Ibid., 231.

29 Ibid., 246.

30 Gene "The Charmer" Walcott with the Johnny McCleverty Calypso Boys, "Is She Is or Is She Ain't?" on *Calypso Records from the West Indies*, Monogram, 1950s. Walcott, who is now known as Louis Farrakhan and is the National Representative of the Nation of Islam, originally released the calypso as a ten-inch shellac 78-rpm record on the Rhythm label in Jamaica before its popularity caused Monogram Records to rerelease it in the US as a seven-inch 45-rpm vinyl disc. A recording of the song can be found at https://www.youtube.com/watch?v=QB-gTmztgVk.

31 Roberta Cowell, *Roberta Cowell's Story by Herself* (London: William Heinemann, 1954), 67.

32 See, for example, the discussion of herstory in Diane Purkiss, *The Witch in History* (London: Routledge, 1996).

33 Cowell, *Roberta Cowell's Story*, 73.

34 Jorgensen, *Christine Jorgensen*, pp. 51–52.

35 Cowell, *Roberta Cowell's Story*, 75.

36 Ibid., 92.

37 Ibid., 87.

38 Ibid., 92.

39 Ibid.

40 Sidney Rodin, "Cowell Sensation," *Sunday Pictorial*, March 14, 1954.

41 Duncan Webb, "Roberta: The Ghastly Truth at Last," *The People*, April 11, 1954.

42 "Come off It 'Roberta,'" *The People*, April 18, 1954.

43 Harry Benjamin, "Transvestism and Transsexualism," *International Journal of Sexology*, 7 (1953): 12–14.

44 "Change of Sex," *British Medical Journal* 1, no. 4863 (1954): 694.

45 "Sex and the Law," *British Medical Journal* 1, no. 4863 (1954): 710–11.

46 Clifford Allen, "Definition of Male and Female," *British Medical Journal* 1, no. 4865 (1954): 816.

47 A. P. Cawadias, "Change of Sex," *British Medical Journal* 1, no. 4866 (1954): 876.

48 Clifford Allen, "Change of Sex," *British Medical Journal* 1, no. 4869 (1954): 1040.

49 Betty Friedan, *The Feminine Mystique* (London: Victor Gollancz, 1963), 17.

50 Susan Stryker, introduction to *Christine Jorgensen: A Personal Autobiography*, by Christine Jorgensen (San Francisco: Cleis Press, 2000), x.

51 Cowell, *Roberta Cowell's Story*, 122.

4 A Death in the Family

1 "Whist Concert Aids St. Dunstan's," *Aberdeen Evening Express*, April 10, 1952.

2 Ewan Forbes, *The Dancers of Don* (Aberdeen: Aberdeen University Press, 1989), 33.

3 "Person's Change of Sex: Will Case Ruling," *Manchester Guardian*, October 4, 1951.

4 "Change in Teacher's Birth Certificate," *The Times*, March 31, 1956.

5 "Changes of Sex," *Belfast News-Letter*, May 6, 1954.

6 "Sex-Changed Father Becomes Bride of Another Father," *Northern Whig*, July 29, 1955.

7 "Sex-Change Sailor Sued by Ex-Wife," *Aberdeen Evening Express*, January 4, 1955; "My Life as Man and Woman," *Belper News*, January 28, 1955.

8 "The Picture That Baffled Six Doctors," *The People*, July 22, 1956.

9 " 'Woman of the Year' at the Embassy," *The Stage*, September 23, 1954.

10 "Dreadful Problems in a Sex-Change," *The Stage*, November 5, 1959.

11 Tom Mangold, " 'It's Love Again,' Coos Sex-Change Chris," *Sunday Mirror*, August 30, 1959. Christine described her fiancé as "an American sailor from the West," and the journalist played on that by ending the piece with "Enter the sailor from the West . . . ," which at that period was a common trope for anal intercourse.

12 "Man Said to Be Changing Sex," *The Times*, July 31, 1957.

13 "Sex Change 2. The Bearded Sailor," *Daily Herald*, August 1, 1957.

14 "Change of Sex by Woman Pilot," *The Times*, January 13, 1958.

15 "Not Cruel of Husband to Want to Be a Woman," *The Times*, May 23, 1958.

16 Dave King, *The Transvestite and the Transsexual: Public Categories and Private Identities* (Aldershot: Avebury, 1993), 41–54.

17 Gregory Woods, *The Homintern: How Gay Culture Liberated the Modern World* (New Haven, CT: Yale University Press, 2016), 7.

18 Money and the Hampsons published a series of guidelines, protocols and recommendations during the 1950s, all suggesting the malleability of gender identity in childhood, and Money repeated his idea of a "gender identity gate" in his popular paperback *Sexual Signatures: On Being a Man or a Woman*.

19 John Money, Joan G. Hampson, and John L. Hampson, "Hermaphroditism: Recommendations Concerning Assignment of Sex, Change of Sex, and

Psychologic Management," *Bulletin of the Johns Hopkins Hospital* 97, no. 4 (1955): 284–300.

20 John Money, Joan G. Hampson, and John L. Hampson, "Imprinting and the Establishment of Gender Role," *AMA Archives of Neurology and Psychiatry* 77, no. 3 (1957): 333–36.

21 Elizabeth Reis, *Bodies in Doubt: An American History of Intersex* (Baltimore: Johns Hopkins University Press, 2009), 143.

22 Money, Hampson, and Hampson, "Hermaphroditism," 286.

23 See Rebecca Skloot, *The Immortal Life of Henrietta Lacks* (New York: Crown, 2010). TeLinde took the unconsented sample, but George Gey developed the cell line.

24 Joanne Meyerowitz, *How Sex Changed: A History of Transsexuality in the United States* (Cambridge, MA: Harvard University Press, 2002), 106.

25 "Florid psychosis" is a medical diagnosis indicating that an individual has lost all touch with reality. It is sometimes present in schizophrenia.

26 Ben Goldacre, *Bad Science* (London: Fourth Estate, 2008), 34.

27 John Bulmer Randell, "Cross Dressing and the Desire to Change Sex" (unpublished MD thesis, University of Wales, 1960).

28 "Sempill Poser—Court May Decide," *Aberdeen Press and Journal*, January 4, 1966.

29 Ivor Brown, "Among the Shadows," *Observer*, September 16, 1951, 6.

30 "Taken Off After One Night," *Manchester Guardian*, July 25, 1952.

31 National Records of Scotland, "Ewan Forbes Sampill" [*sic*], *Statutory Registers: Register of Corrected Entries*, 193/00 001 86, August 30, 1952. The entry and its correction may be viewed at the ScotlandsPeople website by searching first for the birth certificate for Ewan Forbes-Sempill and then by clicking on the link to the correction.

5 Margaret's Fateful Letter

1 "Fintray Public Hall Laying of the Foundation Stone," *Aberdeen Press and Journal*, May 15, 1914.

2 "Deeside Season Ends in Brilliant Fashion," *Aberdeen Press and Journal*, September 15, 1928.

3 "Aberdeen's Fine Response," *Aberdeen Press and Journal*, March 2, 1935.

4 "Rain Spoils Social Side of Lord's Gathering," *Sunday Times*, July 10, 1938.

5 "Commons Amendment to the Criminal Law Amendment Act, 1885," *Hansard*, House of Lords, August 15, 1921, vol. 43, c. 573.

6 Steven Brocklehurst, "Coming Oot: The Fabulous History of Gay Scotland," BBC News, November 28, 2015, http://www.bbc.co.uk/news/uk-scotland -34910016.

7 Harry Gordon Slade, "Modern Country Houses," *Times Literary Supplement*, January 11, 1985, 37.

8 Pearl Murray, "This Scotswoman's Castle Is Her Home—At Last," *Aberdeen Press and Journal*, January 28, 1966.

9 Court of Session, Scotland, *Report of Proceedings in Summary Trial in Petition*

John Alexander Cumnock Forbes-Sempill and the Honourable Ewan Forbes-Sempill, May 15–18, 1967. Judgment given on December 29, 1967. Available from the National Records of Scotland, reference CS258/1991/P892, p. 425.

10 Ibid.

11 Ibid., 421.

12 "Sempill Poser—Court May Decide," *Aberdeen Press and Journal*, January 4, 1966.

13 Dave King and Richard Ekins, "Pioneers of Transgendering: The Life and Work of Virginia Prince," Gendys Conference, 2000, http://www.gender.org.uk/conf/2000/king20.htm.

14 Ibid.

15 Riki Wilchins, *TRANS/gressive: How Transgender Activists Took on Gay Rights, Feminism, the Media & Congress . . . and Won!* (New York: Riverdale Avenue Books, 2017), 25.

16 There is uncertainty about who was present and how they identified when the clientele of the Stonewall Inn on Christopher Street in New York City resisted routine police brutality. At that time, so-called gay clubs usually welcomed all LGBTI people without questioning how they identified.

17 The Homosexual Law Reform Society and the Albany Trust had been formed in 1958, followed by the Committee for Homosexual Equality in 1964. All these groups worked quietly toward the law reform represented by the Sexual Offences Act 1967. By contrast, the Gay Liberation Front, founded on October 14, 1970, by Bob Mellors and Aubrey Walter at the London School of Economics, set out to gain attention and profile for gay issues. One of the first working groups it formed focused on countering the continuing psychopathologization of gay men. See Stuart Feather, *Blowing the Lid: Gay Liberation, Sexual Revolution and Radical Queens* (Winchester: Zero Books, 2015).

18 "BBC Takes a Candid View of Sex Change," *The Times*, November 21, 1966.

19 Harold Garfinkel, *Studies in Ethnomethodology* (Englewood Cliffs, NJ: Prentice-Hall, 1967).

20 John Money and Patricia Tucker, *Sexual Signatures: On Being a Man or a Woman* (London: George G. Harrap, 1976), 75.

21 A full account is given by John Colapinto, *As Nature Made Him: The Boy Who Was Raised as a Girl* (New York: HarperCollins, 2000).

22 *Report of Proceedings in Summary Trial*, 170.

23 Ibid., 158–59, 163–67, 173, 419.

24 Ibid., 416.

25 Ibid., 177.

26 Ibid., 436.

27 Ibid., 161.

28 Ibid., 426.

6 The Medical Examination

1 The will of Margaret Forbes-Sempill can be accessed at the National Records of Scotland in the records of the Aberdeen Sheriff Court, ref. SC1/37/279.

2 "Castle in a Fairy Garden," *Aberdeen Press and Journal*, July 19, 1968, p. 5.

3 Clifford Allen, *A Textbook of Psychosexual Disorders* (London: Oxford University Press, 1962), 252–56.

4 Harry Benjamin, *The Transsexual Phenomenon* (New York: Julian Press, 1966), 93.

5 Harry Benjamin, introduction to *Transsexualism and Sex Reassignment*, ed. Richard Green and John Money (Baltimore: Johns Hopkins University Press, 1969), 1–10.

6 Ira B. Pauly, "Adult Manifestations of Female Transsexualism," in Green and Money, *Transsexualism and Sex Reassignment*, 59–87.

7 A useful discussion of the history and present concerns about trans and intersex involvement in sporting events is provided by Vanessa Heggie, "Testing Sex and Gender in Sports: Reinventing, Reimagining and Reconstructing Histories," *Endeavour* 34, no. 4 (2010): 157–163.

8 Len Adams, "The Astonishing Double Life of Miss Fink," *The People*, September 4, 1966.

9 Court of Session, Scotland, *Report of Proceedings in Summary Trial in Petition John Alexander Cumnock Forbes-Sempill and the Honourable Ewan Forbes-Sempill*, May 15–18, 1967. Judgment given on December 29, 1967. Available from the National Records of Scotland, reference CS258/1991/P892, p. 3.

10 C. N. Armstrong, "Diversities of Sex," *British Medical Journal* (May 1955): 1173–77. Data on incidence of these conditions were not collected in a coherent fashion and so their prevalence is difficult to estimate, beyond recognizing that they were frequent enough to support the work of a small number of interested medical specialists.

11 *Report of Proceedings in Summary Trial*, 32.

12 John Money and Clay Primrose, "Sexual Dimorphism and Dissociation in the Psychology of Male Transsexuals," in *Transsexualism and Sex Reassignment*, ed. Richard Green and John Money (Baltimore: Johns Hopkins University Press, 1969), 115–36. Clay Primrose was a psychology undergraduate at Stanford University working as an intern with Money.

13 *Report of Proceedings in Summary Trial*, 45–47.

14 *Report of Proceedings in Summary Trial*, 396.

15 Ibid., 440.

16 Ibid., 11.

17 Ibid., 8.

18 Ibid., 15.

19 Ibid., 13.

20 Ibid., 76.

7 An Audacious Defense

1 Caroline Richmond, "Professor Paul Polani," *Independent*, March 21, 2006, http://www.independent.co.uk/news/obituaries/professor-paul-polani -6106102.html.

2 Unless otherwise indicated, all information and quotations in this chapter are

from Court of Session, Scotland, *Report of Proceedings in Summary Trial in Petition John Alexander Cumnock Forbes-Sempill and the Honourable Ewan Forbes-Sempill*, May 15–18, 1967. Judgment given on December 29, 1967. Available from the National Records of Scotland, reference CS258/1991/P892.

3 Lewis M. Terman and Catherine Cox Miles, *Sex and Personality: Studies in Masculinity and Femininity* (New York: McGraw-Hill, 1936), 4.

4 C. J. Dewhurst, A. J. N. Warrack, and M. D. Casey, "An XX Hermaphrodite with Male Social Sex," *British Medical Journal* (1963): 221; Milton Diamond, "A Critical Evaluation of the Ontogeny of Human Sexual Behavior," *The Quarterly Review of Biology* 4, no. 2 (June 1965): 147–75.

5 "Sex of Athletes," *British Medical Journal* (January 1967): 185–86.

6 "Disquiet over Forbes-Sempill Secrecy Case," *Glasgow Herald*, December 6, 1968.

7 There are two kinds of lawyers in the UK, solicitors and barristers. Laypeople hire a solicitor for most of their legal business, but if a case is to be heard in a higher court, the solicitor will select a barrister to speak in court. The higher the court, the more experienced the barrister required, with the highest level being Queen's Counsel, or QC for short. In the US, the person who practices law is called an attorney, and the equivalent of a UK barrister is a trial attorney.

8 A. P. Cawadias, *Hermaphroditos: The Human Intersex* (London: William Heinemann, 1943), 31.

9 "Sex of Athletes," *British Medical Journal* (1967): 185–86.

10 Althar Yawar, "Healing in Survivors of Torture," *Journal of the Royal Society of Medicine* 97, no. 8 (2004): 366–70.

8 The Judge's Dilemma

1 See, for example, "How to Urinate Standing Up as a Female," *wikiHow*, June 3, 2021, https://www.wikihow.com/Urinate-Standing-Up-as-a-Female.

2 Jack Dewhurst, *Royal Confinements: A Gynaecological History of the Royal Family* (New York: St. Martin's Press, 1980).

3 Audio recording, "First International Symposium on Gender Identity, London, 1969," USC Digital Library, http://digitallibrary.usc.edu/cdm/ref/collection/p15799coll4/id/1571/rec/7. All quotations from speakers at the symposium are taken from this source.

4 "Selected Proceedings of the First International Congress on Gender Identity, London, England, July 1969," *Archives of Sexual Behavior* 1, no. 2 (1971): 145–74.

5 Jeffrey Weeks, "After the Sexual Offences Act," paper presented at *A Step Forward? 50 Years Since the Sexual Offences Act*, National Archives, July 22, 2017.

6 Richard Green, *Gay Rights, Trans Rights* (self-published, 2018), 154. I was at dinner with Richard and another medical colleague, who revealed Randell's cross-dressing history, much to Richard's shocked astonishment.

7 "Opinion of Lord Hunter," Court of Session, Scotland, *Report of Proceedings in Summary Trial in Petition John Alexander Cumnock Forbes-Sempill and*

the Honourable Ewan Forbes-Sempill, May 15–18, 1967. Judgment given on December 29, 1967. Available from the National Records of Scotland, reference CS258/1991/P892, p. 12. All other quotations from Lord Hunter are from this source.

9 A Perfect Storm

1 April Ashley with Douglas Thompson, *The First Lady* (London: John Blake, 2006), 1.

2 Duncan Fallowell and April Ashley, *April Ashley's Odyssey* (London: Jonathan Cape, 1982), 4–5.

3 *Ibid.*, 10.

4 *Ibid.*, 10, 34.

5 *Ibid.*, 87–88.

6 Ashley with Thompson, *The First Lady*, 124.

7 Ibid., 176.

8 Bowie was photographed in one of them, a cream-and-blue satin dress, for the UK cover of his album *The Man Who Sold the World* in 1971.

9 Fallowell and Ashley, *April Ashley's Odyssey*, 189.

10 Ibid., 210.

11 "Husband Was a Woman," *The Times*, February 28, 1967.

12 D. W. Meyers, "Problems of Sex Determination and Alteration," *Medico-Legal Journal* 36, no. 4 (1968): 174–190. In spite of Meyers's title, the journal indexes the article as "Transsexualism."

13 Roger Ormrod, "The Medico-Legal Aspects of Sex Determination," *Medico-Legal Journal* 40, no. 3 (1972): pp. 78–88.

14 Stephen Gilmore, *Corbett v. Corbett*: Once a Man, Always a Man?," *Landmark Cases in Family Law*, ed. Stephen Gilmore, Jonathan Herring and Rebecca Probert (Oxford: Hart, 2011), 47–72.

15 The UK convention, established in the eighteenth century, is for members of surgical specialties to be titled "Mr., Ms., Miss or Mrs." and for all other doctors to be titled "Dr."

16 *Corbett v. Corbett* [1970] 2 All ER 33.

17 *S v. S* [1962] 3 All ER 55.

18 "Opinion of Lord Hunter," Court of Session, Scotland, *Report of Proceedings in Summary Trial in Petition John Alexander Cumnock Forbes-Sempill and the Honourable Ewan Forbes-Sempill*, May 15–18, 1967. Judgment given on December 29, 1967. Available from the National Records of Scotland, reference CS258/1991/P892, p. 17.

19 Fallowell and Ashley, *April Ashley's Odyssey*, 216.

20 Ashley with Thompson, *The First Lady*, p. 267.

21 "Sir Ewan Gets the Verdict," *Aberdeen Press and Journal*, December 4, 1968.

22 *Burke's Peerage & Baronetage*, 107th edition, volume I, 1454–57.

23 Cecil King, "Enough Is Enough," *Daily Mirror*, May 10, 1968.

24 "Dr. Forbes-Sempill Is Now 11th Baronet of Forbes," *Glasgow Herald*, December 5, 1968.

25 "Disquiet over Forbes-Sempill Secrecy Case," *Glasgow Herald*, December 6, 1968.

26 Fallowell and Ashley, *April Ashley's Odyssey*, 211.

27 Ibid., 214

28 *Corbett v. Corbett* [1970].

29 Ibid.

30 Fallowell and Ashley, *April Ashley's Odyssey*, 215.

31 Fallowell and Ashley, *April Ashley's Odyssey*, 211.

32 *Corbett v. Corbett* [1970]. All other quotations from Lord Ormrod are from this source.

33 For a recent study of the "slip" phenomenon and excuse, see C. Marston and R. Lewis, "Anal Heterosex among Young People and Implications for Health Promotion: A Qualitative Study in the UK," *BMJ Open* 4, no. 8 (2014): 004996, https://bmjopen.bmj.com/content/4/8/e004996.

34 Ivor H. Mills, "Sex and Gender," *The Lancet* 295, no. 7642 (1970): 615.

35 For a detailed discussion of this aspect of Ormrod's judgment, see Christopher Hutton, *The Tyranny of Ordinary Meaning: Corbett v. Corbett and the Invention of Legal Sex* (Switzerland: Palgrave Macmillan, 2019).

36 The case, *Re Kevin* [2001] FamCA 1074, was heard by Judge Chisholm in the Australian Family Court in 2001.

37 Fallowell and Ashley, *April Ashley's Odyssey*, 216.

38 Ormrod, "The Medico-Legal Aspects of Sex Determination," 85.

39 Fallowell and Ashley, *April Ashley's Odyssey*, 222–23

40 Ibid., 224–25.

41 Z. J. Playdon, "Intersecting Oppressions: Ending Discrimination against Lesbians, Gay Men and Trans People in the UK," in *Sexuality Repositioned: Diversity and the Law*, edited by Belinda Brooks-Gordon, Loraine Gelsthorpe, Martin Johnson and Andrew Bainham (Oxford: Hart, 2004), 131–52.

10 Outlawed

1 It was reported on the front page of Ewan's local newspaper, the *Aberdeen Press and Journal*, on February 3, 1970; detail of the court's decision was given in the Sunday newspapers, such as *News of the World*, on February 8, 1970.

2 "Nullity of Marriage Bill," *Hansard*, House of Lords debate, April 22, 1971, vol. 317, cc 817.

3 "Out on a Limbo," *Daily Mirror*, February 10, 1970.

4 "Model April in 'State of Limbo,' " *Newcastle Evening Chronicle*, February 2, 1970.

5 Letter from Edwina Currie, MP, to Virginia Bottomley (then Home Secretary), March 20, 1994. (Author's private collection.)

6 Philippe Sands, "The Ratline," *Intrigue*, Episode 3, BBC Radio 4, September 21, 2018, https://www.bbc.co.uk/programmes/p06lrysn.

7 *Parliamentary Debates: House of Commons Official Report*, Standing Committees Session 1974–75, volume III (London: HMSO, 1975), 102–03.

8 Every Scottish castle has a mains, a nearby collection of outbuildings where

farm workers live and which may include, for example, a laundry or a dairy.

9 Leeds University TV/TS Group, "Conference Report," *Transvestism and Transsexualism in Modern Society* (Leeds, 1974), 18.

10 Dr. Dave King, *Transgender Research Materials*, Wellcome Library: PP/KIN/C/2/3. On October 8, 1976, King recorded in his research notes, "Chat with Alice. C. S. attempting takeover. Wants to exclude gays & tss, ultra masc tvs. C. S. not attending dinner hushed up split. Doesn't think Sylvia can agree. Tomorrow's exec meeting—big punch-up expected."

11 Transsexual Action Organization, *Transsexual Information*, Wellcome Library: PP/KIN/C/16, p. 4.

12 *White v. British Sugar Corporation* [1977] IRLR 121.

13 John Ferris, "When Mr. Becomes Ms.—or Wants To! Transvestism and Transsexuals in the Workplace," *Personnel Management*, July 1988, 44–48.

14 The cases are: New York Supreme Court, *Anonymous v. Anonymous* 1971; Ohio Probate Court, *re Ladrach* 1987; Texas Court of Appeals, *Littleton v. Prange* 1991; Kansas Court of Appeals, *re Estate of Marshall G Gardiner* 2001; Florida District Court of Appeal, *Kantaras v Kantaras* 2004.

15 The cases are: New Zealand, *re T* 1975; South Africa, *W v. W* 1976; Canada, *M v. M (A)* 1984; Australia, *R v. Harris and McGuiness* 1988.

16 Andrea Dworkin, *Woman Hating* (New York: Dutton, 1974), 175.

17 Sheffield Group of the Campaign for Homosexual Equality, *Learning a Little About Transvestism* (Sheffield: CHE, 1976).

18 Betty Friedan, *The Feminine Mystique* (London: Victor Gollancz, 1963), 275–78.

19 Germaine Greer, *The Female Eunuch* (London: MacGibbon & Kee, 1970), 37.

20 "Within feminist thought, the concept of patriarchy has been used in different ways. . . . In some (radical) feminist theory, patriarchy was represented as a universal feature . . . originating in a male nature, which is inherently violent and domineering." Kathleen Lennon and Rachel Alsop, *Gender Theory in Troubled Times* (London: Polity Press, 2020), 80. This problematically homogenizing definition from half a century ago often seems to be the version of "patriarchy" invoked in popular culture today, especially when used to support negative comments about trans women. However, contemporary feminist thought recognizes that patriarchy operates as systemic, sexed and gendered oppression of women (including trans women) through embedded practices across the whole cultural structure.

21 *The Stepford Wives* was made in 1975 and remade in 2004; *Invasion of the Body Snatchers* was originally made in 1956 and remade in 1978; and *Invaders from Mars* was originally made in 1953 and remade in 1986.

22 The book originated as a doctoral thesis under the heading of "Ethics and Society," written for Boston College, a private Jesuit Catholic university, where Raymond was supervised by theologian and radical lesbian feminist Mary Daly. Subsequently, Janice Raymond taught at the University of Massachusetts in Amherst.

23 Susan Stryker and Stephen Whittle, ed., *The Transgender Studies Reader* (London: Routledge, 2006), 131.

24 Carol Riddell, *Divided Sisterhood: A Critical Review of Janice Raymond's The Transsexual Empire* (Liverpool: News from Nowhere, 1980).

25 Author interview with Valerie (her chosen name to protect her identity), July 9, 2017.

26 John Randell, *Sexual Variations* (London: Priory Press, 1973), 78.

27 World Health Organization, *International Classification of Diseases* 1, no. 1 (Geneva: WHO, 1977), 197.

28 The four key principles of biomedical ethics are expressed in the Hippocratic Oath and its variants which medical students usually take when they graduate, and in the UK form the basis of the General Medical Council's benchmark for ethical practice, *Good medical practice*. Their breach comprises professional misconduct. See Kathy Oxtoby, "Is the Hippocratic Oath Still Relevant to Practicing Doctors Today?" *BMJ* 2016; 355:i6629. Validity is concerned with the accuracy of a standard or process and reliability is concerned with its consistency when applied to other subjects or contexts.

29 Eli Coleman, "Toward Version 7 of the World Professional Association for Transgender Health's *Standards of Care*," *International Journal of Transgenderism* 11, no. 4 (2009): 1–7.

30 The HBIGDA *Standards* recommended getting fees in advance, asserted that only "a certified and licensed psychiatrist or psychologist" could prescribe HRT for trans people, and claimed that only a psychiatrist could decide on the provision of reconstructive surgery. Since it was still possible for trans people to self-medicate with HRT and seek private surgery, the HBIGDA tried to block that route by warning surgeons that operating outside the cartel's system would be professional misconduct. Of course, it was all smoke and mirrors. The HBIGDA had no legal power but was simply using bully-boy tactics to protect its own financial interests.

31 Joanne Meyerowitz, *How Sex Changed: A History of Transsexuality in the United States* (Cambridge, MA: Harvard University Press, 2002), 254.

32 The cultural critic Lisa Baraitser defines "warehousing" as "the temporally elongated control of subjugated populations . . . who are imagined as social problems." See Lisa Baraitser, *Enduring Time* (London: Bloomsbury Academic, 2018), 9.

33 Ibid., 4.

34 Harry Benjamin International Gender Dysphoria Association Inc., *Standards of Care: The Hormonal and Surgical Sex Reassignment of Gender Dysphoria Persons*, revised draft 1/80 (San Francisco, 1980), 5–6.

35 American Psychiatric Association, *Diagnostic and Statistical Manual of Mental Disorders* (Washington: APA, 1980).

36 Meyerowitz, *How Sex Changed*, 254.

37 Personal account given to author by Richard Green.

38 Roy Ward Baker, *Dr. Jekyll and Sister Hyde* (Hammer Film Productions,1971); Brian de Palma, *Dressed to Kill* (Filmways, 1980); Jonathan Demme, *The Silence of the Lambs* (Orion Pictures, 1991).

39 Liz Hodgkinson, *Bodyshock: The Truth about Changing Sex* (London: Columbus Books, 1987).

40 "Sex-Change 'Man' Gets a Divorce from Her Wife," *Newcastle Evening Chronicle*, January 19, 1972; "Sex-Change for a TV Music Man," *Daily Mirror*, May 18, 1972; "Oh Sister! Sex-Change Secret of a Monk," *Liverpool Echo*, March 6, 1975; "My Husband, the Sex-Change Para," *Daily Mirror*, April 7, 1977; "Plea for Sex-Change Vicar," *Birmingham Daily Post*, May 30, 1978.

41 Randell, *Sexual Variations*, 146.

42 John Money and Patricia Tucker, *Sexual Signatures: On Being a Man or a Woman* (London: George G. Harrap, 1976), 70, 68.

43 Della Aleksander, Laura Pralet, Rachel Bowen and Jan Ford, *Open Door— Transex Liberation Group*, BBC 2, June 4, 1973. The program can be viewed at https://www.bbc.co.uk/programmes/p06c83f4/player.

44 Renée Richards, *Second Serve: The Renée Richards Story* (New York: Stein and Day, 1983); Anthony Page, *Second Serve* (CBS, 1986).

45 *A Change of Sex*, BBC 2, September 15–17, 1980.

46 Sean Day-Lewis, "Sex and Suffering," *Daily Telegraph*, October 16, 1980; Richard Last, "Stepping out of Line," *Daily Telegraph*, October 17, 1980, 15.

47 Nicholas Mason, "The Transsexual Dilemma: Being a Transsexual," *Journal of Medical Ethics* 6 (1980): 85–89.

48 Mason, "The Transsexual Dilemma," 88.

49 *Rees v. UK* [1986] 9EHRR 56, para. 21.

50 Ibid., para. 44.

11 Another Audacious Defense

1 Letter from Ewan Forbes to Mr. Maitland, April 7, 1985. (Copy in author's collection, courtesy of Fiona Burnett of Leys.)

2 Ewan Forbes, "Craigievar Castle," *Tales from Scottish Lairds* (Norwich: Jarrold & Sons, 1985), 141–44.

3 Ewan Forbes, *The Dancers of Don* (Aberdeen: Aberdeen University Press, 1989), 19.

4 Taken together, trans people's legal exclusion, social ostracism and the forced sterilization of no-choice surgery meet the formal definition of genocide, the biological and cultural eradication of a particular group of people. The distinction between "genocide" and a "crime against humanity" is that genocide requires a specific group to be identified for annihilation. The term was coined to distinguish between the different kinds of atrocities tried after World War II at the Nuremberg Trials. Scholarship has subsequently expanded the original narrow definition of genocide to include all social groups: see Norman M. Naimark, *Stalin's Genocides* (Princeton, NJ: Princeton University Press, 2010).

5 Council of Europe Parliamentary Assembly, *Recommendation 1117 (1989) on the Condition of Transsexuals*; European Parliament, *Resolution of 12 September 1989 on Discrimination Against Transsexuals*.

6 Press for Change, *Working for Civil Rights for All Transsexual and Transgendered People*, information leaflets, c. 1990s.

7 Leslie Feinberg, *Transgender Liberation* (New York: World View Forum, 1992), 5.

8 *Cossey v. UK*, Case 90/20 (1991) 13 EHRR 622, ECHR.

9 *P v. S and Cornwall County Council*, "Statement of P," para. 6.4. (Author's private collection.)

10 Silvan Agius and Christa Tobler, *Trans and Intersex People: Discrimination on the Grounds of Sex, Gender Identity and Gender Expression* (European Commission, 2012). Page 39 identifies P as the source of this argument.

11 Ruki Sayid, "Brother in Sex-Swap Shocker," *Sun*, September 1, 1992.

12 Jim Parker, "Sex Swap Secret of Top Model Bared," *Herald Express*, October 19, 1992.

13 "Wedding of Sex-Swop Man a Sham," *Express & Star*, August 21, 1992.

14 I am indebted to Rosemary Millington for her recollections of shooting with Ewan.

15 Ian Mitchell Davidson, *A Heritage in Stone* (Dingwall: Sandstone Press, 2017), 5–6.

16 Interview with Frank and Linda Smith, August 14, 2020. (Author's private collection.)

17 Kildrummy Church, "Dr the Hon Sir Ewan Forbes, Bart," *Service of Thanksgiving*, October 15, 1991. (Author's private collection.)

18 W. Henry Duncan, *Tribute to the Life of Dr the Hon Sir Ewan Forbes of Craigievar*, Auchindoir & Kildrummy Church, n.d. (Author's private collection.)

19 *P v. S and Cornwall County Council*, Case C-13/94 [1996] IRLR 347, European Court of Justice.

20 Ibid.

21 Deputy Head of General Register Office, "Affidavit of William Jenkins," April 12, 1995, given in *R v. Registrar General for England and Wales Ex parte P & G* [1996], unreported. (Author's private collection.)

22 Ros Wynne-Jones, "Why I Fought for the Right to be Female," *Independent*, May 1, 1996. P's piece was published in an edited form under the title "Trapped in a Man's Body with a Woman's Mind" when it appeared in the *Independent* on May 1, 1996. Press for Change eventually published P's statement in full with its original title, *Living in Truth* (a reference to a collection of essays by Vaclav Havel).

23 An account of the establishment of the forum is given by Dr. Lynne Jones in "The Parliamentarian," *Trans Britain: Our Journey from the Shadows*, ed. Christine Burns (London: Unbound, 2018), 161–86.

24 In 1992, John Money had introduced a new etiology for being trans in which genetic and endocrinological factors predominated, and in 1993, Professor Louis Gooren from Holland gave the Council of Europe's Colloquy on European Law an exhaustive account of the biology of being trans, reinstating it as an intersex condition and demanding that the law should make a provision for trans people as a matter of natural justice. See John Money, "The Concept of Gender Identity Disorder in Childhood and Adolescence After 37 Years," *Gender Identity and Development in Childhood and Adolescence Conference Proceedings, Friday 13 and Saturday 14 March 1992*, St. George's Hospital, London, 3–31: "Causality with respect to gender identity disorder is subdivisible into genetic, prenatal hormonal, postnatal social, and postpubertal hormonal determinants"; and L. J. G. Gooren, "Biological Aspects of

Transsexualism and Their Relevance to its Legal Aspects," *Transsexualism, Medicine and Law: Proceedings of the XXIIIrd Colloquy on European Law*, Vrije Universiteit, Amsterdam, Netherlands, April 14–16, 1993 (Council of Europe Publishing, 1995), 117–143. See also P. T. Cohen-Kettenis, L. J. G. Gooren, and R. Reid, "Psychiatric and Psychological Aspects of Transsexualism," *Transsexualism, Medicine and Law: Proceedings of the XXIIIrd Colloquy on European Law*, Vrije Universiteit, Amsterdam, Netherlands, April 14–16, 1993 (Council of Europe Publishing, 1995), 25–50.

25 Russell Reid et al., *Transsexualism: The Current Medical Viewpoint*, February 2, 1995 (author's private collection). This first edition was presented at the forum's second meeting, on February 2, 1995, and was subsequently issued as a booklet by Press for Change in March 1996.

26 Milton Diamond and H. K. Sigmundson, "Sex Reassignment at Birth. Long-Term Review and Clinical Implications," *Archives of Pediatrics and Adolescent Medicine* 151, no. 3 (1997): 298–304. See also John Colapinto, *As Nature Made Him: The Boy Who Was Raised as a Girl* (New York: HarperCollins, 2000).

27 GIRES began as an offshoot of Press for Change but was obliged to separate from it, since UK charities are not allowed to engage in political action.

28 Z. Playdon, *Report on the Survey of Provision of Medical Care for Transsexualism in UK District Health Authorities Carried out in 1995* (London: Parliamentary Forum on Transsexualism, January 18, 1996). (Author's private collection.)

29 *North West Lancashire Health Authority v. A, D & G* [1999] EWCA Civ 2022.

30 *X, Y and Z v. UK* (1997) 24 EHRR 143, ECHR.

31 *Sheffield and Horsham v. UK* (1998) 27 EHRR 163, ECHR.

32 Department for Education and Employment, *Guide to the Sex Discrimination (Gender Reassignment) Regulations 1999* (Sudbury, Suffolk: Department for Education and Employment Publications Centre, April 1999).

33 Home Office, *Report of the Interdepartmental Working Group on Transsexual People* (London: Home Office Communications Directorate, April 2000).

34 Sally Vincent, "Lost Boys," *Guardian Weekend*, 16 October 1993, pp. 4–8, 37.

35 Suzanne Moore, "The apple of an army's eye," *Guardian*, 2 May 1996, p. 5.

36 "Sex Swap For Queen Mum Doc," *Sunday Mirror*, 31 March 1996, p. 1.

37 *Sun*, 23 August 1996, p. 1.

38 Neil Jordan, *The Crying Game* (1992). The vomiting trope was repeated in, for example, Tom Shadyac's *Ace Ventura: Pet Detective* (1994) and Peter Segal's *Naked Gun 33⅓: The Final Insult* (1994).

39 In advance of the show's screening, for example, the *Daily Telegraph* described "the Israeli transvestite called Dana International" as "she-it-him"; the *Liverpool Echo* included as a clue in its quiz, "What is unusual about Dana International, the Israeli entrant for the Eurovision Song Contest"; and the *Reading Evening Post* published Dana's request for people to "just listen to the song and try to forget my personal story" under the headline "Singer in sex appeal." Boris Johnson, "Why our girl must beat the Euro cheats," *Daily Telegraph*, 4 May 1998, p. 26; "Quiz Time," *Liverpool Echo*, 5 May 1998, p. 10; "Singer in sex appeal," *Reading Evening Post*, 7 May 1998, p. 8.

40 Donna Hay, "Indecent proposal?", *What's on TV*, 26 September–2 October 1998, pp. 6–7.

41 Judith Butler, *Gender Trouble: Feminism and the Subversion of Identity* (New York: Routledge, 1990), p. 33.

42 *Bellinger v Bellinger* [2001] EWCA Civ 1140.

43 *Goodwin v United Kingdom* [2002] IRLR 664.

44 Department for Constitutional Affairs, *Government Policy Concerning Transsexual People*, July 2002. Now archived at https://web.archive.org/web/20080511211217/http://www.dca.gov.uk/constitution/transsex/policy.htm

45 Home Office, *Report of the Interdepartmental Working Group on Transsexual People*, p. 11.

46 Evangelical Alliance Policy Commission, *Transsexualism* (Carlisle: Paternoster Publishing, 2000), pp. 84–5. The document was written in response to the Home Office *Report of the Interdepartmental Working Group on Transsexual People* and formed the basis for objections to the Gender Recognition Act 2004.

47 Jay Walmsley, "The Story of the Sibyls," in *This Is My Body: Hearing the Theology of Transgender Christians*, ed. Christine Beardsley and Michelle O'Brien (London: Darton, Longman and Todd, 2016), 123–28.

48 See, for example, Christina Beardsley, "Taking Issue: The Transsexual Hiatus in *Some Issues in Human Sexuality*," *Theology* 108, no. 845 (2005): 338–46; Helen Savage, "Changing Sex?: Transsexuality and Christian Theology" (unpublished doctoral thesis, University of Durham, 2006).

12 Ewan's Legacy

1 John F. Burns, "British Monarchy Scraps Rule of Male Succession in New Step to Modernization," *New York Times*, October 28, 2011.

2 Countess of Clancarty et al., "Equality for Peeresses," *Daily Telegraph*, May 13, 2013.

3 Equality (Titles) Bill, Parliament: House of Lords, 12, 2013.

4 The successive bills were: Succession to Peerages Bill, Parliament: House of Lords, 16, 2015; Succession to Peerages Bill, Parliament: House of Lords, 33, 2016; Succession to Peerages Bill, Parliament: House of Lords, 5, 2017; Hereditary Titles (Female Succession) Bill, Parliament: House of Commons, 349, 2019; Hereditary Peerages and Baronetcies (Equality of Inheritance) Bill, Parliament: House of Lords, 75, 2020.

5 Thomas Singer, introduction to *Europe's Many Souls: Exploring Cultural Complexes and Identities*, ed. Joerg Rasche and Thomas Singer (New Orleans: Spring Journals, 2016), 1–31.

6 Lord Pannick, "Succession to Peerages," *Hansard*, House of Lords debates, September 11, 2015, column 1619.

7 A private member's bill is one introduced by MPs and Lords who are not government ministers, with the purpose of changing the law as it applies to the general population. Alex Carlile is now Baron Carlile of Berriew and sits in the House of Lords.

8 Gender Identity (Registration and Civil Status) Bill, Parliament: House of Commons, 23, 1995. Stephen Whittle and I were consulted about its contents. Neither of us was happy: Stephen wrote a whole other draft bill as an alternative, but that, too, was ignored. My criticism received the brusque response that "transsexuals should seek to obtain what is possible, nothing more." (Note from Terrence Walton to Zoë Playdon, February 24, 1995; author's private collection.)

9 Lord Filkin, "Official Report of the Grand Committee on the Gender Recognition Bill," *Hansard*, House of Lords debates, January 13, 2004, GC10.

10 Carolynn Gray, "A Critique of the Legal Recognition of Transsexuals in UK Law" (unpublished doctoral thesis, University of Glasgow, 2016), 178.

11 For further discussion of temporality in the Gender Recognition Act 2004, see Emily Grabham, *Brewing Legal Times: Things, Form, and the Enactment of Law* (Toronto: University of Toronto Press, 2016). The current recommended wording for the statutory declaration is: "I have lived as a (insert male or female as appropriate) throughout the period of _ years and I intend to live in that gender until death." The repetition of "live" and "until death" continues to imply that usual ideas of permanence do not apply to gender, while the term "lived as" implies a masquerade that denies the authenticity of trans lives.

12 Lord Tebbit, "Official Report of the Grand Committee on the Gender Recognition Bill," *Hansard*, House of Lords debates, January 13, 2004, GC20.

13 Gender Recognition Act 2004, 9.1.

14 Gail Knudson et al., "Identity Recognition Statement of the World Professional Association for Transgender Health (WPATH)," *International Journal of Transgenderism* 19, no. 3 (2018): 355–56.

15 The World Professional Association for Transgender Health, *Standards of Care for the Health of Transsexual, Transgender, and Gender Nonconforming People*, 7th version (WPATH, 2012). The Harry Benjamin International Gender Dysphoria Association renamed itself WPATH in 2007.

16 American Psychiatric Association, *Gender Dysphoria in the DSM-5*, 2013, http://www.dsm5.org/Documents/GenderDysphoria FactSheet.pdf.

17 Correspondence between Professor Zoë Playdon and Sir Ian Carruthers, CEO, NHS South of England, January 13, 2012, to December 5, 2012. (Author's private collection.)

18 At an NHS England gender identity workshop on November 27, 2014, Dr. John Dean, leader of the team producing the new National Service Specifications, said, "Ultimately, no one is required, or can be required, to have this [sterilization]. They can be pressured, they might be strongly encouraged; there's a fine line between encouraged, advised and pressured."

19 NHS England, Gender Identity Services for Adults (Non-Surgical Interventions), Service Specification No. 1719, September 2018.

20 NHS Specialised Services Circular, *Primary Care Responsibilities in Regard to Requests by Private On-Line Medical Service Providers to Prescribe Hormone Treatments for Transgender People*, SSC 1826, January 16, 2018.

21 Thinkers such as Judith Butler, Hélène Cixous, Rosi Braidotti, Julia Kristeva

and Luce Irigaray took feminist theory on its next intellectual step forward into postfeminism, while Edward Said, Homi Bhabha and Gayatri Spivak produced a distinctively postcolonial critique.

22 Judith Butler, *Undoing Gender* (London: Routledge, 2004), 28.

23 Kathleen Lennon and Rachel Alsop, *Gender Theory in Troubled Times* (London: Polity Press, 2020), 81.

24 Susan Stryker, *Transgender History* (Berkeley, CA: Seal Books, 2008), 134.

25 Julia Serano, *Whipping Girl* (Berkeley, CA: Seal Press, 2007), 14.

26 Ibid., 15–16.

27 Ibid., 166, 91.

28 Ibid., 93, 167.

29 ITV, *Coronation Street*, January 27, 2014, televised at 20:30 GMT.

30 Joey Soloway, *She Wants It* (London: Penguin Books, 2018) (published under the name "Jill Solway").

31 Susan Stryker and Paisley Currah, "Introduction," *Transgender Studies Quarterly* 1, no. 1–2 (2014): 1–18.

32 Rani Baker, " 'The Danish Girl' Stretches Frilly Forced Femme Fantasy Over Actual Trans History," *Harlot Magazine*, November 23, 2015, https://medium.com/@HARLOT/the-danish-girl-stretches-frilly-forced-femme-fantasy-over-actual-trans-history-c5703dbd47a0.

33 Harry Taylor on BBC Free Speech, "Things Not to Say to a Trans Person," May 20, 2015, https://www.facebook.com/watch/?v=641182835981226.

34 Correspondence between Professor Zoë Playdon and Professor Sir Peter Rubin, chair of the General Medical Council, June 25, 2012, to November 27, 2012. (Author's private collection.)

35 Caroline Lucas, "Gender Recognition: Mental Health Services," *Hansard*, House of Commons Written Answers, November 12, 2012, Column 66W.

36 Baroness Gould of Potternewton, "Health: Gender Reassignment," *Hansard*, House of Lords Written Answers, January 19, 2012, Column WA150.

37 Jay McNeil et al., *Trans Mental Health Study 2012* (Edinburgh: Scottish Transgender Alliance, September 2012).

38 Three years later, the GMC dismissed the complaints against Dr. Curtis.

39 Sarah Brown, "It's Time for the Media to Change the Record on Trans Healthcare," *PinkNews*, January 11, 2013, https://www.pinknews.co.uk/2013/01/11/comment-its-time-for-the-media-to-change-the-record-on-trans-healthcare.

40 #TransDocFailAnon tweets can be found at https://twitter.com/TransDocFailAno. "CHx" is West London Mental Health NHS Trust Gender Identity Clinic at Charing Cross Hospital. All tweets were anonymous, since that was the only way trans people felt safe to criticize their doctors.

41 Jane Fae, "The Real Trans Scandal Is Not the Failings of One Doctor but Cruelty by Many," *Guardian*, January 10, 2013, https://www.theguardian.com/commentisfree/2013/jan/10/trans-scandal-doctor-richard-curtis-trans docfail; Charlie Hallam, "As the #transdocfail Hashtag Showed, Many Trans People Are Afraid of Their Doctors," *New Statesman*, January 9, 2013, https://www.newstatesman.com/lifestyle/2013/01/transdocfail-hashtag-showed-many-trans-people-are-afraid-their-doctors.

42 Helen Belcher, "Submission by Trans Media Watch," The Leveson Inquiry, February 8, 2012, https://webarchive.nationalarchives.gov.uk/20140122161236 /http://www.levesoninquiry.org.uk/evidence/?witness=helen-belcher.

43 Julie Burchill, "Transsexuals Should Cut It Out," *Observer*, January 13, 2013, https://www.guardian.co.uk/commentisfree/2013/jan/13/julie-burchill -suzanne-moore-transsexuals (subsequently removed; copy of text in author's private collection).

44 Roz Kaveney, "Julie Burchill Has Ended Up Bullying the Trans Community," *Guardian*, January 13, 2013, https://www.theguardian.com/commentis free/2013/jan/13/julie-birchill-bullying-trans-community.

45 Lili Loofbourow, "The Male Glance," *VQR: A National Journal of Literature and Discussion*, Spring 2018, https://www.vqronline.org/essays-articles /2018/03/male-glance.

46 The designation "trans-exclusionary radical feminist" and its acronym "terf" is sometimes regarded as shifting from being inoffensive to being denigratory. However, as Christopher Davis and Elin McCready point out, "terf" denotes a chosen ideology, rather than being an intrinsic slur. See C. Davis and E. McCready, "The Instability of Slurs," *Grazer Philosophische Studien* 97, no. 1 (2020): 63–85. Accordingly, I retain it here to maintain historical continuity; to reflect the thrust of its arguments that trans people should be excluded from legal, medical and social equality; and to indicate that frequently its protagonists implicitly or explicitly justify their views by appealing to their idea of radical feminism. I have used lowercase to avoid the negative connotations sometimes associated with capitalization, for example, in social media.

47 Heather Saul, "Germaine Greer Defends 'Grossly Offensive' Comments about Transgender Women: 'Just Because You Lop off Your D**k Doesn't Make You a ******* Woman," *Independent*, October 26, 2015, https://www.independent .co.uk/news/people/germaine-greer-defends-grossly-offensive-comments -about-transgender-women-just-because-you-lop-off-a6709061.html.

48 The Yogyakarta Principles were drawn up by an international panel of experts in international law and on sexual orientation and gender identity. They take their name from the location in India where the experts met. The principles were updated in 2016. See yogyakartaprinciples.org.

49 United Nations General Assembly Human Rights Council, *Report of the Special Rapporteur on Torture and Other Cruel, Inhuman or Degrading Treatment or Punishment*, February 1, 2013, A/HRC/22/53.

50 Amnesty International, *The State Decides Who I Am: Lack of Legal Gender Recognition for Transgender People in Europe* (London: Amnesty International, 2014).

51 FRA: European Union Agency for Fundamental Rights, *Being Trans in the European Union: Comparative Analysis of EU LGBT Survey Data* (Luxembourg: Publications Office of the European Union, 2014).

52 Lucy Mangan, "If We Get Bogged Down in the Terf War We'll Never Achieve Anything," *Guardian*, August 9, 2014, https://www.theguardian.com/lifeand style/2014/aug/09/lucy-mangan-terf-war

53 Lennon and Alsop, *Gender Theory in Troubled Times*, 5.

54 Mark Gevisser, *The Pink Line: The World's Queer Frontiers* (London: Profile Books, 2020), 320.

55 Ibid., 320–21.

56 Ibid., 216, 30.

57 Women and Equalities Committee, *Transgender Equality* (London: The Stationery Office, January 14, 2016), 82.

58 Donald Trump (@realDonaldTrump), Twitter, October 7, 2019, https://twitter.com/realDonaldTrump/status/1181232249821388801.

59 The armed forces ban was reversed when President Trump left office.

60 Ruth Pearce, Sonja Erikainen, and Ben Vincent, "TERF Wars: An Introduction," in *TERF Wars: Feminism and the Fight for Transgender Futures*, ed. Ben Vincent, Sonja Erikainen and Ruth Pearce, *The Sociological Review Monographs* 68, no. 4 (2020): 3–24.

61 BBC Radio 4, *Woman's Hour*, "Gender Recognition Act Consultation," October 16, 2018, https://www.bbc.co.uk/programmes/m0000qpk.

62 Channel 4, *Genderquake*, May 8, 2018. Professor Stephen Whittle, who was part of the audience, confirmed that Channel 4 staff encouraged the heckling. The episode is no longer available to watch online.

63 For example, in the US, the exposure of Watergate led to President Richard Nixon resigning from power, while more recently, President Donald Trump was impeached for soliciting Ukrainian interference in American political affairs. In the UK, just four years before Ewan's trial, the Profumo Affair sex scandal almost toppled the government, and in 1969, while Ewan's fate was being decided by the Home Secretary, unknown to the public, the leader of the Liberal Party, Jeremy Thorpe, was becoming involved in a series of events that would lead to his being tried in court for conspiring to murder his ex-lover Norman Scott. Unmasking cover-ups became a staple of twenty-first-century news: a 2010 judicial inquiry exposed the 1972 shooting by the British Army of unarmed British citizens on "Bloody Sunday" in the north of Ireland; after the death of television celebrity Sir Jimmy Savile in 2011, investigations revealed that he had used his position to sexually abuse children for fifty years; another child-abuse inquiry in 2017 showed that when Prime Minister Margaret Thatcher awarded a knighthood to Liberal MP Sir Cyril Smith, she knew he was a pedophile whose activities had been ignored by the security services; and in 2018, the Windrush scandal revealed government's wrongful detainment and deportation of British citizens of color. Globally, WikiLeaks exposed worldwide corruption, while the Harvey Weinstein scandal that triggered the viral #MeToo movement revealed endemic sexual harassment in the entertainment and other industries.

64 Lisa Littman, "Parent Reports of Adolescents and Young Adults Perceived to Show Signs of a Rapid Onset of Gender Dysphoria," *PLoS ONE*, 13(8) doi.org/10.1371/journal.pone.0202330.

65 Florence Ashley, "A Critical Commentary on 'Rapid-Onset Gender Dysphoria,'" in *TERF Wars: Feminism and the Fight for Transgender Futures*, ed. Ben Vincent, Sonja Erikainen and Ruth Pearce, *The Sociological Review Monographs* 68, no. 4 (2020): 105–25.

66 J. K. Rowling, https://www.jkrowling.com/opinions/j-k-rowling-writes-about-her-reasons-for-speaking-out-on-sex-and-gender-issues/.

67 Adrienne Rich, "Compulsory Heterosexuality and Lesbian Existence," *Signs* 5, no. 4 (1980): 631–60. Betty Friedan, one of the leaders of the National Organization for Women, coined the term "lavender menace" in 1969 to describe the threat to the feminist movement that she believed lesbian women constituted. She apologized in 1977.

68 Nick Duffy, " 'Gender Critical' Activists with 'I Heart JK Rowling' Banner Mock Black Lives Matter Protesters in Ugly Confrontation," *PinkNews*, August 31, 2020, https://www.pinknews.co.uk/2020/08/31/gender-critical-posie-parker-jk-rowling-banner-black-lives-matter-protesters-transphobia.

69 Susan Stryker, "Trans Studies Now," *Transgender Studies Quarterly* 7, no. 3 (2020): 299–305.

70 Sally Hines, "Sex Wars and (Trans) Gender Panics: Identity and Body Politics in Contemporary UK Feminism," in *TERF Wars: Feminism and the Fight for Transgender Futures*, ed. Ben Vincent, Sonja Erikainen and Ruth Pearce, *Sociological Review Monographs* 68, no. 4 (2020): 25–43.

71 Gaby Hinsliff, "Whisper It, but Is Anger Giving Way to Decency in Our Politics?," *Guardian*, March 6, 2020.

72 Pearce, Erikainen, and Vincent, "TERF Wars: An Introduction," 5. Liz Truss, the Minister for Equalities, set out this agenda in a speech delivered to the Women and Equalities Committee on April 22, 2020, https://www.gov.uk/government/speeches/minister-for-women-and-equalities-liz-truss-sets-out-priorities-to-women-and-equalities-select-committee.

73 Helena Kennedy, *Eve Was Shamed* (London: Chatto & Windus, 2018), 233.

74 National Centre for Transgender Equality, "The Discrimination Administration: Trump's Record of Action Against Transgender People," https://transequality.org/the-discrimination-administration.

75 Joe Biden (@JoeBiden), Twitter, November 20, 2020, https://twitter.com/JoeBiden/status/1329815610180710401.

76 Royal College of Psychiatrists, *Gender Identity Disorders in Children and Adolescents, Guidance for Management, Council Report CR63* (London: Royal College of Psychiatrists, 1998). Tanner stages, also known as sexual maturity rating, track the development of sex characteristics of children in puberty. Tanner Stage 2 denotes that puberty has commenced. "Blockers" are a temporary intervention, delaying puberty rather than suppressing it: they are never used for prepubertal children.

77 Pearce, Erikainen and Vincent, "TERF Wars: An Introduction," 15.

78 *Bell v. Tavistock* [2020] EWHC 3274 (Admin).

79 Chelsea D. Gilts et al., "Treatment Regret and Quality of Life Following Radical Prostatectomy," *Supportive Care in Cancer* 21, no. 12 (2013): 3337–43.

80 NHS, "Children and Young People: Consent to Treatment," https://www.nhs.uk/conditions/consent-to-treatment/children. The Gillick principle is based on a House of Lords legal case, *Gillick v West Norfolk and Wisbech Area Health Authority* [1986] AC 112. For further discussion of legal consent issues for trans children and adolescents, see Robin Moira White and Nicola

Newbegin, *A Practical Guide to Transgender Law* (Minehead: Law Brief Publishing, 2021).

81 Care Quality Commission, *Tavistock and Portman NHS Foundation Trust Gender Identity Services Inspection Report*, January 20, 2021, 4, https://api.cqc.org.uk/public/v1/reports/7ecf93b7-2b14-45ea-a317-53b6f4804c24?20210301173155

82 Ibid.

83 Paul Jenkins, "Statement in Response to the January 2021 CQC Report on GIDS," Tavistock and Portman NHS Foundation Trust, January 20, 2021, https://tavistockandportman.nhs.uk/about-us/news/stories/statement-response-january-2021-cqc-report-gids.

84 Simona Giordano and Søren Holm, "Is Puberty-Delaying Treatment 'Experimental Treatment'?," *International Journal of Transgender Healthcare* 21, no. 2 (2020): 113–21. GnRH analogues are well-established treatments for adult conditions such as endometriosis and prostate cancer. Pediatric endocrinologists have experience of their licensed use for precocious puberty and their "off license" use in many settings, such as prolonged growing times in children born small for gestational age, children with congenital adrenal hyperplasia, and some survivors of childhood cancers. Their effect on reproductive abilities is wholly reversible.

85 *AB v. Tavistock and Portman NHS Foundation Trust* [2021] EWHC 741 (Fam).

86 Good Law Project, "Our Parental Consent Case Against the Tavistock Has Succeeded," March 26, 2021, https://goodlawproject.org/news/tavistock-success.

87 British Medical Association Media Team, "Leading Doctors Affirm Trans and Non-Binary Rights in Healthcare," September 15, 2020, https://www.bma.org.uk/bma-media-centre/leading-doctors-affirm-trans-and-non-binary-rights-in-healthcare.

88 General Medical Council, "Ethical Guidance for Doctors," November 9, 2020, www.gmc-uk.org/guidance

89 Stonewall, "Stonewall Statement on Gender Recognition Act Reform," September 22, 2020, https://www.stonewall.org.uk/about-us/news/stonewall-statement-gender-recognition-act-reform. By September 2020, the government had shifted its position and proposed only to put the process for applying for a Gender Recognition Certificate online, and to reduce the £140 fee to "a nominal amount." Although this was considered by trans communities to be preferable to the government's initial proposals to reduce equality, it did nothing to improve equality or reduce psychopathologization. Elizabeth Truss, "Response to Gender Recognition Act (2004) Consultation," Statement UIN HCWS4262, September 22, 2020, https://questions-statements.parliament.uk/written-statements/detail/2020-09-22/HCWS462.

90 Robert Booth, "Transgender Man Loses Appeal Court Battle to Be Registered as Father," *Guardian*, April 29, 2020, https://www.theguardian.com/society/2020/apr/29/transgender-man-loses-appeal-court-battle-registered-father-freddy-mcconnell.

91 The writer Jan Morris, transitioning in 1970, records that "the Welfare Officer of the Passport Office sent me a passport without any indication of sex"

to use as she moved from pre- to post-surgery. See Jan Morris, *Conundrum* (London: Faber & Faber, 1974), 106.

92 Luce Irigaray, *I Love to You*, trans. Alison Martin (New York: Routledge, 1996), 53.

93 Lennon and Alsop, *Gender Theory in Troubled Times*, 2.

94 Claire Dyer, "A Fight to Be Born Female," *Guardian*, February 6, 1996.

95 Murad Ahmed, "Male or Female Not Enough as Facebook Offers 50 Genders," *The Times*, 15 February 2014, p. 7.

96 "Top 90 Transgender Blogs and Websites to Follow in 2021," last updated July 22, 2021, https://blog.feedspot.com/transgender_blogs.

97 For example, Roz Kaveney, *Tiny Pieces of Skull* (London: Team Angelica, 2015); Casey Plett, *Little Fish* (Vancouver: Arsenal Pulp Press, 2018) and Andrea Lawlor, *Paul Takes the Form of a Mortal Girl* (New York: Vintage Books, 2019).

98 Nicholas M. Teich, *Transgender 101: A Simple Guide to a Complex Issue* (New York: Columbia University Press, 2012); Ashley Mardell, *The ABC's of LGBT+* (Coral Gables, FL: Mango Media: 2016).

BIBLIOGRAPHY

Archival Sources

This book draws on uncollected materials in the possession of the family and friends of Ewan Forbes as well as on documents in my private collection. I have made use of the following public archives:

Digitized news collections, the London Library, London
Dr. Dave King, Transgender Research Materials, the Wellcome Library, London
EThOs e-theses online service, British Library, https://ethos.bl.uk
Hansard, UK Parliament online, https://hansard.parliament.uk
National Center for Transgender Equality, Washington DC, https://transequality
.org
National Records of Scotland, Edinburgh
Newspaper Collection, British Library, London
Special Collections Centre, University of Aberdeen
TGEU—Transgender Europe, Berlin, https://tgeu.org
Trans-Academic Archives, https://www.jiscmail.ac.uk/cgi-bin/webadmin?A0=trans
-academic
University of Southern California Digital Library, http://digitallibrary.usc.edu
cdm

Books and Journals

Agius, Silvan, and Christa Tobler, *Trans and Intersex People: Discrimination on the Grounds of Sex, Gender Identity and Gender Expression* (European Commission, 2012)
Allen, Clifford, "Definition of Male and Female," *British Medical Journal* 1, no. 4865 (1954): 816
——, "Change of Sex," *British Medical Journal* 1, no. 4869 (1954): 1040
——, *A Textbook of Psychosexual Disorders* (London: Oxford University Press, 1962)
Allen, Robert, *There but for the Grace* (London: W. H. Allen, 1954)
American Psychiatric Association, *Diagnostic and Statistical Manual of Mental Disorders* (Washington: APA, 1980)
American Psychiatric Association, *Gender Dysphoria in the DSM-5*, 2013, http://www.dsm5.org/Documents/GenderDysphoriaFactSheet.pdf
Amnesty International, *The State Decides Who I Am: Lack of Legal Gender Recog-

nition for Transgender People in Europe (London: Amnesty International, 2014)

Andrew, Christopher, *The Defence of the Realm: The Authorized History of MI5* (London: Penguin Books, 2010)

Armstrong, C. N., "Diversities of Sex," *British Medical Journal* (1955): 1173–77

———, "Transsexualism: A Medical Perspective," *Journal of Medical Ethics* 6, no. 2 (1980): 90–91

Ashbee, Henry Spencer ("Pisanus Fraxi"), *Index Librorum Prohibitorum, Being Notes Bio- Biblio- Icono- graphical and Critical on Curious and Uncommon Books*, vols I–III [privately printed 1877] (New York: Documentary Books, 1962)

Ashley, April, with Douglas Thompson, *The First Lady* (London: John Blake, 2006)

Ashley, Florence, "A Critical Commentary on 'Rapid-Onset Gender Dysphoria,'" in *TERF Wars: Feminism and the Fight for Transgender Futures*, ed. Ben Vincent, Sonja Erikainen and Ruth Pearce, *The Sociological Review Monographs* 68, no. 4 (2020): 105–25

Baer, Karl M. [N. O. Body], *Memoirs of a Man's Maiden Years*, trans. Deborah Simon (1907; Philadelphia: University of Pennsylvania Press, 2006)

Baraitser, Lisa, *Enduring Time* (London: Bloomsbury Academic, 2018)

Bashford, Jon, Sherife Hasan, Christina Marriott and Kamlesh Patel, *Inside Gender Identity* (Community Innovations Enterprise, December 2017)

Beachy, Robert, *Gay Berlin: Birthplace of a Modern Identity* (New York: Vintage Books, 2015)

Beardsley, Christina, "Taking Issue: The Transsexual Hiatus in *Some Issues in Human Sexuality*," *Theology* 108, no. 845 (2005): 338–46

———, and Michelle O'Brien, eds., *This Is My Body: Hearing the Theology of Transgender Christians* (London: Darton, Longman and Todd, 2016)

Belcher, Helen, "Submission by Trans Media Watch," *The Leveson Inquiry*, February 8, 2012, https://webarchive.nationalarchives.gov.uk/20140122161236/http://www.levesoninquiry.org.uk/evidence/?witness=helen-belcher

Bendyshe, Thomas, "The History of Anthropology," *Memoirs of the Anthropological Society of London*, volume 1 (London: Trubner and Co., 1863–64)

Benjamin, Harry, "Transvestism and Transsexualism," *International Journal of Sexology* 7 (1953): 12–14

———, *The Transsexual Phenomenon* (New York: Julian Press, 1966)

———, introduction to *Transsexualism and Sex Reassignment*, ed. Richard Green and John Money (Baltimore: Johns Hopkins University Press, 1969), 1–10

Bornstein, Kate, *Gender Outlaw* (New York: Routledge, 1994)

Bottome, Phyllis, *The Challenge* (London: Faber & Faber, 1952)

Bourdieu, Pierre, *The Field of Cultural Production*, ed. Randal Johnson (London: Polity Press, 1993)

Brill, Stephanie, and Rachel Pepper, *The Transgender Child: A Handbook for Families and Professionals* (San Francisco: Cleis Press, 2008)

British Medical Association Media Team, "Leading Doctors Affirm Trans and Non-Binary Rights in Healthcare," September 15, 2020, https://www

.bma.org.uk/bma-media-centre/leading-doctors-affirm-trans-and-non
-binary-rights-in-healthcare

Brooks-Gordon, Belinda, Loraine Gelsthorpe, Martin Johnson, and Andrew
Bainham, eds, *Sexuality Repositioned: Diversity and the Law* (Oxford: Hart,
2004)

Broster, L. R. and H. W. C. Vines, *The Adrenal Cortex* (London: H. K. Lewis, 1933)

Burke's Peerage & Baronetage, 107th edition, volume I

Butler, Judith, *Gender Trouble: Feminism and the Subversion of Identity* (New
York: Routledge, 1990)

———, *Undoing Gender* (London: Routledge, 2004)

Care Quality Commission, *Tavistock and Portman NHS Foundation Trust Gender
Identity Services Inspection Report*, January 20, 2021

Cashford, Jules, "Britain: Autonomy and Insularity in an Island Race," in *Europe's
Many Souls: Exploring Cultural Complexes and Identities*, ed. Joerg Rasche
and Thomas Singer (New Orleans: Spring Journals, 2016), 37–68

Cauldwell, D. O., "Psychopathia Transexualis," *Sexology* 16 (1949): 274–80

Cawadias, A. P., *Hermaphroditos: The Human Intersex* (London: William Heinemann, 1943)

"Change of Sex," *British Medical Journal* 1, no. 4866 (1954): 876

"Change of Sex" *British Medical Journal* 1, no. 4863 (1954): 694

Cohen-Kettenis, P. T., L. J. G. Gooren, and R. Reid, "Psychiatric and Psychological Aspects of Transsexualism," *Transsexualism, Medicine and Law:
Proceedings of the XXIIIrd Colloquy on European Law*, Vrije Universiteit,
Amsterdam, Netherlands, April 14–16, 1993 (Council of Europe Publishing, 1995), 25–50

Colapinto, John, *As Nature Made Him: The Boy Who Was Raised as a Girl* (New
York: HarperCollins, 2000)

Coleman, Eli, "Toward Version 7 of the World Professional Association for Transgender Health's *Standards of Care*," *International Journal of Transgenderism*
11, no. 4 (2009): 1–7

Cooper, Alix, *Inventing the Indigenous: Local Knowledge and Natural History in
Early Modern Europe* (Cambridge: Cambridge University Press, 2007)

Cossey, Caroline, *My Story* (London: Faber & Faber, 1991)

Council of Europe Parliamentary Assembly, *Recommendation 1117 (1989) on the
Condition of Transsexuals*

Court of Session, Scotland, *Report of Proceedings in Summary Trial in Petition
John Alexander Cumnock Forbes-Sempill and the Honourable Ewan Forbes-
Sempill*, May 15–18, 1967 (Scottish Office Ref: CS258/1991/892)

Cowell, Roberta, *Roberta Cowell's Story by Herself* (London: William Heinemann,
1954)

Davidson, Ian Mitchell, *A Heritage in Stone* (Dingwall: Sandstone Press, 2017)

Davis, C., and E. McCready, "The Instability of Slurs," *Grazer Philosophische Studien* 97, no. 1 (2020), 63–85

de Beauvoir, Simone, *The Second Sex*, trans. Constance Borde and Sheila
Malovany-Chevallier (London: Vintage, 2011). First published as *La deuxième sexe* (Paris: Éditions Gallimard, 1949)

Dean, John, Women and Equalities Committee Oral Evidence: Transgender Equality Inquiry, HC390, September 8, 2015 (London: House of Commons, 2016)

Department for Constitutional Affairs, "Government Policy Concerning Transsexual People," July 2002, https://web.archive.org/web/20080511211217/http://www.dca.gov.uk/constitution/transsex/policy.htm

Department for Education and Employment, *Guide to the Sex Discrimination (Gender Reassignment) Regulations 1999* (Sudbury, Suffolk: Department for Education and Employment Publications Centre, April 1999)

Department of Health, *A Guide to Hormone Therapy for Trans People* (London: Department of Health, 2007)

——, *Guidance for GPs, Other Clinicians and Health Professionals on the Care of Gender Variant People* (London: Department of Health, 2008)

——, *Trans: A Practical Guide for the NHS* (London: Department of Health, 2008)

Dewhurst, C. J., A. J. N. Warrack, and M. D. Casey, "An XX Hermaphrodite with Male Social Sex," *British Medical Journal* (1963): 221

Dewhurst, Jack, *Royal Confinements: A Gynaecological History of the Royal Family* (New York: St. Martin's Press, 1980)

Diamond, Milton, "A Critical Evaluation of the Ontogeny of Human Sexual Behavior," *The Quarterly Review of Biology* 4, no. 2 (June 1965): 147–75

——, and H. K. Sigmundson, "Sex Reassignment at Birth. Long-Term Review and Clinical Implications," *Archives of Pediatrics and Adolescent Medicine* 151, no. 3 (1997): 298–304

Dickinson, Tommy, *"Curing Queers": Mental Nurses and Their Patients, 1935–74* (Manchester: Manchester University Press, 2015)

Dillon, Michael, *Self: A Study in Ethics and Endocrinology* (London: Heinemann, 1946)

——, Lobzang Jivaka, *Out of the Ordinary: A Life of Gender and Spiritual Transitions*, ed. Jacob Lau and Cameron Partridge (New York: Fordham University Press, 2017)

Duncan, W. Henry, *Tribute to the Life of Dr the Hon Sir Ewan Forbes of Craigievar*, Auchindoir & Kildrummy Church, n.d. (author's private collection)

Dworkin, Andrea, *Woman Hating* (New York: Dutton, 1974)

Ebershoff, David, *The Danish Girl* (London: Weidenfeld & Nicholson, 2015)

European Parliament, *Resolution of 12 September 1989 on Discrimination Against Transsexuals*

Evangelical Alliance Policy Commission, *Transsexualism* (Carlisle: Paternoster Publishing, 2000)

Fallowell, Duncan, and April Ashley, *April Ashley's Odyssey* (London: Jonathan Cape, 1982)

Fanon, Frantz, *Black Skin, White Masks*, trans. Charles Lam Markmann (London: Pluto Press, 2008)

Fausto-Sterling, Anne, "The Five Sexes," *The Sciences* 33, no. 2 (1993): 20–24

Feather, Stuart, *Blowing the Lid: Gay Liberation, Sexual Revolution and Radical Queens* (Winchester: Zero Books, 2015)

Feinberg, Leslie, *Transgender Liberation* (New York: World View Forum, 1992)

Ferris, John, "When Mr. Becomes Ms.—or Wants To! Transvestism and Transsexuals in the Workplace," *Personnel Management*, July 1988, 44–48

First International Symposium on Gender Identity, 1969, http://digitallibrary.usc.edu/cdm/ref/collection/p15799coll4/id/1571/rec/7

Forbes, Ewan, *The Aul' Days* (Aberdeen: Aberdeen University Press, 1984)

———, "Craigievar Castle," *Tales from Scottish Lairds* (Norwich: Jarrold & Sons, 1985), 141–44

———, *The Dancers of Don* (Aberdeen: Aberdeen University Press, 1989)

Foucault, Michel, *The History of Sexuality*, vol. 1, trans. Robert Hurley (London: Penguin, 1978)

FRA: European Union Agency for Fundamental Rights, *Being Trans in the European Union: Comparative Analysis of EU LGBT Survey Data* (Luxembourg: Publications Office of the European Union, 2014)

Friedan, Betty, *The Feminine Mystique* (London: Victor Gollancz, 1963)

Garfinkel, Harold, *Studies in Ethnomethodology* (Englewood Cliffs, NJ: Prentice-Hall, 1967)

General Medical Council, "Ethical Guidance for Doctors," November 9, 2020, www.gmc-uk.org/guidance

———, *Good medical practice*, www.gmc-uk.org/ethical-guidance/ethical-guidance-for-doctors/good-medical-practice

Gervisser, Mark, *The Pink Line: The World's Queer Frontiers* (London: Profile Books, 2020)

Gibson, James J., *The Ecological Approach to Visual Perception* (Boston: Houghton Mifflin, 1979)

Gilmore, Stephen, "*Corbett v. Corbett*: Once a Man, Always a Man?," *Landmark Cases in Family Law*, ed. Stephen Gilmore, Jonathan Herring and Rebecca Probert (Oxford: Hart, 2011)

Gilts, Chelsea D., et al., "Treatment Regret and Quality of Life Following Radical Prostatectomy," *Supportive Care in Cancer* 21, no. 12 (2013): 3337–43. doi.10.1007/s00520-013-1906-4.

Giordano, Simona, and Søren Holm, "Is Puberty-Delaying Treatment 'Experimental Treatment'?," *International Journal of Transgender Healthcare* 21, no. 2 (2020): 113–21

Goffman, Erving, *Stigma: Notes on the Management of Spoiled Identity* (Englewood Cliffs, NJ: Prentice-Hall, 1963)

Goldacre, Ben, *Bad Science* (London: Fourth Estate, 2008)

Good Law Project, "Our Parental Consent Case Against the Tavistock Has Succeeded," March 26, 2021, https://goodlawproject.org/news/tavistock-success

Gooren, L. J. G., "Biological Aspects of Transsexualism and Their Relevance to its Legal Aspects," *Transsexualism, Medicine and Law: Proceedings of the XXIIIrd Colloquy on European Law*, Vrije Universiteit, Amsterdam, Netherlands, April 14–16, 1993 (Council of Europe Publishing, 1995), 117–43

Gorecki, "Brux Lodge, Aberdeenshire. December 2008," urbexforums.com: Exploring the Unexplored and the Unknown, February 16, 2009, http://

www.urbexforums.com/showthread.php/2991-Brux-Lodge-Aberdeen
shire-December-2008

Gould, Stephen J., *The Mismeasure of Man* (London: W. W. Norton, 1981)

Government Equalities Office, *Government Response to the Women and Equalities Committee Report on Transgender Equality*, Cm 9301 (London: HMSO, July 2016)

——, *LGBT Action Plan*, July 2018

——, "Variations in Sex Characteristics Call for Evidence," January 17, 2019, https://www.gov.uk/government/consultations/variations-in-sex-charac teristics-call-for-evidence

Grabham, Emily, *Brewing Legal Times: Things, Form, and the Enactment of Law* (Toronto: University of Toronto Press, 2016)

Gray, Carolynn, "A Critique of the Legal Recognition of Transsexuals in UK Law" (unpublished doctoral thesis, University of Glasgow, 2016)

Green, Richard, Gay Rights, Trans Rights (self-published, 2018)

——, and John Money, eds., *Transsexualism and Sex Reassignment* (Baltimore: Johns Hopkins University Press, 1969)

Greer, Germaine, *The Female Eunuch* (London: MacGibbon & Kee, 1970)

Haire, Norman, *Everyday Sex Problems* (London: Frederick Muller, 1948)

Halberstam, Judith, *Female Masculinity* (Durham, NC: Duke University Press, 1998)

Hansard, "Commons Amendment to the Criminal Law Amendment Act, 1885," House of Lords, August 15, 1921, vol. 43

——, "Nullity of Marriage Bill," House of Lords Debate, April 22, 1971, vol. 317

——, "Official Report of the Grand Committee on the Gender Recognition Bill," House of Lords, January 13, 2004

——, "Health: Gender Reassignment," House of Lords Written Answers, January 19, 2012

——, "Gender Recognition: Mental Health Services," House of Commons Written Answers, November 12, 2012

——, "Succession to Peerages," House of Lords, September 11, 2015

Harry Benjamin International Gender Dysphoria Association Inc., *Standards of Care: The Hormonal and Surgical Sex Reassignment of Gender Dysphoria Persons*, revised draft 1/80 (San Francisco, 1980)

Heger, Heinz, *The Men with the Pink Triangle* (London: GMP, 1986). First published as *Die Männer mit dem Rosa Winkel* (Hamburg: Merlin-Verlag, 1972)

Heggie, Vanessa, "Testing Sex and Gender in Sports: Reinventing, Reimagining and Reconstructing Histories," *Endeavour* 34, no. 4 (2010): 157–163.

Hines, Sally, "Sex Wars and (Trans) Gender Panics: Identity and Body Politics in Contemporary UK Feminism," in *TERF Wars: Feminism and the Fight for Transgender Futures*, ed. Ben Vincent, Sonja Erikainen and Ruth Pearce, *The Sociological Review Monographs* 68, no. 4 (2020): 25–43

Hirsch, Pam, *The Constant Liberal: The Life and Work of Phyllis Bottome* (London: Quartet, 2010)

Hirschfeld, Magnus, *Transvestites: The Erotic Drive to Cross Dress*, trans. Michael A. Lombardi-Nash (1910; Buffalo: Prometheus Books, 1991)

Hodgkinson, Liz, *From a Girl to a Man* (London: Quartet, 2015)

Home Office, *Report of the Interdepartmental Working Group on Transsexual People* (London: Home Office Communications Directorate, April 2000)

Honey, Maureen, *Creating Rosie the Riveter* (Amherst: University of Massachusetts Press, 1984)

Honigsbaum, Frank, *The Division in British Medicine* (London: Kogan Page, 1979)

Hoyer, Niels (Ernst Ludwig Harthern-Jacobson), ed., *Man into Woman: An Authentic Record of a Change of Sex*, trans. H. J. Stenning (London: Jarrolds, 1933)

Hutton, Christopher, *The Tyranny of Ordinary Meaning: Corbett v. Corbett and the Invention of Legal Sex* (Switzerland: Palgrave Macmillan, 2019)

Ingold, Tim, *Being Alive: Essays on Movement, Knowledge and Description* (London: Routledge, 2011)

Irigaray, Luce, *I Love to You*, trans. Alison Martin (London: Routledge, 1996)

Jenkins, Paul, "Statement in Response to the January 2021 CQC Report on GIDS," Tavistock and Portman NHS Foundation Trust, January 20, 2021, https://tavistockandportman.nhs.uk/about-us/news/stories/statement-response-january-2021-cqc-report-gids

Jones, Lynne, "The Parliamentarian," in *Trans Britain: Our Journey from the Shadows*, edited by Christine Burns (London: Unbound, 2018), 161–86

Jorgensen, Christine, *Christine Jorgensen: A Personal Autobiography* (New York: Eriksson, 1967)

Joyce, James, *Ulysses: The Corrected Text* (London: Bodley Head, 1986)

Kaveney, Roz, *Tiny Pieces of Skull* (London: Team Angelica, 2015)

Kennedy, Helena, *Eve Was Shamed* (London: Chatto & Windus, 2018)

Kennedy, Pagan, *The First Man-Made Man* (New York: Bloomsbury, 2007)

Kildrummy Church, "Dr the Hon Sir Ewan Forbes, Bart," *Service of Thanksgiving*, October 15, 1991 (Author's private collection)

King, Dave, *The Transvestite and the Transsexual: Public Categories and Private Identities* (Aldershot: Avebury, 1993)

———, and Richard Ekins, "Pioneers of Transgendering: The Life and Work of Virginia Prince," Gendys Conference, 2000, http://www.gender.org.uk/conf/2000/king20.htm

King, Florence, *Confessions of a Failed Southern Lady* (New York: St. Martin's Press, 1985)

Kinsey, Alfred C., Wardell B. Pomeroy, and Clyde E. Martin, *Sexual Behavior in the Human Male* (Philadelphia: WB Saunders, 1948)

Knudson, Gail, et al., "Identity Recognition Statement of the World Professional Association for Transgender Health (WPATH)," *International Journal of Transgenderism* 19, no. 3 (2018): 355–56

Lawlor, Andrea, *Paul Takes the Form of a Mortal Girl* (New York: Vintage Books, 2019)

Leeds University TV/TS Group, "Conference Report," *Transvestism and Transsexualism in Modern Society* (Leeds, 1974)

Lennon, Kathleen, and Rachel Alsop, *Gender Theory in Troubled Times* (London: Polity Press, 2020)

Loofbourow, Lili, "The Male Glance," *VQR: A National Journal of Literature and Discussion*, Spring 2018, https://www.vqronline.org/essays-articles /2018/03/male-glance

Mardell, Ashley, *The ABC's of LGBT+* (Coral Gables, FL: Mango Publishing, 2016)

Marston, C., and R. Lewis, "Anal Heterosex among Young People and Implications for Health Promotion: A Qualitative Study in the UK," *BMJ Open* 4, no. 8 (2014): e004996

Mason, Nicholas, "The Transsexual Dilemma: Being a Transsexual," *Journal of Medical Ethics* 6 (1980): 85–89

McBride, Sarah, *Tomorrow Will Be Different* (New York: Three Rivers Press, 2018)

McNeil, Jay, et al., *Trans Mental Health Study 2012* (Edinburgh: Scottish Transgender Alliance, September 2012)

Melville, Michael Leslie, *The Story of the Lovat Scouts: 1900–1980* (Edinburgh: The Saint Andrew Press, 1981)

Meyerowitz, Joanne, *How Sex Changed: A History of Transsexuality in the United States* (Cambridge, MA: Harvard University Press, 2002)

Meyers, D. W., "Problems of Sex Determination and Alteration," *Medico-Legal Journal* 36, no. 4 (1968): 174–90

Mills, Ivor H., "Sex and Gender," *The Lancet* 295, no. 7642 (1970): 615

Ministry of Justice, "The Care and Management of Individuals Who Are Transgender," August 15, 2019

Money, John, Joan G. Hampson, and John L. Hampson, "Hermaphroditism: Recommendations Concerning Assignment of Sex, Change of Sex, and Psychologic Management," *Bulletin of the Johns Hopkins Hospital* 97, no. 4 (1955): 284–300

———, "Imprinting and the Establishment of Gender Role," *AMA Archives of Neurology and Psychiatry* 77, no. 3 (1957): 333–36

———, and Clay Primrose, "Sexual Dimorphism and Dissociation in the Psychology of Male Transsexuals," in *Transsexualism and Sex Reassignment*, ed. Richard Green and John Money (Baltimore: Johns Hopkins University Press, 1969), 115–36

———, and Patricia Tucker, *Sexual Signatures: On Being a Man or a Woman* (London: George G. Harrap, 1976)

———, "The Concept of Gender Identity Disorder in Childhood and Adolescence After 37 Years," *Gender Identity and Development in Childhood and Adolescence Conference Proceedings, Friday 13 and Saturday 14 March 1992*, St. George's Hospital, London, 3–31

Morris, Jan, *Conundrum* (London: Faber & Faber, 1974)

Naimark, Norman M., *Stalin's Genocides* (Princeton, NJ: Princeton University Press, 2010)

National Centre for Transgender Equality, "The Discrimination Administration: Trump's Record of Action Against Transgender People," https://trans equality.org/the-discrimination-administration

National Trust for Scotland, *Craigevar Castle* (Edinburgh: National Trust for Scotland, 2018)

NHS Specialised Services Circular, *Primary Care Responsibilities in Regard to*

Requests by Private On-Line Medical Service Providers to Prescribe Hormone Treatments for Transgender People, SSC 1826, January 16, 2018

NHS England, *Gender Identity Services for Adults (Non-Surgical Interventions)* Service Specification No. 1719, September 2018

NHS, "Children and Young People: Consent to Treatment," https://www.nhs.uk/conditions/consent-to-treatment/children

Nicol, Nancy et al., eds., *Envisioning Global LGBT Human Rights: (Neo)colonialism, Neoliberalism, Resistance and Hope* (London: Human Rights Consortium, 2018)

Ormrod, Roger, "The Medico-Legal Aspects of Sex Determination," *Medico-Legal Journal* 40, no. 3 (1972): 78–88

Oxtoby, Kathy, "Is the Hippocratic Oath Still Relevant to Practicing Doctors Today?" *BMJ* 2016; 355:i6629

Parliamentary Debates: House of Commons Official Report, "Standing Committees Session 1974–75," Vol. III (London: HMSO, 1975), 102–03

Parliamentary Forum on Transsexualism, *Guidelines for Health Organisations Commissioning Treatment Services for Individuals Experiencing Gender Dysphoria and Transsexualism* (London: Parliamentary Forum on Transsexualism, 2005)

Pauly, Ira B., "Adult Manifestations of Female Transsexualism," in *Transsexualism and Sex Reassignment*, ed. Richard Green and John Money (Baltimore: Johns Hopkins University Press, 1969), 59–87

Pearce, Ruth, Sonja Erikainen, and Ben Vincent, "TERF Wars: An Introduction," in *The Sociological Review Monographs* 68, no. 4 (2020): 677–98

Playdon, Z., *Report on the Survey of Provision of Medical Care for Transsexualism in UK District Health Authorities Carried out in 1995* (London: Parliamentary Forum on Transsexualism, January 18, 1996)

———, *Trans People in the New NHS*, conference organised by the Royal College of Psychiatrists, April 16, 2002

———, "Intersecting Oppressions: Ending Discrimination against Lesbians, Gay Men and Trans People in the UK," in *Sexuality Repositioned: Diversity and the Law*, ed. Belinda Brooks-Gordon, Loraine Gelsthorpe, Martin Johnson and Andrew Bainham (Oxford: Hart, 2004), 131–52

Plett, Casey, *Little Fish* (Vancouver: Arsenal Pulp Press, 2018)

Porter, Roy, *Madness: A Brief History* (Oxford: Oxford University Press, 2002)

Pratt, Mary Louise, *Imperial Eyes: Travel Writing and Transculturalism*, 2nd ed. (London: Routledge, 2008)

Press for Change, *Working for Civil Rights for All Transsexual and Transgendered People*, information leaflets, circa 1990s

Purkiss, Diane, *The Witch in History* (London: Routledge, 1996)

Randell, John Bulmer, "Cross Dressing and the Desire to Change Sex" (unpublished MD thesis, University of Wales, 1960)

———, *Sexual Variations* (London: Priory Press, 1973)

Rasche, Joerg, and Thomas Singer, eds., *Europe's Many Souls: Exploring Cultural Complexes and Identities* (New Orleans: Spring Journals, 2016)

Raymond, Janice, *The Transsexual Empire* (New York: Teachers College Press, 1979)

Rees, Mark, *Dear Sir or Madam: The Autobiography of a Female-to-Male Transsexual* (London: Cassell, 1996)

Reid, Russell, et al., *Transsexualism: The Current Medical Viewpoint*, 1st edition (London: Parliamentary Forum on Transsexualism, 1995)

Reis, Elizabeth, *Bodies in Doubt: An American History of Intersex* (Baltimore: Johns Hopkins University Press, 2009)

Rich, Adrienne, "Compulsory Heterosexuality and Lesbian Existence," *Signs* 5, no. 4 (1980): 631–60

Richards, Renée, *Second Serve: The Renée Richards Story* (New York: Stein and Day, 1983)

Riddell, Carol, *Divided Sisterhood: A Critical Review of Janice Raymond's* The Transsexual Empire (Liverpool: News from Nowhere, 1980)

Rorie, David, *The Book of Aberdeen: Compiled for the 107th Annual Meeting of the British Medical Association* (Aberdeen: BMA, 1939)

Rowling, J. K., "J. K. Rowling Writes about Her Reasons for Speaking out on Sex and Gender Issues," June 10, 2020, https://www.jkrowling.com/opinions/j-k-row ling-writes-about-her-reasons-for-speaking-out-on-sex-and-gender-issues

Said, Edward, *Orientalism* (London: Routledge & Kegan Paul, 1978)

Savage, Helen, "Changing Sex?: Transsexuality and Christian Theology" (unpublished doctoral thesis, University of Durham, 2006)

Schulze, Rainer, "Himmler's Crusade Against (Male) Homosexuality and the Continuing Stigmatisation of LGBT People After 1945," in *The Holocaust in History and Memory*, volume 4, *The Pink Triangle: The Long Shadow of the Nazi Persecution of Gay Men*, edited by Rainer Schulze (Colchester: Department of History, University of Essex, 2011), 17–39

"Selected Proceedings of the First International Congress on Gender Identity, London, England, July 1969," *Archives of Sexual Behavior* 1, no. 2 (1971): 145–74

Sengoopta, Chandak, "Glandular Politics: Experimental Biology, Clinical Medicine, and Homosexual Emancipation in Fin-de-Siècle Central Europe," *Isis* 89, no. 3 (1998), 445–73

Serano, Julia, *Whipping Girl* (Berkeley, CA: Seal Press, 2007)

"Sex and the Law," *British Medical Journal* 1, no. 4863 (1954): 710–11

"Sex of Athletes," *British Medical Journal* (1967): 185–86

Sheffield Group of the Campaign for Homosexual Equality, *Learning a Little About Transvestism* (Sheffield: CHE, 1976)

Shepherd, Nan, *The Living Mountain* (Aberdeen: Aberdeen University Press, 1977)

Skloot, Rebecca, *The Immortal Life of Henrietta Lacks* (New York: Crown, 2010)

Slade, Harry Gordon, "Modern Country Houses," *Times Literary Supplement*, January 14, 1984, 37

Smith, S., et al. "Injury Profile Suffered by Targets of Antipersonnel Improvised Explosive Devices: Prospective Cohort Study," *BMJ Open* 7, no. 7 (2017): e014697

Södersten, Per, David Crews, Cheryl Logan et al, "Eugen Steinach: The First Neuroendocrinologist," *Endocrinology*, 155, no. 3 (March 2014): 688–702

Soloway, Joey, *She Wants It* (London: Penguin Books, 2018) (published under the name "Jill Soloway")

Stewart, Jay, "Trans on Telly: Popular Documentary and the Production of Transgender Knowledge" (unpublished doctoral thesis, Goldsmiths College, University of London, 2015)

Stryker, Susan, introduction to *Christine Jorgensen: A Personal Autobiography*, by Christine Jorgensen (San Francisco: Cleis Press, 2000), v–xiii

——, and Stephen Whittle, eds., *The Transgender Studies Reader* (London: Routledge, 2006)

——, *Transgender History* (Berkeley, CA: Seal Books, 2008)

——, and Paisley Currah, "Introduction," *Transgender Studies Quarterly* 1, no. 1–2 (2014): 1–18

——, "Trans Studies Now," *Transgender Studies Quarterly* 7, no. 3 (2020): 299–305

Tata, Jamshed R., "One Hundred Years of Hormones," *EMBP Reports* 6, no. 6 (2005): 490–96.

Tebbutt, Clare R., "Popular and Medical Understandings of Sex Change in 1930s Britain" (unpublished doctoral thesis, University of Manchester, 2014)

Teich, Nicholas M., *Transgender 101: A Simple Guide to a Complex Issue* (New York: Columbia University Press, 2012)

Terman, Lewis M., and Catherine Cox Miles, *Sex and Personality: Studies in Masculinity and Femininity* (New York: McGraw-Hill, 1936)

The New Statistical Account of Scotland, VII (Edinburgh: Blackwood, 1845)

The Yogyakarta Principles: Principles on the application of international human rights law in relation to sexual orientation and gender identity, March 2007, yogyakartaprinciples.org

The Yogyakarta Principles plus 10: Additional principles and state obligations on the application of international human rights law in relation to sexual orientation and gender identity, gender expression and sex characteristics to complement the Yogyakarta Principles, November 10, 2017, yogyakartaprinciples.org

Thompson, Dorothy, *I Saw Hitler* (New York: Farrar & Rinehart, 1932)

Thomson, Matthew, "Disability, Psychiatry and Eugenics," in *The Oxford Handbook of the History of Eugenics*, ed. Alison Bashford and Philippa Levine (Oxford: Oxford University Press, 2010), 116–133

Transsexual Action Organisation, *Transsexual Information*, the Wellcome Library: PP/KIN/C/16

Transsexualism, Medicine and Law: Proceedings of the XXIIIrd Colloquy on European Law, Vrije Universiteit, Amsterdam, Netherlands, April 14–16, 1993 (Council of Europe Publishing, 1995)

Truss, Elizabeth, "Minister for Women and Equalities Liz Truss sets out priorities to Women and Equalities Committee," April 22, 2020, https://www.gov.uk /government/speeches/minister-for-women-and-equalities-liz-truss-sets -out-priorities-to-women-and-equalities-select-committee

——, "Response to Gender Recognition Act (2004) consultation," Statement UIN HCWS4262, September 22, 2020, https://questions-statements.par liament.uk/written-statements/detail/2020-09-22/HCWS462

United Nations General Assembly Human Rights Council, *Report of the Special Rapporteur on Torture and Other Cruel, Inhuman or Degrading Treatment or Punishment*, February 1, 2013, A/HRC/22/53

United Nations Population Fund State of the Population 2020, *Against My Will: Defying the Practices That Harm Women and Girls and Undermine Equality* (New York: UNFPA, 2020)

"Urinate Standing Up as a Female," *wikiHow*, June 3, 2021, https://www.wikihow.com/Urinate-Standing-Up-as-a-Female

von Krafft-Ebing, Richard, *Psychopathia Sexualis* (Stuttgart, 1886), authorized English adaptation of last revised German edition (New York: Pioneer Publications, 1947)

Weeks, Jeffrey, "After the Sexual Offences Act," paper presented at *A Step Forward? 50 Years Since the Sexual Offences Act*, conference held at the National Archives, July 22, 2017

White, Robin Moira, and Nicola Newbegin, *A Practical Guide to Transgender Law* (Minehead: Law Brief Publishing, 2021)

Wilchins, Riki, *Read My Lips: Sexual Subversion and the End of Gender* (New York: Firebrand Books, 1997)

———, *TRANS/gressive: How Transgender Activists Took on Gay Rights, Feminism, the Media & Congress . . . and Won!* (New York: Riverdale Avenue Books, 2017)

Women and Equalities Committee, *Transgender Equality* (London: The Stationery Office, January 14, 2016)

Woods, Gregory, *The Homintern: How Gay Culture Liberated the Modern World* (New Haven, CT: Yale University Press, 2016)

World Health Organization, *International Classification of Diseases* 1, no. 1 (Geneva: WHO, 1977)

World Professional Association for Transgender Health, *Standards of Care for the Health of Transsexual, Transgender, and Gender Nonconforming People*, 7th version (WPATH, 2012)

Yawar, Althar, "Healing in Survivors of Torture," *Journal of the Royal Society of Medicine* 97, no. 8 (2004): 366–70

Zhou, Jiang-Ning, Michel A. Hofman, Louis J. G. Gooren, and Dick F. Swaab, "A Sex Difference in the Human Brain and Its Relation to Transsexuality," *Nature* 378, no. 6552 (1995): 68–70

Newspaper Reports

"Fintray Public Hall Laying of the Foundation Stone," *Aberdeen Press and Journal*, May 15, 1914

"Deeside Season Ends in Brilliant Fashion," *Aberdeen Press and Journal*, September 15, 1928

"Aberdeen's Fine Response," *Aberdeen Press and Journal*, March 2, 1935

" 'Woman' Changes Her Sex," *Yorkshire Post and Leeds Intelligencer*, May 29, 1936

"He Was Formerly Woman Athlete," *Portsmouth Evening News*, August 11, 1936

"How Unlike a Woman!," *Daily Mail*, November 18, 1937

"Rain Spoils Social Side of Lord's Gathering," *Sunday Times*, July 10, 1938

"Funeral of Gwendolen Lady Sempill," *Aberdeen Press and Journal*, March 6, 1944

"Clan Banners Will Be Flown at Aboyne," *Aberdeen Press and Journal*, September 3, 1946

Ivor Brown, "Among the Shadows," *Observer*, September 16, 1951

Person's Change of Sex: Will Case Ruling," *Manchester Guardian*, October 4, 1951

"Whist Concert Aids St. Dunstan's," *Aberdeen Evening Express*, April 10, 1952

"Taken Off After One Night," *Manchester Guardian*, July 25, 1952

"Public Notices," *Aberdeen Press and Journal*, September 12, 1952

"Doctor's Birth Re-Registered," *Daily Telegraph*, September 13, 1952

"Exclusive Statement by Dr Ewan Forbes-Sempill," *Aberdeen Press and Journal*, September 15,1952

"Dr. Ewan Forbes-Sempill Weds His Housekeeper," *Aberdeen Evening Express*, October 11, 1952

Sidney Rodin, "Cowell Sensation," *Sunday Pictorial*, March 14, 1954

Duncan Webb, "Roberta: The Ghastly Truth at Last," *The People*, April 11, 1954

"Come off It 'Roberta,' " *The People*, April 18, 1954

"Changes of Sex," *Belfast News-Letter*, May 6, 1954

" 'Woman of the Year' at the Embassy," *The Stage*, September 23, 1954

"Sex-Change Sailor Sued by Ex-Wife," *Aberdeen Evening Express*, January 4, 1955

"My Life as Man and Woman," *Belper News*, January 28, 1955

"Sex-Changed Father Becomes Bride of Another Father," *Northern Whig*, July 29, 1955

"Change in Teacher's Birth Certificate," *The Times*, March 31, 1956

"The Picture That Baffled Six Doctors," *The People*, July 22, 1956

"Man Said to Be Changing Sex," *The Times*, July 31, 1957

"Sex Change 2. The Bearded Sailor," *Daily Herald*, August 1, 1957

"Change of Sex by Woman Pilot," *The Times*, January 13, 1958

"Not Cruel of Husband to Want to Be a Woman," *The Times*, May 23, 1958

Tom Mangold, " 'It's Love Again,' Coos Sex-Change Chris," *Sunday Mirror*, August 30, 1959

"Dreadful Problems in a Sex-Change," *The Stage*, November 5, 1959

"Sempill Poser—Court May Decide," *Aberdeen Press and Journal*, January 4, 1966

Pearl Murray, "This Scotswoman's Castle Is Her Home—At Last," *Aberdeen Press and Journal*, January 28, 1966

Len Adams, "The Astonishing Double Life of Miss Fink," *The People*, September 4, 1966

"BBC Takes a Candid View of Sex Change," *The Times*, November 21, 1966

"Husband Was a Woman," *The Times*, February 28, 1967

Cecil King, "Enough Is Enough," *Daily Mirror*, May 10, 1968

"Sir Ewan Gets the Verdict," *Aberdeen Press and Journal*, December 4, 1968

"Dr. Forbes-Sempill Is Now 11th Baronet of Forbes," *Glasgow Herald*, December 5, 1968

"Disquiet over Forbes-Sempill Secrecy Case," *Glasgow Herald*, December 6, 1968

"Model April in 'State of Limbo,' " *Newcastle Evening Chronicle*, February 2, 1970

"April's Husband Taken to Hospital," *Aberdeen Press and Journal*, February 3, 1970

"Judgment on April," *News of the World*, February 8, 1970

"Out on a Limbo," *Daily Mirror*, February 10, 1970

"Sex-Change 'Man' Gets a Divorce from Her Wife," *Newcastle Evening Chronicle*, January 19, 1972

"Sex-Change for a TV Music Man," *Daily Mirror*, May 18, 1972

"Oh Sister! Sex-Change Secret of a Monk," *Liverpool Echo*, March 6, 1975

"My Husband, the Sex-Change Para," *Daily Mirror*, April 7, 1977

"Plea For Sex-Change Vicar," *Birmingham Daily Post*, May 30, 1978

Sean Day-Lewis, "Sex and Suffering," *Daily Telegraph*, October 16, 1980

Richard Last, "Stepping out of Line," *Daily Telegraph*, October 17, 1980

"Obituary of Sir Ewan Forbes of Craigievar, Bt," *Daily Telegraph*, October 1, 1991

"Wedding of Sex-Swop Man a Sham," *Express & Star*, August 21, 1992

Ruki Sayid, "Brother in Sex-Swap Shocker," *Sun*, September 1, 1992

Jim Parker, "Sex Swap Secret of Top Model Bared," *Herald Express*, October 19, 1992

Sally Vincent, "Lost Boys," *Guardian Weekend*, October 16, 1993

Claire Dyer, "A Fight to Be Born Female," *Guardian*, February 6, 1996

"Sex Swap for Queen Mum Doc," *Sunday Mirror*, March 31, 1996

Ros Wynne-Jones, "Why I Fought for the Right to be Female," *Independent*, May 1, 1996

P, "Trapped in a Man's Body with a Woman's Mind" *Independent*, May 1, 1996

Suzanne Moore, "The Apple of an Army's Eye," *Guardian*, May 2, 1996

Boris Johnson, "Why Our Girl Must Beat the Euro Cheats," *Daily Telegraph*, May 4, 1998

"Quiz Time," *Liverpool Echo*, May 5, 1998

"Singer in Sex Appeal," *Reading Evening Post*, May 7, 1998

Donna Hay, "Indecent Proposal?," *What's on TV*, September 26–October 2, 1998

Caroline Richmond, "Professor Paul Polani," *Independent*, March 21, 2006, http://www.independent.co.uk/news/obituaries/professor-paul-polani-6106102.html

John F. Burns, "British Monarchy Scraps Rule of Male Succession in New Step to Modernization," *New York Times*, October 28, 2011

Charlie Hallam, "As the #transdocfail Hashtag Showed, Many Trans People Are Afraid of Their Doctors," *New Statesman*, January 9, 2013, https://www.newstatesman.com/lifestyle/2013/01/transdocfail-hashtag-showed-many-trans-people-are-afraid-their-doctors

Jane Fae, "The Real Trans Scandal Is Not the Failings of One Doctor but Cruelty by Many," *Guardian*, January 10, 2013, https://www.theguardian.com/commentisfree/2013/jan/10/trans-scandal-doctor-richard-curtis-transdocfail

Sarah Brown, "It's Time for the Media to Change the Record on Trans Healthcare," *PinkNews*, January 11, 2013, https://www.pinknews.co.uk/2013/01/11/comment-its-time-for-the-media-to-change-the-record-on-trans-health-care

Roz Kaveney, "Julie Burchill Has Ended Up Bullying the Trans Community," *Guardian*, January 13, 2013, https://www.theguardian.com/commentis-free/2013/jan/13/julie-birchill-bullying-trans-community

Julie Burchill, "Transsexuals Should Cut It Out," *Observer*, January 13, 2013, https://www.guardian.co.uk/commentisfree/2013/jan/13/julie-burchill -suzanne-moore-transsexuals (subsequently removed)

Murad Ahmed, "Male or Female Not Enough as Facebook Offers 50 Genders," *The Times*, February 15, 2014

Countess of Clancarty, "Equality for Peeresses," *Daily Telegraph*, May 13, 2013

Lucy Mangan, "If We Get Bogged Down in the Terf War We'll Never Achieve Anything," *Guardian*, August 9, 2014, https://www.theguardian.com/life andstyle/2014/aug/09/lucy-mangan-terf-war

Heather Saul, "Germaine Greer Defends 'Grossly Offensive' Comments about Transgender Women: 'Just Because You Lop off Your D**k Doesn't Make You a ******* Woman," *Independent*, October 26, 2015, https://www .independent.co.uk/news/people/germaine-greer-defends-grossly-offen sive-comments-about-transgender-women-just-because-you-lop-off -a6709061.html

Steven Brocklehurst, "Coming Oot: The Fabulous History of Gay Scotland," BBC News, November 28, 2015, http://www.bbc.co.uk/news/uk-scotland -34910016

Gaby Hinsliff, "Whisper It, but Is Anger Giving Way to Decency in Our Politics?," *Guardian*, March 6, 2020

Robert Booth, "Transgender Man Loses Appeal Court Battle to Be Registered as Father," *Guardian*, April 29, 2020, https://www.theguardian.com/society /2020/apr/29/transgender-man-loses-appeal-court-battle-registered -father-freddy-mcconnell

Nick Duffy, "'Gender Critical' Activists with 'I Heart JK Rowling' Banner Mock Black Lives Matter Protesters in Ugly Confrontation," *PinkNews*, August 31, 2020, https://www.pinknews.co.uk/2020/08/31/gender-critical-posie -parker-jk-rowling-banner-black-lives-matter-protesters-transphobia

Legal Cases

The key to the following abbreviations is at the start of the Notes section on page 299.

AB v. Tavistock and Portman NHS Foundation Trust [2021] EWHC 741 (Fam)

Anonymous v. Anonymous 67 Misc. 2d 982 (N.Y. Sup. Ct. 1971)

Bell v. Tavistock [2020] EWHC 3274 (Admin)

Bellinger v. Bellinger [2001] EWCA Civ 1140

Chessington World of Adventures v. Reed [1997] IRLR 556, EAT

Corbett v. Corbett [1970] 2 All ER 33

Cossey v. UK, Case 90 / 20 (1991) 13 EHRR 622, ECHR

Gardiner (Estate of) Re 42 P.3d 120 (Kan. 2002)

Gillick v. West Norfolk and Wisbech Area Health Authority [1986] AC 112

Goodwin v. United Kingdom [2002] IRLR 664

John Alexander Cumnock Forbes-Sempill v. The Hon Ewan Forbes-Sempill (1967) unreported, Scottish Court of Administration

Kantaras v. Kantaras 884 So. 2d 155 (Fla. Ct. App. 2004)
Kevin (Validity of Marriage of a Transsexual), Re [2001] FamCA 1074
Ladrach, Re 513 N.E.2d 828 (Ohio Misc. 1987)
Littleton v. Prange 9 S.W.3d 223, 224 (Tex. Ct. App. 1999)
M v. M (A) (1984) 42 RFL (2d) 267
North West Lancashire Health Authority v. A, D & G [1999] EWCA Civ 2022
P v. S and Cornwall County Council Case C-13/94 [1996] IRLR 347, ECJ
R v. Harris and McGuiness (1988) 17 NSWLR 158
R v. Registrar General for England and Wales Ex parte P & G (16 February 1996)
      unreported
Rees v. UK (1986) 9EHRR 56
S v. S [1962] 3 All ER 55
Sheffield and Horsham v. UK (1998) 27 EHRR 163, ECHR
Smith and Grady v. UK (1999) 29 EHRR 493
T, Re [1975] 2 NZLR 449, McMullin J
Talbot v. Talbot (1967) 111 SJ 213
W v. W 1976(2) SALR 308
White v. British Sugar Corporation [1977] IRLR 121
X Petitioner [1957] SLT (Sh. Ct.) 61
X, Y and Z v. UK (1997) 24 EHRR 143, ECHR

UK Statutes, Bills and Statutory Instruments

Criminal Law Amendment Act 1885
Representation of the People Act 1918
Representation of the People Act 1928
Administration of Justice (Scotland) Act 1933
Sexual Offences Act 1967
Equal Pay Act 1970
Nullity of Marriage Act 1971
Sex Discrimination Act 1975
Gender Identity (Registration and Civil Status) Bill 1996
House of Lords Act 1999
Sex Discrimination (Gender Reassignment) Regulations 1999
Gender Recognition Act 2004
Mental Capacity Act 2005
Mental Health Act 2007
Equality Act 2010
Succession to the Crown Act 2013
Equalities (Titles) Bill 2013
Succession to Peerages Bill 2015
Succession to Peerages Bill 2016
Succession to Peerages Bill 2017
Hereditary Titles (Female Succession) Bill 2019
Hereditary Peerages and Baronetcies (Equality of Inheritance) Bill 2020

Film, Television, Radio, Vinyl and social media

Film

1915, *Birth of a Nation*, dir. D. W. Griffiths

1915, *A Woman*, dir. Charlie Chaplin

1926, British Pathé, "Stag Lane Aerodrome. Prince Chichibu. Crown Prince of Japan Enjoys His First Actual 'Joy Ride,' " https://www.britishpathe.com /video/prince-chichibu/query/Chichibu

1932, *The Steinach Film*, Austrian Federal Film Agency

1939, British Pathé, "Denbigh Eisteddfod," https://www.britishpathe.com/video /denbigh-eisteddfod

1940, *Jud Süss*, dir. Veit Harlan

1947, *Mine Own Executioner*, dir. Anthony Kimmins

1953, *Invaders from Mars*, dir. William Cameron Menzies

1956, *Invasion of the Body Snatchers*, dir. Don Siegel

1968, *The Killing of Sister George*, dir. Robert Aldrich

1970, *Performance*, dir. Donald Cammell and Nicolas Roeg

1971, *Dr. Jekyll and Sister Hyde*, dir. Roy Ward Baker

1975, *The Stepford Wives*, dir. Bryan Forbes

1978, *Invasion of the Body Snatchers* remake, dir. Philip Kaufman

1986, *Invaders from Mars* remake, dir. Tobe Hooper

1980, *Dressed to Kill*, dir. Brian de Palma

1986, *Second Serve*, dir. Anthony Page

1991, *The Silence of the Lambs*, dir. Jonathan Demme

1992, *The Crying Game*, dir. Neil Jordan

1994, *Ace Ventura: Pet Detective*, dir. Tom Shadyac

1994, *Naked Gun 33⅓: The Final Insult*, dir. Peter Segal

2004, *The Stepford Wives* remake, dir. Frank Oz

2015, *The Danish Girl*, dir. Tom Hooper

2017, *A Fantastic Woman*, dir. Sebastián Lilo

Television

BBC 2, Della Aleksander, Laura Pralet, Rachel Bowen and Jan Ford, *Open Door—Transex Liberation Group*, June 4, 1973, https://www.bbc.co.uk/pro grammes/p06c83f4/player

BBC 2, *A Change of Sex*, September, 15–17 1980

Netflix, *Orange Is the New Black*, 2013–19

Amazon Prime, *Transparent*, 2014–17

ITV, *Coronation Street*, January 27, 2014 (series from 1960–present day)

BBC 2, *Boy Meets Girl*, 2015–16

Channel 4, *Genderquake*, May 8, 2018

Radio

BBC Radio 4, Philippe Sands, "The Ratline," *Intrigue*, Episode 3, September 21, 2018, https://www.bbc.co.uk/programmes/p06lrysn

BBC Radio 4, *Woman's Hour*, "Gender Recognition Act Consultation," October 16, 2018, https://www.bbc.co.uk/programmes/m0000qpk

Vinyl

Gene "The Charmer" Walcott with the Johnny McCleverty Calypso Boys, "Is She Is or Is She Ain't?" on *Calypso Records from the West Indies*, Monogram, 1950s, https://www.youtube.com/watch?v=QB-gTmztgVk

David Bowie, *The Man Who Sold the World*, Parlophone, 1971

The Kinks, "Lola," Pye, 1970

Social Media

Biden, Joe, @JoeBiden, November 20, 2020
https://twitter.com/JoeBiden/status/1329815610180710401

Daughters' Rights: Legislation to End Discrimination https://www.facebook.com/DaughtersRightsUK

BBC Free Speech, "Things Not to Say to a Trans Person," May 20, 2015 https://www.facebook.com/watch/?v=641182835981226

"Top 90 Transgender Blogs and Websites to Follow in 2021," last updated July 22, 2021, https://blog.feedspot.com/transgender_blogs/

Trump, Donald, @realDonaldTrump, October 7, 2019 https://twitter.com/realDonaldTrump/status/1181232249821388801

#TransDocFail, https://twitter.com/hashtag/transdocfail

ACKNOWLEDGMENTS

My first thanks must go to Julia Simpson and Ben MacIntyre for paving my way to United Agents, where St John Donald, Sarah Ballard and Eli Keren suggested making Sir Ewan Forbes the focus of what was then a lengthy research report. Sarah put me in touch with Alexis Kirschbaum, my wonderfully collaborative editor at Bloomsbury, and Eleanor Jackson did the same with my similarly wonderful editor at Scribner, Kathy Belden. Thanks, everyone, for making the book happen.

Relocating the focus meant learning a lot more about the Forbes-Sempill family's lives, and my biggest debt of gratitude goes to Sir Ewan's youngest niece, Gabriel Forbes-Sempill, her sisters Kirstie and Janet Forbes-Sempill, and the family and friends Gabriel introduced me to: Nadya Menuhin, Petroc Menuhin, Sir Archibald Grant, Lady Harriot Tennant, the late Mark Tennant of Balfluig, Fiona and Jamie Burnett of Leys, historian Andrew Kerr, Frank and Linda Smith, and Rosemary Millington. A chance meeting in Alford led to my meeting some of Ewan's former patients: thank you, Brenda Glass, for introducing me to Sheena Esson and Betty Reach and for sharing your memories of Ewan, and thank you, Patty Murray, for telling me how your father pulled Ewan's Land Rover from the Don. Jamie Burnett's contacts helped me to identify the mysterious Aline Scott Elliot, who played a pivotal role in Ewan's life, and thanks go to Caroline Ayles, Alastair Baxter, Angus Baxter and Robin Baxter.

Some of my research took me to the usual academic haunts of librarians and archivists, and in particular I should like to thank National Records of Scotland and ScotlandsPeople for helping me find my way around their remarkable resources. Other research took me into less usual locations, and I am grateful to the National Trust for Scotland for the visits I made to Craigievar Castle and to Jennifer Melville in particular for introducing me to Gabriel. William Evans, gunsmiths in St. James, explained why Ewan might prefer a sixteen-bore to the usual twelve-bore (I like detail), and I learned much by television producer Jules Hussey helpfully suggesting I join her at the Lonach Gathering. Jeffrey Pilkington at Christie's Archives identified an auction item for me, and Iain Stoddart generously shared photographs of the Forbes-Sempill family and the former Fintray House. Photography for the book was not easy, since there are almost no original images left of Ewan and his milieu, and I am grateful to Sara Hannant for putting her remarkable talents to use. Another friend and colleague, the Reverend John Nicholas Latham, kindly explained some of the theological tensions that have existed between different Christian churches in the past and set out the possibilities for an increasing ecumenicism and inter-religious dialogue in the future.

Without my former history teacher Dr. John Roberts, I would never have found Ewan's hidden case. Similarly, this story would not exist without the work and commitment of my legal colleagues, and I want to thank in particular Madeleine Rees and Ramby de Mello, who initiated the *P* case and together with Baroness Helena Kennedy, QC, thereby rewrote human rights law internationally. But the LGBTI legal work in which I was involved was done by many hands: Lord Pannick, QC; Dame Laura Cox; Ben Emerson, QC; Stephanie Harrison, QC; Malek Wan Daud; Jonathan Cooper; Vereena Jones from the Equal Opportunities Commission; and Ceri Edwards and John Wadham from Liberty (the National Council for Civil Liberties) all taught me a great deal. Alongside my legal colleagues were my fellow attendees of the Parliamentary Forum on Gender Identity: we all owe an unpayable debt to Dr. Lynne Jones, MP, for co-founding it and chairing its work so ably for so many years. In a similar vein, the work of the Government Equalities Office and the Women and Equalities Committee must be acknowledged: their persistent explorations of trans equality have advanced government debate, whether aided or hindered by its ministers.

The work of Professor Stephen Whittle at Press for Change, of Terry and Bernard Reed at GIRES, of Susan Stryker at *TSQ: Transgender Studies Quarterly*, and of Susie Green at Mermaids are monumental achievements in trans activism: my regret is that I am unable to acknowledge every trans activist, whether working individually or nationally, who has striven to regain the civil liberties removed from trans people in the 1960s. But since activism has been increased exponentially by the growth of the internet, it would be wrong not to mention Zagria's remarkable virtual encyclopaedia (https://zagria.blogspot.com), which provides information and speculation about thousands of trans, intersex, cis and other persons, both famous and obscure. Similarly, I am grateful to Professor Alex Sharpe for signposting specific documents and to members of various trans internet forums, such as Trans-Academic, Trans Forum UK and Trans London, for their sharing of ideas and resources.

Four old friends died during the course of writing, and I shall miss the views of playwright Vincent Mahon, activist Terry Reed, family doctor Joyce Martin and geologist Alan Cook, while remaining grateful for the supportive criticism of Vincent's daughters, Emily and Molly Marler. I owe a permanent debt to Jules Cashford for her clarity of thought over the three decades we have known each other. All those years at the deanery taught me much about the inner workings of medicine, and I especially enjoyed the company of the clinical colleagues with whom I had such a creative time, notably Dr. Hugh Seeley, Dr. Jolyon Oxley and Professor David Black, as well as the pleasure of working with the hospital consultants, family doctors and NHS managers who were my students and colleagues. Some of my colleagues remain permanent friends and have nobly tolerated me talking about my research for the last six years: Professor Jo Winning, Schuyla Van Dyke de Curtis, Kathleen Sullivan and Steven Wallace. As well, my fellow council members at the Association for Medical Humanities have been generous in giving me space to share ideas through our conferences, seminars and business meetings. To tune into the non-academic world, I attended two Arvon residential courses and am grateful for the support of their tutors, Marina Benjamin, Hilary

Benn, Alexander Masters and Cathy Rentzenbrink, and for the enthusiastic companionship of the fellow writers I met there: you are all invited to the book launch.

In my birth family, nephew Adam has rooted out arcane references for me while his mother, Pauline, has been steadfastly supportive all of our twinned lives. My enduring debt, however, is to Catherine, who has proofread, edited, corrected and commented on endless drafts: I owe her a lifetime of treats and favors.

INDEX